CW00969428

Studies in Modern History

General Editor: J. C. D. Clark, Joyce and Elizabeth Hall Distinguished Professor of British History, University of Kansas

Titles include:

James B. Bell
A WAR ON RELIGION
Dissenters, Anglicans and the American Revolution

James B. Bell
THE IMPERIAL ORIGINS OF THE KING'S CHURCH IN EARLY AMERICA
1607–1783

Joe Bord
SCIENCE AND WHIG MANNERS
Science and Political Style in Britain, c.1790–1850

Jonathan Clark and Howard Erskine-Hill (*editors*)
SAMUEL JOHNSON IN HISTORICAL CONTEXT

Edward Corp
THE JACOBITES AT URBINO
An Exiled Court in Transition

Eveline Cruickshanks and Howard Erskine-Hill
THE ATTERBURY PLOT

Diana Donald and Frank O'Gorman (*editors*)
ORDERING THE WORLD IN THE EIGHTEENTH CENTURY

Richard D.Floyd
CHURCH, CHAPEL AND PARTY
Religious Dissent and Political Modernization in Nineteenth-Century England

Richard R. Follett
EVANGELICALISM, PENAL THEORY AND THE POLITICS OF CRIMINAL LAW
REFORM IN ENGLAND, 1808–30

Andrew Godley
JEWISH IMMIGRANT ENTREPRENEURSHIP IN NEW YORK AND LONDON
1880–1914

William Anthony Hay
THE WHIG REVIVAL
1808–1830

Mark Keay
WILLIAM WORDSWORTH'S GOLDEN AGE THEORIES DURING THE
INDUSTRIAL REVOLUTION IN ENGLAND, 1750–1850

Kim Lawes
PATERNALISM AND POLITICS
The Revival of Paternalism in Early Nineteenth-Century Britain

Marisa Linton
THE POLITICS OF VIRTUE IN ENLIGHTENMENT FRANCE

Karin J. MacHardy
WAR, RELIGION AND COURT PATRONAGE IN HABSBURG AUSTRIA
The Social and Cultural Dimensions of Political Interaction, 1521–1622

James Mackintosh
VINDICIÆ GALLICÆ
Defence of the French Revolution: A Critical Edition

Robert J. Mayhew
LANDSCAPE, LITERATURE AND ENGLISH RELIGIOUS CULTURE, 1660–1800
Samuel Johnson and Languages of Natural Description

Jeremy C. Mitchell
THE ORGANIZATION OF OPINION
Open Voting in England, 1832–68

Paul Monod, Murray Pittock and Daniel Szechi (editors)
LOYALTY AND IDENTITY
Jacobites at Home and Abroad

Marjorie Morgan
NATIONAL IDENTITIES AND TRAVEL IN VICTORIAN BRITAIN

James Muldoon
EMPIRE AND ORDER
The Concept of Empire, 800–1800

F. D. Parsons
THOMAS HARE AND POLITICAL REPRESENTATION IN VICTORIAN BRITAIN

Julia Rudolph
WHIG POLITICAL THOUGHT AND THE GLORIOUS REVOLUTION
James Tyrrell and the Theory of Resistance

Lisa Steffen
TREASON AND NATIONAL IDENTITY
Defining a British State, 1608–1820

Lynne Taylor
BETWEEN RESISTANCE AND COLLABORATION
Popular Protest in Northern France, 1940–45

Anthony Waterman
POLITICAL ECONOMY AND CHRISTIAN THEOLOGY SINCE THE
ENLIGHTENMENT
Essays in Intellectual History

Doron Zimmerman
THE JACOBITE MOVEMENT IN SCOTLAND AND IN EXILE, 1746–1759

Studies in Modern History
Series Standing Order ISBN 978-0-333-79328-2 (Hardback) 978-0-333-80346-2 (Paperback)
(outside North America only)

You can receive future titles in this series as they are published by placing a standing order. Please contact your bookseller or, in case of difficulty, write to us at the address below with your name and address, the title of the series and the ISBN quoted above.

Customer Services Department, Macmillan Distribution Ltd, Houndmills, Basingstoke, Hampshire RG21 6XS, England

Loyalty and Identity
Jacobites at Home and Abroad

Edited By

Paul Monod
Barton Hepburn Professor of History, Middlebury College, USA

Murray Pittock
Bradley Professor of English Literature, University of Glasgow

Daniel Szechi
Professor of Early Modern History, University of Manchester

First published 2010 by
PALGRAVE MACMILLAN

Palgrave Macmillan in the UK is an imprint of Macmillan Publishers Limited,
registered in England, company number 785998, of Houndmills, Basingstoke,
Hampshire RG21 6XS.

Palgrave Macmillan in the US is a division of St Martin's Press LLC, 175 Fifth
Avenue, New York, NY 10010.

Palgrave Macmillan is the global academic imprint of the above companies
and has companies and representatives throughout the world.

Palgrave® and Macmillan® are registered trademarks in the United States,
the United Kingdom, Europe and other countries

ISBN 978-0-230-22257-1   hardback

This book is printed on paper suitable for recycling and made from fully
managed and sustained forest sources. Logging, pulping and manufacturing
processes are expected to conform to the environmental regulations of the
country of origin.

A catalogue record for this book is available from the British Library.

A catalogue record for this book is available from the Library of Congress.

10   9   8   7   6   5   4   3   2   1
19   18   17   16   15   14   13   12   11   10

Printed and bound in Great Britain by
CPI Antony Rowe, Chippenham and Eastbourne

In Honour of Eveline Cruickshanks

Contents

List of Illustrations, Appendices and Tables

Illustrations

Appendices

Tables

Preface: Eveline Cruickshanks, an Appreciation

Dr. Eveline Cruickshanks, to whom this volume is dedicated, has made a salient contribution to our understanding of eighteenth-century British politics. While the seventeenth century, and now the sixteenth, are currently seen as sites of profound ideological disagreement and diverse visions of their own futures, the eighteenth century, from the last years of William III almost to the first of the younger Pitt, was dominated by one story: the triumph of the Whigs. Was there a real source-based historian writing of this period during the period, such as Clarendon on the seventeenth-century civil wars? Apparently not; even Hume, and later the great Lingard, cut off their narratives at 1688. In these circumstances, and at first almost single-handed, Eveline Cruickshanks challenged this example of what the late Edward Thompson called 'winners' history'. She has never wished to supplant the Whig narrative with a Tory narrative. It has rather been her aim to uncover the complexity of the period: its radically diverse aims, its conflicting ideologies, and the different hopes for its future held by eighteenth-century people themselves.

Her thought on these issues was first made clear in the History of Parliament volumes of Romney Sedgwick (ed.), *The House of Commons, 1715–54* (2 vols., London, 1970). A Namierite project (Sir Lewis Namier and John Brooke edited *The House of Commons, 1754–1790* in 1964), it sought in the first place to explain the political conduct of MPs by their material and family interests. The considerable new archival research involved did indeed uncover much that Namier would have desired. It also revealed, however, a quite well-organised though effectively proscribed Tory party, riven by a serious international Jacobite movement which lasted from 1689 to 1759. No criticism of Namierite method is here intended. It came up with what it was expected to come up with; but it came up also with much that was less expected. That is true empiricism.

The Commons, 1715–54 is a collaborative project under its General Editor. Individual entries are, however, printed over the initials of their author. Section V of the 'Introductory Survey', 'The Tories' (i. 62–78), was the work of Dr. Cruickshanks. E. C.'s individual entries (not all of which are on Tories and Jacobites) are worth special study. The entries on Oxford and Oxford University (i. 305–7) may be singled out, as may that on Sir John Hynde Cotton, Bt. (i. 584–5). Her work stands out generally for its exploitation of the enormous archive of Stuart MSS. at Windsor Castle (a source which, it may be thought, requires special knowledge and skills to interpret) and of the Harrowby MSS. (made available to the nation relatively recently by the Earl of Harrowby) in which the now decoded diary of Sir Dudley Ryder reveals, among much else, the seriousness with which Sir Robert Walpole regarded the Jacobite threat in his last years.

When one looks back on the career of Dr. Cruickshanks one sees, what she has herself pointed out, the significance of her background, she having been a child of Anglo-Scottish and French ancestry, but having lived and worked long now in the United Kingdom. Her University of London doctoral thesis (1956) was on a French subject: the contest to succeed Cardinal Fleury in the direction of foreign policy under Louis XV. What was her concept of history at this early stage? It was pragmatic, not ideological. She was well-appraised of all the powers, all the moves, on the chess-board of European politics. In a display of virtually Namierite political analysis, each contender to succeed Fleury (chiefly individuals but in one case a group) is considered in the light of family background, economic circumstances, personal connections, and the particular skills with which one or the other might make an effective claim. The nature of the court of Louis XV is well considered. There are only three brief mentions of Jacobitism, a matter which Cardinal de Tencin, pro-tégé and friend of James III and a contender for Fleury's place, resolved not to touch.

After *The Commons, 1715–54*, Cruickshanks published *Political Untouchables: The Tories and the '45* (London, 1979), on the English and French sides of the '45. It is a telling account in which the serious design of France to send military assistance to the Jacobites after their early success is emphasised, and, on the crucial point of whether Prince Charles should have advanced further south from Derby with his small army, Cruickshanks decides that it was 'a narrow kind of Scottish nationalism' in his Council which compelled him to retreat (p. 100). After this, her preferred mode was for some time the edited collection of essays by several hands which she would introduce and to which she would contribute: *Ideology and Conspiracy: Aspects of Jacob-itism 1689–1745* (Edinburgh, 1982); with Jeremy Black, *The Jacobite Challenge* (Edinburgh, 1988); *By Force or By Default? The Revolution of 1688–1689* (Edin-burgh, 1989); with Edward Corp, *The Stuart Court in Exile and the Jacobites* (London, 1995); and *The Stuart Courts* (Stroud, 2000). Based on conferences in which the exchange of ideas could readily take place, these volumes betokened a desire to find common interests, relevant to the new picture of eighteenth-century Toryism and Jacobitism, among scholars of diverse ori-entation and specialism. The conference which launched *Ideology and Conspiracy* was especially well-judged and successful in this regard, revealing new directions for many who were hitherto sceptical or uninterested, and unsealing many ancient fountains. Of her own contributions, her essay on 'The Revolution and the Localities' in *By Force or By Default* stands out for its cool pouring of cold water on the 'Glorious Revolution' in its earlier stages – cold water well-sourced.

In 2002 was published *The House of Commons 1690–1715*, volume i., edited by David Hayton, volumes ii. to v. edited by Eveline Cruickshanks, Stuart Handley and David Hayton. Many entries appear over the initials: 'E. C.'

In 2004 *The Atterbury Plot* was published, a book written in collaboration but one in which Dr. Cruickshanks bore the greater part. It presents a substantial amount of new evidence on the nature of the plot with which Atterbury's name has been long associated, evidence which the previous authority on Atterbury, G. V. Bennett, either did not know of, or, knowing it, did not wish to consider.

The most recent event in the academic career of Eveline Cruickshanks has been the Jacobite Studies Conference, first held at the British Academy in July 2007. The aim was, as usual, to invite as wide a range of scholars as possible. Contributors ranged from famous European intellectuals such as Emmanuel Le Roy Ladurie to very young scholars, one Scots, one French, still working on their doctorates. A truly inspiring number of distinguished scholars now in their middle years, but whom Eveline encouraged quite long ago, gave a dazzling array of papers: Jonathan Clark, Edward Corp, Paul Monod, Éamonn Ó Ciardha, Murray Pittock, Nathalie Genet-Rouffiac, Daniel Szechi were among these. Christopher Duffy, the military historian, gave a paper on a neglected figure in the '45: the Prince of Hesse. David Womersley read a subtle paper on that subtle satirist Swift; and Anne Barbeau Gardiner, who has kept a few non-Whiggish flags flying in the U.S.A., heart of Whig historiography, one on Dryden. Notable contributions were made by Patrick O'Brian, Aidan Bellenger, Patrick Clarke de Dromantin, Stéphane Genet, Kieran German, Gabriel Glickman, Ian Higgins, Richard Sharp and Andrew Starkie. Interesting papers were also read by Steve Murdoch, Alan Hobson and Jonathan Oates.

At the end of this Conference (the first of which it is hoped will be a triennial series, with the next to be held in Glasgow) I said, addressing myself chiefly to younger scholars in the field: 'Fear no more the frown o' th' great': they need not become the next generation of Whig historians. They need not, for example, work on the Hon. Spencer Compton when they find Sir John Hynde Cotton more interesting. Yet more work on Addison or Shaftesbury will not be *de rigueur* while Charles Leslie and William Law cry out for attention. By the same token, the Jacobite risings in Scotland, perennially interesting, seem for the moment well-worked over by comparison with the enormous Jacobite diaspora on the continent of Europe. Much remains to be done. But, thanks to Eveline Cruickshanks, it may all be seen in a wider and more generous perspective.

Howard Erskine-Hill

Notes on Contributors

J. C. D. Clark is an historian of the British Isles in the 'long eighteenth century.' His best-known books are *English Society 1660–1832* (2nd edn., 2000) and *The Language of Liberty 1660–1832* (1994). Although trained as an historian of Whig politics, he has come to accept the importance of the Jacobite challenge. He has explored its literary dimensions in *Samuel Johnson* (1994) and in two volumes jointly edited with Howard Erskine-Hill: *Samuel Johnson in Historical Context* (2002) and *Samuel Johnson in Historical Perspective* (in progress).

Patrick Clarke de Dromantin, *docteur en droit et en histoire*, is a member of the *Centre d'Etudes des Mondes Moderne et Contemporain* of the University of Bordeaux III and of the *Académie Montesquieu*. The *Presses Universitaires de Bordeaux* published his two doctoral theses, under the titles *Les Oies Sauvages. Mémoires d'une famille irlandaise réfugiée en France (1690–1914)* (1995), and *Les réfugiés jacobites dans la France du XVIIIe siècle, l'exode de toute une noblesse pour cause de religion* (2005). He is also the author of numerous articles on the Jacobite diaspora, which has been his domain of research for more than twenty years.

Edward Corp is Professor of British History at the University of Toulouse, and is completing a study of the Stuart Court in Rome and Bologna (1719–66) for Cambridge University Press. His books include *The King over the Water: Portraits of the Stuarts in Exile after 1689* (2001), *A Court in Exile: The Stuarts in France, 1689–1718* (2004) and *The Jacobites at Urbino: An Exiled Court in Transition* (2009). He has also edited four collections of essays, including *The Stuart Court in Rome: The Legacy of Exile* (2003).

Christopher Duffy studied at Balliol College, Oxford, before joining the academic staff of the RMA Sandhurst in 1961. He left in 1996 as Senior Lecturer in War Studies to take up a research professorship at De Montfort University, Bedford. Since 2002 he has worked voluntarily for the Court Witness Service. He has published widely on military history, with an emphasis on that of the eighteenth century in Central Europe. He will shortly publish a full-length study on the Hessian corps in Scotland in 1746, and is up-dating his substantial *The '45'* (2003).

Howard Erskine-Hill is Emeritus Professor of Literary History in the Faculty of English at Cambridge University and Fellow of Pembroke College, Cambridge. He is author of *The Social Milieu of Alexander Pope* (1975), *The Augustan*

Idea in English Literature (1983), *Poetry and the Realm of Politics* (1996), *Poetry of Opposition and Revolution* (1996), as editor, *Alexander Pope, Selected Letters* (2000), as editor with Jonathan Clark, *Samuel Johnson in Historical Context* (2002), and with Eveline Cruickshanks *The Atterbury Plot* (2004). He has published essays on Donne, Vaughan, Milton, Dryden, Swift, Pope and Johnson. He is currently working on a new biography of Alexander Pope.

Nathalie Genet-Rouffiac was trained at the *Ecole Nationale des Chartes* in France. As a *conservateur en chef du patrimoine*, she is in charge of military archives at the *Service historique de la Défense*, Vincennes. Since her doctoral dissertation on the first generation of Jacobite exiles in Paris and Saint-Germain-en-Laye, she has written several articles in French and English, as well as a book, *Le Grand Exil* (2007). She is co-founder of the *Société d'études militaires franco-irlandaises (SEMFI)* and co-organiser of the first Franco-Irish military conference *(Franco-Irish Military connections, 1580–1945*, eds. David Murphy and Nathalie Genet-Rouffiac, 2009). She is presently working on a biography of James II.

Kieran German is currently completing a doctoral dissertation at the University of Aberdeen. His thesis focuses on the Jacobite movement in the north-east of Scotland. Kieran's wider research interests include Jacobitism, Scots Episcopacy and Scottish national identity.

Ian Higgins is Reader in English literature at The Australian National University in Canberra. He is the author of *Swift's Politics: A Study in Disaffection* (1994) and *Jonathan Swift* (2004), as well as of several articles on Swift and Jacobite authors. He is an editor (with Claude Rawson) of *Gulliver's Travels* (2005) and is a general editor of *The Cambridge Edition of the Works of Jonathan Swift* (2008).

Paul Kléber Monod is Barton Hepburn Professor of History at Middlebury College, Vermont. His doctoral dissertation at Yale University became his first book, *Jacobitism and the English People, 1688–1788* (1989), which was awarded the John Ben Snow Prize by the North American Conference on British Studies. He has also written *The Power of Kings: Monarchy and Religion in Europe, 1588–1714* (1999), *The Murder of Mr. Grebell: Madness and Civility in an English Town* (2004), and a textbook, *Imperial Island: A History of Britain and Its Empire, 1660–1837* (2009). He is currently working on a study of the occult in the British Enlightenment.

Steve Murdoch is Reader in History at the University of St. Andrews. His research interests include migration from the British Isles in the seventeenth century and all forms of interaction between early modern Scotland and the Wider World. His most recent monograph is *Network North: Scottish*

Kin Commercial and Covert Associations in Northern Europe, 1603–1746 (2006). His major edited collections include (with Alexia Grosjean), *Scottish Communities Abroad in the Early Modern Period* (2005). He is currently completing a monograph on Scottish Maritime Warfare, 1513–1713.

Éamonn Ó Ciardha holds an MA from the National University of Ireland and a PhD from Cambridge. He has published numerous articles on Jacobitism, law and order and the use of Irish-language sources for seventeenth- and eighteenth-century Ireland. Formerly visiting professor at St. Michael's College, University of Toronto and at the Keough Institute for Irish Studies, University of Notre Dame, and IRCHSS post-doctoral Fellow at Trinity College Dublin, he now teaches at the University of Ulster. His *Ireland and the Jacobite Cause, 1685–1766: 'A Fatal Attachment'* (2002) appeared in paperback in 2004.

Murray Pittock is Bradley Professor of English Literature at the University of Glasgow, and formerly held senior appointments at the universities of Manchester, Edinburgh and Strathclyde. A former prizewinner of both the Royal Society of Edinburgh and the British Academy, he is the author of a number of key works on Jacobitism, Romanticism and contemporary identities, most recently *Scottish and Irish Romanticism* (2008), *The Road to Independence?* (2008) and *The Myth of the Jacobite Clans* (2nd edn, 2009).

Richard Sharp read History at Jesus College, Cambridge before migrating to Oxford to begin research on the High Church tradition in eighteenth-century England. As an independent scholar he has continued to work on this subject, developing a particular interest in the influence of Nonjuring thought and in the production and distribution of engraved portraiture. He is author of *The Engraved Record of the Jacobite Movement* (1996). From 1995–2002 he was a Senior Research Fellow of Worcester College, Oxford. He now lives in Northumberland and is Honorary Secretary of the Literary and Philosophical Society of Newcastle.

Daniel Szechi is a graduate of the University of Sheffield and St. Antony's College, Oxford, and was appointed Professor of Early Modern History at the University of Manchester in 2006. He is a Fellow of the Royal Society of Edinburgh and the Royal Historical Society and Professor Emeritus at Auburn University, Alabama. His books include: *1715. The Great Jacobite Rebellion* (2006), *George Lockhart of Carnwath 1689–1727: A Study in Jacobitism* (2002); and *Jacobitism and Tory Politics, 1710–14* (1984).

A Bibliography of the Works of Eveline Cruickshanks

1956
Pidansat de Mairobert, *Memoirs of Madame du Barry*, ed. with an introduction (London, 1956).

1957
Hogarth's England: A Selection of Engravings with Descriptive Text (London, 1957).

1960
Memoirs of Louis Philippe, Comte de Ségur, partly retranslated with an introduction (London, 1960).

1969
'101 Secret Agent' [François de Bussy], *History Today*, 19 (April 1969), pp. 273–6.

1973
'The Tories and the Succession to the Crown in the 1714 Parliament', *Bulletin of the Institute of Historical Research*, 46 (1973), pp. 176–85.

1979
Political Untouchables: The Tories and the '45 (London and New York, 1979).
'The House of Commons Vote on the Transfer of the Crown, 5 February 1689' (with John Ferris and David Hayton), *Bulletin of the Institute of Historical Research*, 52 (1979), pp. 37–47.

1980
'Divisions in the House of Lords on the Transfer of the Crown and other Issues, 1689–94: Ten New Lists' (with David Hayton and Clyve Jones), *Bulletin of the Institute of Historical Research*, 53 (1980), pp. 56–87; reprinted in Clyve Jones and David Lewis Jones (eds), *Peers, Politics and Power: The House of Lords 1603–1911* (London, 1986).

1982
(ed.) *Ideology and Conspiracy: Aspects of Jacobitism, 1689–1759* (Edinburgh, 1982).

1983

Charles XII of Sweden: A Character in Two Poems, with an introduction (Brisbane, 1983).

1984

'The Political Management of Sir Robert Walpole, 1720–42', in Jeremy Black (ed.), *Britain in the Age of Walpole* (Basingstoke, 1984), pp. 23–43.

'Ashby v. White: the Case of the Men of Aylesbury, 1701–4', in Clyve Jones (ed.), *Party and Management in Parliament* (Leicester, 1984), pp. 87–106.

1985

'The Waltham Black Act and Jacobitism' (with Howard Erskine-Hill), *Journal of British Studies*, 24 (1985), pp. 358–65.

1986

'Multi-biographical Analysis as an Approach to British Parliamentary History', in Françoise Autrand (ed.), *Prosopographie et Genèse de l'Etat Moderne* (Paris, 1986), pp. 335–44.

'Lord Cornbury, Bolingbroke and a Plan to Restore the Stuarts, 1731–1735', *Royal Stuart Paper*, 27 (1986).

'The Convocation of the Stannaries of Cornwall: the Parliament of Tinners 1703–1752', *Parliaments, Estates and Representation*, 6 (1986), pp. 59–67.

1987

'Religion and Royal Succession: the Rage of Party', in Clyve Jones (ed.), *Britain in the First Age of Party 1680–1750: Essays Presented to Geoffrey Holmes* (London, 1987), pp. 19–43 (reprinted as, *Royal Stuart Paper*, 50, 1997).

1988

(ed., with Jeremy Black), *The Jacobite Challenge* (Edinburgh, 1988).

'Lord North, Christopher Layer and the Atterbury Plot, 1720–23', in *The Jacobite Challenge*, pp. 92–106.

1989

(ed.) *By Force or By Default? The Revolution of 1688–1689* (Edinburgh, 1989).

'The Revolution and the Localities: Examples of Loyalty to James II', in *By Force or By Default*, pp. 28–43.

1994

'Lord Cowper, Lord Orrery, the Duke of Wharton and Jacobitism', *Albion*, 26 (1994), pp. 27–40.

1995

(ed., with Edward Corp) *The Stuart Court in Exile and the Jacobites* (London, 1995).

'Attempts to restore the Stuarts, 1689–96', in *The Stuart Court in Exile*, pp. 1–13.

'Le XVIIIè Siècle, de la Glorieuse Révolution à la Révolution Française', in Bernard Cottret, Eveline Cruickshanks and Charles Giry-Deloison (eds), *Histoire des Îles Britanniques du XVIè au XVIIIè siècle* (Paris, 1995).

'The Political Career of the Third Earl of Burlington', in Toby Barnard and Jane Clark (eds), *Lord Burlington: Architecture, Art and Life* (London, 1995), pp. 201–15.

'Parliamentary Lists for the House of Commons 1660–1764' (with David Hayton), in *British Parliamentary Lists, 1660–1800: A Register* (London, 1995), pp. 99–136.

'The Oglethorpes: a Jacobite Family, 1689–1760', *Royal Stuart Paper*, 45 (1995).

1996

'La Unión con Escocia y el Problema de la Identidad Nacional Escocesa', in Conrad Russell and José Andrés-Gallego (eds), *Las Monarquías del Antiguo Régimen, ¿Monarquias Compuestas?* (Madrid, 1996), pp. 57–64.

1998

'Charles Spencer, Third Earl of Sunderland and Jacobitism', *English Historical Review*, 113 (1998), pp. 65–76.

1999

(ed.) *Royal Stuart Miscellany*, 1999 (London, 1999).

2000

The Glorious Revolution (Basingstoke, 2000).

(ed.), *The Stuart Courts* (Stroud, 2000).

'The Second Duke of Ormonde and the Atterbury Plot', in Toby Barnard and Jane Fenlon (eds), *The Dukes of Ormonde, 1610–1745* (Woodbridge, 2000), pp. 243–53.

2001

'The Households of Charles II, James II, Catherine of Braganza and Mary of Modena, 1660–1689', in Klaus Malettke and Chantal Grell (eds), *Hofgesellschaft und Höflinge an Europäischen Fürstenhöfen in der Frühen Neuzeit (15–18. Jh.)/Société de Cour et Courtisans dans l'Europe de l'Époque Moderne (XVe–XVIIIe Siècle)* (Münster, 2001), pp. 69–76.

2002

'Tory and Whig "Patriots": Lord Gower and Lord Chesterfield', in Jonathan Clark and Howard Erskine-Hill (eds), *Samuel Johnson in Historical Context* (Basingstoke, 2002), pp. 146–68.

'Jacobites, Tories and "James III"', *Parliamentary History*, 21 (2002), pp. 247–54.

2004

The Atterbury Plot, with Howard Erskine-Hill (Basingstoke, 2004).

2006

'Walpole's Tax on Catholics,' *Recusant History*, 28 (2006), pp. 95–102.

Contributions to *The Oxford Dictionary of National Biography*

Sir Edward Atkyns (1630/31–1698)
James Grahme (1650–1730)
George Granville, Lord Lansdowne (1666–1735)
Bevil Higgons (1670–1736)
Jane Stuart (c.1654–1742)

The History of Parliament

Romney Sedgwick (ed.), *The History of Parliament: The House of Commons 1715–1754* (2 vols. London, 1970).
Cruickshanks wrote 456 biographies, including Sir John Barnard, James Barry, 4th Earl of Barrymore, Charles Caesar, John Campbell, Lord Glenorchy and Sir John Hynde Cotton, 3rd Bt., and 57 constituency histories, including Cornwall, London, Westminster, and Middlesex.

At the request of Romney Sedgwick, Eveline Cruickshanks wrote the section on the Tories for the Introductory Survey, which he cut down and accepted. Sir John Neale, a member of the Editorial Board, then insisted that the whole survey should be published under Romney Sedgwick's name only, which he refused to do, saying he regarded plagiarism as 'the Sin against the Holy Ghost'. A rather lame compromise was suggested by the Editorial Board, to which Cruickshanks agreed so that Sedgwick, who had worked for years without any financial reward, would be able to see the volumes in print in his lifetime.

B. D. Henning (ed.), *The History of Parliament: The House of Commons 1660–1690* (3 vols. London, 1983).
Cruickshanks wrote 249 biographies, including James Grahme, Sir Richard Grahme, Lord Preston, Sir Thomas Osborne, (later Earl of Danby),

Sir George Saville, (later Earl of Halifax), Sir Richard Temple 3rd Bt., and Hon. Thomas Wharton; and twenty-one constituency histories, including London, Westminster and Middlesex.

Eveline Cruickshanks, David Hayton and Stuart Handley (eds), *The History of Parliament: The House of Commons 1690–1715* (5 vols, Cambridge, 2002).

Cruickshanks wrote 982 biographies, including Hon. Benedict Leonard Calvert, Sir Charles Carteret, Sir Ralph Delaval, John Fitzgerald, 18th Earl of Kildare, James Grahme, George Granville, (later Earl of Lansdowne), John Manley, Thomas Tonkin, and Hon. Thomas Wharton and also sixty-five constituency histories, including Cornwall, which formed the basis of that section of David Hayton's introductory survey, together with her article on the Cornish Parliaments (*op. cit.*), Buckinghamshire, Cheshire, Cumberland, Lancashire, Northumberland and Yorkshire.

Reviews

'The Radicals' Predicament', review of Linda Colley, *In Defiance of Oligarchy: The Tory Party 1714–1760*, in *Times Literary Supplement*, 4130 (28 May 1982), p. 581.

Mark Blackett-Ord, *Hell-fire Duke*, in *Parliamentary History*, 4 (1985), p. 234.

'Re-Viewing the Eighteenth Century', review of David G. Chandler, *Sedgemoor, 1685: An Account and an Anthology*; J. C. D. Clark, *English Society, 1688–1832*; Daniel Szechi, *Jacobitism and Tory Politics, 1710–1714*; A. J. Youngson, *The Prince and the Pretender: A Study in the Writing of History*, in *Journal of British History*, 25 (1986), pp. 500–4.

L. L. Bongie, *The Love of a Prince: Bonnie Prince Charlie in France, 1744-1748*, in *American Historical Review*, 92 (1987), pp. 1207–8.

J. Kent Clark, *Goodwin Wharton*, in *Parliamentary History*, 6 (1987), p. 342.

Horace Walpole, *Memoirs of George II*, John Brooke (ed.), in *Parliamentary History*, 7 (1988), p. 179.

Daniel Szechi (ed.), *Letters of George Lockhart of Carnwath, 1698–1732*, in *Parliamentary History*, 11 (1992), p. 168.

Tim Harris, *London Crowds in the Reign of Charles II: Propaganda and Politics from the Restoration until the Exclusion Crisis*, in *American Historical Review*, 95 (1990), p. 162.

Jeremy Black, *Culloden and the '45*, in *Archives*, 19 (1991), p. 331.

Hugh Douglas, *Jacobite Spy Wars: Moles, Rogues and Treachery*, in *Albion*, 32 (1999–2000), pp. 648–9.

Introduction: Loyalty and Identity

Paul Kléber Monod, Murray G. H. Pittock and Daniel Szechi

The study of Jacobitism is at a crossroads. From the 1970s, when Eveline Cruickshanks and Howard Erskine-Hill re-established it as a serious area of research, the main emphasis among those who work on Jacobitism has been on its disruption of the prevailing trends of the contemporary societies of the British Isles through risings, conspiracies, riots, seditious words and a language of dissidence that resonated in literature, song, art, glass and textiles. This new research disrupted a traditional historiography which in response has generally sought to ignore rather than counter it. The traditional view identified Jacobitism not as a real threat to the stability of the British kingdoms, but rather as a defiant pose that never translated into a coherent ideological alternative, a marginal politics outside the social, religious and political mainstream. To be a Jacobite was to be a backward-looking absolutist rather than a forward-looking Briton.

The inaugural conference of the Jacobite Studies Trust was held at the British Academy on 11th and 12th July 2007, the proceedings being opened by Professor Emmanuel le Roy Ladurie. The essays that follow are a selection of the lively discussion engendered there on new ways forward for Jacobite scholarship. It was fitting that the opening paper came from Jonathan Clark, whose *English Society 1688–1832* (1985, 2000) simultaneously advanced the explosive argument that the eighteenth century was less forward-looking and stable than had been supposed, and that, logically and conversely, Jacobitism was therefore by no means so *outré* as a political option as those who had seen '1688' as the tipping-point for modernity had sought to determine. The title 'English Society' also showed Clark's wisdom in declining to incorporate Scotland and Ireland into a Procrustean 'British' historical model. In the essay which opens *Loyalty and Identity*, Clark argues in more detail the case that the treatment of Jacobitism by that historical model has been partial and inadequate. In part this is because the very existence of the British and later British-Irish union were predicated on the suppression and final defeat of the forces Jacobitism represented.

1

Several other trends in recent research are addressed in the papers that follow. The first of these has been the recognition that British nation-building was neither an inevitable nor an entirely straightforward process. The Scots nationalism that only a few decades ago seemed quaint or absurd to many observers has revived as a powerful political movement. With its successes has come a realisation of the fragility of British national identity. The nationalist aspirations of eighteenth-century Scots Jacobites no longer seem atavistic or strange; nor does criticism of the Union fall outside the sphere of acceptable political discourse. Allan Macinnes's *Clanship, Commerce and the House of Stuart* (1996), Murray Pittock's *The Myth of the Jacobite Clans* (1995, 1999, 2009) and Daniel Szechi's *1715* (2006) have all informed major developments in this field, while in the present volume Paul Monod's essay on Thomas Carte shows that English Jacobites, by contrast, were far from immune to the appeal of Britishness.

A second trend has been the rediscovery of Irish Jacobitism, especially in studies of Gaelic poetry. In the cultural world of Catholic Ireland, Jacobite attachments seem to have been the norm rather than the exception, and it was representatives of the Protestant British state who were regarded as interlopers. The desire to bring back a Catholic – to many a native – monarchy, which did not always equate with personal affection for the Stuarts, remained very strong among Catholics in Ireland until 1760, and even beyond. To a certain extent, the reconstruction of Irish Jacobitism has turned the paradigm of the Jacobite as outsider on its head, and has opened up a new point of view as well as a sphere of research. The key text here is Éamonn Ó Ciardha's *An Unfortunate Attachment* (2002), and his chapter in this book suggests new directions in the still largely unexplored territory of Irish Jacobitism.

Related to both of these has been a third, highly important trend towards studying English and Scottish Jacobitism in a local context. This has illustrated the degree to which Jacobites were integrated into the social and economic milieu of their localities, even if their political attitudes set them apart. Nobody lived every aspect of their lives as a Jacobite. Even Nonjurors had to make compromises with the world around them, and seek the acceptance of those who did not share their opinions. Local studies have revealed that people with Jacobite sympathies did not remove themselves from social contacts or broader influences. They have also shown that 'Whig society' was not uniform or monolithic on a local level, and had to make accommodations with those who did not share its premises. Daniel Szechi's *George Lockhart of Carnwath* (2002) and Margaret Sankey's *Jacobite Prisoners of the 1715 Rebellion* (2005) are important studies in this area. In the present collection, the essays by Christopher Duffy, Kieran German and Szechi himself all contribute to the further opening of discussion in this field of research, while Richard Sharp's essay revisits the long neglected topic of Nonjuror identity. Recent work on local history by Alan Hobson and Jonathan Oates was also unveiled at the conference.

A fourth trend in Jacobite history has been to examine diasporic communities outside the British Isles. In France, Spain, Sweden and many other parts of Europe, Jacobites were both outsiders and insiders, who used their connections with England, Scotland or Ireland to enhance their economic ventures and promote their social advancement. They blended with local communities while remaining, in certain important ways, Scots or Irish or English. Their attitudes were not regarded as backward or unusual – in fact, they were often seen as enlightened or progressive – and it was assumed in many European countries that the majority of their countrymen at home secretly shared the aversion of the émigrés to the post-1688 settlement. This is a vast field, and has links to associational and club culture among diasporic communities in Europe and possibly the Americas. Some important early works have come from Rebecca Wills (*The Jacobites in Russia*, 2002), Doron Zimmermann (*The Jacobite Movement in Scotland and in Exile*, 2003), Geoffrey Plank (*Rebellion and Savagery*, 2005), Steve Murdoch (*Network North*, 2006) and Nathalie Genet-Rouffiac (*Le Grand Exil: Les Jacobites en France*, 2007). In the collection that follows, Nathalie Genet-Rouffiac, Patrick Clarke de Dromantin and Steve Murdoch explore different aspects of the lives of Jacobite émigrés, from their military service to their economic activities and their social networking.

The study of Jacobite literature, culture and discourse is a fifth trend which informs all the previous four. If Jacobites adopted a complex and potent oppositional agenda, how was it communicated? Who were its poets? Where did its songs come from? What were the symbols used in its textiles or its objects of connoisseurship? What was its relationship to Freemasonry or to other associational groupings which constituted the early development of domestic and diasporic public spheres throughout Europe? Here Paul Monod's *Jacobitism and the English People* (1989) provided many indications of directions for future research, but much is still undeveloped. Geoffrey Seddon's monograph on *Jacobite Glass* (1995) and Robin Nicholson's *Bonnie Prince Charlie and the Making of a Myth* (2002) have addressed the evidence of material artifacts and visual culture. Works by Howard Erskine-Hill (*Poetry of Opposition and Revolution*, 1996), Murray Pittock (*Poetry and Jacobite Politics*, 1994, 2006, 2008), Kathryn King (*Jane Barker, Exile*, 2000) and Pat Rogers (*Pope and the Destiny of the Stuarts*, 2005) have all contributed substantially to the debate over the role of Jacobitism in literature, as has the research of Ian Higgins (*Swift's Politics*, 1994, 2008). An essay by Higgins on Swift and Charles Leslie appears in this volume.

An offshoot of the new attention that is paid to the Jacobite diaspora has been the study of the Jacobite courts. These were once seen as pathetic islands of fantasy on which the later Stuarts isolated themselves from the reality of their situation. Thanks to the scholarship of Edward Corp

(*A Court in Exile*, 2003) and others, we now know that this was far from the case. The Jacobite courts at St. Germain, Bar-le-Duc, Urbino, Rome (which Corp examines in his essay here) and even Florence operated, as much as was possible, like other princely or royal courts. They adhered to strict rules of ritual and etiquette. They hummed with the activities of courtiers and servants and ambassadors. They were centres of artistic and musical patronage. They provided opportunities for exercising clientage and showing off personal wealth or influence. They helped to tie the exiled community to the Stuart monarch. Occasionally, they served as focal points for plots and conspiracies, but this was not their main purpose. While its budget was restricted and visitors often had to be anonymous, little else in its functions set the exiled court apart from that in Westminster.

Through all of these new avenues of research, the study of Jacobitism has become less alienated from the principal currents of eighteenth-century studies. At the same time, nobody has sought to deny the basically dissident viewpoint of the Jacobites. Throughout the British Isles, those who maintained an attachment to the Stuart cause were always dissatisfied with the political and social consequences of the change in dynasty, although the level of their dissatisfaction varied enormously. They were also running some risk, since any expression of Jacobitism could be prosecuted or lead to public denunciation. The dissident and hazardous nature of Jacobitism should never be forgotten. At the same time, it has to be understood in the context of a complicated series of exchanges with broader influences and the wider world.

By combining an interest in the peculiarities of Jacobitism with an awareness of the varied ways in which it made an impact, scholars have gradually moved from the study of Jacobitism to what might be called Jacobite Studies. In other words, they are using the defining features of Jacobitism in order to explore wider questions of identity, political adaptation, social integration and cultural expression. This has taken them far beyond questions that centre on the personalities of the exiled monarchs, the level of support they enjoyed or the chances a particular plot or rising may have had of ultimate success. While these questions are interesting and important, they are limited and do not convey the full impact of Jacobitism. The essays in this volume generally follow different intellectual paths, and can be seen as illustrative of the emergence of Jacobite Studies.

Jacobite Studies points towards numerous avenues of future research. First, new primary sources remain to be identified and explored. The Catholic Church's archives in Rome have barely been touched, but we already know from those pioneering scholars who have delved there that they contain within them a great deal that is of relevance to Jacobite Studies. The French archives have been more thoroughly explored, but there are still plenty of possibilities for finding new material, most notably in the military archives at Vincennes. The Spanish government archives have also been very lightly investigated and a flurry of research there could well turn up material that would revise our understanding of the Jacobite phenomenon. As for the Portuguese, Savoyard, Modenese, Swedish, Prussian and Habsburg archives, they are virtually unexplored territory. There is also still the possibility of new source material re-emerging in the British Isles. The Wemyss papers are still closed, yet we know that the portion of Lord Elcho's memoirs published at the beginning of the twentieth century was only a small portion of the whole. The Scots Catholic Archives contain over 600 encoded letters by the Jacobite activist and sometime agent Father James Carnegy. An attempt systematically to decipher this potentially rich source is currently underway, but as with so much else in modern historical research this ultimately depends on successful funding applications. And there are doubtless other undiscovered gems languishing unrecognised in the private archives that still dot the British Isles.

Secondly, diaspora scholarship is one of the most exciting new fields which are opening up the history of Jacobitism. The creation, and sustaining, of a Jacobite government and multiple centres of Jacobite culture in exile defined the movement both in the British Isles and abroad. Without these overseas bases, with a royal court at their heart, Jacobitism must quickly have dissipated and died. Hence the importance of understanding how the court and other Jacobite communities functioned. The Jacobite communities abroad also made enormous contributions – military, economic, social and artistic – to the countries in which they were located. In this field, there is much more to do. Though the Jacobite impact on France and Russia has been tentatively explored, the role of the Jacobites in Spain, the Netherlands, Sweden, Prussia and the Habsburg Empire has barely been touched. Here the intersection between Diaspora Studies and Jacobite Studies is likely to be mutually beneficial to both.

Thirdly, just as the diaspora is an important topic of further research, so is the locality. While Jacobites throughout these islands never ceased to talk, think and dream of restoring the Stuarts, they also had to get on with their lives. There were businesses and estates to run, children to educate, loves to pursue and lawsuits to prosecute. Plots, riots and uprisings were actually quite rare events in the life of an enduring, dynamic community. Like the Christian and dissident underground in the pre-1989 Soviet bloc, the Jacobites were generally pretty well known as such to their kin, friends and neighbours, yet their community survived for at least three generations. Jacobites were aided, either implicitly or explicitly, by a great many non-Jacobites. The Hanoverian Tory clergyman who continued to buy books from a Nonjuring bookseller; the Walpolian Whig landowner who renewed the lease on a farm to a family he knew were Jacobites; the Opposition Whig burgess who stood surety for the errant son of a Jacobite neighbour, are all examples of this. Their motives were without doubt individual, personal and unique; but there is a pattern there that can tell us a great deal about the warp and weft of contemporary society. How did the Jacobites do it? What kind of business and social networks supported their continued existence? Where did they negotiate compromises with the system? When did their strength begin to drain away?

Fourthly, despite continuing interest and some significant scholarship in the last twenty years, Jacobite culture in all its forms – principally associational and material – has not received the systematic attention it might have done. It is important not only because it established means of communication and exchange within local or diasporic groups, and because it allows us to examine Jacobitism's role in early modern consumer culture, but also because it perpetuated a Jacobite discourse beyond the end of Jacobite politics as an effective option.

This is turn feeds into a fifth possible area for future Jacobite Studies, the Jacobite legacy. Many scholars in the field have noticed the lingering shadow of Jacobitism on phenomena as varied as the Wilkites and the Irish volunteers of the early twentieth century, but there has been no systematic exploration of the Jacobite legacy as a whole. As a consequence we currently have no answer to the simple question of, what next? Where did old (and some not so old) Jacobites go after 1766? How were the skills used, for example, to etch hidden white roses into drinking glasses redeployed when there was no longer a market for such paraphernalia? Individual Jacobites did not dry up and blow away with the accession of George III. They continued to pursue their callings. We need to follow them on and investigate the way Jacobite ideas, motifs, tropes and approaches influenced culture and society in the late eighteenth century and beyond.

A sixth area for future research in Jacobite Studies is the long-neglected one of religion, particularly as the somnolence of English Jacobitism when it really mattered is made all the more puzzling by the clear evidence that further research has provided of the influence of the Nonjurors in England. The breadth of the network of subscribers described below by Richard Sharp is very striking, and the same is true of the trust organised by Thomas Carte. Was Jacobite scholarship and idealism, most visibly transmitted by the Nonjurors, a kind of intellectual earthquake, whose reverberations echoed and re-echoed through the very fabric of eighteenth-century intellectual life until they were intrinsic to it rather than disruptive of it? Extensive work on the Nonjuring community in England in the modern era still remains to be done. The same might be said of the Scottish Episcopal Church. Meanwhile, Gabriel Glickman's research should cast new light on the role of Jacobitism in the English Catholic community. Jacobitism within the Irish Catholic Church awaits a major investigation.

If Jacobite Studies is to be a legitimate field, surely some part of it will have to be devoted to a seventh possible path for future research: anti-Jacobitism. This will require a more detailed examination of the question of how the sympathies of Jacobites were used by their opponents in order to create the taint of 'Otherness'. How were the supporters of a regime that had once enjoyed broad popularity and held power as recently as 1688 turned into the avatars of everything negative, destructive and alien? To what extent was this 'profiling' successful among the public? How did the concern with Jacobitism, which became at time almost an obsession, shape not just the policies but the self-image of the British state in the century after 1688? Lastly, how did the British state manage to survive *without* the Jacobite bogeyman in the years after 1760? It is far from clear when that bogeyman entirely disappeared – for many radicals of the 1760s and 70s, George III had learned his principles from the Jacobite Lord Bolingbroke, and most of his ministers secretly longed for the restoration of the Stuarts. Moreover, the bogeyman survived in the minds of scholars, and purging it at last may be the most important mission of Jacobite Studies.

Some will no doubt argue that the whole concept of 'Jacobite Studies' rests on uncertain ground. Its subject matter aside from the most explicit oppositionalism – is notoriously difficult to identify, and to pin down consistent Jacobite behaviour can be an extremely slippery task. Jacobitism may have appealed to a substantial proportion of people in Scotland, and perhaps a majority of Catholics in Ireland, but it attracted only a minority in the largest kingdom, England, and many of them were not very consistent in their attachment to it. Moreover, it is often unclear to what extent Jacobitism can be assumed to have influenced those interactions that were not directly related to political resistance.

Jacobite Studies also stands on a relatively restricted territory, unlike, say, Gender Studies or Urban Studies, which encompass vast areas of human experience. That territory, however, is clearly demarcated: not so much by individuals who can certainly be labeled Jacobites, but by the principles, arguments, ideas, expressions and slogans that can collectively be called Jacobitism. In this sense, although Jacobitism was a global phenomenon, its inherent interdisciplinarity renders it more akin to area studies than to thematic approaches, and it obviously has very strong links with Scottish and Irish Studies in particular. The shifting and often complicated relationship of people, movements, literary works and cultural artifacts to the force-field, wavering in strength but always detectable, of Jacobite language, code, symbol and action, determines the subject matter of Jacobite Studies.

Pursuing answers to the questions raised by Jacobite Studies will open the way to new insights on contemporary society in all three kingdoms. The nature of Jacobitism challenged British identity at its core throughout much of the eighteenth century. That is why Jacobite Studies have been so long repressed, ignored or dismissed in so many quarters: they interrogate the value, security and reality of the state that succeeded in defeating them. That too is why Jacobite Studies is contemporary, necessary and compelling, and why the next generation of Jacobite scholarship must succeed in

rewriting the history of the eighteenth century which it has already succeeded in putting on the defensive. The essays that follow, and the scholarship that underpins them, are a small – a very small – part of that process.
The Jacobite Studies Trust's research projects will be taking the process to
the next stage in the years that lie ahead.

1

The Many Restorations of King James: A Short History of Scholarship on Jacobitism, 1688–2006

J. C. D. Clark

From 1688 to the 1770s: Whig presentism

On 1 January 1766, in Rome, died James Francis Edward Stuart: to his supporters, still King James III and VIII of England, Scotland, Ireland and France; to his opponents, still the Old Pretender. In Catholic eyes, he had suffered for his faith, surrendering worldly advantage rather than pay the price of conversion to Protestantism that his restoration would have required. Pope Clement XIII decided on a royal funeral, against James's wishes, and his exequies were of great magnificence. At his lying in state in St. Peter's, a sombre event commemorated by one of the most impressive of Jacobite engravings,[1] a crown was placed on his head, an orb and a sceptre in his hands; twenty-two cardinals attended his requiem mass. The Catholic Church still took James seriously.[2]

Yet after four months of negotiation and reflection, and with an eye to the wider interests of Catholicism, Clement declined to recognise James's son Charles Edward Stuart as king, despite the absence of any doubt as to Charles's paternity. Too much had changed since James's birth in 1688. The mental world in which Bishop Bossuet, Robert Brady, Roger L'Estrange, Nathaniel Johnston and Samuel Parker once published had given way to that of Adam Ferguson, Edward Gibbon, David Hume, Richard Price, Joseph Priestley and John Wilkes. The Peace of Paris in 1763 had transformed the strategic balance of Europe; the Stamp Act had been passed in 1765, and Britain's relations with her North American colonies were already conducted in a language of politics that neither James nor Charles Edward spoke. James's death made almost no ripples in London.

Jacobitism, at that date, was scarcely a subject for British historians. Contemporary writings had of course addressed the Jacobite rebellions, but as a series of immediate practical problems. Such writings were generally normative rather than historical, like *An Enquiry into the Cause of the Late Rebellion: and the Proper Methods for Preventing the Like Misfortune for the Future* (London, 1746). Accounts had appeared of the rebellions of 1715

9

and 1745, but as episodes in the military history of armed rebellion, written in the conventions established by celebration of the Revolution. In 1691, Guy Miege's account of 1688 was intended to celebrate 'Our Wonderful and Happy Deliverance'. Jacobites were merely 'Misguided by an erroneous Principle', suffering 'the greatest Infatuation that Men were ever guilty of'. Laurence Echard in 1725 similarly treated the Revolution as 'a great *Deliverance*'. From this premise, the analysis followed. In 1717, Robert Patten depicted the Fifteen as 'the last Resort of desperate Men' and did not need to investigate 'what Principles either of Honour or Conscience these Men proceeded upon'. Peter Rae in 1718 described the Jacobites' attempts as 'pernicious Endeavours' against the 'undoubted Right and Title' of George I.[3]

Henry Fielding, in 1745, similarly imputed the motives of Charles Edward and his followers to the 'wicked Principles' of violent 'Popery'. James Ray, a volunteer under Cumberland, recorded a rebellion 'carried on by a Set of Men whose desperate Fortunes, and unreasonable Prejudices, made them fit Instruments for our common Enemy to work upon' to 'set on the Throne of these Realms, an abjured Pretender; bred up and instructed in Popish Superstition, and Arbitrary Principles; to the utter Subversion of our Religion, our Laws, our Liberties and Properties'. In 1746 John Marchant concentrated on the events of the rebellion, 'from whatever Cause it took its rise', although he was confident that it was an attempt to deprive Englishmen of 'Religion', 'Liberty' and 'Property', chiefly devised by France but backed at home by 'Legions of Popish Priests'. He took the view, inauspicious for further enquiry, that 'It might, perhaps, be for the Honour of the British Nation, if this Part of its History should never find a Place in our Annals', caused as it was by 'a small Company of Desperadoes' who, humiliatingly, achieved so much against an unprepared England. In 1747 Samuel Boyse termed the Forty-five an 'unnatural and desperate Rebellion', undertaken in spite of the unqualified blessings enjoyed under the House of Hanover. In 1748, Andrew Henderson analysed Jacobitism merely as 'a Spirit of arbitrary Power'.[4] Even in 1779, a Scottish Whig account had to urge that 'The greater part of the kingdom [of Scotland] did not favour his [Charles's] family and pretensions'; a military history, it gave minimal space to the invasion of England and most attention to Charles's escape after Culloden and his subsequent conduct in France.[5] The political sensitivity of the subject meant that any deeper historical understanding of it could scarcely yet be attempted. Whig efforts to disparage Jacobitism took precedence over any attempt to reconstruct it historically; and these efforts were to continue, in different settings, in later centuries.

The emergence of Jacobitism as a subject for serious historical analysis was neither as easy nor as obvious as it is assumed to have been by those who treat it as a matter of sentiment and nostalgia. To present Jacobitism as a symptom of emotional weakness or self-deception turned it into a nat-

urally-arising default mode and so diminished the need for historical investigation: the answers were known in advance. Moreover, an overview of its
academic development over time highlights a feature that it shares with
few other themes in professional historiography. Not only has Jacobitism
as a subject markedly ebbed and flowed within the academic arena, attention to it being concentrated in distinct phases; its presence there was from
the 1740s rhetorically contested as improper, as if to select it for study were
to make a normative claim in its favour, or as if to exclude it from serious
attention were to record a correct moral verdict against the principles that
its supporters were supposed to have championed. The effects of that normative resistance will be examined in this essay. Jacobite studies have also
followed importantly different trajectories in England, Scotland, Ireland
and Wales, in ways that cannot for reasons of space be traced here.
Nevertheless, some shared patterns emerge from this complex picture, and
the historiography may be broadly distinguished into successive chronological phases.

The emergence of serious study: Boswell, Dalrymple, Macpherson

The first phase was one in which the subject of Jacobitism could, for the
first time, be treated candidly. This emergence of historical analysis was not
easy. In 1777 James Boswell told Samuel Johnson of his, Boswell's, wish for
'an authentick history' of the Forty-five, a work that he would (with
remarkable neutrality) entitle a *History of the Civil War in Great-Britain in
1745 and 1746*. He confessed that he could not publish it 'in my life-time';
Johnson suggested Boswell might publish it in Holland.[6] This was a problem that they had already gingerly skirted, for Johnson and Boswell gave
revealingly different accounts of their Highland tour of August–November
1773. Both men kept diaries, but where Boswell's account, published in
1785, could discuss the Jacobite echoes and associations that their progress
uncovered, Johnson's version, printed in 1775, carefully avoided comment
on what Boswell more candidly recorded.[7] Even so, Johnson's book evoked
instant criticism, for Scots Whigs still had to minimise the significance of
the rising. Andrew Henderson, who had published a history of the Forty-
five in 1748, objected that Johnson had implied that 'the whole part' of
Scotland had been 'in actual rebellion' whereas 'there were but few, not
above the hundredth part of the inhabitants being Jacobite, even in the
year 1715'.[8] Scots of a Whig persuasion needed strategies to cope with
their marginalisation within the British state. Yet Johnson's reticence was
understandable. For Johnson (1709–84) the Jacobite question was real and
dangerous; for Boswell (1740–95) it was already receding into the past,
becoming not only discussable but exploitable for literary advantage. In
1785 Boswell could even pursue George III at his levee with questions

about Stuart royal titles,[9] a provocation that would have had dire consequences if offered to George II. Boswell's chosen sub-title for his account
of the tour referred explicitly to the fortunes of 'the grandson of King James
II', an implicit rejection of the Whig 'warming pan' myth that denied royal
paternity to James Francis Edward. Where Johnson published his cautious
account in 1775, Boswell brought out his audacious version only after
Johnson's death. Murray Pittock has argued that Boswell had stronger
inclinations towards the Stuart cause than has conventionally been allowed;[10]
if so, his greater openness on the subject from the 1780s is the more
remarkable.

One way of covertly addressing the history of Jacobitism was through
historical discussion of Mary Queen of Scots (1542–87), a theme that
attracted both Whig and Jacobite historians from the 1750s to the 1780s.[11]
But these discussions could only be elliptical and allusive; the most recent
Stuarts were beyond the historically permissible until the 1770s. Boswell's
greater candour by 1785 may have been facilitated by a debate initiated in
Scotland, for an early response of the Scottish intelligentsia to the problem
of the posthumous interpretation of Jacobitism had importantly opened up
serious historical debate. This growing freedom on the part of Whigs to
question Whig hagiography without seeking to overturn the Whig project
itself was especially evident in the work of two men, Sir John Dalrymple
(1726–1810) and James Macpherson (1736–96). The historical achievement
of both was obscured by their hostile reception in England. Even the Tory-
Jacobite Samuel Johnson, although he approved of Dalrymple's 'discoveries
to the prejudice of Algernon Sydney and Lord Russell' and thought
Dalrymple 'an honest fellow', disparaged him as an historian: 'nothing can
be poorer than his mode of writing; it is the mere bouncing of a school-
boy', mere 'foppery'. Johnson's relations with Macpherson were soured
from the early 1760s by Johnson's disbelief in the authenticity of
Macpherson's Ossian poems, and their antagonism descended to mutual
threats of violence in January 1775. Johnson regarded the Ossianic phenomenon as 'another proof of Scotch conspiracy in national falsehood',
and evidently ignored Macpherson's *History*.[12]

Yet the scholarship of Dalrymple and Macpherson was significant.
Dalrymple was securely entrenched as a member of the Scottish Whig legal
establishment, a minor author, inventor and campaigner for Catholic
relief.[13] His chief historical work, based on an unprecedented degree of
archival research, was published in 1771–3.[14] He anticipated the reaction it
evoked:

I have been told, that I shall draw enemies upon myself from the
descendents of some great families, whose actions I have represented in
colours belied by the principles and actions of their posterity; and that it
was not to be expected, that a man of a whig family should have been

the first to expose to the public the intrigues of the Whig-party at St. Germains. I am sensible, that here I tread upon tender ground.

His justification was an appeal to historical truth; that he had first been alerted to 'whig-intrigues with St. Germains' by David Hume; and that he had consulted Charles Yorke, the Lord Chancellor, who refused to allow him to 'quit the subject' after such discoveries. Perhaps unwisely, Dalrymple appealed to the new climate of reconciliation after 1760:

> Some persons have complained to me, that, in the second part of this work, I speak too favourably of King James [II]; I gave them this answer, That, though I would draw my sword against his family, I would not do injustice to any of their characters; and that I lived under a Prince [George III] who will not think the worse of his subjects for avowing such sentiments.

In some quarters, this would have been read as a provocation. Dalrymple began with a portentous eulogy: 'The history of England is the history of liberty, and of the influence which the spirit of it, kept alive during a long revolution of ages, has had upon the constitution, the religion, the wealth, the power, and, above all, upon the dignity of the national character of the English.'[15] But this only threw the conduct of the Whigs into higher relief.

Dalrymple's researches indeed produced sensational results. The Popish Plot he presented as deliberately contrived for Whig advantage. He emphasised the plans of Essex, Sidney, Hampden and Russell as conspirators to murder Charles II and James, Duke of York, in the Rye House Plot, 'partly because they were determined deists, and partly because they who believe they have a right over their own lives, are always masters of those of other men': men who approved of suicide were contemptuous of others. Burnet's *History of His Own Times*, continued Dalrymple, whenever checked, was always wrong. Sunderland in 1686 was duplicitous: 'There is good reason to believe, that he enjoyed pensions from the Prince of Orange, Louis the XIV and James, all at one time; pretending to each of these princes, a separate attention to his interest.' Admiral Russell was in correspondence with James II after 1689 while commanding a fleet for William III.[16] In 1773 Dalrymple's second volume, drawing on the papers of the French ambassador, Barillon, revealed a series of Whig MPs, including Algernon Sidney (1622–83), as in receipt of money from the French crown in Charles II's reign. This evidence proved that

> There is no political party in this country which has a right to assume over another from the merit of their ancestors; it being too plain, from the following papers, that whigs and tories, in their turns, have been

equally the enemies of their country, when their passions and interests misled them.

Not only was this an affront to Whigs, but it seemed to echo the premise of George III's schemes to rise above dependence on any political party. Dalrymple professed his Whig purity: 'when I found in the French dispatches Lord Russel intriguing with the court of Versailles, and Algernon Sidney taking money from it, I felt very near the same shock as if I had seen a son turn his back in the day of battle'.[17] But in 1771–3, Dalrymple presented a political target.

Sections of English opinion were outraged. Joseph Towers spoke for the Dissenting interest, inconsistently arguing both that the charges were untrue, resting only on Barillon's evidence, and also that the Whig heroes were justified: 'If Russel and Sydney were of opinion, that by intriguing with the court of France, they might prevent Charles from enslaving England, they might be no more criminal than those who intrigued with the Prince of Orange against James II and thereby brought about the Revolution'.[18] The Bedford faction also joined the fray, using an edition of the letters of William, Lord Russell's widow as a vehicle for a substantial introduction satirising Dalrymple's 'strict, self-denying regard to truth and justice' that did not allow him to suppress evidence of Russell's duplicity; 'How laudable are such sacrifices of inclination and party! How rare such instances of impartiality in this degenerate age! Industriously to seek for materials at home and abroad, from enemies as well as friends, to ascertain, if not destroy, the characters of the best friends of his country, and who had sealed a life of patriotism, in the worst of times, with their blood!'[19]

Other commentators used more inflammatory language. One associated Dalrymple with George III's alleged political misconduct: 'The wish of Majesty seems to be to silence all pens but those of panegyric.' No. 45 of *The North Briton* was right; the 'principles of government' currently did not bear scrutiny; '*we are fond of alliances with Catholic Princes since the accession of his present Majesty*'. George III's 'great love for historical truth' was the subject of ironical denial; Dalrymple was one of '*his Scotch friends*'. Not coincidentally, David Hume, 'when secretary to the embassy at Paris, was caressed by the French', and was the first to have access to the French archives. 'Hume's history is exploded and condemned for assertions totally void of truth', but Dalrymple's was 'a *maiden name*, and a journey to Paris might cover the deception'. Even so, 'It is not difficult to convict both these gentlemen of errors in their histories. Partialities are flagrant in almost every page.' 'Contempt and infamy are the proper rewards' of Dalrymple's historical method, betrayed by 'zeal and warmth on the Tory side'. He was 'Artful and designing, but the principles and views of such an editor, cannot escape the notice of a discerning public'. Dalrymple had printed a letter, undated but evidently from 1693, allegedly from Lord

Godolphin to William III. It was not Godolphin's letter, replied the critic, but expressed well the policy of the court in 1773. The letter had argued:

> And if it pleased God to grant your Majesty [William III] an honourable peace, and you would then be pleased to set up for *a party of your own*, and let all the people see, that if they expected *your* favour, they must depend upon *you* for it, and not let any one hope for promotion for being true to a faction, but by *serving of you*; I presume to say, that the war being ended, a new Parliament called and such measures pursued, your Majesty would quickly find that the *Jacobites* would turn moderate churchmen and *loyal subjects*, and the Whigs much more obsequious courtiers, and easier servants than now they are.

Such a letter, argued the anonymous pamphleteer, could have been 'wrote *very lately*'. The whole supra-party project, associated with Bute and Mansfield, was 'abominably wicked'.[20] It did not matter that Dalrymple was a Whig; the polemics of the 1770s required his denigration.

It mattered equally little, in England, that James Macpherson's background and sympathies were different from Dalrymple's. Born in a Jacobite community in the north east of Scotland, he was educated at Aberdeen, perhaps under the classicist Thomas Blackwell. His 'Ossian' poems of 1762 and 1763 were retro-Homeric, but were soon swept up into the elegiac sentimentalism of proto-Romanticism, expressing 'a romanticization of ... loss'.[21] Nevertheless, Macpherson's Ossianic heroes were not explicitly Jacobites, and expressed a bid for Scotland's retrospective membership of classical culture.[22] It was this element in the poems' reception that was steadily emphasised until his death in 1796.

Given the widespread scepticism that 'Ossian' evoked south of the Border, Macpherson may have sought redress against English Whigs through his historical writing. After political service in America and the West Indies, he returned to Britain in 1766, was awarded a government pension, and became a newspaper writer in the government cause, enjoying the patronage of Lord Bute. In this sensitive position, he was cautious about method; as he claimed, 'Unwilling to advance any matter of fact, without proof, he has printed his materials'[23] in two quarto volumes. Published in 1775, this collection of documents seemingly provided evidence for, among other things, the Prince of Orange's 'intrigues for mounting the throne' as early as 1681; Admiral Edward Russell's duplicity during the Revolution; and Queen Anne's inclination, towards the end of her reign, that James Francis Edward Stuart should succeed her. Macpherson suggested that the crucial vote in the House of Lords on 5 April 1714 which had swung the succession to the House of Hanover by 'a small majority' was decided by defections from the Tories of men of whom it could be said that 'Their principles ... were not the sole motives of their desertion.' The papers revealed 'more solid grounds'. Indeed both Whigs and Tories were shown to be in touch with both Stuarts and Hanoverians before 1714, hedging their bets against the moment of Queen Anne's death.[24]

In his *History*, another two substantial quartos published the same year, Macpherson professed that he 'felt no predilection for any party', and indeed described James II's rule as 'despotism ... Nothing ... could divert this infatuated Prince from the mad purpose of propagating his own faith.' Yet he forthrightly asserted that 'The conduct of the King, exclusive of religion, merited every praise.' Throughout his *History*, the dynastic rivals were implicitly treated as on a par. Of James II, Macpherson wrote: 'An enthusiasm similar to his own, precipitated him from his throne, and not those manly principles which deem every government unjust that is not free.' The Convention Parliament acted without authority:

> The members of parliaments, regularly dissolved, met upon the invitation of a person vested with no authority recognised by the laws. They devolved a power, which they possessed not themselves, upon a Prince who had not even the small advantage of being a native of England. He exerted his fictitious authority, and summoned an assembly, who, by virtue of powers derived solely from himself, conferred upon him the crown.

Consequently, William III 'reigned over a divided people'. Thanks to this and to Admiral Russell's self-serving, 'The fate of the British kingdoms depended upon accident. Had [the French admiral] Tourville arrived on the coast of Normandy a few days before, or had the winds retarded him till Russel's proposed return to his old station, the crown of England would have been transferred to the late King, without contest.' Chance dictated the naval dispositions that led to the Williamite victory in the battle of La Hougue.[25]

Even after that naval battle, continued Macpherson, by 1693 the grievances of the English

> had increased, to a surprising degree, the party of the abdicated King. The Whigs were equally forward with the Tories; and more dangerous, as they were more resolute in their political views. In the list of noble correspondents with the court of St. Germains, the two parties were blended with one another, in the present year. James [II] had received the most solemn assurances from four dukes, four marquises, twenty earls, four viscounts, eleven barons, besides the Roman Catholics, in every degree of nobility.

Those in contact with St. Germain included the Duke of Marlborough. Even as late as 1714, had the queen lived longer 'and continue[d] her favour for the Pretender' Bolingbroke and Marlborough 'would probably have paved his way to the throne'.[26]

One opponent claimed at once that Macpherson was part of a government-inspired movement involving David Hume, Sir John Dalrymple, John Shebbeare and Samuel Johnson, the last of these 'a writer whose partiality to the exiled family of Stuart shines in every page of his works ... pensioned by a prince who holds his crown not by hereditary right, but by the choice of the people'. Its critic saw the object of this movement as an attempt to magnify the power of George III and to diminish the Whigs, always bulwarks against absolutism. Not surprisingly, Macpherson had besmirched the 'brightest ornaments' of the last age; he had 'most certainly undertaken an invidious task: – To tear the laurels from the brows of deceased heroes'; such discoveries 'tend to debase every spark of patriotism into self interest', much to the advantage of the current minister and the detriment of 'the cause of Liberty'. Macpherson's message was essentially that 'James II was the best of Men and of Kings, and that William III was the worst of both; that the Revolution was a state trick, contrived by a parcel of scoundrels, only to save their necks; a measure so detested by every man without exception, in these realms, that even they who had brought it about, wished it undone again, and entered into measures to overthrow it'.[27]

Although Macpherson and Dalrymple were careful to refer to the Stuarts as pretenders, and to Catholicism as a politically dangerous 'Popery', their political narrative and constitutional analysis constituted an indictment of what had happened between 1688 and 1714. They met with substantial opposition in England as the nobility attempted to vindicate their ancestors, or Whigs attempted to defend the Revolution. Consequently, in Dalrymple and Macpherson Scottish historiography failed to establish a working relationship with an English audience which would have launched a proper attention to Jacobitism and all that it signified. That relationship was worked out instead in the realm of literature, in a second phase of Jacobite studies. English praise of Scots historians was meanwhile reserved instead for Hume and Robertson, in whose work the earlier Stuarts featured (sometimes problematically) but the Jacobites after 1688 did not. Even Hume, whose *History* extended to the Revolution, and who condemned 'many gross falsehoods' propagated by subsequent Whig historians in 'despicable' compositions, exploiting their party's dominance ('Rapin Thoyras, Locke, Sidney, Hoadley, &c.') did not specify their mistakes. For Hume, the Revolution, 'By deciding many important questions in favor of liberty, and still more, by that great precedent of deposing one King, and establishing a new family ... gave such an ascendant to popular principles, as has put the nature of the English constitution beyond all controversy.'[28] Such a judgement was designed to terminate scholarship on Jacobitism, not to facilitate it.

Scotland's capitulation: Burns, Scott

This second phase, although expressed in the literary realm, was similarly difficult and ambiguous. In the reintegration of Jacobitism, Robert Burns (1759–96) was not as influential as his later cult status suggests. He turned to Jacobitism for a purpose unusual in the 1780s, using it as an epitome of plebeian counter-cultural protest. *Poems, Chiefly in the Scottish Dialect* (1786) owed nothing to 'Ossian', but also perhaps little to the Jacobite tradition of Scots Gaelic.[29] Indeed Burns expressed in an unsigned letter published in *The Edinburgh Evening Courant* of 22 November 1788 the view that he had been 'Bred and educated in revolution principles' and that the prerogatives of the Stuarts were 'inimical to the happiness of a nation and the rights of subjects'. 'That they [the Stuarts] failed [in 1715 and 1745], I bless my God most fervently; but cannot join in the ridicule against them.'[30] It was a very limited apology, whatever glasses Burns may have raised to the Stuarts' memory. In Burns's poetry Charles Edward became a symbol of nationhood because he was a hero to plebeians, more than a dynastic hero. How much potential there was for an extended version of this Jacobite plebeian image in the political world that emerged after 1815 was hardly tested.[31] Burns was a farmer, not an industrial worker engaging with any new, post-agrarian social nexus; and his death aged thirty-seven averted a cultural debate or collision with the man who became dominant as an image-maker for Scotland.

The central agent in the cultural assimilation of Jacobitism was Walter Scott (1771–1832), especially through his novel *Waverley* (1814).[32] Scott's earliest loyalties were complex. His great-grandfather was a Jacobite; his grandfather converted to the Whig cause, and, according to Sir Walter, 'fetched back' Sir Walter's father and uncle from their attempt to join Charles Edward in the Forty-five;[33] later, the father sided with the Whigs. As a child, Scott heard stories of the Forty-five from his family and their circle, including from one man, Alexander Stewart, who had himself been out in both that episode and the Fifteen. Scott recorded his own 'very strong prejudice in favour of the Stuart family, which I had ori-ginally imbibed from the songs and tales of the Jacobites'.[34] As a result, Scott wrote that he 'became a valiant Jacobite at the age of ten years old'.[35] This did not last; but his attitude to Jacobitism, as to the Union, was ambiguous.

He was therefore much closer than Boswell to the events of 1745–6, although he was Boswell's junior in years. Scott accepted by 1806–8, or was obliged to claim, that 'the time is now past away when the theme would have had both danger and offence in it' since the stories of those times 'have so strangely vanished from our eyes'.[36] Yet Scott acknowledged his intellectual conviction that the victory of the Whig cause was inevitable and right:

> Seriously I am very glad I did not live in 1745 for although as a lawyer I could not have pleaded Charles's right and as a clergyman I could not have prayed for him yet as a soldier I would I am sure against the convictions of my better reason have fought for him even to the bottom of the gallows. But I am not the least afraid nowadays of making my feelings walk hand in hand with my judgement though the former are Jacobitical, the latter inclined for public weal to the present succession.[37]

So Scott redefined Jacobitism to be a thing of the heart, not of the head. His Toryism was of an early nineteenth-century, not an early eighteenth-century, variety. Disbelieving in 'Ossian',[38] Scott fashioned a new image of the Highland hero to match his position on the Stuart cause.

In 1808 he began work on a novel, published in 1814 as *Waverley, or 'tis Sixty Years Since*, that reflects considerable historical knowledge of the events of 1745–6. With *Waverley*, Jacobitism became, almost for the first time in English, a literary entertainment.[39] Scott, ever one to seize the moment, followed the success with *Rob Roy* (1817) and *Redgauntlet* (1824). In the introduction to the last, for the collected edition of his novels in 1832, he wrote that 'The Jacobite enthusiasm of the eighteenth century, particularly during the rebellion of 1745, afforded a theme, perhaps the finest that could be selected, for fictitious composition, founded upon real or probable incident. This civil war and its remarkable events were remembered by the existing generation without any degree of the bitterness of spirit which seldom fails to attend internal dissension.' This last was a highly questionable argument, and points to reconciliation as Scott's goal.

Scott presented reconciliation as a response to economic necessity. In *Waverley* he made sweeping claims for his country's social transformation since 1746:

> There is no European nation which, within the course of half a century, or little more, has undergone so complete a change as this kingdom of Scotland. The effects of the insurrection of 1745, – the destruction of the patriarchal power of the Highland chiefs, – the abolition of the heritable jurisdictions of the Lowland nobility and barons, – the total eradication of the Jacobite party, which, averse to intermingle with the English, or adopt their customs, long continued to pride themselves upon maintaining ancient Scottish manners and customs, commenced this innovation. The gradual influx of wealth, and extension of commerce, have since united to render the present people of Scotland a class of beings as different from their grandfathers, as the existing English are from those of Queen Elizabeth's time. The political and economic effects of these

changes have been traced by Lord Selkirk with great precision and accuracy. But the change, though steadily and rapidly progressive, has, nevertheless, been gradual; and, like those who drift down the steam of a deep and smooth river, we are not aware of the progress we have made until we fix our eye on the now-distant point from which we set out.

Selkirk had presented a similar claim of 'rapid change', but admitted that he had no 'immediate or local connexion with the Highlands', and that his knowledge derived chiefly from a single 'extensive tour' in 1792. Selkirk's purpose in presenting this assertion was to argue for the inevitability of emigration from Scotland in the absence of provision for the Highlanders of 'new branches of industry', emigration being an economically beneficial process.[40] His work is therefore not strong evidence for the reality of Walter Scott's image. Changes there had been; but whether they had been sufficient to prove Scott's case, and whether or not Selkirk had proved them, they allowed Scott to present his argument, debatable as it was, as a natural process.

Recent scholarship has implicitly questioned Scott's account, pointing out the 'continuous efforts of intrusive central government to undermine clanship from the outset of the seventeenth century': 'Absentee landlordism, indebtedness, rent-raising and the removal and relocation of clansmen were not products of the Forty-Five, but part of an ongoing process of commercialism and cultural assimilation that can be traced back to the early seventeenth century'.[41] Indeed the metaphor of the river was Scott's only proof; but it made it plausible for him to argue for the harmlessness of political Jacobitism. There were some, he continued:

who, in my younger time, were facetiously called, 'folks of the old leaven,' who still cherished a lingering, though hopeless attachment, to the house of Stuart. This race has now almost entirely vanished from the land, and with it, doubtless, much absurd political prejudice; but also, many living examples of singular and disinterested attachment to the principles of loyalty which they received from their fathers, and of old Scottish faith, hospitality, worth, and honour.[42]

In order to define a noble cultural nexus of loyalty and honour, and to secure for that nexus an acceptable place in national life, Scott conceded the political case: Jacobitism was 'absurd political prejudice'. Historians largely agreed.

Yet this was not a reluctant concession on Scott's part. 'It is the object of this history', he wrote, 'to do justice to all men'.[43] Scott's purpose was reconciliation, Highlander with Lowlander, Scots with English. *Waverley*'s main object was to explain the Highlander to his southern neighbours and render him attractive and harmless,[44] but for a Scots audience the book also depicted English officers as equally honourable as their Scottish Jacobite antagonists. The novel shows representative individuals of the two sides coming to understand each other, and ends with the Duke of Cumberland granting a pardon to the English convert to Jacobitism Edward Waverley, since Waverley had on the battlefield saved the life of the English Whig Colonel Talbot, who now intercedes for him. The battle of Culloden, and the atrocities which followed, do not feature in Scott's novel. The symbolic loser is the executed Highland chief, Fergus Mac-Ivor, brave and principled but, in Scott's narrative, inevitably sacrificed so that a wider reconciliation may emerge from the conflict. Flora Mac-Ivor, his sister, acknowledges that 'it was impossible it [the rising] could end otherwise than thus'.[45] The most famous outcome of this strategy was the visit of George IV to Scotland in 1822, a ratification of Scotland's final loyalty to the dynasty which was as politically effective as it was culturally and historiographically compromising. Yet Scott succeeded in this programme of political assimilation, and Queen Victoria was to be its triumphant beneficiary.

'Romance' was a term used unashamedly in Scott's novel. Its narrator, Edward Waverley, was happy 'to give himself up to the full romance of his situation' in the Highlands, excited by 'a fund of circumstances for the exercise of a romantic imagination, and all enhanced by the solemn feeling of uncertainty at least, if not of danger!'[46] As Claire Lamont, Scott's editor, wrote in 1981: 'From the beginning the reader is assumed to share the social experience of Edward Waverley – that of enjoying the romance of Jacobitism while (until he disavows it) safely under the protection of the Hanoverian government ... Nothing more clearly marks the defeat of Jacobitism and the destruction of Highland society than the fact that by 1814 they may be presented in contrast to a largely undescribed Hanoverian way of life which we are all tacitly assumed to share'.[47]

The theme of 'romance' was not an excuse for indulging in sentiment, but rather Scott's device for explaining Edward Waverley's decision to join Charles Edward's cause: 'romance' was harmless in a way that national sentiment, self-interest, religion or ideology were not. Although later widely blamed for the invention of tartanry, Scott's vision was influential because it presented itself as historically soundly based.[48] Yet, remarkably, religion and ideology were largely absent from *Waverley*. Scott provided a rationale for subsequent Scots cultural distinctiveness, not for Scots political independence. Others devalued his message, turned Charles Edward into 'Bonnie Prince Charlie', and used new technologies to decorate with nineteenth-century images of the prince on the lids of biscuit tins; although Scott's novel was a considerable achievement of literature, and stooped to no such depths, he had removed the barriers to this next step.

By Scott's day, Jacobitism was pictured as a securely Scottish allegiance. In the eighteenth century, by contrast, the very division of Scottish society over the issue of the dynasty had been a key to Jacobitism's failure. Charles

Edward, on the run after Culloden, told Malcolm MacLeod that he did not fear the slow-moving government troops, but 'the Highlanders who were against him'.[49] Elsewhere Scott was explicit about the existence of pro-Hanoverian clans,[50] but in *Waverley* the cultural image of unanimous Highland loyalty now overrode this earlier reality. Jacobitism was not only Scottish; Walter Scott's cultural stereotypes cemented the identification of Jacobitism specifically with the Highlander. It later became clear that this was an exaggeration: Murray Pittock's research indicates that Prince Charles's army, at its peak, had about 6,750 men in regiments drawn primarily from the Highlands, 5,400 from chiefly Lowland regiments, and 830 Franco-Scots and Irish, joined by 300 English.[51] This diversity was increasingly overlooked, as was the large contingent of Scots who fought *against* Charles Edward.[52] Scott's ideas of loyalty, honour and nationality contradicted the cosmopolitanism of early eighteenth-century dynastic culture, and eclipsed them. Boswell recorded Malcolm MacLeod, who watched one night over Charles Edward when on the run after Culloden, as saying that the prince spoke in his sleep in French, Italian and English.[53] By degrees, however, Charles's image was transformed from that of a European prince into that of a patriotic Highland Scot.[54] Whether from Robert Burns or Sir Walter Scott, Victorian Scots could find in Jacobitism various sorts of consolation and inspiration; but their distance from the historic eighteenth century steadily grew.

Assimilation: Clarke, Home, Chambers

Where Scots historiographical initiatives in the 1770s had often met strident opposition in England, English reactions were sometimes different later in the century, and such a shift of sentiment identifies a third phase in Jacobite studies. This was notably the case in the circle of the Prince of Wales, later George IV. The Rev. James Stanier Clarke (1765?–1834) launched his career by serving with the prince in the Channel fleet in the 1790s and winning his patronage. A domestic chaplain at Carlton House in 1799, librarian there from 1805, he rose to be historiographer to the king in 1812. His edition of *The Life of James II* by Lewis Innes (1651–1738) in 1816 was later termed by J. K. Laughton in the *Dictionary of National Biography* 'a *servile* attempt to portray James II in heroic colours'.[55] But it was part of the wider strategy of the late Hanoverians to re-appropriate the legitimacy of the Stuarts: the pension granted by George III to Henry Benedict in 1799; the Prince of Wales's symbolic contribution to Canova's memorial to the Stuarts in St. Peter's in 1819; the securing of the Stuart papers and their bestowal at Windsor Castle;[56] George IV's tartan-bedecked visit to Edinburgh in 1822. Also part of this phase of scholarship was Johnstone's *Memoirs of the Rebellion in 1745 and 1746* (1820). The editor, 'J. B.', a Scot, defended himself in the second edition (1821): his position was that 'too favourable an opinion was generally entertained' of Charles Edward, and he had corrected the picture. Nevertheless, he recorded that 'It is certain ... from the archives of the Stuart family, now in the King's library, that a very great proportion of the English aristocracy were Jacobites'.[57] It was an ineffective protest: key English voices were now bent on assimilation.

James Stanier Clarke, as editor, reminded his readers that 'The Nation' was indebted for the survival of the Stuart papers to 'the zeal and unremitting exertions' of the Prince Regent; indeed 'the House of Brunswick from the first displayed a noble regard for the feelings of The Stuart Family', a remarkable claim. Clarke's rationale for publication was that 'This Life of James bears also a striking analogy with those events which have so recently convulsed and demoralised a considerable part of Europe.'[58] Innes's early eighteenth-century account had been very different: a Catholic panegyric that depicted James as 'the darling of the Nation' until he adopted Catholicism, when he 'was sett upon every side as the common Enemy'. James II was 'the most Heroical, the most oppressed, and the most Christian Prince, the world has seen for many ages'. Whig arguments to the contrary were deceitful rhetoric: 'It is the main drift of all promoters of Sedition and treason, to get possession of those specious titles of being the Assertors and Restorers of Liberty, Property and Religion, and then they are sure the work is more than half perform'd'; so that 'the deluded Patriots ... to avoid an imaginary servitude embraced a real one' to William III.[59]

But Innes's purpose was swamped by and subsumed in the project of George IV and Sir Walter Scott to recruit the Jacobite phenomenon as an imaginative prop to the Hanoverian monarchy in an age of revolution, and the book did not sell. Between Innes's death in 1738 and the publication of his work in 1816, too much had changed. The nature of this change of mood can be discerned in the contrast between two Scotsmen's histories of the Forty-five, one by the Presbyterian, Unionist Whig John Home (1802) and the other by the Episcopalian, unsuccessful nationalist Robert Chambers (1827). Together, they illustrate the impact of the interpretation most publicly championed by Sir Walter Scott.

John Home (1722–1808), an aspiring clergyman in the Moderate party of the Church of Scotland, graduated from Edinburgh University in 1742; in September 1745 he enlisted in a corps of volunteers to defend the city against the Jacobite threat. When Edinburgh fell he joined Sir John Cope's forces, fought in Hawley's army at Falkirk, was captured, and escaped. Following this unambiguous testimony of his Whig convictions, he received a parish, although his attention was soon distracted by 'the kind of reading to which his inclination led, that of the historians and classics of Greece and Rome'.[60] His most famous play, *Douglas* (1756), in effective fashion identified Caledonia with ancient Athens and paved the way for James Macpherson's response, the retro-Homeric inventions of the poems of 'Ossian' which implicitly dignified the Highlander against Whig disparagement.[61] Home was a Scots Whig, and a politically aware one. After the outcry caused among severer Calvinists by a clergyman's having written a play, Home resigned his parish, moved to London, acted as Lord Bute's secretary and secured a handsome pension from George III on his accession. Home had evidently begun his *History of the Rebellion* in 1746 or 1747,[62] and returned to it after his career as a playwright stalled in the 1770s.

Hume's *History* finally appeared in 1802, dedicated effusively to the Hanoverian king. Yet the book belonged intellectually to the 1740s. Instead of outlining the history of Jacobitism, Home's Preface established its author's allegiance with an eulogy of the Revolution of 1688:

> To the Revolution it is owing, that the people of this island have ever since enjoyed the most perfect system of liberty that ever was known amongst mankind. To the Revolution it is owing, that at this moment, in the year 1801, Great Britain stands the bulwark of Europe; whilst her fleets and armies, in regions the most remote, defend the cause of Government and Order, against Anarchy and Confusion.[63]

This excused deeper reflections on the cultural phenomenon of Jacobitism. Home's *History* therefore really began with the landing of Charles Edward in 1745, and ended with the prince's return to France in September 1746.

Home was aware of counter-factuals, but dealt gingerly with them. He touched briefly on the potential danger of Charles Edward's marching into England towards Newcastle, the centre of the coal trade, immediately after the battle of Prestonpans, and did not deal in depth with the decision to retreat from Derby or the strategic threat posed by an advance on London. Home knew that the Forty-five was 'only a fragment of the original design' and gave space to the much more serious French invasion attempt of 1744.[64] Yet he never openly discussed the possibility, which he must have known to have been a reality, that the Hanoverian cause might have lost.

This was so not least because, although he gave attention to those Highland clans that refused to join Charles Edward even after Prestonpans, his essential explanatory model of Jacobitism was that of the Highlands versus the rest. After 1688, 'every rebellion was a war carried on by the Highlanders against the standing army'. The Fifteen was an action by 'the Highlanders'; and the Highlanders were 'essentially different from the other inhabitants of Britain'.[65] Except for one individual,[66] Home said little about the motives of the participants; the Jacobites were merely 'the rebel army' in a political and military history. Home was no Romantic, aiming instead to echo the role of 'Xenophon and Caesar' as historians and participants. His work did not stop at the battle of Culloden, but thereafter only traced Charles Edward's months as a fugitive. Home avoided any reflection on the impact on Scotland of the rebellion's failure.[67] Henry Mackenzie indeed suggested that Home had chosen to 'weaken and soften down' his original criticisms of the conduct of the Duke of Cumberland after Culloden.[68] Home's was a history of Whig triumph. It was a story of the political and military events in which a rebellion was frustrated, and did not extend a real effort of historical understanding to the losing party.

Although Robert Chambers's *History* appeared only twenty-five years after Home's, it belonged to a changed world. Chambers was of a wholly different generation, born in 1802 and surviving to 1871, part of a newly burgeoning popular literary culture of booksellers and opportunistic authors, owing his living to the market rather than to noble patronage. Home's *History* had appeared in quarto, like Dalrymple's and Macpherson's. In 1827, Chambers's two duodecimo volumes on the Forty-five looked more like novels than works of history.

Indeed Chambers admitted that his 'chief object' had been 'scarcely so much to write a history, in the accepted sense of the word'. Instead, 'I have been induced to forego what is called the philosophy of history, by a conviction in my own mind, that the merit of the subject, does not lie in any political questions which it involves, but purely in its externally romantic character.' This created a market opportunity, since 'there is in reality no work upon the subject at all suitable to the spirit of modern literature' which could gratify the 'increasing curiosity of the public, regarding this transaction of their ancestors'. Chambers set out to provide a work 'uniting the solid information of an historical narrative with the amusement and extensive popularity of a historical novel'. Political involvement was hardly a danger, even from 'the Jacobite party – those few and fast disappearing votaries of a perished idea'. But the image of these people served, according to Chambers, a present day cultural purpose. They 'still survive to dignify this world of expediency, liberality, and all uncharitableness, with their stately old manners and primitive singleness of heart'.[69]

Chambers was a Scots Episcopalian:[70] his work betrayed mounting sympathy for the cause he recorded, and distaste for Whigs. Of the many writings on the Forty-five, 'most ... run riot in religious and political cant, and in still more loathsome adulation of the triumphant party'. Yet Chambers gave away his case. James II, he wrote, had been a 'devoted and bigoted Catholic'; the Revolution of 1688 had been brought about by 'a coalition of Whigs and Tories'. The Convention Parliament's declaration that James II had abdicated was 'sanctioned by the exigency of the occasion'. Chambers identified the Hanoverians as a 'foreign race of sovereigns' who had involved Britain in ruinous wars; allegiance was so divided on their accession that 'very little was wanting in 1715 to achieve the restoration of the House of Stuart' except military leadership; but, if the country had been so divided, the Stuarts' failure was all the more puzzling.[71]

In outlining the military balance in 1745, Chambers's literary priorities took over from his historical ones:

> In one of the parties we see many of the features of chivalry: – a love of desperate deeds for their own sake, and a pure and devoted spirit of loyalty, such as might have graced the wars of the Roses, or glowed in the pages of Froissart. In the other we are disgusted with the alarms of a parcel of ancient civil officers – with the vile cant of a pack of affected patriots – and with the contemptible technicalities of a military frippery, the most ostentatious in pretension, and the most feeble in practice, that ever disgraced a country.

Prince Charles was by contrast fired by a 'purer and loftier spirit – that peculiar spirit of chivalry and high-souled feeling – which, in some measure, might be said to form the mental atmosphere of his adherents'.[72]

Throughout, Chambers drew a contrast between the grace and glamour of Jacobitism and 'the commonplace feelings of the modern world'. Despite the material motives of many who backed Prince Charles, 'Jacobitism was a generous sentiment, arising from a natural love of abstract justice, and nourished by the disposition, equally natural, to befriend the oppressed and unfortunate'. So the Jacobites 'sacrificed fortune, and favour, and all that men hold dear on earth, for the sake of a mere emotion of their feelings, for the associations of the times that were past, or at least for principle which they believed to be right; whilst the Whigs alone were the men with whom the suggestions of prudence and expediency had any weight, and who could reasonably hope for advantage, national or individual, from the issue of the contest'.[73] This had not always been the case, however: 'We must allow that Jacobitism, in its earlier stages, had all the gross and ordinary features of mere political partisanship; but we cannot help asserting, as the result of elaborate research and consideration, that it has been purified and refined away before the occurrence of the last insurrection, to the spirit which we have above attempted to describe. Hence the comparative merit of the *Forty-five* over the *Fifteen*, as a subject of history, or as a matter of poetical reflection'.[74]

Chambers wrote with contempt that this altruistic cause secured 'not a single recruit' on Charles's march into England; at that time the Englishman 'required to be pretty sure of his ultimate success before risking the pains of treason'. This political pragmatism was far from the cultural Jacobitism that Chambers had defined for Scotland; and Chambers's sources were all Scots. He knew nothing of English, Welsh or Irish Jacobitism. To him, the 'English churls' were 'wrapped up in their own selfish notions' and unable to understand the 'enthusiasm' of the Scottish army for a 'national and romantic' cause; the Welsh 'Jacobite squires' who could, he thought, have turned out large numbers of men, were excused from participation by Charles's retreat, and 'had all their lives afterwards the cheap satisfaction of only boasting in their cups, how far each of them had gone in testification of his valour and loyalty'.[75] Charles's retreat from Derby was ascribed to 'Providence' rather than Scots parochialism or miscalculation; the Scots were 'at length obliged to yield to a fate which they could no longer brave', when they saw that 'the venture which lay before them was too much for mortal man to dare'.[76]

Sometimes Chambers's proclivities got the better of him, and he set out counter-factuals in which the Jacobites might have won. After Cope's defeat at Prestonpans, if Charles had marched at once on England, 'considering the terror of his name, the rapidity with which he could have marched, and the general idea which at this moment prevailed, that there was nothing impossible to his arms, he might have dislodged his Majesty from London, and changed, for a time at least, and probably for ever, the titles of King and Pretender'. At Culloden, 'the fortune of the day was very doubtful, and that indeed the tide of courage, which had hitherto sustained the hearts of the Duke [of Cumberland]'s soldiers, was just beginning to turn and ebb, when the Highlanders relieved them by retreating'.[77] In general, however, Chambers's vision of cultural Jacobitism rested on the premise of Jacobitism's political futility.

Chambers wrote at length of the 'extreme of cruelty' and 'fiendish wickedness' shown by Cumberland's troops after the battle, murdering the wounded in cold blood even some days after the action. He continued with an even longer account of Charles Edward's sufferings as a fugitive, the 'rapine and massacre' of Cumberland's suppression of the Highlands, the trials and executions that followed the rising, and the Prince's subsequent experiences in France. As a result of this military repression, 'for some time Scotland might be said to have been treated throughout its whole bounds as a conquered country, subjected to the domination of military law'.[78]

Such a resounding condemnation of the Whigs seems as if it should have issued in a programme for political action in 1827. It did not do so. Chambers was obliged to cover George IV's visit to Edinburgh with abject flattery. 'National independence', a prospect held out by Prince Charles, was a 'visionary idea'.[79] Summing up the respective claims of the Jacobite and Whig positions, Chambers concluded that 'both parties were to a certain extent right, and to a certain extent wrong'. The Jacobites' reverence for the person of their monarch 'refused all alliance with reason, and ... was in fact superstitious'. Their temperament was of 'that inconsiderate and poetical sort, which finds gratification in the joy of others, and is disposed to forego all earthly good for the sake of a visionary idol'. At a later period, Jacobitism became 'a spirit more pure and melancholy'. 'The romance of the party may be said to have reached its height in 1745'.[80]

The high tide of Whig disparagement

Like Sir Walter Scott, although with more open indignation, Chambers
neutralised political Jacobitism in order to invent a consoling cultural
Jacobitism. Again like Sir Walter, Chambers invented this set of cultural
stereotypes only for Scotland. After the Fifteen the Highlands seemed 'the
only portion of the British dominions that actively disputed King George's
title'.[81] Such a diminished movement can have stood no serious chance of
victory. Even as a cultural phenomenon, Scott and Chambers had defined a
Scottish Jacobitism that had only limited political and historiographical
impact in nineteenth-century Britain. Although the publication of records
continued and gathered pace,[82] there was an hiatus in serious historical
attention to the Jacobite question until a remarkable flowering of interest
in the last decade of the nineteenth century. What work there was in the
meanwhile was normatively dismissive of Jacobitism to a remarkable
degree. This was notoriously the case in the works of Thomas Babington
Macaulay (1800–59), especially his *History of England* (5 vols., London,
1849–61). Such normative perspectives constituted the fourth of our
phases.

   The self-evident admissibility of such disparagement was widely evidenced. In 1875 A. C. Ewald (1842–91), a senior clerk in the Public Record
Office who exploited its collections during his working hours to produce
history books for a wider audience, reported that the failure of writers to
use the archives meant that although the rising of 1745 was 'a thrice-told
tale … nothing worthy to be called a biography of Prince Charles had been
written'.[83] He drew on Earl Mahon's edition of the letters of Sir Horace
Mann, English envoy in Florence, which reported fully on the later years of
the prince.[84] Ewald's predispositions were clear, however; Clementina
accepted James's offer of marriage in 'an evil hour'; the young Prince
Charles was surrounded by 'bigoted intriguers, whose one prayer was that
England might return to the Catholic faith'; the Stuarts were 'a God-cursed
dynasty' whose annals were 'but the history of bloodshed and oppression,
failure and intrigue'; James III was 'Irresolute, narrow-minded, and miserably weak'; he had an affair with the Countess of Inverness that fatally dis-
torted his judgement. Charles Edward may have been taught 'to believe in
Brady and Filmer, rather than in that development of Parliamentary
Government which was gradually making the House of Commons the
centre and force of the State'. Jacobite plots were disparaged; the Forty-four
was not taken seriously; the Forty-five was solely the undertaking of 'the
Highlanders'. Even so, the decision not to advance from Derby was a strategic mistake that reflected ill on the Jacobite commanders. In Rome, priests
and monks had contributed money to Charles Edward's cause in the hope
of seeing Catholicism re-established in England: 'Posterity may congratulate itself upon their disappointment.' Although Ewald was eloquent in

condemnation of the brutality of Cumberland after Culloden, he was clear that Charles Edward's moral degradation thereafter meant that he 'lived too long for his reputation' into 'a manhood debased by vice, a temper rendered querulous and suspicious by disease, no refinement, no delicacy, nothing but humanity's coarsest grain'.[85]

From this historiographical dismissal, novelists failed to rescue their subject. The leading Jacobite novel of this period was *Kidnapped* (1886), set in the Highlands in 1751 and exploring the aftermath of the Forty-five. In it, Robert Louis Stevenson (1850–94) promoted the same great theme as *Waverley*: reconciliation within a Whig outcome.[86] Stevenson's fiction is essentially about the friendship and collaboration of two opposites, the Jacobite man of action Alan 'Breck' Stewart and the Whig heir David Balfour. Both are presented as attractive characters, especially Stewart. Yet the adversity they face together is more the result of the inherent and chance injustice of all things than of the iniquity of one political cause in particular. Thanks to their joint triumph over vicissitude, reconciliation is symbolised by David Balfour's reclaiming his estate from his grasping uncle Ebenezer: this wider drama of legitimacy and benevolence re-established (but within a Whig settlement) is therefore one to which the many injustices triggered by the Jacobite risings are only temporary hindrances. Within this wider scheme, Highland loyalty and Lowland legal wisdom are presented as not inconsistent. Stevenson's harshest words are reserved for Scots Whigs like the Campbells who fail to pursue the path of reconciliation; even the repressions of government troops after the Forty-five are not painted in the harshest colours. Above all, Jacobitism is not presented as a serious alternative to Whig prosperity, but as a generous misjudgement. The denouement is provided by a lawyer, Mr. Rankeillor, depicted as living in an age (by implication, long past) 'when there were two parties in the state, and quiet persons, with no very high opinions of their own, sought out every cranny to avoid offence to either'. Appropriately, the last words of the book in its recent printings are David Balfour's: 'The hand of Providence brought me in my drifting to the very doors of the British Linen Company's bank.'[87]

The second spring: *fin de siècle* and after

Despite this historiographical disarming, in the late nineteenth century, especially after an influential exhibition in London in 1888–9,[88] interest in the Stuart dynasty widely conceived grew considerably: these years saw a new wave of writing on Jacobitism, lasting until the First World War, and forming a fifth phase. Although the subject was now addressed in an idiom at its best more indebted to positivist history, late nineteenth century Romanticism produced a subtly different setting for archivally-based Jacobite studies[89] as the final arrival of an urban-industrial society created the need for cultural antitheses. The cultural hegemony of a muscular Protestantism, in alliance with the positivist assumptions of high modernism, still excluded Jacobitism from the historical mainstream, but now gave it a particular appeal to cultural minorities. It has been explained as 'a reaction by the artistic and literary classes against the values of material progress, and the burgeoning worlds of imperial and industrial power'.[90] This reaction coincided with the maturing of Irish romantic nationalism, with echoes of that movement in Scotland, and with major crises in Ireland that produced the Liberal policy of 'Home Rule All Round' in 1894. But Jacobite studies' contributions to these political movements were small compared with the contributions that *völkisch* history was then making to nationalism in continental Europe. It may be suggested that its political weakness in the British Isles had much to do with the hegemonic structure of explanation indebted not least to Sir Walter Scott.

The *fin de siècle* nevertheless saw a distinct phase of normative legitimism that has yet to find its historian. The Order of the White Rose was founded in 1886, dedicated to a revival of Jacobite culture; from 1890 to 1905 it published a journal entitled *The Royalist*.[91] In 1891 the Legitimist Jacobite League of Great Britain and Ireland was founded, dedicated to an actual Stuart restoration; from 1893 it published a journal, *The Jacobite*, as well as a series of pamphlets.[92] The Society of King Charles the Martyr was formed in 1894; the same year was published *The Legitimist Kalendar*, which was still going in 1910. From 1895 was published in London *The White Cockade: A Jacobite Journal*. Such publications reflected a distinct, if specialised, social phenomenon; the purposes of their authors deserve further study.[93]

Yet Irish literary nationalism did not prominently invoke Jacobitism. Daniel Corkery's book *The Hidden Ireland: A Study of Gaelic Munster in the Eighteenth Century* (1925), a pioneering study that famously evoked a Gaelic culture, strangely avoided much explicit mention of Jacobite allegiance. Even the *aisling* (vision) poems are presented as lacking the Stuart dimension that their Scots Gaelic equivalents had; 'The place that the Stuarts themselves occupy in the Scottish poems is occupied in the Irish poems by Ireland herself'.[94] English collective solidarities depended even less on romantic nationalist images. Consequently, the Jacobite scholarship of c. 1880–1914 never recovered from Sir Walter Scott's translation of it from the political to the social sphere. The little world of clubs and journals was far more a social than a political one, an aesthetic protest against utilitarianism and materialism but also an attempt to create a secret space, insulated from these Protestant pressures. It was at this point that it was noted that the French term *prétendant* (best translated as 'claimant' but generally rendered as 'pretender') 'is somehow suggestive of fraud to ordinary minds'.[95] It was the reaction that John Henry Newman (1801–90) had met with from his antagonist Charles Kingsley (1819–75) and that had led to Newman's *Apologia Pro Vita Sua* (1864). 'Pretender' had originally echoed the 'warming pan myth', but as this receded in time, the term took on another meaning: by the mid- and late-nineteenth century it came to imply a social pretence, a disguised unmanliness, indeed sometimes a covert homosexuality, an implication that survived beyond 1945 but then evaporated.

This fifth phase of scholarship was terminated in 1914 when the person then acknowledged as the senior Stuart descendant, the Bavarian Prince Rupprecht, served as a Field Marshal in the German army.[96] However eccentric this neo-Jacobitism seems from the perspective of the present, it nevertheless coincided with, and encouraged, a distinct intellectual formation: from the 1880s to the First World War, Jacobite studies enjoyed another golden age.

By this point, Scottish and English perspectives were, to an extent, elective affinities. Andrew Lang (1844–1912) was shrewdly identified by his friend R. L. Stevenson as 'an Oxford kind of Scot'. Born in Selkirk, educated at the Edinburgh Academy, St. Andrews, Glasgow and Oxford, a journalist and prolific author in many fields, he made his living as a writer in the London market. His 'cavalier temperament and distaste for the Whiggish and Presbyterian bias of so much existing Scottish historiography moved him to produce a series of books devoted to a single ambitious question: was it possible to defend the Stuarts?'[97] It was a question which he ultimately answered in the negative.

His *Pickle the Spy* (1897) sought to puncture much Romantic myth about Highland loyalty; it showed a Prince Charles betrayed by a chief and barely escaping a ruthless Hanoverian secret service. Lang's most influential work was his life of Charles Edward Stuart, based on substantial archival research, but presenting its subject as 'the centre and inspirer of old chivalrous loyalty ... one who would have brought back a lost age, an impossible world of dreams. Romance was in Charles's blood.' To confirm that aesthetic, it was necessary to depict Jacobitism as a hopeless cause before 1745, and this Lang did: in 1743 'the Jacobite party in England and Scotland was practically broken up, and quite disorganized ... In fact the country, while it flattered James and Charles in toasts and sentiments, was entirely resolved to have a Protestant on the throne, even a Hanoverian Protestant.' The aborted rising of 1744 was not taken seriously. At that point, 'To cool reflection, it seems that the exiled family should simply have withdrawn from hopes and projects, and accepted a good pension from England'. In that country, the Jacobite party, 'we repeat ... was a chaos of cross-worked plots, and internecine quarrels'. A quick invasion of England after Prestonpans would have been 'insane'. There was nothing for it to link with in England: 'Little has been said, hitherto, on the political aspect of the dynastic struggle, because Jacobitism was so much a matter, not of politics, but of sentiment.' The French court 'liked to have a Pretender, to annoy England with pinpricks, but had neither the resolution, the money, the ships, nor even the desire, to restore the House of Stuart'. English county families 'had learned their lesson of timidity' in the Fifteen, and did not stir as Charles Edward marched south. Once at Derby, none of the alarm in England 'proves that the Highlanders had a chance of entering the capital'. Lord George Murray 'was compelled to look at the situation in the light of what he knew. Charles beheld it in the spirit of romance.' In his months on the run after Culloden, 'romance reaches a happy moment'.[98] For the London market in 1900, Jacobitism was still essentially amusing literature, not disturbing history. And in these respects Lang may have answered for many of the Jacobite clubs of his time.

The Anglicised Lang provided little contrast with another significant scholar who moved in the opposite direction. Charles Sanford Terry (1864–1936), born in the mountain fastnesses of Newport Pagnell, educated at Cambridge, pursued a career as an academic in the newly developing subject of history, from 1898 at Aberdeen; from 1903 to 1930 he held a chair there, and made notable contributions to Scottish history as well as writing standard works on J. S. Bach. By 1900, the state of printed primary materials was such that Terry could publish two volumes offering coherent narratives of the Jacobite risings through lengthy quotations selected from original sources, with minimal editorial commentary.[99] The books had, however, certain important features.

First, they appeared as volumes III and IV in a series, *Scottish History from Contemporary Writers*. Jacobitism was now almost wholly a Scottish subject: English, Welsh and Irish Jacobitism hardly featured, still less the European dimension. Going further in this direction, Terry even depicted the Forty-five as chiefly a 'racial struggle' by 'Celticism' against 'Teutonism' in which 'Celtic patriotism fought its last fights in the service of James the Seventh, his son the Chevalier de St. George, and his grandson Prince Charles'.[100] Second, Terry ultimately did not take his subject seriously. At the crucial moment of the Forty-five, at Derby, Terry offered the opinion that the Jacobite army would have been militarily overwhelmed, even if it had succeeded in reaching London; Prince Charles's 'assent to the retreat from Derby was therefore wisely, albeit reluctantly given'.[101] Third, Terry wrote a history of events. He made little use of the 'enormous number of pamphlets which, while they illustrate the spirit and the passions in which the contest was waged, do not throw light upon its events'. Political ideology was not integral to his story. Terry concluded his volume on the Forty-five by quoting as if it were fact the passage from Scott's *Waverley* (chapter xliii) noted above, as a summary of the economic transformation of Scottish society in the following half century and as an account of the lasting appeal of cultural Jacobitism.[102] But, like Scott, he had implicitly abandoned the reality of early eighteenth-century political Jacobitism.

Lang and Terry were part of a cluster of scholarship on Jacobitism in c. 1890–1914 which often used the vehicle of biography. The first decade of the twentieth century even saw a flurry of works on James Francis Edward, hitherto a figure largely ignored.[103] In a biography of 1907 that began to tap French and Italian sources, Alice Shield and Andrew Lang explicitly attempted to rescue their subject from the memorable disparagement of his character by William Makepeace Thackeray (1811–63) in his novel *Henry Esmond* (1852) and from the apparent inevitability of the Revolution of 1688 after 'two crowded centuries of glorious history'. Yet the effect of this was undone by the authors' not taking seriously the Fifteen and the Forty-five. 'From first to last there was no hope in it', they wrote of the first; the negotiations that prepared the ground for the second 'are of scant interest'. James did not 'share the dreams' of Charles Edward. The French invasion plans of 1744 received two lines. The authors were more concerned to defend James's moral character from the charge of having had an affair with Lady Inverness, wife of James's Secretary of State, a charge that had aroused the moral indignation of A. C. Ewald in 1875.[104]

In 1907, an able study of James Francis Edward by 'Martin Haile' [i.e. Mary Hallé] was based on even more substantial archival research, and took a more positive and Anglocentric line: 'It was of absorbing interest to find how large a share Jacobitism held in the life of England during the seventy-eight years between the downfall of James II and the death of his son; and how great a mistake it is to regard the insurrections of 1715 and '45 as isolated occurrences; they were but the overflowing of a persistent current, which it required all the power and skill of William III and the first two Georges and their Ministers, and of the Whigs and Hanoverians in the time of Anne, to stem and to suppress.' Indeed, had the campaign of the Fifteen been led by the Duke of Berwick rather than the Earl of Mar, it might have had 'a different result'. The plans of 1744, too, were taken seriously; in 1745, had Marshal Saxe landed a French army in England, he would have succeeded. For Haile, it was Henry Benedict's acceptance of a cardinal's hat in 1747 rather than the battle of Culloden that was fatal to the cause. Even then, Haile recorded the serious intent of the French invasion attempt of 1759.[105] But it seems that these arguments did not widely register within British historiography.

Henry Benedict was dealt with in a similar time frame, with biographies in 1899, 1906 and 1908.[106] Yet these studies necessarily became primarily works on the history of the Catholic Church in eighteenth-century Italy and said almost nothing on the dimensions of Jacobitism in the British Isles. The books also shared a pessimistic view on the prospects for a successful restoration, possibly as a means of winning more attention for their subject against the entrenched assumptions of their age. Henry Vaughan wrote that Henry Benedict had performed a great service to Britain by accepting a cardinal's hat, so dealing 'the deathblow to a cause now irreparably lost'.[107] Andrew Lang used his Introduction to Alice Shield's study to accept that 'James VII [and II] had convinced England and

Scotland that the experiment of subjecting a Protestant country to the rule of a Catholic king was never again to be risked'; for Henry Benedict, 'there was never any hope'; his cardinalate was 'an abdication'; the Stuarts were extinguished by a merciful 'Fate'.[108] Alice Shield closed her volume with equally pessimistic counter-factual reflections on what would have happened had the Stuarts regained their throne in 1708 or 1745–6. Would not malcontents at home, wars abroad, the demands of Catholicism have produced the 'old story over again; the wars of Charles I; the Revolution; banishment or the scaffold?' Rather than 'conjecture ... we are glad to believe that all is for the best in this best of all possible worlds'.[109]

Where the Scottish historians had convinced themselves of Jacobitism's essential Scottishness, their English counterparts were beginning to adopt a Europe-wide perspective. But these English authors were evidently often Catholic, like 'Martin Haile',[110] and this gave their work, along with that of similar contemporaries, a recognisable identity (Kelly's *Life of Henry Benedict Stuart* carried the Imprimatur of Herbert Vaughan, Cardinal Archbishop of Westminster). These works of the early decades of the twentieth century often belonged to a reviving Catholic consciousness more prominently represented by Hilaire Belloc and G. K. Chesterton;[111] and although this ensured for it a certain currency, it also ensured that such currency would be strictly limited. Haile, Lang and Shield were not university teachers, and their work did not command entry to university curricula. This helped to deny it lasting impact. After the real achievements of the scholarship of c. 1890–1914, the next few decades saw in many ways a falling off.

Jacobite scholarship debased? Academic disengagement, 1914–1970

The work of the years c. 1914–70, often slighter in its intellectual calibre and self-indulgent in its commercial sentimentalisation, constituted a sixth phase. After 1907, the next life of James Francis Edward followed in 1934; it was markedly inferior.[112] After 1908, the next life of Henry Benedict was in 1958; it too was a far lesser work.[113] Even Alistair and Henrietta Tayler, zealous archival scholars, could not reverse this ebbing tide of academic seriousness.[114]

Academic exclusion also told against the history of the Nonjurors. Macaulay's polemical disparagement of them remained hegemonic. If moderate High Churchmanship inspired historians of the Nonjuring movement in 1845[115] and 1902,[116] this almost guaranteed for it exclusion from the historical mainstream. Overton's 1902 study also sought to rehabilitate those churchmen by downplaying their Jacobitism,[117] a strategy that condemned the Nonjurors to even greater irrelevance. The next major scholarly survey, in 1924, sold so few copies that it was eventually pulped by Cambridge University Press, and has become the rarest book in Jacobite scholarship.[118]

L. M. Hawkins's London PhD thesis was published in 1928, but the effect of her slim volume was subverted by G. P. Gooch's Foreword, claiming that the 'political ideas' of the Nonjurors 'have seemed too preposterous to deserve detailed analysis ... the conduct of James II made it impossible for the average man and even for the average Churchman to swallow the Gospel of Divine Right'. In 1688, Gooch continued,

> The Nation as a whole declined to believe that the only choice was between tyranny and anarchy; and accepting the assurance of Locke that a mixed government was both possible and desirable, proceeded with the leisurely construction of our liberties. The Revolution Settlement was the triumph of common sense. The last of the Die-hards were brushed aside because the modern Englishman is practical, prosaic, and empirical, inclined to compromise, caring nothing for mysticism and little for logic, but testing the value of institutions and principles by their fruits alone.[119]

Within such a normative mind-set, widespread in academe, Nonjuring religion and Jacobite ideology could command no attention.

The Catholic tradition did much to sustain what scholarship there was on Jacobitism in these decades of decline, as in the work of Sir Charles Petrie (1895–1977). Petrie's Catholicism also gave him a European perspective on events. In the first edition of his study, in 1932, he wrote: 'This book is the outcome of ten years of research in the subject of which it treats, and it is an attempt to tell the story of Jacobitism, not as a romance, but as a definite political movement.' In 1948, he added: 'To those who are accustomed to regard Jacobitism as a purely insular affair a disproportionate amount of space may appear to have been devoted to the background of international politics, but my defence is that to understand the Movement properly it must be viewed in the setting of the general European situation.'[120] But this appeal found few echoes within the British historical profession as it stood in that year. Petrie was more widely regarded as symbolising a late Romanticism born of prior social and denominational commitment rather than standing for a new tradition of archival or transnational scholarship. His main thesis, that Jacobite commitment was widespread and its chances of success real, was not widely identified.

Suspicion of Catholicism must be distinguished from another but more pervasive impediment to Jacobite studies. In retrospect, it is too easy to label the nineteenth century as the era of 'Romanticism', without making appropriate distinctions. Yet in this area at least the evidence suggests that the real age of trivialising sentimentality was not the early nineteenth century but the early twentieth. It was now, in this sixth phase, that the peculiar habit spread of referring to Charles Edward Stuart as 'Bonnie

Prince Charlie', a subtle denigration that implied its subject's descent into a slightly fey irrelevance. Robert Chambers suggested in 1827 that 'The reason why Charles's name is so generally diminished in this manner by popular parlance, seems to be, that the Erse or Gaelic translation of Charles is Charlich or Charli. The Lowlanders must have adopted the name generally given to him by his adherents.'[121] But the next step was more decisive.

The adjective 'bonnie' was authentic eighteenth-century Scots;[122] the locution 'bonnie prince' appeared first in song, was known but unusual in the eighteenth century, and spread to be common usage only by the 1830s.[123] A chapbook of the 1830s was revealingly titled *History of Prince Charles Edward Stuart, called by some "The Young Pretender," but more frequently, in the North, the Young Chevalier, or Bonnie Prince Charlie* (Newcastle upon Tyne, [c. 1832–7]). The earliest literary adaptations were a play by William Moncrieff in 1887 and a novel by G. A. Henty in 1888.[124] From song and literature, the transfer to politics and historical writing was not swift. Apart from one slight provincial work in 1903,[125] the earliest significant examples were from the 1910s, 1928 and 1932.[126] From there, however, the usage snowballed, and may be analysed as itself an historical phenomenon.[127] The student of historiography frequently discovers a considerable disjuncture between academic history and popular history. So it is here. None of the biographies of Charles Edward Stuart before Frank McLynn's in 1988 raised their subject to academic respectability. The fact that they were so numerous had itself the opposite effect.

By the inter-war period the sentimentalised aesthetic of the sixth phase was securely established. It was sustained in England not least by an Oxford-educated Scot, a son of the manse, John Buchan (1875–1940). His novel *Midwinter: Certain Travellers in Old England* (London, 1927), depicted (without evidence) Samuel Johnson as 'out' in the Forty-five. Even Buchan did not take his subject entirely seriously, for he evoked as his political yardstick a mystical vision of 'Old England' that was essentially neutral between Stuart and Hanover, priest and parson. He did not add to the plausibility of this idea of Old England by placing it in some undefined relation to what he termed 'Fairyland'.[128]

In 1933 Grant Francis still had no doubt that he was 'dealing with Jacobite romance' which was but a branch of a wider phenomenon:

> Little as it is possible for romance to manifest itself in the rush and turmoil of life in this prosaic twentieth century, it needs but the opportunity, and although – in comparison with the more spectacular occasions in medieval days of chivalry – it is difficult enough to invest the mud and blood-stained figures of the Great War with what we understand by 'Romance', there can be no question of it being present all the time.

However, Jacobitism was 'the very quintessence of modern "Romance"', and 'created such romantic incidents and stories as no thrilling fiction of these modern days can excel'. The failure of the movement was ascribed chiefly to the 'fate which dogged the footsteps of the Stuarts for generations'.[129] Francis combined antiquarian zeal with a prominent authorial voice which sounded convinced that it was imparting valuable information and imaginative involvement. Whether that was the case may be doubted.

Once these aesthetic assumptions had been laid down, however, works could be published which operated unreflectively and without any obvious need for justification within these guidelines.[130] No historical topic in recent writing was so compromised by this form of commercialisation, with the exception of the marital adventures of Henry VIII. Against this sentimentalisation, professional historians reacted strongly. The authors of a bibliographic survey of recent Jacobite scholarship, published in 1939, felt obliged to assure their readers that 'Jacobitism is dead', and to disparage what they recorded: 'Lost causes frequently have feline vitality, and bibliographically they nearly always do'. In the nineteenth century, 'As Scottish nationalism was merged with English and the word "British" became a reality, Jacobitism was rejuvenated to a harmless and rather sentimental virility.' One piece of genealogical research attracted a sneer: it 'listed names and titles of royal personages who would then have been ruling except for the fact that someone else was'. Whiggish works were treated differently: G. M. Trevelyan on Queen Anne was 'splendid' and Winston Churchill on Marlborough was 'monumental'.[131]

Even historians who questioned some aspects of the hegemony of modernism unthinkingly accepted others. In particular, they rejected any consideration of counter-factual analysis, the serious study of alternative pathways of development. It may today be objected that this is an essential component of all historical explanations, as well of those things that did happen as of those that did not: the claim that '*a* caused *b*' is also the claim that 'if *a* had not been present, *b* would not have occurred'. All history therefore involves counter-factual analysis; but this was, by many, indignantly denied and by others trivialised. In 1931 Herbert Butterfield, writing in *The Whig Interpretation of History*, that famous subversion of complacent Protestant teleologies, explained why historians were interested in the past for more than its present relevance. They became, he argued, drawn in, fascinated by the specific case: 'we cannot save ourselves from tumbling headlong into it and being immersed in it for its own sake; and very soon we may be concentrated upon the most useless things in the world – Marie Antoinette's ear-rings or the adventures of the Jacobites.'[132] Even Butterfield, who began to challenge positivist assumptions about overdetermined outcomes by the reintroduction of ideas of 'vicissitude' or 'chances and changes'[133] did not yet seriously entertain the counter-factual; certainly not on so outrageous a topic.

In his *Autobiography*, published in 1939, the Oxford philosopher and historian R. G. Collingwood outlined in layman's terms the philosophy of history he was later to encapsulate in the sentence 'The history of thought, and therefore of all history, is the re-enactment of past thought in the historian's own mind.'[134] Yet despite his historically-sensitive assertion that the historian must discern the problem as the past actor saw it, Collingwood too was dismissive of the counter-factual, in a key case refusing an effort of understanding to an alternative analysis that might have given a decisive battle a different outcome: 'Naval historians think it worth while to argue about Nelson's tactical plan at Trafalgar because he won the battle. It is not worth arguing about Villeneuve's plan. He did not succeed in carrying it out, and therefore no-one will ever know what it was. We can only guess. And guessing is not history.'[135] Serious historians of Jacobitism contended against this sentimentalisation and denial of the counter-factual largely in vain.

From the 1970s to the present

The idiom of writing on Jacobitism established after 1914 persisted into the 1970s, yet the unspoken assumptions underpinning Jacobite studies were eventually reversed; and this reversal constitutes a seventh phase. In the 1890s, the last Stuarts exercised a widespread aesthetic appeal, but it was as widely conceded that their cause stood no practical chance of achieving a restoration. That, indeed, was what gave glamour to what was presented as the politics of the hopeless gesture, the badge of a secret status or identity. By the 1980s a new generation of scholars had arisen, non- or anti-Romantic, who shared little or nothing of their predecessors' sentimental proclivities, but who began to treat Jacobitism as a movement with, at times, a significant chance of success. This last was the real heresy in the eyes of many scholars committed to the inevitability of the wider scenario of late modernism. It is, of course, not the case that Jacobitism deserves serious study only if it had stood a realistic chance of success: failed and successful causes are equally entitled to historical attention. But the opposite attitude was long powerful: the assumption that Jacobitism had stood no chance of success acted to discourage scholarship on the subject.

This reversal of assumptions from those of the 1890s may be analysed thematically. By the 1980s, a more hospitable climate was created for Jacobite studies by the growing acceptance of six themes: first, parliamentary psephology; second, the 'three kingdoms' model of the British Isles; third, the continental European dimension; fourth, literary and cultural studies; fifth, religion; and sixth, counter-factual analysis.[136]

First, parliamentary psephology. In 1970 were published the early eighteenth-century volumes of *The History of Parliament*, containing a key section by Eveline Cruickshanks on the Parliamentary Tory party.[137] Sir Lewis Namier had died in 1960, but his model of non-party politics was still dominant a decade later; the Sedgwick volumes were therefore doubly shocking, not only for uncovering strongly-etched party alignments but for asserting that a powerfully surviving Jacobite commitment created the ideological polarity that underpinned them. Cruickshanks depicted a Tory Parliamentary party heavily implicated in Jacobite conspiracy; the French invasion attempt of 1744 was co-ordinated with domestic plans, and had every chance of success had a French army been landed; Charles Edward might have won even in the much less auspicious circumstances of the Forty-five. There were allied studies, but as yet they did not constitute a critical mass. In 1975 Paul Fritz's monograph,[138] showing the seriousness with which English ministers regarded Jacobitism between 1715 and 1745, was diminished in its impact by the absence of related studies and by his residence in Canada, far from the epicentre of the debate. In 1979 Cruickshanks developed these themes at greater length, and in a more overtly European setting, in a monograph which proved to be decisive in changing the prevailing assumptions of historical scholarship.[139] It came as a revelation to many to see the evidentiary sources hitherto most associated with Namierites being made to yield such ideologically rich results, and to reveal a world in which Whig as well as Tory manoeuvre was dedicated so clearly but so anxiously to dynastic goals.

In retrospect, we can appreciate how the work of some political historians, however indifferent in scholarly calibre, became epitomes of an older scheme of explanation. Nowhere was this more true than in Cambridge, where J. H. Plumb (1911–2001) used the black arts of patronage and manoeuvre to sustain a world view. When his model of eighteenth-century politics[140] was undermined in 1970 by the publication of the 1714–54 volumes of *The History of Parliament*, and unavoidably challenged in 1979 by the publication in separate form of the research of Eveline Cruickshanks, Plumb reacted, as sometimes did his pupils, in re-enactments of the normative comment that had characterised reactions to Jacobite studies since the 1770s. Linda Colley had written a Cambridge PhD thesis under Plumb's supervision, depicting the early eighteenth-century Tory party in Plumbian terms as a body owing its coherence to gentry patronage rather than to ideology, and loyal to George I and George II; this argument could not now be reversed, and when published in 1982 the resulting book contained the same claim.[141] Colley defended this increasingly weak position by arguing in 1992 that the 'obvious strategy' of dismissing Jacobite attempts at a restoration as unfeasible because inimical to the interests of 'the bulk of Britain's trading sector' was 'rarely adopted' by historians because 'a disproportionate number of those who write about Jacobitism are themselves Jacobites who shut their eyes to the less attractive aspects of their cause'.[142] She produced no evidence of this, yet her reaction was not unique. David Cannadine, Linda Colley's husband from 1982, denounced in 1986 'the new Jacobite view of history, a wilfully perverse celebration of such obscurantist troglodytes as the Young Pretender', a view which 'makes even the embittered splutterings of Hilaire Belloc seem models of fair-mindedness and tolerance by comparison'. Cannadine sensed that Jacobite studies posed a threat to a scenario of British history that reached its apogee in the 1960s and 70s and that depicted 'a vision of the national past which was highly usable and very relevant to contemporary Britain', a scenario 'simultaneously dramatic yet benign'.[143] Pronouncements like this were notable for their stridency, but shared a number of more serious features that distinguish them from the normative opposition that had met authors of the subject from Dalrymple and Macpherson onwards: a sense that a secure historical teleology had been overturned; a desperate attempt to reclaim the high ground of moderation; and a reaching (whether sincerely or not) for late nineteenth- and early twentieth-century social stereotypes.

From 1979 the academic challenge to that scenario fortuitously paralleled the challenge which the British electorate was posing to equally deep-seated assumptions about the inevitable extension of collectivism and state provision in national life. Politically-committed historians of the 1960s and 70s who had invested heavily in this world view could be deeply disconcerted by claims of parity for what might be presented as its opposite. Although Jacobite scholarship had nothing substantively in common with the intellectual premises of Thatcherism (indeed was not connected to them), it was therefore often loudly resisted in the academic arena as if it did. Those who resisted it could reach for the cultural stereotypes that had been so dominant from the 1890s to the 1930s to depict Jacobite studies as a movement with a cultural if not a political agenda. 'Those who work on Jacobitism have been accused of "revisionist obscurantism" and nostalgia', protested one historian.[144] Yet this dismissive response rested on a false analysis and consequently failed to damage its target. Jacobite studies grew.

Second, the 'three kingdoms' model changed the setting within which English Jacobitism had been weighed. To see the civil wars of the 1640s as expressing a dynamic between England, Scotland and Ireland was the achievement of scholars of the seventeenth century in and after the 1970s. Yet it had an unanticipated result. Twentieth-century historians of the eighteenth century who disparaged or diminished Jacobitism generally focused on England. They employed an older set of historical assumptions in which England was made to stand proxy for Scotland, Ireland and Wales, and in which England was explained in terms of a secular, contractarian model of modernity. The discrediting of both these assumptions meant a reconsideration of the essential nature of English society, and opened up a larger field of comparison in which the political commitments of Scotland, Ireland and Wales carried far more weight.[145] The relative quiescence of English Jacobitism no longer looked decisive if, as in the 1630s and 40s, events in England could be determined by what happened in Scotland and Ireland. Moreover, the flourishing of historical writing in Scotland and Ireland in recent decades had allowed Scots and Irish historians to use the 'three kingdoms' model to highlight writing that in reality focused only on Scotland or on Ireland.

Third, a growing attention to Europe floated the theme of Jacobitism also. The reigning overview of Jacobitism from 1954 had given attention to diplomatic history, but had taken a sceptical line. George Hilton Jones, its author, judged that 'Any man now can see' that James III was 'wasting his energies in claims when his only profit must have lain in renunciation'. Rather, Jones depicted the Jacobite claimants as pawns in European diplomacy, used by the powers that backed them from time to time for their own purposes but standing no chance of success.[146]

If diplomatic history was the loser from the rise of new fashions in historiography during the 1960s and 70s, the diplomatic history of Europe in the eighteenth century was the area most widely abandoned. Its resuscitation was the work of several scholars. Eveline Cruickshanks, educated in England and France, used her knowledge of the French archives to important effect in her monograph of 1979. Studies of the Forty-five, she noted, had 'largely ignored the European context out of which the '45 arose and in which alone it could succeed'.[147] In 1981, Frank McLynn underlined France's good prospects of success in 1745–6, had she 'seized all the opportunities presented'.[148] Jeremy Black, who began his career as an historian of diplomacy, applied it to the Forty-five in a monograph published in 1990. Taking seriously the diplomatic background revealed that the Forty-five was 'the most serious crisis to affect the eighteenth-century British state' not least because he challenged the assumption that 'a successful rebellion required an invading foreign army'; the historian could not conclude that 'the Stuart cause was bound to fail'. On the contrary, there were many points in the campaign at which the Prince's army could have achieved even more than it did. And taking the campaign as a whole, including Cumberland's 'planned savagery' in the Highlands after Culloden, disposes of 'eighteenth-century Britain appearing as a "polite and commercial society", as indeed the country ... is most commonly presented to modern audiences'. Rather, such atrocities assimilate Britain to the wartime experiences of many continental European states, and refute the image of Britain as a place of 'peace and stability, liberty and property, politeness and tolerance'.[149]

Fourth, literary and cultural studies began to make increasing contributions to political history as late modernism's grasp weakened. Jacobitism had been imaginatively represented (or misrepresented) to mainstream historians chiefly through the novels of Scott, Stevenson and Buchan; but from the 1970s scholars of English literature began to uncover a mental world of eighteenth-century letters quite different in its sensibilities from that imagined by the Romantics. This was a slow process. Important studies by Douglas Duncan in 1965 and David Greenwood in 1969 were initially largely ignored.[150] Another pioneer was William Donaldson, whose PhD thesis of 1974 was published only in 1988;[151] yet it was wholly concerned with Scotland, and was not immediately recognised in England. There, from the 1970s, almost a lone voice in literary scholarship, Howard Erskine-Hill, began to recover a very different Jacobite aesthetic in English literature that had much to do with the Latinate culture of late humanism.

His research on Alexander Pope (1688–1744) led via an archival route to a new insight. The largest number of Pope's extant letters had been exchanged with John Caryll (1667–1736), member of a consistently Jacobite family in Sussex. Erskine-Hill's monograph on Pope[152] attracted the attention of Eveline Cruickshanks, and Erskine-Hill gave an important paper to the pathbreaking conference on Jacobite studies held at the Institute of Historical Research, London, on 2–4 July 1979.[153] It was possibly the first academic conference on the subject in recent decades, and had an important effect, evident in subsequent years, in rehabilitating Jacobitism as a subject for serious academic study. It had the further effect of establishing a bridge between literary studies and Parliamentary political history; but it also met resistance of a familiar kind. G. V. Bennett's review of the volume resulting from the conference[154] was a good example of the agitated response of one who had formerly defined Walpole's regime as offering 'stability and moderation', had identified personally with those virtues, and now found himself associated with a position that was shown to have been as substantive as those which he uneasily repudiated.

Erskine-Hill applied these insights into dynastic politics to Samuel Johnson in 1984,[155] and a remarkable academic conflict over the political and religious identity of Johnson unfolded in the following years. This controversy was characterised by the extreme language of Donald J. Greene and his followers who sought to defend an older image of Johnson as a Lockeian, proto-Evangelical, non-political or pro-Hanoverian figure. Not only was the new hypothesis of Johnson as a Nonjuror, drawn in early life to the Stuart cause, rejected as wrong; it was, in the eyes of Greene and his circle, improper and scandalous to advance it; it could only be explained in *ad hominem* terms, and could only be resisted by disparaging the scholars who proposed it. Here Greene set the tone of debate in 1996 by invoking in the same article Senator Joseph McCarthy and the John Birch Society, Marx, Hitler, Lenin, and Stalin, the Gestapo and the KGB, Nietzsche, Cecil Rhodes, Oswald Spengler, Mussolini, Mao, Pearl Harbor, William Joyce, Pétain, neo-Fascism, and Hilaire Belloc, evidently in an attempt to associate his opponents with extremism. Remarkably, Greene protested against the suggestion that his remarks had embodied 'a certain *ad hominem* rhetoric'. Thomas M. Curley added: 'Let it be remembered that to label him [Johnson] a Jacobite is to stigmatize him with the very worst of English crimes.'[156] Greene's opponents, it was implied, were not merely mistaken; they were morally and politically disreputable to advance such arguments. The rhetorically heightened nature of this response was however evidence that much more was at stake, and evidence that that an older position was losing the debate. Indeed, it already had: in the same year Erskine-Hill's magisterial studies of the relationship between literature and politics showed how such themes could be explored across a much wider canvas and for all parts of the political spectrum.[157]

Literary scholarship also underpinned the growing study of identity, thanks not least to the work of Murray Pittock, and informed awareness of the role of the Stuarts as symbolic redeemer-kings like Arthur (Owain), Fionn and Cuchulainn, part, at times, of a fertility myth. Such a role in creating and sustaining a myth was 'no accretion of sentimental Jacobitism: it was contemporaneous with Stuart rule, and not merely nostalgic'. Not only Jacobite ideology survived; so did Jacobite poetry and song, as vehicles for this myth, and myths were component parts of the wider question of national identities within the British Isles.[158]

A growing interest in material culture (now, in the sense of the cultural significance of artifacts) contributed to Jacobite studies as much as it did to bolster the historical model of eighteenth-century England as commercial, secular and politically pragmatic. Medals were part of 'a propaganda war', as was made clear by Noel Woolf in 1988.[159] Prints and portraiture were not less important. In 1994 and 1996, Eirwen Nicholson and Richard Sharp revealed the rich tradition of iconography that sustained the image of the Stuarts and their supporters into the 1740s and after; in 2002 Robin Nicholson showed how the plausible early eighteenth-century image of essentially European princes was Scotticised and then trivialised by sentimental nineteenth-century portraiture.[160] Until the 1740s, and except in newspaper and pamphlet publishing, the propaganda war was evidently won by the Stuarts rather than the Hanoverians, a discovery that helped restore credence to the political possibilities of a Stuart restoration in that decade.

In 1989, Paul Monod argued that Jacobitism was best understood as a 'culture' rather than as an ideology, or judged by its capacity to raise a military insurrection. As such, his use of evidence from cultural and social history established links with the fashionable historiographical methods of the 1990s to reveal the wide extent of Jacobitism even among English plebeians: a culture of demonstrations, crime, riots and seditious words, going far beyond the elegant artifacts and self-interested caution of the English elite. No longer could Jacobitism be dismissed by historians as 'a reactionary vice'.[161] It was an index of popular sentiment and allegiance to a degree that modernist historians had failed to appreciate.

Fifth, the rehabilitation within academe of religion permitted a reassessment of Jacobite motives and Jacobite ideology.[162] 'Ecclesiastical history' had been implicitly defined by the mainstream of the historical profession as a harmless irrelevance, persisting only in protected enclaves; increasingly from the 1980s it was re-integrated into the mainstream, and this revealed not only the social constituencies of political action but a wide land-scape of ideological conflict. The model of eighteenth-century society originating with T. H. Buckle, G. M. Trevelyan and others, carried forward by Basil Williams and Charles Stuart, luxuriating in the 1960s and 70s with such authors as E. P. Thompson, J. H. Plumb, John Cannon, H. T. Dickinson, W. A. Speck, Paul Langford and others had been either unthinkingly or programmatically secular. From the 1980s, the new group of historians who dispensed with this pre-commitment found themselves drawn to the subject of religion as a good predictor of the social constituencies within which men and women acted, and an indispensable element in explaining personal motivation and allegiance in the past. Historical interpretations not only of Jacobites but of Whigs were profoundly modified. Jacobites, instead of being a tiny minority of anachronistic survivals, found themselves at the contested centre of a new historical landscape in which both Whigs and Tories deployed a language of dynastic politics and divine right.

This language could be explained in other ways than as an ideology. Late modernism had profoundly shaped perceptions of what past *mentalités* could have been. Not only was dynastic politics the sphere of the irrational; to entertain it in the eighteenth century, as in the late twentieth, was to entertain 'the politics of nostalgia'.[163] Only in the 1990s was it observed that 'nostalgia' is not an eighteenth-century concept, not appearing in Samuel Johnson's *Dictionary* (1755). In retrospect, it is more evident how little the early students of *mentalité* actually explored *mentalités*: from the 1980s, research agendas gradually expanded.

These developments decisively changed the role ascribed to the churches. Now, the small communities of English and Scots Catholics emerged from the shadows to be a group successfully resisting two centuries of oppression, and finding in Jacobitism a political voice: contrary to previous assumptions, the English Catholic response to the Fifteen in the North was 'overwhelming'.[164] English Nonjurors ceased to be an historiographical aberration and became the tip of an iceberg of unknown but menacing size. Formerly, 'Nonjurors' were identified with (in England) a small group of clergy, ejected from their livings, who thereafter worshipped in separated congregations; now, it was realised that the term applied to that much larger number of laymen who, unwilling to swear, might often have avoided having the oaths tendered to them. Dispossessed Scots Episcopalians were no longer a backdrop to the inevitable victory of Presbyterian Moderatism, and became a major and unreconciled recruiting ground for Jacobite risings; the religious composition of the clans now became an important predictor (though not the only predictor) of their allegiance, not least with the spread of Presbyterianism.[165] Finally, and belatedly, the large community of Irish Catholics ceased to be an implicit yardstick of the presumed primitiveness of Irish society and became a valid folk culture, waiting for a catalyst to create a national movement.[166] In respect of personal faith, as Daniel Szechi summed it up:

> Essentially, from the exiled Stuart royal family downwards the term that best characterises Jacobite religious practice is *dévot*. Whether they were Catholic or Protestant, most of the men and women who were involved in Jacobitism were piously, deeply committed to their respective faiths. Indeed, it was through religious motifs that Nonjurors, Anglicans and Scots Episcopalians all shared, such as the doctrines of passive obedience, non-resistance and indefeasible hereditary right, that Jacobitism was able consistently to draw fresh recruits from among the more devout Tories (its best source of new blood).[167]

Such developments were promoted also by historians whose focus was still primarily on Scotland; among them, Bruce Lenman importantly showed how the major social constituency for Scots Jacobitism was provided not by Catholics but by Episcopalians, and revealed the world view of that community.[168]

Sixth, counter-factual analysis was reasserted. It was no coincidence that from the 1970s the decline of modernism coincided with growing attention in historical circles to the themes of contingency and counter-factuality. Yet these themes too were bitterly resisted. Richard J. Evans, giving the Butterfield lecture at The Queen's University Belfast in 2002, dismissed the genre as 'entertainments rather than serious intellectual endeavours': 'Imagining what might have happened is always fun' (why it should be 'fun' to ask what might have happened if, for example, Hitler had won in 1940 is not clear). Evans argued that an assertion about 'what might have happened implies an agenda as to what should or should not have happened'.[169] If this were inevitably true, the revival of interest in Jacobite studies would have been peculiar indeed (was its aim in 2002 a restoration of the *status quo ante* 1688?) Although the charge is easy to make, the evidence to support it is still absent. To explain the revival in Jacobite studies, we must trace the additional causes explored above.

More telling is Evans's modernist argument that attention to counter-factuals privileges the histories of politics, ideas, policies and events over the histories of 'processes, structures, cultures, societies, economies';[170] but, if so, the tension between the historical methodology of, say, R. G. Collingwood and that of reductionist social history is much older and wider than the tensions created by the recent revival in Jacobite studies. Nor does scholarship fail to transcend such boundaries: recent work by Paul Monod and Daniel Szechi employs social-anthropological evidence in ways that many social historians would find congenial. An article on Jacobitism in *Annales* itself confirms the acceptability of that theme in those circles at an early stage of revived British attention to the subject.[171]

The problem lay with late modernism rather than with Jacobite studies. The over-determination of outcomes that typified many schools of historical interpretation within the mental world of modernism was consciously challenged by the rise of counter-factual analysis, often in the work of very senior scholars. John Pocock reflected on the possibility of civil war recurring in mainland Britain after the treaty of Limerick and the massacre of Glencoe;[172] Conrad Russell showed how it was possible to construct a plausible scenario in which William of Orange's attempt in 1688 failed, so that the Henrician Reformation was reversed.[173] By the 1990s, systematic counter-factual analyses of large historical themes became not only popular but indispensable.[174] This gave unintended support to estimates that, had Charles Edward's army advanced from Derby to London, 'Victory was surely theirs for the asking', whatever might have happened afterwards.[175]

In 1985, Frank McLynn argued for the lasting importance of the threat of dynastic regime change: 'Until Hawke's victory at Quiberon Bay [in 1759], no one could be certain that Charles Edward would not come again to Scotland for another trial of strength'. Indeed 'the Jacobite risings are respectable counterfactual candidates … they did not represent a hopeless and anachronistic fantasy of counter-revolution'.[176] We might add larger counter-factuals that can be simply stated. In 1745 France did not intervene militarily to a significant degree, and a rising was militarily suppressed; in 1778 France intervened effectively, and a rising succeeded. These strategic realities are unavoidable; perhaps the thing most deserving of historiographical enquiry is why, at certain times and in certain quarters, they were so vehemently denied.[177]

This moral was greatly reinforced by the discoveries that the Atterbury plot of 1721–2 disclosed a culture of continued conspiracy, only frustrated by Walpole's ruthless and illegal methods;[178] that for thirteen years after the Forty-five 'the Jacobite movement persisted as a viable threat to the Hanoverian dynasty and the British state';[179] that the last French-backed Jacobite invasion attempt occurred in 1759.[180] It is this contradiction, implicit or explicit, of the Whig myth of British uniqueness that provides the most general reason why Jacobite studies continue, in some quarters, to be so passionately resisted. For it is certainly the case, as it has been since the 1770s, that scholarship on this question continues to be met with resistance or even *ad hominem* denigration. For deep-seated reasons, this disparagement seems likely to continue. Whether it will prove effective, as it has in checking earlier stages of Jacobite studies, remains to be seen.

Notes

1 Richard Sharp, *The Engraved Record of the Jacobite Movement* (Aldershot, 1996), pp. 37, 101.

2 For some of the complexities of the Catholic Church's relations with the deposed Stuarts see Edward Gregg, 'The Exiled Stuarts: Martyrs for the Faith?', in Michael Schaich (ed.), *Monarchy and Religion: The Transformation of Royal Culture in Eighteenth-Century Europe* (Oxford, 2007), pp. 187–213.

3 [Guy Miege, 1644–?1718], *A Complete History of the Late Revolution, from the First Rise of it to this Present Time* (London, 1691), p. 80; [David Jones], *The Life of James II. Late King of England* (London, 1702); *Memoirs of the Life of the Chevalier de St. George* (London, 1712); Robert Patten, *The History of the Late Rebellion. With Original Papers, and Characters of the Principal Noblemen and Gentlemen Concern'd in it* (London, 1717; 4th edn., 1745), p. 3; [Peter Rae], *The History of the Late Rebellion; Rais'd against His Majesty King George By the Friends of the Popish Pretender* (Dumfries, 1718), p. iii; Laurence Echard [?1670–1730], *The History of the Revolution, and the Establishment of England in the Year 1688* (London, 1725), sig. A4v.

4 [Henry Fielding, 1707–54], *The History of the Present Rebellion in Scotland* (London, 1745; 2nd edn., 1934), pp. 4–6, 12, 14–18, 23, 27, 29–30, 33, 37; [Dougal Graham, 1721–79], *A Full, Particular and True Account of the Rebellion in the Years 1745–6* (Glasgow, 1746; 9th edn., Falkirk, 1812) was 'basically metrical journalism' (*Oxford Dictionary of National Biography*); *The History of the Rise, Progress and Extinction of the Rebellion in Scotland, in the Years 1745 and 1746. With a particular account of the hardships the young Pretender suffered after the battle of Culloden, until he landed in France on the 10th of October, 1746* (London, [?1746]); John Marchant, *The History of the Present Rebellion* (London, 1746), pp. iii, v; James Ray 'of Whitehaven', *A Compleat History of the Rebellion, From its First Rise in 1745, to its Total Suppression at the Glorious Battle of Culloden, in April 1746* (Manchester, [?1747]), p. vi; Samuel Boyse, *An Historical Review of the Transactions of Europe, From the Commencement of the War with Spain in 1739, to the Insurrection in Scotland in 1745 ... To which is Added, An Impartial History of the late Rebellion* (2 vols., Reading and London, 1747), I, sig. A2v; II, pp. 59–60 bis; [Andrew Henderson], *The History of the Rebellion: 1745 and 1746. Containing, a Full Account of its Rise, Progress and Extinction* (Edinburgh and London, 1748; 5th edn., 1753), p. 24.

5 *A Short and True Narrative of the Rebellion in 1745 ... The whole being the shortest and most Authentic Account That can be given of that troublesome time* (Edinburgh, 1779), p. 10.

6 James Boswell, *The Life of Samuel Johnson LL.D.* (2 vols., London, 1791), sub 19 September 1777. Boswell in 1791 looked forward to John Home's history (for which, see below) that, although Hanoverian, would 'do justice to the other side' (*ibid.*).

7 Samuel Johnson, *A Journey to the Western Islands of Scotland* (London, 1775; ed. J. D. Fleeman, Oxford, 1985); James Boswell, *The Journal of A Tour to the Hebrides: with Samuel Johnson LL.D. ... with an authentick account of the distresses and escape of the grandson of king James II in the year 1746* (London, 1785; eds Frederick A. Pottle and Charles H. Bennett, 2nd edn., New York, 1961).

8 Andrew Henderson, *A Letter to Dr. Samuel Johnson, on His Journey to the Western Isles* (London, [1775]), pp. 47–8.

9 Murray Pittock, *James Boswell* (Aberdeen, 2007), p. 79.

10 Pittock, *Boswell*, pp. 69–79.

11 Pittock, *Boswell*, pp. 22–7.

12 Boswell, *Life of Samuel Johnson*, sub 3, 30 April 1773; 20 January, 7 February 1775.

13 Nicholas Phillipson, 'Sir John Dalrymple', *Oxford Dictionary of National Biography*. For his belief that the ideological conflict over resistance and non-resistance was pragmatically resolved in 1688 – both sides 'in reality could only differ about the degree of provocation which justified resistance' – see [Sir John Dalrymple], *The Address of the People of Great-Britain to the Inhabitants of America* (London, 1775), p. 14.

14 Sir John Dalrymple, *Memoirs of Great Britain and Ireland. From the Dissolution of the Last Parliament of Charles II. until the Sea-battle Off La Hogue* (2 parts, London and Edinburgh, 1771, 1773). *Idem.*, *Memoirs of Great Britain and Ireland: From the Battle Off La Hogue till the Capture of the French and Spanish Fleets at Vigo Volume Second* [actually third] (Edinburgh and London, 1788; new edn., 1790), carried the story from 1691 to 1702.

15 Dalrymple, *Memoirs*, I, pp. vii–viii, 1.

16 Dalrymple, *Memoirs*, I, pp. 43–5; Book I, pp. 21, 28, 34, 91; Part II, p. 199.

17 Dalrymple, *Memoirs*, II, pp. vi–vii, 132–4, 260–4.

18 Joseph Towers, *An Examination into the Nature and Evidence of the Charges brought against Lord William Russel and Algernon Sydney, by Sir John Dalrymple, Bart. In his Memoirs of Great Britain* (London, 1773), pp. 5–6, 9, 15–16, 25–6, 30–1.

19 [Thomas Sellwood, ed.], *Letters of Lady Rachel Russell from the Manuscript in the Library at Woburn Abbey. To which is prefixed, An Introduction, Vindicating the Character of Lord Russell Against Sir John Dalrymple, &c.* (London, 1773), pp. i–ii.

20 *Observations On a late Publication entitled 'Memoirs of Great-Britain, by Sir John Dalrymple', in which Some Errors, Misrepresentations, and the Design of that Compiler and his Associates are detected* (London, 1773), pp. 4, 6–7, 9–11, 15, 21–2, 25, 28. The author included an appendix (pp. i–xiv) of articles and letters in the newspaper press attacking Dalrymple and 'Scotch Principles'.

21 Murray Pittock, *The Invention of Scotland: The Stuart Myth and the Scottish Identity, 1638 to the Present* (London, 1991), p. 72.

22 In the same idiom was [Ralph Griffiths], *Ascanius, or, The Young Adventurer: A True History* (London, 1746), a reference to the son of Aeneas in Virgil's *Aeneid*, destined to have a part in the founding of Rome.

23 James Macpherson, *The History of Great Britain, from the Restoration to the Accession of the House of Hannover* (2 vols., London, 1775), p. iii.

24 James Macpherson, *Original Papers; Containing the Secret History of Great Britain, from the Restoration, to the Accession of the House of Hannover. To which are prefixed Extracts from the Life of James II. as written by Himself* (2 vols., London, 1775), I, pp. 116, 242; II, 175, 222, 364, 522–3, 538.

25 Macpherson, *History*, I, pp. vii, 430, 473, 487, 546, 557; II, pp. 3, 15.

26 Macpherson, *History*, II, pp. 51, 416–17, 502, 639, 651.

27 *A Letter to James Macpherson, Esq. With an Address to the Public on his History of Great Britain, and his Original Papers* (London, 1775), pp. iii–iv, 1, 3.

28 David Hume, *The History of Great Britain Containing the Commonwealth, and the Reigns of Charles II and James II* (London, 1757), II, pp. 443, 445.

29 For a different view see Pittock, *Invention of Scotland*, pp. 79–84; cf. Ian McIntyre, *Dirt and Deity: A Life of Robert Burns* (London, 1995), pp. 123, 201: 'It is possible to make too much of Burns's Jacobitism: the evidence is that he

used it as a sort of poetic fashion-accessory – it was a minor form of exhibition-ism rather than a matter of conviction.'

30 'For the Edinburgh Evening Courant', Nov. 8 [1788], in James DeLancey Ferguson (ed.), *The Letters of Robert Burns* (2nd edn., Oxford, 1985), I, pp. 332–5.

31 For some echoes see Keith Webb, *The Growth of Nationalism in Scotland* (Glasgow, 1977), pp. 33–5.

32 Cited here from Sir Walter Scott, *Waverley; or, 'Tis Sixty Years Since*, ed. Claire Lamont (Oxford, 1981). A properly nuanced account of Scott demands consideration of his other novels; reasons of space prevent such a discussion in this essay, which is more concerned with Scott's reception.

33 Sir Walter Scott, *Waverley*, ed. P. D. Garside (Edinburgh, 2007), p. 311. I owe this reference to Murray Pittock.

34 J. G. Lockhart, *Memoirs of the Life of Sir Walter Scott, Bart* (7 vols., Edinburgh, 1837–8), I, pp. 3–4, 17–18, 69–71.

35 H. J. C. Grierson (ed.), *The Letters of Sir Walter Scott* (12 vols., London, 1932–7), *Letters 1787–1807*, pp. 342–3; Arthur Melville Clark, *Sir Walter Scott: The Formative Years* (Edinburgh, 1969), pp. 65–70.

36 Scott to Robert Surtees, 17 December 1806 and 4 April 1808, in Grierson (ed.), *Letters …1808–1811*, pp. 37, 342–3.

37 Scott to Miss Clephane, 13 July 1813, Grierson (ed.), *Letters … 1811–1814*, III, pp. 301–3, at 302.

38 James Anderson, *Sir Walter Scott and History* (Edinburgh, 1981), pp. 25, 29, 93–4.

39 Henry Fielding's *The History of Tom Jones* (1749) had references to the Forty-five, but that was not its main point, and Jacobitism was there dismissed with conventional Whig rhetoric about liberty and popery. A Jacobite work, [?Neil MacEachen], *Alexis; or, The Young Adventurer: A Novel* (London, 1746; 30 pp.) and a Whig response, *Alexis; or, The Worthy Unfortunate* (London, 1747; 114 pp.) were more propaganda than significant literary achievements.

40 [Thomas Douglas, Earl of Selkirk], *Observations on the Present State of the Highlands of Scotland* (London, 1805), pp. 2–3, 67–8, 76–7.

41 Allan I. Macinnes, *Clanship, Commerce and the House of Stuart, 1603–1788* (East Linton, 1996), pp. ix–x.

42 Scott, *Waverley*, p. 340.

43 Scott, *Waverley*, p. 171.

44 Robert Clyde, *From Rebel to Hero: The Image of the Highlander, 1745–1830* (East Linton, 1995).

45 Scott, *Waverley*, p. 323.

46 Scott, *Waverley*, p. 78.

47 Claire Lamont, in Scott, *Waverley*, pp. xiv–xv.

48 He drew, for example, on the Whig histories of the Forty-five by James Ray (1747) and John Home (1802): Lamont, in Scott, *Waverley*, p. xix.

49 Boswell, *Journal of a Tour*, ed. Pottle and Bennett (1961), p. 129.

50 Anderson, *Sir Walter Scott and History*, p. 24.

51 Alastair Livingstone of Bachuil, Christian W. H. Aikman and Betty Stuart Hart (eds), *Muster Roll of Prince Charles Edward Stuart's Army* (Aberdeen, 1984); Murray Pittock, *The Myth of the Jacobite Clans* (2nd edn., Edinburgh: forthcoming). I am grateful to Murray Pittock for this information in advance of publication.

52 For a modern study of these diversities see Murray Pittock, *The Myth of the Jacobite Clans* (Edinburgh, 1995); for other historians' repeated inattention to them, pp. 10–14.

53 Boswell, *Journal of a Tour*, eds Pottle and Bennett, p. 131.
54 For the visual aspect of this process see Robin Nicholson, *Bonnie Prince Charlie and the Making of a Myth: A Study in Portraiture, 1720–1892* (Lewisburg, 2002).
55 J. S. Clarke (ed.), [Lewis Innes], *The Life of James the Second, King of England, &c. Collected out of Memoirs writ of his Own Hand ... Published from the Original Stuart Manuscripts in Carlton-House* (2 vols., London, 1816).
56 For which see Alistair and Henrietta Tayler, *The Stuart Papers at Windsor* (London, 1939), Introduction.
57 James Johnstone, Chevalier de Johnstone (1719–1800), *Memoirs of the Rebellion in 1745 and 1746 ... Translated from a French ms. originally deposited in the Scots College at Paris, and now in the hands of the publishers* (London, 1820), pp. iv, xlviii–xlix, xxxvi, xxxix.
58 Clarke (ed.), *Life of James the Second*, I, pp. ix, xii, xxvi.
59 Clarke (ed.), *Life of James the Second*, I, p. 487; II, pp. 2, 190, 225, 243, 292.
60 Henry Mackenzie, *An Account of the Life and Writings of John Home Esq.* (Edinburgh, 1822), pp. 6, 32–3.
61 James Macpherson, *Fragments of Ancient Poetry, Collected in the Highlands of Scotland, and Translated from the Galic or Erse Language* (Edinburgh, 1760); idem., *Fingal. An Ancient Epic Poem ... composed by Ossian* (London, 1762); idem., *Temora, an Ancient Epic Poem ...composed by Ossian* (London, 1763). Among the Scots who attacked Johnson for his scepticism over Ossian was Andrew Henderson, author of a history of the Forty-five: 'Ossian' offered the possibility for Scots of all parties to make common cause.
62 Mackenzie, *Home*, p. 67.
63 John Home, *The History of the Rebellion in the Year 1745* (4to., London, 1802), pp. iii, vii. The work reached a second edition (8vo., Edinburgh, 1822).
64 Home, *History*, pp. 24–33, 123, 146.
65 Home, *History*, pp. 3, 16, 19, 130–5.
66 The exception was James Hepburn of Keith, who ostentatiously affirmed his allegiance to Prince Charles, even though Keith 'disclaimed the hereditary indefeasible right of kings', because he 'condemned the Union between England and Scotland, as injurious, and humiliating to his Country'; Whigs deplored the fact that 'this accomplished gentleman, the model of ancient simplicity, manliness and honour, should sacrifice himself to a visionary idea of the independence of Scotland': Home, *History*, p. 101.
67 Home, *History*, pp. v, 237–61.
68 Mackenzie, *Home*, pp. 68–9.
69 Robert Chambers, *History of the Rebellion in Scotland in 1745, 1746* (2 vols., Edinburgh and London, 1827), I, pp. v–viii. The work reached a seventh edition in 1869.
70 Sondra Cooney, 'Robert Chambers', *Oxford Dictionary of National Biography*. Chambers included an eloquent discussion of the persecution of the Scots Episcopalian Church after Culloden: *History*, II, pp. 293–9.
71 Chambers, *History*, I, pp. vi, x–xi, 12, 29.
72 Chambers, *History*, I, 50, 63–4.
73 Chambers, *History*, I, pp. 182, 203–4.
74 Chambers, *History*, I, p. 304.
75 Chambers, *History*, I, pp. 222, 224, 233.
76 Chambers, *History*, I, pp. 228, 230.
77 Chambers, *History*, I, p. 174, II, p. 105.
78 Chambers, *History*, II, pp. 108, 112, 136, 125–285, 141.

79   Chambers, *History*, I, pp. 115–16, 119.

80   Chambers, *History*, II, pp. 287–9.

81   Chambers, *History*, I, p. 34.

82   For example, in Philip Henry, 5th Earl Stanhope, *'The Forty Five'. Being the Narrative of the Insurrection of 1745, extracted from Lord Mahon's History of England. To which are added, Letters of Prince Charles Stuart, from the Stuart Papers … at Windsor* (London, 1851).

83   Alex. Charles Ewald, *The Life and Times of Prince Charles Stuart, Count of Albany, commonly called The Young Pretender. From the State Papers and Other Sources* (2 vols., London, 1875), I, p. 5.

84   Lord Mahon (ed.), *The Decline of the Last Stuarts: Extracts from the Dispatches of British Envoys to the Secretary of State* (Roxburgh Club, vol. 59, London, 1843).

85   Ewald, *Prince Charles Stuart*, I, pp. 2, 6–7, 20–1, 40, 92, 95, 301–2; II, pp. 38–47, 206.

86   For an argument that Stevenson should not be interpreted as a 'Jacobite-inspired reactionary' see Frank McLynn, *Robert Louis Stevenson: A Biography* (London, 1993), p. 4 and *passim*. McLynn argues that Stevenson's interest in Jacobitism was driven by a psychological preference for a 'Jacobite sensibility' over a Calvinist one, p. 262.

87   Robert Louis Stevenson, *Kidnapped: Being Memoirs of the Adventures of David Balfour in the Year 1751* (London, 1886), pp. 76–7, 284, 331. Until the publication of Stevenson's *Catriona* (1893), the book ended with a paragraph open to a more favourable reading of Jacobitism: '[Just there, with his hand upon his fortune, the present editor inclines for the time to say farewell to David. How Alan escaped, and what was done about the murder, with a variety of other delectable particulars, may be some day set forth. That is a thing, however, that hinges on the public fancy. The editor has a great kindness for both Alan and David, and would gladly spend much of his life in their society; but in this he may find himself to stand alone. In the fear of which, and lest any one should complain of scurvy usage, he hastens to protest that all went well with both, in the limited and human sense of the word "well;" that whatever befell them, it was not dishonour, and whatever failed them, they were not found wanting to themselves.]', p. 311, parentheses original. I owe this reference to Howard Erskine-Hill.

88   The New Gallery, *The Royal House of Stuart* (London, 1889).

89   This subject has yet to receive extended investigation, although see Murray Pittock, 'By the Statue of King Charles: the Jacobite Revival of the 1890s', in Pittock, *Spectrum of Decadence: The Literature of the 1890s* (London, 1993), pp. 96–101. Pittock diagnoses the phenomenon as 'symbolic politics' or 'gesture politics', 'another approach to the absolute in the Symbolist hunt for Beauty', part of 'the deliverance of the artist from materialist, mechanist, capitalist, and Puritan bondage', pp. 99, 101.

90   Pittock, *Invention of Scotland*, pp. 120–33, at 120 (Pittock contributes insights on the English case also).

91   It ran from 1890 to 1905. Publication resumed in 1948, it must be assumed, a rather different social milieu, and ran until 1962.

92   Few survive. No. 14 was Henri de Massue de Ruvigny, 2nd Marquis Ruvigny and Raineval, *Legitimism in England* (?1897); no. 18 was Walter Clifford Meller, *Objections Answered* (?1899).

93   Ian Fletcher, 'The White Rose Rebudded: Neo-Jacobitism in the 1890s', in Fletcher, *W. B. Yeats and His Contemporaries* (Brighton, 1987), pp. 83–123;

Victoria Horley, 'The Jacobite Clubs of the Victorian Era', *The Jacobite: Journal of the 1745 Association*, no. 71 (1989), pp. 4–9; F. Peter Lole, *A Digest of Jacobite Clubs* (Royal Stuart Paper LV, 1999). The Royal Stuart Society was a later foundation, dating from 1926.

94 Daniel Corkery, *The Hidden Ireland: A Study of Gaelic Munster in the Eighteenth Century* (Dublin, 1925), pp. 130–1, 134; inconsistently, see pp. 258, 286, 299. Murray Pittock reminded me of this book.

95 Herbert M. Vaughan, *The Last of the Royal Stuarts: Henry Stuart, Cardinal Duke of York* (London, 1906), p. 103.

96 Pittock, *Invention of Scotland*, p. 123.

97 William Donaldson, 'Andrew Lang', *Oxford Dictionary of National Biography*.

98 Andrew Lang, *Prince Charles Edward Stuart: The Young Chevalier* (1900; 2nd edn., London, 1903), pp. 4, 54, 57, 66, 76, 83, 173, 175, 183–4, 206, 217, 219, 297.

99 Charles Sanford Terry (ed.), *The Rising of 1745* (London, 1900; 2nd edn., 1903); for a valuable bibliography of Jacobite studies to that date, revised in the 2nd edn., see pp. 227–319; *idem.* (ed.), *The Chevalier de St. George and The Jacobite Movements in his Favour 1701–1720* (London, 1901).

100 Terry, *Rising of 1745*, pp. v–vi. In *The Chevalier de St. George*, ch. I, Terry used Lockhart's *Memoirs* to establish 'Antiquity of Scotland – Persistent attempts of England to reduce Scotland – The Scots a brave, generous, and polite people ... Superiority to the English ... The Union of 1603 the beginning of Scotland's ruin', p. xiii.

101 Terry, *Rising of 1745*, p. 98.

102 Terry, *Rising of 1745*, pp. vi, 224–5.

103 This enthusiasm even floated into print in as slight a work as Oxford's Stanhope Essay for 1904: Henry D. Roome, *James Edward the Old Pretender* (Oxford, 1904). It attributed James III's failure to his 'faults of character', took care to deny the claims of the Stuart dynasty, and announced that a restoration would have meant 'despotism', pp. 68, 71–2.

104 Alice Shield and Andrew Lang, *The King Over the Water* (London, 1907), pp. v–vii, 1, 224–5, 231, 257, 367–81, 412–13.

105 Martin Haile, *James Francis Edward: The Old Chevalier* (London, 1907), pp. v–vii, 377–89, 401, 416, 444.

106 Bernard W. Kelly, *Life of Henry Benedict Stuart, Cardinal Duke of York* (London, 1899); Vaughan, *Last of the Royal Stuarts* (1906); Alice Shield, *Henry Stuart: Cardinal of York and His Times* (London, 1908).

107 Vaughan, *Last of the Royal Stuarts*, p. 282.

108 Lang, in Shield, *Henry Stuart*, pp. x–xi.

109 Shield, *Henry Stuart*, pp. 307–9.

110 'Haile' also wrote *Queen Mary of Modena: Her Life and Letters* (London, 1905); *Life of Reginald Pole* (London, 1910); *Life and Letters of John Lingard, 1771–1851* (London, [1911]); *An Elizabethan Cardinal: William Allen* (London, 1914).

111 Ian Ker, *The Catholic Revival in English Literature, 1845–1961* (Notre Dame, 2003).

112 Alistair and Henrietta Tayler, *The Old Chevalier: James Francis Stuart* (London, 1934).

113 Brian Fothergill, *The Cardinal King* (London, 1958).

114 Their many works included *Jacobites of Aberdeenshire and Banffshire in the Forty-Five* (Aberdeen, 1928); *The Old Chevalier* (1934); *Jacobites of Aberdeenshire and Banffshire in the Rising of 1715* (Edinburgh, 1934); *1715: The Story of the Rising* (London, 1936); *A Jacobite Exile* (London, 1937); *The Stuart Papers at Windsor*

(London, 1939); *John Graham of Claverhouse* (London, 1939); *Jacobite Epilogue* (London, 1941).

115 Thomas Lathbury, *A History of the Nonjurors: Their Controversies and Writings* (London, 1845).

116 J. H. Overton, *The Nonjurors: Their Lives, Principles and Writings* (London, 1902).

117 Overton, *Nonjurors*, pp. 12, 14, 64, 66, 158, 359, 416–17.

118 Henry Broxap, *The Later Non-Jurors* (Cambridge, 1924). J. C. Findon's important PhD thesis, 'The Nonjurors and the Church of England, 1689–1716' (Oxford, 1978) remains unpublished.

119 L. M. Hawkins, *Allegiance in Church and State: The Problem of the Nonjurors in the English Revolution* (London, 1928), Foreword by G. P. Gooch, pp. vii–viii. Hawkins's position was hardly more robust: pp. 162, 167.

120 Sir Charles Petrie, Bt., *The Jacobite Movement* (London, 1932); 2nd edn. as *The Jacobite Movement: The First Phase 1688–1716* (London, 1948), p. xi; *idem.*, *The Jacobite Movement: The Last Phase 1716–1807* (London, 1950).

121 Chambers, *History of the Rebellion in Scotland*, I, p. 283. The Gaelic for Charles is, rightly, 'Tearlach': ex inf. Niall MacKenzie. See also MacKenzie, 'The "poetical Performance" between John Roy Stewart and Lord Lovat (1736)', *Eigse: A Journal of Irish Studies*, 34 (2004), pp. 127–40.

122 As in *Ye banks and braes of bonny Down ... the words by the celebrated Robt. Burns* [London, 1796?].

123 *Five Popular Songs ... Bonnie Charlie* (Falkirk, [1825 or 1826]); William Lovell Phillips, *Bonnie Prince Charlie: A Song* (London, [c. 1830]); James Dewar, *Bonnie Prince Charlie, the favourite Jacobite song* (Edinburgh: [c. 1830]); *Bonnie Prince Charlie's Song Book* [Newcastle upon Tyne, c. 1832–7]; William Henry West, *Bonnie Prince Charlie, a celebrated Scotch ballad* (London, [c. 1840]); John Liptrot Hatton, *Bonnie Prince Charlie, a favourite Scotch ballad* (Liverpool, [c. 1840]), etc.

124 William Thomas Moncrieff, *Bonnie Prince Charlie* (London, [1887]); G. A. Henty, *Bonnie Prince Charlie: A Tale of Fontenoy and Culloden* (London, [1888]); it was last reprinted in 1955.

125 J. A. Wheatley, *Bonnie Prince Charlie in Cumberland* (Carlisle, 1903).

126 W. T. Fyfe, *Bonnie Prince Charlie: The Story of the Forty-five* (Edinburgh, n.d. [publication assigned in different catalogues to 1910, 1917 and 1920]); Donald Barr Chidsey, *Bonnie Prince Charles: A Biography of the Young Pretender* (London, 1928); Clennell Anstruther Wilkinson, *Bonnie Prince Charlie* (London, 1932).

127 Henrietta Tayler, *Bonnie Prince Charlie* (London, n.d. [1945]); Dorothy Middleton, *Bonnie Prince Charlie* (London, 1948); Winifred Duke, *In the Steps of Bonnie Prince Charlie* (London, n.d. [1953]); Sylvia T. Haymon, *Bonnie Prince Charlie* (London, 1969); Moray McLaren, *Bonnie Prince Charlie* (London, 1972); David Daiches, *Charles Edward Stuart: The Life and Times of Bonnie Prince Charlie* (London, 1972); Lawrence du Garde Peach, *Bonnie Prince Charlie* (London, 1975); Alexander Bruce Tulloch, *Adventures of Bonny Prince Charlie and the Battle of Culloden* (Newtongrange, 1981); Kenneth Bailey, *Bonnie Prince Charlie* (Edinburgh, 1982); Fitzroy Maclean, *Bonnie Prince Charlie* (London, 1988); Rosalind Marshall, *Bonnie Prince Charlie* (Edinburgh, 1988); Mollie Hunter, *Flora MacDonald and Bonnie Prince Charlie* (London, 1988); Jimmie MacGregor, *In the Footsteps of Bonnie Prince Charlie* (London, 1988); Susan Maclean Kybett, *Bonnie Prince Charlie* (London, 1988); Carolly Erickson, *Bonnie Prince Charlie: A Biography* (New York, 1989); Alan Norman Bold, *Bonnie Prince Charlie* (London, 1992); John Ure, *A Bird on the Wing: Bonnie Prince Charlie's Flight from Culloden Retraced* (London, 1992); Hugh Douglas, *Bonnie Prince Charlie in Love:*

The Private Passions of Charles Edward Stuart (Stroud, 1995); Diana Preston, *The Road to Culloden Moor: Bonnie Prince Charlie and the '45 Rebellion* (London, 1995); George Forbes, *Rebellion: Bonnie Prince Charlie and the 1745 Jacobite Uprising* (Glasgow, n.d. [?1995]); Barbara Mure Rasmusen, *Bonnie Prince Charlie* (Oxford, 1996); Kirsty White, *Over the Sea to Skye: A Tale of Bonnie Prince Charlie* (London, 1997); David R. Ross, *The Story of Bonnie Prince Charlie* (New Lanark, 1998); Josh Brooman, *Bonnie Prince Charlie: Hero or Failed Pretender?* (Harlow, 1998); Sandra Woodcock, *Bonnie Prince Charlie* (London, 2000); Hugh Douglas, *The Flight of Bonnie Prince Charlie* (Stroud, 2000); David R. Ross, *On the Trail of Bonnie Prince Charlie* (Edinburgh, 2000).

128 John Buchan, *Midwinter: Certain Travellers in Old England*, intro. Allan Massie (Edinburgh, 1993), p. 115.
129 Grant R. Francis, *Romance of the White Rose: A Jacobite Portrait Gallery. Narrating the Romantic Activities of the Principal Characters of the Jacobite Movement* (London, 1933), pp. xi, 13, 118, 154.
130 E.g. Ernest George Macdonald, Baron Porcelli, *The White Cockade: The Lives and Adventures of James Francis Edward Stuart and his son "Bonnie Prince Charlie" and Cardinal York* (London, [1949]).
131 Dorothy A. Guthrie and Clyde L. Grose, 'Forty Years of Jacobite Bibliography', *Journal of Modern History*, 11 (1939), pp. 49–60, at 49–51, 56.
132 Herbert Butterfield, *The Whig Interpretation of History* (1931; Harmondsworth, 1973), pp. 19–20.
133 Butterfield, *Whig Interpretation*, pp. 36–7, 54, 56.
134 R. G. Collingwood, *The Idea of History* (Oxford, 1946), p. 215.
135 R. G. Collingwood, *An Autobiography* (1939; Oxford, 1978), p. 70.
136 The way in which these themes flowed together can be well seen in a survey like Murray Pittock, *Jacobitism* (Basingstoke, 1998).
137 Eveline Cruickshanks, 'The Tories', in Romney Sedgwick (ed.)., *The History of Parliament: The House of Commons, 1715–1754* (2 vols., London, 1970), I, pp. 62–78.
138 Paul Fritz, *The English Ministers and Jacobitism between the Rebellions of 1715 and 1745* (Toronto, 1975).
139 Eveline Cruickshanks, *Political Untouchables: The Tories and the '45* (London, 1979). The seriousness of French attempts to support the Forty-five was further enforced by Frank McLynn, *France and the Jacobite Rising of 1745* (Edinburgh, 1981).
140 Best exemplified in J. H. Plumb, *The Growth of Political Stability in England 1675–1725* (London, 1967).
141 Linda Colley, *In Defiance of Oligarchy: The Tory Party, 1714–1760* (Cambridge, 1982).
142 Linda Colley, *Britons: Forging the Nation, 1707–1837* (New Haven, 1992), p. 72.
143 David Cannadine, 'The State of British History', *Times Literary Supplement*, 10 October 1986, pp. 1139–40.
144 Jeremy Black, *Culloden and the '45* (Stroud, 1990), p. vii.
145 E.g. Brendan Bradshaw and John Morrill (eds), *The British Problem, c. 1543–1707* (London, 1996); Brendan Bradshaw and Peter Roberts (eds), *British Consciousness and Identity: The Making of Britain, 1533–1707* (Cambridge, 1998); Glenn Burgess (ed.), *The New British History: Founding a Modern State, 1603–1715* (London, 1999); Jim Smyth, *The Making of the United Kingdom, 1660–1800* (Harlow, 2001); Allan I. Macinnes and Jane Ohlmeyer (eds), *The Stuart Kingdoms in the Seventeenth Century: Awkward Neighbours* (Dublin, 2002).

146 George Hilton Jones, *The Main Stream of Jacobitism* (Cambridge, Mass., 1954), p. 196. A copy with the ownership inscription of the Namierite historian John B. Owen (author's collection) is unmarked, and shows no sign of use.

147 Eveline Cruickshanks, *Political Untouchables: The Tories and the '45* (London, 1979), p. v.

148 Frank McLynn, *France and the Jacobite Rising of 1745* (Edinburgh, 1981), pp. 1–3.

149 Black, *Culloden*, pp. x, 2–4, 126, 184, 192, 202–4, 213; on the non-inevitability of the Jacobites' defeat in 1745, arguing (p. 213) against W. A. Speck, *The Butcher: The Duke of Cumberland and the Suppression of the '45* (Oxford, 1981).

150 Douglas Duncan, *Thomas Ruddiman: A Study in Scottish Scholarship of the Early Eighteenth Century* (Edinburgh, 1965); David Greenwood, *William King: Tory and Jacobite* (Oxford, 1969).

151 William Donaldson, *The Jacobite Song: Political Myth and National Identity* (Aberdeen, 1988).

152 Howard Erskine-Hill, *The Social Milieu of Alexander Pope: Lives, Examples and the Poetic Response* (New Haven, 1975).

153 Subsequently published as Howard Erskine-Hill, 'Literature and the Jacobite Cause: Was There a Rhetoric of Jacobitism?', in the proceedings of the conference, Eveline Cruickshanks (ed.), *Ideology and Conspiracy: Aspects of Jacobitsm, 1689–1759* (Edinburgh, 1982), pp. 49–69.

154 *English Historical Review*, 99 (1984), pp. 386–9.

155 Howard Erskine-Hill, 'The Political Character of Samuel Johnson', in Isobel Grundy (ed.), *Samuel Johnson: New Critical Essays* (London, 1984), pp. 107–36.

156 Donald J. Greene, in *The Age of Johnson*, 7 (1996), pp. 60, 63–4, 69, 75, 84, 87–8, 91, 95, 109, 118, 124, 127–8; Curley, p. 141.

157 E.g. Howard Erskine-Hill, *Poetry and the Realm of Politics: Shakespeare to Dryden* (Oxford, 1996); *idem., Poetry of Opposition and Revolution: Dryden to Wordsworth* (Oxford, 1996).

158 Pittock, *Invention of Scotland*, pp. 1–6, 8, 31, 41, 64; *idem., Inventing and Resisting Britain: Cultural Identities in Britain and Ireland, 1685–1789* (Basingstoke, 1997); *idem., Celtic Identity and the British Image* (Manchester, 1999).

159 Noel Woolf, *The Medallic Record of the Jacobite Movement* (London, 1988), p. [ii].

160 Eirwen Nicholson, 'English Political Prints and Pictorial Political Argument c. 1640–c. 1832: a study in historiography and methodology (Edinburgh PhD thesis, 1994); Sharp, *The Engraved Record* (1996); Nicholson, *Bonnie Prince Charlie and the Making of a Myth*; for a critique of established historiography for ignoring visual evidence, see p. 87.

161 Paul Kléber Monod, *Jacobitism and the English People 1688–1788* (Cambridge, 1989), pp. 7–8, 345. Monod's book represented a breakthrough. By contrast, Paul Chapman's Cambridge PhD thesis of 1984, 'Jacobite Political Argument in England, 1714–1766', remains unpublished.

162 By contrast with the theme of religion, there were few studies of Jacobite *mentalités* originating from other subject areas. See however Theodore Harmsen, *Antiquarianism in the Augustan Age: Thomas Hearne, 1678–1735* (Oxford, 2000).

163 Isaac Kramnick, *Bolingbroke and His Circle: The Politics of Nostalgia in the Age of Walpole* (Cambridge, Mass., 1968).

164 Monod, *Jacobitism*, p. 134; on religion in general, pp. 126–58.

165 Macinnes, *Clanship, Commerce*, pp. 173–81.

166 Breandán Ó Buachalla, *Aisling Ghéar: Na Stíobhartaigh agus an tAos Léinn, 1603–1788* (Baile Atha Cliath, 1996); Éamonn Ó Ciardha, *Ireland and the Jacobite Cause, 1685–1776: A Fatal Attachment* (Dublin, 2002).
167 Daniel Szechi, *The Jacobites: Britain and Europe 1688–1788* (Manchester, 1994), pp. 15–21, 26.
168 Bruce Lenman, *The Jacobite Risings in Britain, 1689–1746* (London, 1980); *idem., The Jacobite Clans of the Great Glen, 1650–1784* (London, 1984).
169 R. J. Evans, 'Telling It Like It Wasn't' and 'Response', *Historically Speaking*, 5 (March 2004), pp. 11, 31.
170 *Ibid.*, p. 13.
171 Guy Chaussinand-Nogaret, 'Une élite insulaire au service de l'Europe: les Jacobites au XVIIIè siècle', *Annales*, 28 (1973), pp. 1097–122.
172 J. G. A. Pocock, 'The Fourth English Civil War: Dissolution, Desertion and Alternative Histories in the Glorious Revolution', *Government and Opposition*, 23 (1988), pp. 151–66.
173 Conrad Russell, 'The Catholic Wind', in *idem., Unrevolutionary England* (London, 1990), pp. 305–8.
174 Niall Ferguson (ed.), *Virtual History: Alternatives and Counterfactuals* (London, 1997); Philip E. Tetlock, Richard Ned Lebow and Geoffrey Parker (eds), *Unmaking the West: "What If" Scenarios that Rewrite World History* (Ann Arbor, Michigan, 2006).
175 Pittock, *Jacobitism*, p. 103.
176 Frank McLynn, *The Jacobites* (London, 1985), pp. 123, 210.
177 For the 'rejectionists' see Daniel Szechi, *The Jacobites: Britain and Europe 1688–1788* (Manchester, 1994), pp. 5–8. Much more might be written on this theme.
178 Eveline Cruickshanks and Howard Erskine-Hill, *The Atterbury Plot* (Basingstoke, 2004).
179 Doron Zimmermann, *The Jacobite Movement in Scotland and in Exile, 1746–1759* (Basingstoke, 2003), p. 1. See especially 'The Modern Historical Debate on Jacobitism', pp. 3–13.
180 Claude Nordmann, 'Choiseul and the Late Jacobite Attempt of 1759', in Eveline Cruickshanks (ed.), *Ideology and Conspiracy: Aspects of Jacobitism, 1689–1759* (Edinburgh, 1982), pp. 201–17.

2

'A lot done, more to do': The Restoration and Road Ahead for Irish Jacobite Studies[1]

Éamonn Ó Ciardha

On 6 May 2008, in their last official engagements as Taoiseach and First Minister of the new Northern Ireland Assembly, Mr. Bertie Ahern and the Reverend Dr. Ian Paisley opened the new Battle of the Boyne Heritage Centre. It would be difficult to exaggerate the symbolic importance of this meeting of old ideological foes on one of Europe's great battlefields. Ian presented Bertie with a seventeenth-century copy of the King James Bible, to accompany his previous gift of a 'Jacobite' musket which had been discarded after the rout in July 1690. 'The Big Man' entertained an attentive, appreciative audience with a lively, if somewhat skewed, historical discourse on the 'Glorious Revolution'. Castigating the bigoted tyrant King James and 'Lying Dick Talbot', the ever-dependable whipping-boys of Whig history, he invoked a motley crew of Protestant heroes – William the Silent, James I, Charles I, William III, Governor Walker and the Apprentice Boys – in a speech which bristled with timeless Protestant rhetoric. The First Minister and/or his speech-writers ignored recent reappraisals of a divisive historical legacy, drawing instead on the venerable authority of Lord Macaulay and the Reverend Thomas Hamilton, first President of Queen's University Belfast.[2]

Pocketing a potentially embarrassing gift with undue haste, Bertie's gracious retort judiciously avoided any whiff of historical controversy. Forgoing any reference to King James II, Patrick Sarsfield, French allies, divisive historical argument or the pathos-filled quatrains of the Irish Jacobite poets Dáithí Ó Bruadair or Aogán Ó Rathaile, his address resonated with the 'Republican Party' rhetoric of liberty and equality and democracy, while soft-pedalling on the vexed question of Irish unification. The exchange between Ahern and Paisley marks an apposite moment to appraise both Whig intellectual decommissioning and recent Jacobite historical re-armament, processes which began in the watery meadows of County Meath and are coming to fruition in the pages of *Eighteenth-century Ireland*.

Before assessing more recent developments in Irish Jacobite studies, it is necessary to provide a brief historical context. Irish Catholic loyalty to the House of Stuart first manifested itself following the accession of the Protestant King James VI of Scotland to the English throne and Irish crown as James I in 1603.[3] The first *de facto* monarch of the whole country, the new king's martyred Catholic mother, his impeccable (fabricated) Gaelic genealogies and the strategic diplomatic and theological trimming of Irish friars and theologians in Louvain, Rome and Salamanca, ensured that he had no rivals for Irish royalist affections.[4] This loyalty survived the trauma of the 'Wars of the Three Kingdoms', the Interregnum and the political frustrations and disappointments of Charles II's reign. On the succession of James II in 1685, many Irishmen looked to the new Catholic monarch to abolish anti-Catholic legislation and restore lands that they had lost fighting for his father and brother against Cromwell and the English Parliament. Disillusionment and military defeat initially dimmed but did not extinguish Irish enthusiasm for his fallen house. Through the course of the late-seventeenth and eighteenth centuries, Irish Jacobites looked to the exiled Stuarts to restore their confiscated lands, dissolve the anti-Catholic penal laws against land and religion, and reverse the political, social and cultural domination of the Protestant ascendancy. Like their English, Scottish and European counterparts, they tailored Jacobitism to suit the particular needs of their community: the cause would even be invoked to demand the right to bear arms, dispossess and drive out Protestants, take out leases, vote in elections and restore and promote the Irish language and Gaelic culture.

Although early-modern Ireland arguably expended more blood and treasure on behalf of the Stuarts than their English and Scottish counterparts, they wielded much less influence at court, whether in London, Dublin, Saint-Germain, Avignon or Rome and have, until recently, been under-represented in the Jacobite historical chronicle.[5] Lord Macaulay claimed that the fallen dynasty meant absolutely nothing to the Irish who regarded the 'foreign sovereign of his native land with the feeling with which a Jew regarded Caesar'.[6] Indeed, Professor Clark's comprehensive review of English and Scottish Jacobite history and historiography bears testimony to the fact that English and Scottish historians have, until recently, shown little interest in Irish Jacobitism; those who have tend to underplay or dismiss the phenomenon after 1691.

The contrasting fate of the first two contemporary Irish accounts of the 'Glorious Revolution' provides a suitable metaphor for the negation of Irish Jacobitism. Archbishop King's *State of the Protestants in Ireland* (London, 1692) became a foundation-text of Irish Protestant identity and has gone through numerous editions, invariably issued at moments of acute political crisis for Irish Protestants, from the 1798 Rebellion through Catholic Emancipation and Repeal to the third Home Rule bill.[7] In stark contrast, the Rev. Charles Leslie's devastating rebuttal (*An Answer to the book entitled 'The State of the Protestants in Ireland under the late King James' Government'*, London, 1692) has never been reprinted. Furthermore, its author, the evangelist of Nonjuring English Jacobitism and the prolific 'reasoner who could not be reasoned against', to use Dr. Johnston's immortal phrase, has never merited a serious scholarly biography.[8]

Other canonical texts for the study of Irish Jacobitism are un-catalogued, un-edited, un-translated, unpublished (or published abroad,) out of print or inaccessible to those who do not read Irish, Latin or French. Some of Nicholas Plunkett's 'Light to the Blind', a key Jacobite narrative of the war and its aftermath, has never appeared in print. The full text, divided between two large manuscripts housed in the Bodleian, Oxford, and the National Library of Ireland, also contains numerous unpublished pamphlets which shed much light on dynastic, political, military, economic and financial aspects of Irish Jacobitism, as well as presenting some fascinating counter-factuals (a key facet of Irish Jacobite letters).[9] Other inaccessible and out-of-print Jacobite texts include Roderick O'Flaherty's *Ogygia, seu rerum Hibernicarum chronologia* (London, 1688), Charles O'Kelly's allegorical *Marcariae Exidium: The Destruction of Cyprus* (Dublin, 1850), Hugh Reilly's *Ireland's Case Briefly Stated* (Paris/Louvain, 1695), Matthew Kennedy's *Chronological, Genealogical and Historical Dissertation of the Royal Family of the Stuarts...*(Paris, 1705) and the Abbé MacGeoghegan's *Histoire d'Irlande* (Paris, 1758–62).[10]

Some of the most important repositories for Jacobite studies have barely been tapped for the Irish side of the story. The Stuart Archives at Windsor Castle, ignored by Irish historians until the 1990s, contain more untold riches than the specifically Ireland-related material published in Dr. Patrick Fagan's two-volume *Ireland in the Stuart Papers* Dublin, 1996).[11] Early-modern Irish scholars have long mined the French, Spanish and Vatican archives with profit, but there has been greater focus on seventeenth century, with particular emphasis on the political, diplomatic, military and religious history. Finally, and crucially, an enormous amount of Irish Jacobite poetry and prose is neither edited nor translated, and there has, to date, been little understanding of, or engagement with, its contemporary political, literary and historical contexts.[12]

The lack of serious engagement with the Jacobite phenomenon also derives from the association of royalism with defeat, confiscation, persecution and the emergence of republicanism as the ascendant political ideology within Irish nationalism. The heroes of the Irish nationalist and republican tradition disdained the worthless Stuarts. Even at the Boyne, General Patrick Sarsfield, darling of the Irish Jacobite army, wished to exchange kings and fight again.[13] A century later in the 1790s, Theobald Wolfe Tone, the United Irish leader and father of Irish republicanism, scoffed at the suggestion of a Stuart restoration, while James Connolly, the socialist republican martyr of the 1916 Rising, dismissed James II as 'the most worthless representative of a worthless race that ever sat on a throne'.[14] It is no surprise, therefore, that the Irish state found no place in its national pantheon for the absolutist Stuart king who deserted the country in its hour of need.

In spite of these intellectual and ideological impediments, Jacobitism hovered on the Irish academic horizon in the centuries after James' fall, linking itself to many of the other political, cultural, literary and scholarly subjects which preoccupied Irish letters; the 1641 Rebellion,[15] the Ossian controversy,[16] the Penal Laws, Catholic Relief and the Roman Catholic mission,[17] the Irish military diaspora,[18] the Oath,[19] the evolution from Jacobitism through Jacobinism to the crypto-royalism of O'Connellism,[20] the long-running Hidden Ireland controversy and the importance of Irish-language poetry as a source for early-modern Irish history.[21]

Influential Irish historians and commentators have suggested that ignorance and apathy rather than hostility characterised Irish attitudes towards the Stuarts. Thomas D'Arcy Magee, the Young Irelander *cum* Canadian federalist, noted that King William III was acknowledged by all but the extreme Jacobites as *de facto* king. His history focused on Irish inaction during the Jacobite rebellions, although he did concede on Franco-Irish military, economic and logistical support for the '45. John Mitchel, republican firebrand and apologist for Southern slavery, seized on the lack of an Irish response to James II's infamous 1693 Declaration to show that the Irish 'had had enough of Righ Seamus at the Boyne'.[22] W. E. H. Lecky concluded that no great enthusiasm existed among Catholics in the eighteenth century for a return of the Stuarts, and that the surviving gentry did not wish to risk their estates again.[23] Catholic historians such as Canon W. P. Burke and Daniel McCarthy, in their eagerness to show the injustices of the penal laws against Catholics in the eighteenth century, underplayed Irish Jacobitism and the Jacobite threat, citing inaction in 1715 and 1745 as a suitable yardstick of Catholic apathy for the fallen dynasty. Similarly, Reginald Walsh believed that Catholics had been reduced to such an extremity that the government had not the slightest reason to apprehend any disturbance, and dismissed the penal laws as 'a mere pretext for satisfying its hatred of the ancient faith'.[24]

Catholic amnesia and republican disdain also manifested themselves in the Irish literary tradition. Edward Walshe suggested that his Jacobite 'Reliques' were 'dear to people for being in their native tongue, rather than for their political sentiments'. Indeed, he argued that 'they sang them in their beautiful native airs without troubling themselves much about the Pretender'.[25] John O'Daly, a pioneer editor of the finest Jacobite poems and songs, regarded James II as 'the most dastardly poltroon that ever set foot on Irish ground'. He underplayed the significance of Ireland's Jacobite literary past, asserting that 'it would be wrong to consider these songs purely

Jacobite (in the Scotch sense) for the Irish cared less for a king than for a deliverer of that land which they loved with an intensity beautifully shown in the ballads'.[26] James Hardiman, another prolific editor of Jacobite verse, believed that the Irish supported the Jacobite cause 'more out of principle than allegiance, with perhaps a vain hope of regaining their estates, than from any particular attachment to himself or his ungrateful race'. Accusing 'the pusillanimous king' (James II) of betraying them 'on the very verge of victory', he contradicted the subject-matter of his two-volume minstrelsy by claiming that the Irish moved 'neither tongue, pen or sword...in their favour during the rebellions of 1715 and 1745'.[27]

The context in which Walshe, O'Daly and Hardiman collected their 'reliques' and penned their dismissive forewords should also be borne in mind. By the mid-nineteenth century, the 'dejacobitisation' of the Irish political tradition, initiated by Cornelius Nary, continued by the Hanoverian accommodationists Charles O'Conor, John Curry, Fr. Arthur O'Leary and the United Irishmen Miles Byrne, Charles Teeling and Micheál Óg Ó Longáin, had achieved its purpose.[28] Despite occasional royalist posturings by Daniel O'Connell, there was no equivalent in the Irish literary or political experience to the contemporary 'Balmoralisation' of the British royal family or of the Scottish Jacobite romantic history concocted by Sir Walter Scott and Lady Carolina Nairne.[29] Ireland had moved on.[30] The Irish harp had been re-strung and tuned for a republican air.

This disdain for the Stuarts and their luckless cause also manifested itself in popular historical and literary discourse. In the 1950s, Brian O'Higgins confidently rehearsed these broad historical themes and cultural certainties to a popular readership in the *Wolfe Tone Annual*, a magazine which might have may have passed through young Bertie's hands as a student at St. Aidan's Christian Brothers, Drumcondra. O'Higgins reiterated the conventional view that James II and William of Orange 'faced each other across the Boyne as antagonists for the crown of England' and believed that 'they had no interest in Ireland or its freedom, except in so far as it might be useful as a granary, a breeder of soldiers, a strategic outpost and a source of revenue'. He censured those who 'despised the people of Ireland who lived through the terrible penal days because they endured so much without rising out against their oppressors because of their slavish loyalty to the mean and worthless Stuarts'.[31]

Trinity College Dublin, having long ago exorcised the unwelcome spectre of Jacobitism,[32] echoed with a similar refrain. T. W. Moody suggested that 'the Old English and the Old Irish shared a common ruin, fighting on the side of one English king [James II] against another rival English king [William III]'.[33] Similarly, R. B. McDowell's prodigious scholarship resonated with a contemptuous impatience for Jacobite Ireland, its literature and the political sentiments of Irish-speaking people.[34] Irish Jacobitism also became the victim of its most authoritative historian; J. G. Simms concluded his seminal *Jacobite Ireland* (London, 1969, repr., Dublin, 2000) with the resounding defeat of the Irish Jacobite nation in 1691.[35] Marcus Beresford, also trained in the Trinity stable, claimed that 'a combination of time and penal laws stifled temporarily the political ambitions of Catholics,' an opinion which can certainly be challenged by even a cursory examination of Irish Jacobite literature, the voluminous Irish correspondence in the Stuart Papers, as well as many published and unpublished writings of the Irish diaspora.[36] The reasons advanced for this 'collapse of Catholic political will' include the crushing finality of the Williamite victory, the fact that 'the greater proportion of the wealth of the country lay in the hands of a small minority', and the 'erosion of the natural leaders of the Irish Catholic political nation'.[37] Similarly, David Dickson's *New Foundations* treated the decapitation of St. Ruth at the Battle of Aughrim in 1691 as a metaphor for the definitive truncation of Jacobite Ireland.[38] Other historians have followed suit. Thomas Bartlett referred to the destruction of the Jacobite cause at the Boyne and Aughrim eight times in the first forty pages of his *Fall and Rise of the Catholic Nation*. Similarly, David Hayton stated that after Jacobite War 'without their natural leaders it was unthinkable that the common people could rebel'.[39]

Despite this impressive and long-standing historical and historiographical consensus, the arguments are not entirely persuasive and have been refracted through a Whiggish prism of historical hindsight; and the act of refraction, by definition, causes deviation. Catholic Ireland had been vanquished and disarmed in 1691 and the greatest proportion of land and wealth had indeed passed into the hands of the Protestant minority.[40] It should be remembered, however, that Catholic Ireland had been comprehensively crushed in the 1650s, but within three years of James' succession Dick Talbot had effectively seized control of the kingdom and successfully held his charge for his master's cause. It would take King William, with a large army of continental veterans and mercenaries, funded to the tune of £2,000,000 by the English Parliament, to bring divided, impoverished Jacobite Ireland to its knees. The Protestant Ascendancy would be further secured by the wholesale disarmament of Catholic Ireland, in defiance of the terms of the Treaty of Limerick, and the provision of a standing army which was billeted throughout the kingdom. Furthermore, when Sarsfield led the Irish Jacobite army from Limerick in 1691, neither he, nor his Catholic or Protestant contemporaries, believed that exile would terminate their involvement in Irish political affairs. In addition, the prodigious research of Cullen on the Catholic middle-classes, of Power on the suspect political loyalties of Protestant converts, of Whelan on the 'underground gentry', of Leighton on the Catholic *ancien régime* and of Fenning and Fagan on the Catholic Church, all suggest that the political shipwreck and ideological bankruptcy of the Catholic political interest in the eighteenth century has been exaggerated.[41]

Until the early 1990s, there was no article or review, much less a monograph on post-1691 Irish Jacobitism, the ideology which principally sustained Irish Catholic political identity in the hundred years between 1688 and the French Revolution. Although English and Scottish Jacobite history has recently experienced yet another resurgence,[42] Irish Jacobitism languished outside the mainstream of an eighteenth-century Irish history which was still dominated by ascendancy history, high politics, the Church of Ireland, the Volunteers, 1798 and the Roman Catholic Church.[43] Slowly, however, calls did begin to resound in Irish academic circles for an appraisal of Jacobitism. In an otherwise glowing review of Sean Connolly's *Religion, Law and Power: The Making of Protestant Ireland* (1992), Marianne Elliott concluded that the age-old issue of whether Catholic Ireland posed a serious Jacobite threat would not be resolved until further research had exhaustively explored Irish-language, and continental, as well as British and Irish sources.[44] Toby Barnard's authoritative overview of eighteenth-century Irish historiography concurred, highlighting Jacobitism as a key area for further scholarly exploration.[45]

Breandán Ó Buachalla's review of Eveline Cruickshanks and Jeremy Black's *The Jacobite Challenge* (1988) provided the only modern commentary on post-1691 Irish Jacobitism when I embarked on my own doctoral research in 1992.[46] Three years later, Michael Fry and Dr. Joan Pittock-Wesson responded favourably to my request to include an Irish 'Jacobite' dimension to the University of Aberdeen's Quincentennial international conference on 'Jacobitism, Scotland and the Enlightenment' (29 July 1995). Ó Buachalla duly delivered a key-note address, while Mícheál Mac Craith, Vincent Morley and I formed a panel, the first major Irish scholarly representation at an international Jacobite conference. These scholars have subsequently published their work and their findings will be considered during the course of this essay. It is not a coincidence that this Jacobite 'awakening' occurred at the same time as the foundation of *Eighteenth-century Ireland*, a bilingual, interdisciplinary academic journal which would play a key role in mainstreaming Irish Jacobite studies. Not only did the new journal publish Ó Buachalla's aforementioned review, but it also carried paradigm-shifting analytical articles and sources by Pádraig Breathnach, Vincent Geoghegan, Mícheál Mac Craith, Vincent Morley, Diarmuid Ó Muirithe and Breandán Ó Buachalla.[47]

Ó Buachalla aired many of his major findings, both archival and interpretative, on royalism, messianism and Jacobitism in peer-reviewed journals and edited collections,[48] thereby whetting Irish academic appetites for the appearance of his monumental *Aisling Ghéar: na Stíobhartaigh agus an tAos Léinn* (1996), one of the most important books published on early modern Irish history and literature in the last fifty years. His close re-readings and contextualisations have rescued Irish Jacobite poetry (and prose) from the 'Charlie over the Waterism' and the literary nostalgia which plagued it for nearly two hundred years. Unfortunately the inability of many Irish historians to engage with the massive corpus of source-material used by Ó Buachalla means that the book is more referenced than read.[49]

More recently, Sean Connolly's online review of my own book, *Ireland and the Jacobite cause, 1685–1766* (2002, repr. 2004) is in itself a ringing endorsement of the emergence of Jacobitism as a serious subject in early modern Irish historical discourse.[50] Connolly pens an engaging, and challenging review which assesses the work and acknowledges its engagement with a broad, if incomplete, range of literary, official and continental sources. His critical commentary also helps to plot a future course for Irish Jacobite studies. However, he does question the originality of my findings, citing a broad range of eighteenth-century Irish historical scholarship from Maureen Wall, through Brían Ó Cuív, J. G. Simms, Louis Cullen, Roy Foster, Thomas Bartlett and David Dickson. I would contend that these scholars, and many others who have written about Irish Catholic politics, ideology, religion and literature in the post-war period, have failed to locate Jacobitism, the main political ideology on the island, at the centre of their discussions. They have also tended to over-emphasise the 'shipwreck' of Jacobite Ireland after 1691. This is not an invalid historiographical position, but it views Ireland through the distorting prism of hindsight, which is at odds with a broad array of Jacobite and anti-Jacobite sources which have been utilised and interrogated in the book.

In volume three of the *New History of Ireland*, Brían Ó Cuív offered an original and insightful overview of political themes in Gaelic literature; my study, both drawing upon and supplementing the work of MacCraith, Morley and Ó Buachalla, attempts to provide a thorough examination of Irish Jacobite poetry in its Irish, 'British' and European military and political contexts. Simms drew the curtain on Jacobite Ireland after 1691. Moreover, his sections on the Irish in continental Europe in the *New History of Ireland* do not view the Irish clerical and military diaspora as an integral part of the Irish Jacobite 'nation', as they were perceived by Jacobites and anti-Jacobites alike. By his own admission, and possibly smarting from Ó Buachalla and O'Riordan's trenchant criticisms, Cullen acknowledged that he understated the level of politicisation in Irish poetry in his re-appraisal of Daniel Corkery's *The Hidden Ireland: A Study of Gaelic Munster in the Eighteenth Century* (Dublin, 1925).[51]

The 'underground culture' which Roy Foster speaks of is only 'underground' – as the 'Hidden Ireland' is only really hidden – to those historians who have not (or cannot) engage with its literary remains. Furthermore, this literature is by no means 'visionary' by the mid-eighteenth century, as he would have us believe, if examined in its proper political context.[52] In the period covered by my book, Catholics remained both unwilling and unable to build on the 'new foundations' upon which Dickson constructed his masterful survey of Ireland from the Restoration (1660) to the Act of Union (1800). Bartlett defined the Catholic question as 'the issue of the re-admission of Catholics to full civil, religious and political equality in both Britain and Ireland'. Although Jacobitism undoubtedly provided one of the main impediments to their participation, and the single most important ideology of his Irish Catholic 'nation', it is ignored in his work.

The Irish Catholic polity, Jacobite or otherwise, should not be viewed as an ideological monolith and no Irish scholar would advocate a return to Corkery's shared common culture between big house and lowly peasant's hut.[53] Throughout the period in question, tensions continually bubbled beneath the surface of Irish Jacobitism, best exemplified in the Old English/Old Irish bias in Plunkett's 'Light to the Blind' and O'Kelly's '*Marcariae Excidium*: the destruction of Cyprus', as well as in the writings and correspondence of Thomas Sheridan, John Riley, the anonymous writer of 'The Groans of Ireland', the '*Lettre d'un officier irlandais à son fils*', and in numerous letters, memoirs and missives to the Stuart court.[54] They also occasionally surfaced in struggles between the regular and secular clergy, doctrinaire Jacobites and Hanoverian accommodationists, in the 'court poetry' of Ó Bruadair and Mac Cárthaigh and the folkloric verse of those who dismissed James II as a coward who had failed Ireland. However, it should be remembered that what lords Fingall and Delvin, Cornelius Nary, Charles O'Conor, John Curry and Arthur O'Leary had in common with the Jacobite poet Eoghan Rua Ó Súilleabháin, who decried the indignity of the penal laws[55] or the Galway peasant who 'loved King James in his heart',[56] was that they suffered political and religious discrimination in their own country for most of the eighteenth century, a discrimination which was directly related to their refusal to abjure the Stuarts. That their spiritual leader (the Pope) continued to recognise James Francis Edward Stuart as the true king of Ireland, England and Scotland (not Britain) until 1766, giving him exclusive rights to nominate all bishops who would serve on the Irish mission, made it exceedingly difficult to wriggle clear of this political and ideological strait-jacket.[57] Indeed, Ó Buachalla traces an emergent, virulent strain of anti-clericalism in contemporary Irish poetry to this period, when the Pope's refusal to recognise Charles Edward's claim facilitated a strategic accommodation with the House of Hanover.[58]

Connolly also poses pertinent questions on the nature of Irish Jacobitism, its core religious and political characteristics and the relative importance of dynastic allegiance and religious solidarity. These could be addressed through a broader inventory and closer comparative readings, as well as historical and literary contextualisation of English, Irish and Scots-Gaelic Jacobite poetry, prose, pamphlets and historical texts.[59] A wide range of Irish political commentators and pamphleteers, some unconsciously pre-empting and reflecting 'James II's advice to the Prince of Wales',[60] contemplated Ireland's position in the event of a Stuart restoration; Nicholas

Plunkett,[61] Thomas Lally,[62] and Ulick Burke,[63] among others, considered the Jacobite cause in its three-kingdom, European and global contexts. There is little evidence emanating from Jacobite Ireland which suggests any desire to abandon a lost cause in favour of erstwhile French or Spanish allies. This is no great surprise, given that Louis XIV did not offer himself or any of his family as alternative candidates before 1715. It became a political impossibility until the outbreak of the War of Jenkins' Ear in 1739 as the Regent, the Abbé Dubois and Cardinal Fleury had all sacrificed the Stuarts on the altar of French political, military and economic expediency. Although Philip V of Spain tried to emulate his Habsburg namesake by dispatching armadas against Protestant England and Scotland (with similar success, one might add), he showed little interest in pursuing a Spanish claim to the English and Irish thrones. However, further focused investigation in major European repositories, following the trail blazed by Marcus Beresford, and more recently Liam Swords, Tom Connors, Marian Lyons, Éamonn Ó Ciosáin, Eoghan Ó hAnnracháin, Oscar Morales, Ciaran O'Scea and Natalie Genet-Rouffiac, might uncover supplementary evidence or alternative views.

A number of reviews draw attention to the hotly-contested debates which have raged within the English, and to a lesser extent Scottish, academy on the related subjects of Tory politics, the stability of the Hanoverian regime and the Jacobite question, and warn the unwary and uninitiated of the dangers of nailing one's flag to a single ideological mast.[64] All serious scholars of a complex, contentious and multi-faceted movement and ideology should endeavour to read widely, engaging with the latest English, Scottish and European research. However, historians of Irish Jacobitism will search in vain for any meaningful treatment of Ireland, particularly among the Jacobite 'refusniks'. Dr. Eveline Cruickshanks and Professor Linda Colley have taken contrary positions which have both contributed to, and driven, a fruitful if sometimes intemperate debate among colleagues and acolytes. Until recently, Ireland rarely featured in this discourse. From the 'Anglocentric' world of the History of Parliament,[65] Cruickshanks has since blazed a trial through the Royal Archives, French and Spanish sources, a vital European context for Irish Jacobite studies, and has provided a ready conduit for the work of literary critics and continental historians. These are vital repositories for Irish Jacobite scholars, while the European political, military, diplomatic, religious, or mercantile networks, and crucial historical and literary continental contexts, provide key portals for the cosmopolitan Irish Jacobite world. Similarly, Professor Howard Erskine-Hill's 'rhetoric of Jacobitism' isolated common themes in English Jacobite verse; hereditary right, the rights of the lawful prince, disdain for the corrupting influence of foreigners and the inevitability of a Stuart restoration as the only solution to the nation's problems; some though not all of these themes also resonated through Irish and Scots-Gaelic verse.[66]

Paul Monod's study of English Jacobitism provides an invaluable, if some-times problematic, comparative model for Ireland,[67] Daniel Szechi's 'Jacobite theatre of death' included an Irish gibbet, and Frank McLynn's and Jeremy Black's work argued convincingly for the lasting threat of 'dynastic regime change'.[68]

Connolly urges caution in dealing with the optimistic, exaggerated testi-monies of Jacobite agents and Whig accusers and calls for a clear demarca-tion between the actual extent of Jacobite conspiracy and establishment fears. He also stresses the need to differentiate between varying levels of acceptance and non-acceptance of the revolution. Sage advice, no doubt, but it is extremely difficult to quantify 'active' Jacobitism amongst an Irish Catholic community which had been defeated and disarmed at home and effectively excluded from the decision-making processes at Saint-Germain, Avignon and Rome.[69] Besides, 'activity' is a fluid concept and an unreliable yard-stick for evaluating a proscribed political movement or ideology; Charles II's sarcastic commentary on the throngs which lined his route to London in 1660 immediately springs to mind. Connolly is on less sure ground, at least in relation to Irish Catholics, when suggesting that men of all political opinion saw some level of contact with the Stuarts as an accept-able insurance policy.[70] There is evidence of resignation but little by way of popular acceptance of the Revolution among Irish Catholics, at home or abroad, during the first half of the eighteenth century. In the first instance, Irish Catholics had been effectively excluded from the political process and papal recognition of the Stuart claim until 1766 also hampered any realistic attempts to secure a strategic accommodation with the House of Hanover. They would continue to struggle with the oath through the 1770s, even when the Stuart cause had dissolved in Charles Edward's alcoholic stupor.[71] Indeed, the Hanoverian monarchy would sacrifice Pitt the Younger and Henry Dundas, and defy the 'Iron Duke',[72] before the laurels of Catholic Emancipation would be prised from their reluctant hands by Daniel O'Connell, the 'Uncrowned King' and penultimate inheritor of the mes-sianic Stuart mantle.[73]

The possibility of ever accurately assessing the Jacobite threat to the Hanoverian state may prove even more elusive than separating perceptions and actualities, real conspiracies and sham plots, unbridled Jacobite opti-mism and Whig paranoia. More research is certainly needed, particularly in Stuart Papers and in continental, Jacobite-related political, military, diplo-matic and Masonic archives. Neither should one discount 'Irish' economic and maritime interests, the sinews of a prospective Jacobite war-machine. Anton Murphy's biography of Richard Cantillon,[74] Sylvie Walshe's recent doctoral dissertation on Antoine Walshe of Serrant,[75] who bankrolled the '45, and Natalie Genet-Rouffiac's ongoing researches on the Arthurs' banking dynasty could be complemented by additional works on the Waters, Cantillon and Drumgoole families, as well as broader 'Franco-Irish' and 'Spanish-Irish' banking, mercantile, maritime, privateer and slaving interests.[76]

Rumours of alleged and real links between Ireland-based Jacobites and their continental counterparts might be further explored in the voluminous correspondence of James, 2nd Duke of Ormonde, 'Sir' Patrick Lawless, 'Sir' Daniel O'Brien, Colonel Arthur Dillon, the O'Brien Viscounts Clare, 'Sir' John O'Rourke, Thomas Arthur Lally, 'Sir' Charles Wogan and other prominent Irish Jacobites, which survive in the Stuart Archives and the national repositories of France, Spain, Italy, Germany, Austria, Sweden and Russia. A good start has already been made here and scholars eagerly await the publication of the findings of the PRTLI/Centre for Irish-Scottish Studies French Mercenary Project which has been completed under the auspices of the Irish-Scottish Research Institute at Trinity College Dublin.[77] It should be pointed out, however, that large numbers of those recruiting for the Irish regiments in both France and Spain would not have considered themselves mercenaries.

Neither should one discount the efficacy of the newly re-habilitated historical biography in raising, engaging and answering some of these key questions. For example, Thomas Arthur Lally's Jacobite background, chequered martial career and tragic end provide a fascinating microcosm of the complex, interconnected struggles for dynastic, political, diplomatic and military hegemony between Irish Catholics and Protestants, Hanoverian and Stuart royalism and Franco-British imperialism. His intrigues and travails followed a broad trajectory from the West of Ireland, through the home counties of England, the Lowlands and Highlands of Scotland, to the Iberian Peninsula, Imperial territories and the Russian Steppe, providing a fitting testimony to the mobility, cultural fluidity and political vulnerability of the exiled Irishman in eighteenth-century Europe. They also shed valuable light on the vagaries of the Irish exile, in particular the need to balance loyalty to the Stuarts with political and military duty to the French (or Spanish) Bourbons.[78] Lally's gradual rise and spectacular fall maps a political and military journey from the Boyne and Aughrim, through the Scottish Highlands to the battlefields and battlements of Dettingen, Fontenoy, Lauffelt, Bergen-op-Zoom, Madras, Pondicherry and Wandewash, to the executioner's block at the Place de Grève. His spectacular triumphs and heroic defeats provide tantalising counter-factuals for the history of eighteenth-century Ireland, Britain, Europe and the second British Empire, best evidenced by his astute and unheeded advice to D'Argenson 'du cabinet', the French foreign minister, and Louis XV, on the need to restore the Stuarts and drive the British out of America and India.[79]

Lally cannot be dismissed as either a sentimental, tippling Jacobite squireen or an opportunist Franco-Irish military careerist. At once an inveterate Jacobite and close confidant of the Stuart prince, he had risen to the highest echelons of the French military less as a consequence and more in spite of his Jacobite pedigree. He eagerly grasped the opportunity to revive flagging French political and military fortunes on the Indian sub-continent and appointed hardened veterans of the Franco-Irish regiments to senior and sensitive commands; men who had joined Saxe's abortive invasion in 1744 and others who would give evidence of their Jacobite zeal on the battlefields of Falkirk, Prestonpans and Culloden. This has implications for the importance of Jacobitism as an ideological glue which cemented a far-flung, disabused military contingent in adverse political and military circumstances.[80] Biographical studies of the Rev. Charles Leslie, Charles Barry, 4th Earl of Orrery, Sir Charles Wogan, 'the Irish Don Quixote', James Butler, 2nd Duke of Ormonde, Robert McCarthy, 5th Earl of Clancarthy, Count John O'Rourke, Daniel O'Brien, the O'Brien Viscounts Clare, Michael and Charles Edward Rothe and the Irishmen of Moidart (George Kelly, Thomas Sheridan and John William O'Sullivan) would do much to uncover their elusive ideology and clandestine activities.

Trans-continental investigations of this nature should also be complemented by additional work on Irish Jacobite communities or interests in Ireland and Britain, with particular focus on political, military, economic, diplomatic, ecclesiastical, professional and cultural networks. Patrick Melvin's,[81] Paul Hopkins'[82] and Peter Linebaugh's[83] varied research on Irish plotters, Jacobite agents, recruiters and criminals could be expanded to focus on the broader Irish expatriate community in England, carried into the eighteenth century, and moved 'over the water' to the 'Irish' on the continent.[84] John Bergin and Liam Chambers' reconstruction of the geographical, literary cultural milieu of London-based Irish legal interests might also shed light on their elusive alliances, allegiances and cultures.[85] At home, a reconsideration of the dynamics of Irish Jacobitism might be also served by a quantitative, geographical stock-taking of the surviving Irish-language manuscripts and libraries and a comprehensive study of Irish Catholic institutional and clerical links with the exiled court and its ambassadorial networks. Other means of evaluating its overall strength and significance would be an extensive prosopographical examination of the Irish Catholic episcopate and higher clergy, recruitment for the Irish Brigades, and Irish clerical, educational, legal and mercantilist networks on the continent.

The 'British' nature of Irish Jacobitism has been the subject of a lively academic debate between Professor Connolly and Dr. Morley, though this need not detain us here.[86] Academic imports such as 'old' or 'new' British History, J. C. D. Clark's 'ancien régime' and E. P. Thompson's 'moral economy' may have re-invigorated early modern Irish history, but they need to spend considerably more time in quarantine.[87] Irish Jacobitism was not a 'British' ideology, either in a geographical, political or literary sense, although it drew political, literary and visual inspiration from its English, Scottish and European strains. There were Jacobites of Irish, Scottish and English origin in every port, city and country from Cadiz to St. Petersburg. No political entity called Britain existed before 1707, and it never included Ireland during the Jacobite period; moreover Jacobites of all hues opposed the Anglo-Scottish Union. That a pre-revolutionary 'British' ideology existed in the mind of James VI and I and some of his subjects is beyond doubt. However, it proved a problematic ideological bequest to Charles I, Charles II and James II. Morley shows that the term 'British' never gained popular currency among the Irish Gaels, in stark contrast to their Scottish counterparts.[88] Moreover, there is little evidence to suggest that Irish royalists or Jacobites saw themselves as holding any sort of 'British' ideology. In 1603 the poet Eoghan Rua Mac an Bhaird alluded to the three crowns in king James's charter ('trí coróna i gcairt Shéamais') on the Stuart accession to the thrones, not to some sort of three-tiered imperial British tiara.[89] One would imagine that the 'Redeat Magnus Ille Genius Britanniae', which emblazoned numerous imprints of Roettier's medals, would have had as little relevance for Liam Inglis as for Linda Colley.[90] Mac an Bhaird's Irish Jacobite successors at home and abroad realised that their exiled king would need to be restored to his English inheritance before the Irish crown could be secured. The discerning reader will find little more than passing reference to London, Edinburgh or Dublin in Irish Jacobite poetry. Paris, Madrid and Rome were the capitals of Gaelic Ireland, and the Irish literati knew, as did 'James III', that it was from power bases in these great continental, Catholic capitals that the House of Stuart would be restored. Even so, the Irish kingdom and its political, military, economic and cultural welfare, was the main focus of their concerns.

Although Bertie and the 'Soldiers of Destiny' may have been oblivious to Jacobitism, or uncomfortable with its problematic historical legacy, Irish Jacobite studies could easily adopt Fianna Fáil's most recent political slogan: 'A lot done, more to do'. Fifteen years since commencing my own doctoral research, a great deal of work has been completed and more needs to be done on both sides of the Irish Sea and English Channel before we can fully evaluate its importance. To date, the research of Mac Craith, Morley and Ó Buachalla, in addition to my own, into the emergence, extent, and evolution of Jacobitism from the succession of James II to the death of Charles Edward in the context of Irish, British and European politics, has re-habilitated it as a serious academic subject. However, a great deal of archival research, editorial recovery and close literary and antiquarian reading is required before we can fully evaluate its importance.[91] Morley's seminal study of Ireland and the American Revolution has influenced and supported my postscript remarks on the Jacobite 'Twilight'. As well as stifling the emergence of a popular Hanoverian royalism, Jacobitism was crucial to the ease with which American and French-inspired republicanism penetrated Irish society in the 1790s. Similarly, Ó Tuathaigh's, Ó Buachalla's and Uí Ógáin's theses show that a messianic Jacobite residue survived the collapse of United Irish republicanism and manifested itself in the popular cult of O'Connell.[92]

This Jacobite 'chimera' merits further investigation, in view of the fact that the long eighteenth century has now reached the 1830s.[93] An examination of the residual Jacobite influence on, and the motivation behind, late-eighteenth and nineteenth-century literature, folklore and antiquarian investigations might also shed light on its political, literary and cultural legacy.[94] This would necessitate a thorough investigation of the published works, writings, manuscripts, airs, libraries and cultural milieux of Charlotte Brooke,[95] her Irish evangelist Muiris Ó Gormáin,[96] his peers and successors Peadar Ó Gealcháin, Art Mac Bionaid and Nicholas Ó Cearnaigh, John O'Daly, Edward Walsh, Thomas Davis, Emily Lawless, Thomas Moore, James Clarence Mangan, Douglas Hyde and Emily Lawless, among others.[97] There is obvious scope for comparison with English and Scottish poets and writers such as Samuel Johnson, James Boswell, Robert Burns, Joseph Ritson, James Hogg, Lady Carolina Nairne and Sir Walter Scott as researches and lively scholarly exchanges in these realms have provided fruitful avenues of scholarly enquiry for scholars of English and Scottish Jacobitism.[98] Even a cursory perusal of Rolf and Magda Loeber's recently published *Guide to Irish Fiction, 1650–1900* (2006) raises the sub-conscious literary spectres of Wild Goose, smuggler, outlaw and ruined Jacobite houses and families – Irish versions of Scott's *Redgauntlet* and *Waverley* or Stevenson's *Master of Ballantrae*.[99]

Dickson concluded his recent masterful re-appraisal of Jacobitism in eighteenth-century Ireland, another ringing endorsement of its new found importance, with a call to investigate the contribution of Munster writers to the shaping of Irish cultural nationalism.[100] The 'Literary Revival' and the foundation of the Irish National Theatre and Conradh na Gaeilge support his call and Stalin's truism that writers are the engineers of men's souls. No Irish Jacobite scholar would recruit Yeats for the Jacobite cause (much less Swift,[101] Berkeley,[102] Heaney[103] or, more recently, MacCóil[104]) although he did attend Charles Edward's requiem mass in 1888, flirted briefly with the White Rose Society and drew inspiration from the 'Wild Geese', 'Red Hanrahan's daughter' and the doleful laments of Aogán Ó Rathaille.[105] Dubhghlas de hÍde, founder of An Conradh and first president of Ireland, reached back to the Jacobite literary tradition for his nom de plume ('An Craoibhín Aoibhinn'), as did Pádraig Ó Siochfhradha ('An Seabhac'), another leading 'engineer' of Irish cultural nationalism.[106] Four of the seven signatories of the 1916 proclamation (Thomas MacDonagh, Seán Mac Diarmada, Éamonn Ceannt and Pádraig Mac Piarais) edited and translated Irish Jacobite poetry, which may explain why 'Óró 'sé do bheatha abhaile', a re-packaged, republicanised Jacobite tune, became the anthem of the Irish Volunteers in 1916.[107] One should not too readily dismiss the rejuvenation of the Irish language and culture (in the event of a Stuart restoration) as a totally unrealistic prospect. It is often forgotten, and certainly so by early-modern Irish historians, that Irish was still the main language and literary culture on the island in the Jacobite period. A restoration of sorts, particularly in Dickson's Jacobite heartland, had already taken place after the Cromwellian era, and in the lifetime and memory of the earlier Jacobite poets. Some 200 years later Éamon de Valera, more often associated with Machiavellianism than messianism, put the restoration of the Irish language and the promotion of Irish culture at the centre of his Fianna Fáil political agenda. However, unrealistic or unsuccessful this might have been (Zhou Enlai's cautious advice on the French Revolution springs to mind)[108] his successor Brian Cowen would not dare (and as a fluent Irish speaker would be disinclined, one would imagine) to publicly consign the Irish language to the dustbin of history.

Notes

1 I would like to thank Marie-Claire Harrigan, Micheál Mac Craith, Don MacRaild, James McConnel, Vincent Morley and Micheál Ó Siochrú for their insightful comments on various drafts of the text.

2 Speech by Ian Paisley at the Joint Official Opening of the Battle of the Boyne site, 6 May 2008, Cain Webservicehttp://cain.ulst.ac.uk/issues/politics/docs/dup/ip060508.htm. See also Speech by the Taoiseach, Mr. Bertie Ahern, TD, at the Joint Official Opening of the Battle of the Boyne Site with First Minister, at http://www.taoiseach.gov.ie/index.asp?locID=582&docID=3880.

3 B. Ó Buachalla, 'James Our True King: The ideology of Irish royalism in the seventeenth century', in D. G. Boyce, R. Eccleshall and V. Geoghegan (eds), *Political Thought in Ireland Since the Seventeenth Century* (London, 1993), pp. 1–35. See also *idem, The Crown of Ireland* (Galway, 2006), *passim.*

4 *Idem, Aisling Ghéar: Na Stíobhartaigh agus an tAos Léinn, 1603*–1788 (Dublin/B.Á.C., 1996), pp. 3–67.

5 Allan Macinnes would disagree on the strength of Irish-Scottish influence at the exiled court but has stressed the need for further research; Macinnes, 'Jacobitism in Scotland: Episodic cause or national movement', *Scottish Historical Review, lxxxvi,* 2, no. 222 (Oct. 2007), p. 230.

6 T. B. Macaulay, *The History of England from the Accession of James II* [ed. C. H. Firth] (6 vols., London, 1913–15), *iii*, p. 1472; R. Hayes, 'Ireland and Jacobitism', in *Studies, xxxviii* (1949), pp. 101–6.

7 T. Bartlett, *The Fall and Rise of the Irish Nation. The Catholic Question, 1690–1830* (London, 1992), p. 7.

8 J. C. D. Clark, 'The many restorations of Jacobite Studies, 1766–2006', address to the opening conference of the Jacobite Studies Trust, The British Academy, London, 11 July 2007. I would like to thank Professor Clark for making the text of his lecture, which appears in this volume, available to me.

9 'Tracts and pamphlets by [Nicholas] Plunkett c. 1690–1715 (N.L.I., Ms 476–7); 'Nine treatises on Irish subjects by [N] Plunkett, c. 1700–15 (Bodl., Ms 229). Also see P. Kelly, 'A light to the blind: the voice of the dispossessed elite in the generation after defeat at Limerick', *Irish Historical Studies, xxiv* (1985), pp. 431–62.

10 For re-readings of the Abbè Macgeoghegan's *Histoire d'Irlande* and the *Life of the 2ⁿᵈ Duke of Ormonde*, see Vincent Geoghegan, 'A Jacobite history. The Abbè Macgeoghegan's History of Ireland', *Eighteenth-century Ireland*, vi (1991), pp. 37–55; Éamonn Ó Ciardha, 'The unkinde deserter and the bright duke: the dukes of Ormond in the Irish royalist tradition', in T. Barnard and J. Fenlon (ed.), *The Dukes of Ormonde, 1610–1745* (London, 2000), p. 179.

11 Éamonn Ó Ciardha, Review of Patrick Fagan (ed.), *Ireland in the Stuart Papers*, in *History Ireland*, iv, no 2 (1996), pp. 53–5.

12 Mícheál Mac Craith, Review Article, 'Breandán Ó Buachalla, *Aisling Ghéar: Na Stíobhartaigh agus an tAos Léinn, 1603–1788*', in *Eighteenth-century Ireland*, xiii (1998), p. 171; D. Dickson, 'Jacobitism in eighteenth-century Ireland: A Munster perspective', *Éire-Ireland*, 39:3/4 (2004), pp. 38–99.

13 Éamonn Ó Ciardha, *Ireland and the Jacobite Cause, 1685–1766: A Fatal Attachment* (Dublin, 2002, repr. 2004), p. 22.

14 James Connolly, *Labour in Irish History* (Dublin, 1910), pp. 9–10. A proposal had been made to Tone by the French Directory in the 1790s to place 'Henry IX', Cardinal York, brother of the deceased 'Charles III' (Charles Edward) on an Irish throne, T. W. Moody, R. B. McDowell and C. J. Woods (eds), *The Writings of Theobald Wolfe-Tone* (3 vols., Oxford, 2001), ii, pp. 157, 160. There are many other examples of disrespect for the Jacobite tradition in Irish politics and literature; B. Ó Buachalla, *Aisling Ghéar*, pp. 650, 652.

15 J. Curry, *Historical and Critical Review of the Civil Wars in Ireland* (2 vols., Dublin, 1786); C. O'Conor, and J. Curry, *The case of the Roman Catholics of Ireland wherein the principles and conduct of that party are fully explained and vindicated* (Dublin, 1755); C. O'Conor, *A vindication of a pamphlet lately published entitled 'The case of the Roman Catholics of Ireland'* (London, 1755); J. A. Froude, *The English in Ireland in the Eighteenth Century* (3 vols., London, 1872–4); For a comprehensive overview, see T. C. Barnard, '1641: a bibliographical essay', in B. Mac Cuarta (ed.), *Ulster in 1641: Aspects of the Rising* (Belfast, 1993), pp. 177–8.

16 Mícheál Mac Craith, 'Charlotte Brooke and James Macpherson', *Litteraria Pragensia*, Vol. 10, 20 (2000), pp. 5-17; *idem*, 'Cúlra Seacaibíteach James Macpherson', in Máirtín Ó Briain agus Pádraig Ó Héalaí (eds), *Téada dúchais: aistí in ómós do Bhreandán Ó Madagáin* (Cló Iar-Chonnachta, 2002), pp. 91–110.

17 O'Conor and Curry, *Case of the Roman Catholics of Ireland*; O'Conor, *A Vindication*; M. Wall, *Catholic Ireland in the Eighteenth Century*, ed. G. O'Brien (Dublin, 1989); H. Fenning, *The Irish Dominican Province, 1698–1797* (Dublin, 1990); Idem, *The Undoing of the Friars* (Louvain, 1972); P. Fagan, *Divided Loyalties: The Question of an Oath for Catholics* (Dublin, 1997); idem, *Dublin's Turbulent Priest: Cornelius Nary, 1658-1738* (Dublin, 1991); J. Kelly, 'A Wild Capuchin of Cork: Arthur O'Leary (1709–1778)', in G. Moran (ed.), *Radical Irish Priests* (Dublin, 1998), pp. 39–62; S. Connolly, 'Jacobites, Whiteboys and Republicans: Varieties of disaffection in eighteenth-century Ireland', *Eighteenth-Century Ireland*, xviii (2003), pp. 63–80; Vincent Morley, 'Catholic disaffection and the oath of allegiance of 1774' (forthcoming, 2009). I would like to thank Dr. Morley for making his article available to me prior to publication.

18 J. C. O'Callaghan, *History of the Irish Brigades in the Service of France*, repr. (Shannon, 1969); M. O'Conor, *Military History of the Irish Nation* (Dublin, 1845). See also '*The Irish Sword*', *Journal of the Military History Society of Ireland* (Dublin, 1949).

19 P. Fagan, *Divided Loyalties*; Kelly, 'A Wild Capuchin of Cork, pp. 39–62; S. Connolly, 'Jacobites, Whiteboys and Republicans', pp. 63–80; V. Morley, 'Catholic disaffection and the oath of allegiance of 1774'.

20 J. Smyth, *The Men of No Property. Irish Radicals and Popular Politics in the Late Eighteenth Century* (Dublin, 1993), passim; K. Whelan, *Tree of Liberty: Radicalism, Catholicism and the Construction of Irish Identity, 1760–1830* (Cork, 1996), p. 47; G. Ó Tuathaigh, 'Gaelic Ireland, popular politics and Daniel O'Connell', *Galway Historical and Archaeological Society Journal, xxxiv* (1974–5), pp. 21–34; B. Ó Buachalla, *Aisling Ghéar*, pp. 596–662.

21 Cullen, L., 'The Hidden Ireland: the re-assessment of a concept', *Studia Hibernica, ix* (1969), pp. 7–48; B. Ó Buachalla, 'An mheisiasacht agus an aisling', in P. De Brún, S. Ó Coileáin and P. Ó Riain, P. (eds), *Folia Gadelica* (Cork, 1983), pp. 72–87; M. O'Riordan, 'Historical perspectives on the Hidden Ireland', *Irish Review, iv* (1988), pp. 73–82; L. Cullen, The *Hidden Ireland: The Re-assessment of a Concept*, repr. (Gigginstown, 1988). See also Dickson, 'Jacobitism in eighteenth-century Ireland', p. 68; Connolly, 'Jacobites, White-boys and Republicans', pp. 63–80. For overview, see Ó Ciardha, *Ireland and the Jacobite Cause*, pp. 38–51.

22 J. Mitchel, *The History of Ireland, Ancient and Modern, Taken from the Most Authentic Records, and Dedicated to the Irish Brigade. By the Abbè Mac-Geoghegan. With a Continuation from the Treaty of Limerick to 1852 by John Mitchel* (New York, 1853), pp. 11, 43–4, 59–70.

23 W. E. H. Lecky, *A History of Ireland in the Eighteenth Century*, 5 volumes (London, 1872), *i*, p. 413. Indeed, Lecky finds common cause with his old antagonist Froude on this point; J. A Froude, *The English in Ireland, i*, pp. 402–6. J. O'Donoghue's M.A. thesis provides a useful overview of early Jacobite historiography, see O'Donoghue, 'Ireland and the Jacobite threat, 1700–1727' (unpublished MA thesis, University College Cork, 1992), introduction.

24 W. P. Burke, The *Irish Priest in Penal Times, 1660–1760*, repr. (Shannon, 1969), p. 111. D. McCarthy (ed.), *Collections on Irish Church History from the Manuscripts of the late very rev. Laurence F. Renehan* (Dublin, 1861), pp. 88–9; R. Walsh, 'Glimpses of Irish Catholicism in penal times', *Irish Ecclesiastical Record, xx* (1906–11), p. 260; Connolly, 'Jacobites, Whiteboys and Republicans', p. 78.

25 E. Walsh (ed.), *Reliques of Irish Jacobite Poetry* (Dublin, 1866), p. iv.

26 [J. O'Daly] (ed.), *The Poets and Poetry of Munster* (Dublin, 1848), p. 31. See also Proinsias Ó Drisceoil, *Seán Ó Dálaigh: Éigse agus iomarbhá* (Cork, 2007).

27 J. Hardiman (ed.), *Irish Minstrelsy* (2 vols. repr., Shannon, 1972), *ii*, p. 7. Joep Leerssen provides a useful context for Hardiman's work; Joep Leerssen *Remembrance and Imagination* (Cork, 1996), pp. 176–8. This distaste for Jacobitism and 'Charley-over-the-Waterism' pervaded Irish literature; R. Breathnach, 'The end of a tradition. A survey of eighteenth-century Gaelic literature', *Studia Hibernica, i* (1960), p. 147; E. Knott (ed.), *The Poems of Tadhg Dall Ó h-Uiginn* (2 vols., London, 1922–6), *i*, p. lxiii; M. O' Conor, *Military History of the Irish Nation* (Dublin, 1845), p. 115.

28 P. Fagan, *The Second City: A Portrait of Dublin* (Dublin, 1986), p. 148; R. Ward and C. Ward (eds), The *Letters of Charles O'Conor of Belanagare* (Ann Arbor, Michigan, 1980), p. 29 and no. 94; O' Conor and Curry, *The Case of the Roman Catholics of Ireland*, pp. 43–4; C. Teeling, *History of the Rebellion of 1798*, repr. (Shannon, 1972), pp. 103–5; [M. Byrne], *The Memoirs of Miles Byrne*, repr. (Shannon, 1972), p. 7; M. O'Reilly, *The Irish at Home, at Court and in the Camp, with Souvenirs of the 'Bridage'. Memoirs of an Emigrant Milesian* (New York, 1856),

p. 33. J. Kelly, 'A Wild Capuchin of Cork', pp. 39–63. See also Ó Ciardha, *Ireland and the Jacobite Cause*, postscript.

29 There are other examples of O'Connell's royalism; O. MacDonagh, *Daniel O'Connell* (London, 1991), pp. 441, 453, 462; Leerssen, *Remembrance and Imagination*, pp. 77–9. Indeed Thomas Davis, Ireland's national bard, and his contemporaries Emily Lawless and A. M. and T. D. Sullivan, had effectively 'disinfected' Irish history, and the cult of the Irish Brigades in particular, from any references to Jacobitism. See also B. Ó Buachalla, *The Crown of Ireland* (Galway, 2006), p. 45. This is, of course, in stark contrast to Sir Walter Scott's stage-managing of George IV's visit to Edinburgh in 1822, where he met the Highland chiefs, and so began the rehabilitation of Scottish Jacobitism.

30 Clark, 'Many restorations of Jacobite studies'.

31 These sentiments also infuse the perennially popular and influential *Ireland's Own*, a magazine which is worthy of future examination.

32 I. Campbell-Ross, 'Was Berkeley a Jacobite? Passive obedience revisited', *Eighteenth-century Ireland*, *xx* (2005), pp. 17–30.

33 T. W. Moody, 'Irish history and Irish mythology', in C. Brady (ed.), *Interpreting Irish history: The Debate on Historical Revisionism* (Dublin, 1994), pp. 72, 76.

34 Vincent Morley, *Irish Opinion and the American Revolution, 1760–83* (Cambridge, 2002), p. 2; idem, *Washington i gceannas a ríochta* (Dublin/B.Á.C., 2005), p. xi.

35 See also J. Childs, *The Williamite Wars in Ireland, 1688–1691* (London, 2007), p. 494. Needless to say, Irish Jacobites at home and abroad did not see things in these terms.

36 M. de la Poer Beresford, 'Ireland in the French strategy, 1691–1789' (unpublished M. Litt. thesis, University of Dublin, 1975), pp. 3–4. See also S. Connolly, *Religion, Law and Power: The Making of Protestant Ireland, 1660–1760* (Oxford, 1992), pp. 244–6.

37 M. de la Poer Beresford, 'Ireland in the French strategy, 1691–1789', pp. 3–4. See also P. Kelly, 'A light to the blind', p. 431.

38 Simms, *Jacobite Ireland*; Dickson, *New Foundations*, p. 32; Ó Buachalla, 'Review of Cruickshanks and Black', pp. 186–90.

39 Bartlett, *Fall and Rise*, pp. 2, 9–10, 17, 24, 31, 34–5, 38; D. Hayton, 'Walpole and Ireland', in J. Black (ed.), *Britain in the Age of Walpole* (London, 1984), p. 96.

40 Connolly, 'Jacobites, Whiteboys and Republicans', p. 71. For opposing views, see Morley 'The continuity of disaffection', *passim* and Clark, 'The many restorations of Jacobite Studies'.

41 L. Cullen, 'Catholic social classes under the penal laws', in T. Power and K. Whelan (ed.), *Endurance and emergence: Catholics in Ireland in the Eighteenth Century* (Dublin, 1990), pp. 57–84; idem, 'Catholics under the penal laws', *Eighteenth-century Ireland*, *i* (1986), pp. 23–37; T. Power, 'Converts'; in Power and K. Whelan (ed.), *Endurance and Emergence*, pp. 101–28; Fenning, *Undoing of the friars*; idem, *Irish Dominican Province*; Fagan, *Dublin's Turbulent Priest*; idem, *An Irish Bishop*; Leighton, *Catholicism*; Whelan, *Tree of Liberty*, pp. 3–56. See also Bartlett, *Fall and Rise*, p. 49; Ó Buachalla, *Aisling Ghéar*, pp. 221, 315.

42 Six, according to J. C. D. Clark, 'The many restorations of Jacobite Studies, 1766–2006', *passim*. See also J. Hill, 'Convergence and conflict in eighteenth-century Ireland', *The Historical Journal*, *xl*, 4 (2001), pp. 1039–63.

43 B. Ó Buachalla, 'Seacaibíteachas Thaidhg Uí Neachtain', *Studia Hibernica*, *xxvi* (1990–91), pp. 31–64.

44 M. Elliott, 'Irishry down to the roots', in *The Guardian*, 24 July 1993. See also O'Donoghue, 'Jacobite threat', p. 30. Irish Jacobitism after 1714 had been

described as *'terra incognita'*; Smyth, *Men of no Property*, p. 41. Similarly, James Kelly stated that 'Jacobite activity, overwhelmingly if not exclusively Catholic, remains little studied'; J. Kelly, 'The glorious and immortal memory: commemoration and Protestant identity in Ireland, 1660–1800', *Proceedings of the Royal Irish Academy*, xciv (1994), p. 32.

45 The review also noted Professor Connolly's general discomfort in dealing with Irish Catholic political consciousness and questioned his contradictory thesis on the Penal laws; T. Barnard, 'Farewell to Old Ireland', *Historical Journal*, xxxiv, no. iv (1993), pp. 910, 916, 919. In another review the same author expressed the view that Connolly's book focused 'on the worlds and values of the Castle and College Green'; Barnard, Review of S. Connolly, *Religion, Law and Power: The Making of Protestant Ireland, 1660–1760* (Oxford, 1992), *Irish Historical Studies*, xxviii (1993), p. 321. He also noted that although Bartlett's *Fall and Rise of the Irish Nation* (1992) had stretched the parameters of eighteenth-century Ireland to breaking-point, it remained heavily weighted towards the last decades of the eighteenth century and expended little time or energy on collective or individual mentalities, ideas or ideologies; Barnard, 'Farewell to Old Ireland', pp. 910–12.

46 Ó Buachalla, Review of Cruickshanks and Black, pp. 186–90; *idem, Aisling Ghéar*. See also Mac Craith, 'Filíocht Sheacaibíteach na Gaeilge', pp. 57–75; V. Morley, *An crann os coill. Aodh Buí Mac Cruitín* (Dublin/B.Á.C., 1995); *idem*, 'Idé-eolaíocht an tSeacaibíteachais in Éirinn agus in Albain', *Oghma*, ix (1997), pp. 14–24.

47 P. Breathnach, 'Oral and written transmission of poetry in eighteenth-century Ireland', *Eighteenth-century Ireland*, ii (1987), pp. 57–67; Mac Craith, 'Filíocht Sheacaibíteach na Gaeilge', pp. 57–75; V. Morley, 'Aodh Buí Mac Cruitín; File Gaeilge in Arm na Fraince', *Eighteenth-century Ireland*, viii (1993), pp. 39–58; D. Ó Muirithe, ''Tho' Not in Full Stile Compleat': Jacobite songs from Gaelic manuscript sources', *Eighteenth-century Ireland*, vi (1991), pp. 93–104; Ó Buachalla, 'Irish Jacobitism in official documents', *Eighteenth-century Ireland*, viii (1993), pp. 138–48.

48 B. Ó Buachalla, 'Irish Jacobite poetry', *Irish Review*, xii (1992), pp. 40–50; *idem*, 'Irish Jacobitism and Irish nationalism: the literary evidence', in M. O'Dea and K. Whelan (eds), *Nations and nationalisms: France, Britain, Ireland and the Eighteenth-century context* (Oxford, 1995), pp. 103–16; *idem*, 'Seacaibíteachas Thaidhg Uí Neachtain', pp. 31–64.

49 Irish-language scholars have unanimously lauded Ó Buachalla's enormous scholarly achievement; A. Titley, *Saol*, Feabhra 1998; MacCraith, 'Review article', *passim*; L. P. Ó Murchú, *Foinse*, 23 Samhain 1997; Ó Murchú, 'Breandán Ó Buachalla, *Aisling Ghéar*: Na Stíobhartaigh agus an tAos Léinn, 1603–1788', in É. Ó Ciardha, F. Sewell and A. Titley (eds), *The Oxford History of the Irish Book: The Irish Book in Irish from 1567*, forthcoming (Oxford, 2009). In contrast, there has been a deafening silence from Irish historians. Indeed, one scholar has cited Ó Buachalla's 800-page tome and uses my own 500-page monograph by way of a translation; J. Hill, 'Convergence and conflict', p. 1042. Likewise, it is astonishing that Professor David Hayton would hold court on what he considers the narrow source-base of Ó Buachalla's book, a work which he has evidently not read; D. W. Hayton, 'Review of Éamonn Ó Ciardha, *Ireland and the Jacobite Cause, 1685–1766*', *Eighteenth-century Ireland*, xviii, (2003), p. 155. For the enormous flexibility of Irish poetry as a source, see Mícheál. Mac Craith's review article, p. 166. Besides, even a cursory perusal of

Aisling Ghéar's one hundred page bibliography bears testimony to a staggering range of manuscript, newspaper, printed primary and secondary sources in Irish, Scots-Gaelic, English, French, Spanish, German, Welsh, Italian and Latin.

50   S. Connolly, 'Review of Éamonn Ó Ciardha, *Ireland and the Jacobite Cause, 1685–1766*', *Reviews in History*, Institute of Historical Research, Senate House, London, Jan 2003. http://www.history.ac.uk/reviews/paper/ociardha.html. See also the author's reply.

51   For a synopsis of these discussions, see Ó Ciardha, *Ireland and the Jacobite Cause*, pp. 38–51; Dickson, 'Jacobitism in eighteenth-century Ireland', p. 68. Professor Connolly has continued to cite the 1969 edition of Cullen's essay; S. Connolly, 'Approaches to Irish popular culture', *Bullán*, ii (1996), p. 84; idem, 'Jacobites, Whiteboys and Republicans: Varieties of disaffection in eighteenth-century Ireland', *Eighteenth-century Ireland*, xviii (2003), p. 74; idem, *Divided Kingdom, Ireland 1630–1800* (Oxford, 2008), p. 298.

52   Ó Buachalla, *Aisling Ghéar*, Mac Craith's review article, pp. 168–9. For an opposite view, see Connolly, 'Jacobites, Whiteboys and Republicans', p. 75; Macinnes, 'Jacobitism in Scotland', p. 233.

53   D. Corkery, *The Hidden Ireland: A Study of Gaelic Munster in the Eighteenth Century* (Dublin, 1925), p. 52; S. Connolly, *Divided Kingdom*, p. 328.

54   Ó Ciardha, *Ireland and the Jacobite Cause, passim.*

55   Ó Buachalla, *Aisling Ghéar*, p. 594.

56   Ó Ciardha, *Ireland and the Jacobite Cause*, p. 331.

57   C. Giblin, 'The Stuart nomination of bishops, 1687–1765', *Proceedings of the Irish Catholic Historical Committee* (1955–7), pp. 35–47; Fagan, *Divided Loyalties, passim*; Ó Ciardha, *Ireland and the Jacobite Cause*, pp. 358–67; Dickson, 'Jacobitism in eighteenth-century Ireland', pp. 53–71, 93–8.

58   Mac Craith, 'Review article', p. 170; Connolly, 'Jacobites, Whiteboys and Republicans', p. 64; Dickson, 'Jacobitism in eighteenth-century Ireland', p. 65.

59   This is already in hand, as evidenced by the recent editorial and analytical work; M. Comer Bruen and D. Ó hÓgáin, *An Mangaire Súgach* (Dublin/B.Á.C., 1996); B. Ó Buachalla, *An caoine agus an chaointeoireacht* (Dublin/B.Á.C., 1998); M. Ní Úrdail, *The Scribe in Eighteenth- and Nineteenth-century Ireland* (Münster, 2000); P. Riggs (ed.), *Dáibhí Ó Bruadair: His Historical and Literary Context* (Dublin, 2001); D. Binéid, *Searc na Suadh: Gnéithe de fhilíocht Dháibhí Uí Bhruadair* (Dublin/B.Á.C. 2003); Ú. Nic Éinrí, *Canfar an Dán: Uilliam English agus a chairde* (An Daingean, 2003); B. Uí Chatháin, *Éigse Chairbre: Filíocht ó Chairbreacha i gContae Chorcaí agus ón gceantar Máguaird, 1750–1850* (Dublin/ B.Á.C, 2007); P. Ó Drisceoil, *Seán Ó Dálaigh: éigse agus iomarbhá* (Cork, 2007); Ó Buachalla (ed.), *Aogán Ó Rathaille* (Dublin/B.Á.C., 2007); V. Morley (ed.), *Aodh Buí Mac Cruitín*, forthcoming; B. Ó Croinín, 'Filíocht Phiarais Mhic Gearailt' (PhD, in progress at the University of Limerick).

60   J. S. Clarke, *Life of James II* (2 vols., London, 1816), ii, p. 636.

61   N. Plunkett, 'A light to the Blind' (N.L.I., MS 746, ff. 469–70, 743); idem, 'To the Irish nobility at St. Germain, a memorandum' (N.L.I., 477); idem, 'To the re-enthroned king: a method of governing England, Scotland and Ireland' (N.L.I., MS 477); idem, 'The case of the Roman Catholics of Ireland' (N.L.I., MS 477); idem, The improvement of Ireland' (Bodl. Carte MC 229).

62   L. Graecen, *Voltaire's Last Case: The Death of Thomas Lally*, forthcoming (Irish Academic Press).

63   Ó Ciardha, *Ireland and the Jacobite Cause*, p. 267; Connolly, 'Jacobites, Whiteboys and Republicans', p. 72.

64   S. Connolly, *Religion, Law and Power*, *passim*; Connolly, 'Jacobites, Whiteboys and Republicans', p. 78; Hayton, 'Review of Ó Ciardha', p. 157.

65   Macinnes, 'Jacobitism in Scotland', p. 228.

66   H. Erskine-Hill, 'Literature and the Jacobite cause: Was there a rhetoric of Jacobitism?', in E. Cruickshanks (ed.), *Ideology and Conspiracy: Aspects of Jacobitism* (Edinburgh, 1982), pp. 49–70. See also Murray Pittock, *Poetry and Jacobite Politics in Eighteenth-century Britain and Ireland* (Cambridge, 1994), *passim*; Mac Craith, 'Filíocht Sheacaibíteach', pp. 57–75; Morley, 'Idé-eolaíocht an tSeacaibíteachais in Éirinn agus in Albain', pp. 14–24; *idem*, 'Continuity of disaffection in eighteenth-century Ireland', *passim*; Ó Ciardha, 'The Stuarts and deliverance in Irish and Scots-Gaelic poetry', in S. Connolly (ed.), *Kingdoms United: Scotland and Ireland since 1500* (Dublin, 1998), pp. 78–94.

67   P. Monod, *Jacobitism and the English People, 1688–1788* (repr., Cambridge, 1993), *passim*; Ó Ciardha, *Ireland and the Jacobite Cause*, pp. 31, 38–9, 49.

68   F. McLynn, *The Jacobites* (London, 1985), pp. 123–210; D. Szechi, 'The Jacobite theatre of death', in Cruickshanks and Black (eds), *The Jacobite Challenge*, pp. 57–73; J. Black, 'Could the Jacobites have won?', *History Today*, xl (1995), pp. 24–30; Clark, 'The many restorations of Jacobite Studies'.

69   Macinnes, 'Jacobitism in Scotland', pp. 230, 231, 233, 236.

70   Clark, 'Many restorations of Jacobite studies'.

71   P. Fagan, *Divided Loyalties*, passim; J. Kelly, 'A wild Capuchin of Cork', pp. 39–62; S. J. Connolly, 'Jacobites, Whiteboys and republicans', p. 64. Morley, 'Catholic disaffection and the oath of allegiance'.

72   Wellington is often remembered for expressing disdain for the land of his birth. However, he vigorously supported Catholic Emancipation in the House of Lords, reminding his political opponents that 40% of his all-conquering Peninsular army were Irish Catholics.

73   B. Ó Buachalla, *The Crown of Ireland* (Galway, 2006). Éamonn de Valera and Charles J. Haughey, the iconic leaders of Fianna Fáil, might have also staked their claim. Indeed, the latter regularly employed the Jacobite anthems 'We'll rise and follow Charlie' and 'Charlie is my darling' during electoral hustings.

74   A. Murphy, *Richard Cantillon: Entrepreneur and Economist* (Oxford, 1986).

75   S. Walsh, 'Antoine-Vincent Walsh et autres marchands nantais d'origine irlandaise' (unpublished PhD dissertation, University of Ulster, 2006).

76   For a useful comparative Scottish model, see S. Murdoch, *Network North: Scottish Kin, Commercial and Covert Associations in Northern Europe, 1603–1746* (Brill Academic Publishers, 2006). See also Macinnes, 'Jacobitism in Scotland', pp. 233, 249–50.

77   Hector McDonnell, 'Some documents relating to the involvement of the Irish Brigade in the rebellion of 1745', *Irish Sword*, xvi (1985), pp. 3–21; E. Ó h-Annracháin, 'An analysis of the Fitzjames Cavalry Regiment, 1737', *Irish Sword*, xix (1995), pp. 253–76; *idem*, 'The Irish Brigade at Laffelt: Pyrrhic victory and aftermath', *Journal of the Cork Historical and Archaeological Society*, cii (1997), pp. 1–22; *idem*, 'Irish veterans in the Invalides: the Tipperary contingent', *Tipperary Historical Journal* (1998), pp. 158–90. See also Trinity College Dublin PRTLI/Centre for Irish-Scottish Studies. French Mercenary Project, September 2002.

78   Scottish Jacobite exiles had similar dilemmas; Macinnes, 'Jacobitism in Scotland', p. 230.

79   Graecen, *Voltaire's Last Case: The Death of Thomas Lally*, forthcoming in 2009 from Irish Academic Press. Lally's opinion is not at odds with recent historio-

graphy; F. McLynn, *France and the Jacobite Rising of 1745* (Edinburgh, 1981), pp. 1–3.

80　It would, for example, be fascinating to deduce how many of these Franco-Irish veterans joined the forces of the British East India company, or opted for the service of Hyder Ali; cf. A. MacKillop, *The Scots and Irish in the East India Company*, forthcoming (Manchester, 2009).

81　P. Melvin, 'Irish soldiers and plotters in Williamite England (part 1)', *Irish Sword*, viii, 52 (1979), pp. 256–67; (part 2); xiii, 53 (1979), pp. 353–68; (part 3); xiv (1981), pp. 271–86.

82　P. A. Hopkins, 'Aspects of Jacobite conspiracy in the Reign of William III' (unpublished PhD dissertation, Cambridge, 1981), *passim*; *idem*, 'Sham Plots and Real Plots in the 1690s', in Cruickshanks (ed.), *Aspects of Jacobitism*, pp. 89–110.

83　P. Linebaugh, *The London Hanged. Crime and Civil Society in eighteenth-century London* (London, 1991), *passim*.

84　C. Bailey, 'The Irish network: a study of ethnic patronage in London, 1760–1840' (unpublished PhD dissertation, University of London), 2004.

85　J. Bergin and L. Chambers (eds), 'The library of Dennis Molony (1650–1726), an Irish Catholic lawyer in London', *Analecta Hibernica*, forthcoming. See also Dickson on the lingering and persuasive survival of Jacobitism among London expatriates such as Garrett Nagle and David Rochfort; Dickson, 'Jacobitism in eighteenth-century Ireland', p. 83.

86　These vigorous exchanges between two prolific and engaging historians provide invaluable teaching-tools for postgraduate students and are ringing endorsements of Jacobitism's centrality to early-modern Irish history. Of course, the reader can make his/her own decision as to who claims the laurels.

87　Connolly's, and, more recently, Cadoc Leighton's attempt to squeeze Ireland into the strait-jacket of J. C. D. Clark's 'Ancien Regime' should serve as a warning; S. Connolly, *Religion, Law and Power*, *passim*; Connolly, 'Jacobites, Whiteboys and Republicans', p. 78; Hayton, 'Review of Ó Ciardha', p. 157; C. Leighton, *Catholicism in a Protestant Kingdom* (Dublin, 1994), *passim*. As far as many Irish Catholics were concerned, the king was a usurper, the established church was heretical and the aristocracy comprised the sweepings of the streets of London who had been established in their confiscated estates by Cromwell and his regicides. Cf. Dickson for evidence to the contrary in eighteenth-century Munster, focusing on intermarriage, kinship networks, close personal friendships and collaboration between the two groups, Dickson, 'Jacobitism in eighteenth-century Ireland', p. 91.

88　Vincent Morley, 'The idea of Britain in eighteenth-century Ireland and Scotland', *Studia Hibernica*, xxxiii (2004–5), *passim*. See also *idem*, 'The continuity of disaffection', *passim*.

89　B. Ó Buachalla, *The Crown of Ireland* (Galway, 2006), *passim*.

90　É. Ó Ciardha, 'A voice from the Jacobite underground: Liam Inglis', in G. Moran (ed.), *Radical Irish Priests, 1660–1970* (Dublin, 1998), pp. 16–39; Connolly, 'Jacobites, Whiteboys and Republicans', p. 69.

91　Ó Buachalla's close reading of Irish Jacobite poetry, *Párliament na mBan* (*idem*, 'The making of a Cork Jacobite', pp. 469–98) and various eighteenth-century '*caointe*' (*idem*, *An caoine*); Morley's comprehensive collection of the Irish-language poems of the American Revolution (*Washington i gceannas a ríochta*) are shining examples of the untold riches which await the intrepid explorer in the unchartered, unedited collections of Irish manuscripts in Ireland, Britain, Europe and North America.

92 B. Ó Buachalla 'From Jacobite to Jacobin', in T. Bartlett, D. Dickson and K. Whelan (eds), *1798: A Bicentenary Perspective* (Dublin, 2003), pp. 75–96; idem, *The Crown of Ireland*, pp. 36–48; Ó Tuathaigh, 'Gaelic Ireland, popular politics and Daniel O'Connell', pp. 21–34; R. Uí Ógáin, *Immortal Dan: Daniel O'Connell in Irish Folklore* (Dublin, 1995).

93 Bartlett, *Fall and Rise*, *passim*.

94 Guy Beiner's ground-breaking intellectual re-habilitation and contextualization of Irish folk history, memory and antiquarianism and B. Mac Suibhne's splendid reconstruction of the Gothic political landscape of post-rebellion Ulster from the writings of John Gamble provide obvious templates for such scholarly endeavours; G. Beiner, *Irish Folk History and Social Memory* (Madison, 2007); G. Ó Tuathaigh, 'Once upon a time in the West', *Field Day Review*, iv (2008), pp. 315–25; B Mac Suibhne, 'Afterworld: the Gothic travels of John Gamble (1770–1831)', *ibid.*, pp. 63–113. See also L. Ní Dhonnchadha, 'An Mílean-nachas agus Meisiasachas i litríocht na Gaeilge idir 1780–1820' (unpublished MA thesis, NUI Galway, 2005). W. Hamrick, 'Literary and cultural manifestations of Jacobitism' and S. Hamrick, 'Appropriation of Irish language and culture in nineteenth-century Ireland' (University of Notre Dame, PhD dissertations in progress).

95 Charlotte Brooke, *Reliques of Irish Poetry*, edited and annotated with a new introduction by Lesa Ní Mhunghaile (Dublin, 2009).

96 N. Mac Cathmhaoil, 'Muiris Ó Gormáin: Saol agus saothair' (University of Ulster. PhD dissertation, in progress).

97 Recent and ongoing research on Irish book history would provide a useful guide; R. Gillespie and W. Mailey (eds), *The Oxford History of the Irish book: The Irish Book in English, 1500-1800*, vol III (Oxford, 2006); É. Ó Ciardha, F. Sewell, and A. Titley (eds), *The Oxford History of the Irish Book: The Irish Book in Irish since 1567*, vol II (Oxford, forthcoming).

98 See Clark, 'The many restorations of Jacobite studies' for an extensive survey of this material.

99 R. and M. Loeber, *A Guide to Irish Fiction, 1650–1900* (Dublin, 2006). See also J. M Cahalan, *Great Hatred, Little Room: The Irish Historical Novel* (Syracuse, 1983), *passim*.

100 Macinnes' warning on the danger of confusing nationalist aspirations of the eighteenth century with the present should not deter this type of investigation; Macinnes, 'Jacobitism in Scotland', p. 228.

101 Ó Ciardha, *Ireland and the Jacobite Cause*, pp. 171–2, 202, 215–16.

102 Campbell-Ross, 'Was Berkeley a Jacobite?', *passim*.

103 Like Yeats, Seamus Heaney has also drawn inspiration from the Jacobite canon, as evidenced by his stunning rendition of Ó Rathaille's 'Gile na Gile': L. De Paor (ed.) *Leabhar Sheáin Uí Thuama* (Dublin/B.Á.C., 1997), p. 105.

104 L. Mac Cóil, *Fontenoy* (Gaillimh, 2005).

105 It is, therefore, no great surprise that his brief dalliance with the White Rose Society is not addressed in Foster's chapter on 'Secret Societies'; R. Foster, *W. B. Yeats: A Life* (2 vols., Oxford: Oxford University Press, 1997–2003), I: 89–112.

106 Ó Siochfhradha's cultural milieu could be explored with reference to his extensive library which has recently returned to Coláiste Íde, An Daingean; D. Ní Loinsigh, 'An exploration of the bibliographical legacy of "An Seabhac"',

in Ó Ciardha, Sewell, and Titley (eds), *The Oxford History of the Irish Book*, forthcoming.

107 *Abair Amhrán, an 8ú cló* (Béal Feirste, 1981), p. 25. Ireland had moved on, but when and how far are questions which still need to be answered.

108 It is alleged that when Zhou Enlai, Mao Zedong's wily premier, was asked about the significance of the French Revolution, he cautiously retorted that it was too early to tell.

3
Jacobite Politics in Aberdeen and the '15

Kieran German

On September 20th 1715, James Francis Edward Stuart was proclaimed King James VIII at the Mercat cross in Aberdeen. George Keith, 9th (and last) Earl Marischal of Scotland, led the proceedings. He was flanked by his younger brother, James Francis Edward Keith, members of the Aberdeenshire nobility and gentry, and a significant contingent of the town's merchant burgesses and trades guild members. They had good reason to make a scene. The '15, which had been simmering for months, had finally been unleashed at Braemar two weeks earlier. The proclamation was shaded by rioting and the town's magistrates and councillors evacuated the Tolbooth, Aberdeen's municipal headquarters. These, the town's leading citizens, were otherwise absent from the occasion. The Jacobites took control of Aberdeen swiftly. Despite the rioting, there was little resistance and no need for violence. This is somewhat surprising, when one considers that the town's pro-Hanoverian magistracy was equally in-tune with the political and military developments taking place in the summer and autumn of 1715. The town, indeed the whole country, was psyched up for a Jacobite crescendo of some sort. What we know is that even if the magistrates did not support the Jacobite insurrection, and even if they were loath to regard James Stuart proclaimed king in their burgh, they did not do much to stop it.[1]

Were they being coy? What does their attitude suggest? The urban dynamic has been overlooked in the historiography of the '15 which, by and large, has explained the situation in Aberdeen as a competition between Jacobite Episcopalian landed gentry and Hanoverian Presbyterian urban magistrates.[2] But that needs to be reconciled to the reputation of both the town and county of Aberdeen as a very significant Jacobite area. The north-east of Scotland is commonly called 'the Jacobite heartlands'; the two university towns have been conjointly termed 'the intellectual citadel' of Jacobitism; the Church north of the Tay the 'nursery' of Jacobitism.[3] If such an environment is to be believed, and it should be, there is every reason to believe that there was a conscientious and educated

Jacobite community within the region's greatest city. There was; but often dismissed as 'the trades', they have not been properly profiled and, if anything, their eminence has been underestimated (and perhaps downplayed). This is not to say that the cause of King James commanded universal assent. Yet there is hitherto unexplored depth to the context of Aberdeen's urban elite, which undoubtedly influenced the ways in which the contrary forces of the well-affected magistracy and the indigenous Jacobites engaged with the rising and with one another during it, and which consequently illustrates a more equivocal picture of Aberdeen in the '15. A broader contextualisation of the urban elite of Aberdeen is demanded, and leads, inevitably, to a re-analysis of the town's contribution to the rising.

Aberdeen's urban elite was drawn exclusively from the burgess guild. Burgesses, by definition, were elite. They alone were allowed to conduct overseas trade. They were also privileged with authority. Of an available nineteen seats on the town council, seventeen were reserved for burgesses, and the town's magistrates were always burgess councillors. On the basis of these privileges, the burgesses were the most economically vital and the most influential of the town's citizens. This was no mean status; Aberdeen was the regional hub of the north-east as well as a point of international trade. Within the elite, a further distinction can be made. Aberdeen's council was self-perpetuating. At Michaelmas each year, as a matter of course, it was selected by the outgoing council, with four councillors or magistrates retained for continuity. Such a system made the council vulnerable to domination by a small group. In the council rolls of the seventeenth century a few family names recur almost continuously.[4] This community could be characterised as the ruling elite.

After the Revolution, Aberdeen's ruling elite maintained blatant Jacobite and Episcopalian principles which were obnoxious to the new government of Scotland. The town did not have a meaningful Presbyterian presence at all, let alone in the urban elite.[5] There is also little to suggest that a well-affected Williamite faction was available to take the reins of the council. When, in 1691, a visitation from the General Assembly of the Church arrived in town to implement the Presbyterian church settlement, the town council engineered a riot to resist the commissioners. The Privy Council was incensed. It perceived the event as a systematic transgression by a disaffected council with which it had repeatedly been forced to intervene. The Privy Council ordered the deposition of the provost and produced a list of burgesses unacceptable for election to the town council. Subsequently, the town council made a symbolic gesture of concurrence with the prevailing pro-Presbyterian policies of the Scottish government by indicting one of the town's most high-profile Episcopalian clerics, Dr. George Garden. Nevertheless, it remained necessary to moderate election to the council in following years. The Duke of Argyll was intervening in the composition of the council until as late as 1700 to ensure it was suitably affected.[6]

Thereafter, the council began to develop a meaningful and energetic working relationship with the Presbytery of Aberdeen. The council promoted the career of the energetic and intelligent Presbyterian minister, Thomas Blackwell. In 1710, the council was responsible for his appointment to Marischal College, which was otherwise dominated by Episcopalians. Earlier that year Blackwell had dedicated a book to the town council. Its laudatory dedication praises their Christian energy thus far, but can be read as an exhortation to spread their influence further.[7] In the following two years the council repeatedly investigated and prosecuted dissention from the Presbyterian Kirk within the town in accordance with the Presbytery's intimations. Moreover, leading members of the council provided enormous financial support to Blackwell, who undertook an extended visit to London to lobby the government against passing the Act of Toleration and the Act to Restore Patronages. These acts had been precipitated by the legal limbo of Episcopalian ministers who read the English Liturgy in Scotland, a case of which was presently vexing the Aberdonian magistrates. In his endeavour Blackwell also sought to gain support for the town council in their broader designs to neutralise Episcopalian activism within Aberdeen. It is indicative of their conviction that by 1711 the town council's positioning on religious matters was confrontational to Episcopalians within the burgh and at odds with the government's and the Queen's preferences and policies. Blackwell warned the council to be more sensitive to the religious sentiments of the queen and the government.[8] By 1715, Aberdeen's council was monopolised by the Presbyterian community, even though its interests diverged from the majority of the demographic it represented.[9]

The coincidence of Jacobitism and Episcopalianism was marked in Aberdeen in the '15, but can such a thing imply Jacobitism as characteristic of Episcopacy before the rising? Episcopalianism did not automatically equate to Jacobitism. In spite of the Scots Bishops' non-juring some Episcopalians made efforts to reconcile themselves to the post-Revolution regime. Indeed, in the wake of the Revolution, the most resounding address to the Convention Parliament to advocate a form of Episcopalian conciliation with both William and the Presbyterians came from senior Episcopalian ministers from Aberdeen.[10] Similarly, the succession of Queen Anne in 1702 raised Episcopalian hopes of toleration. George Garden made a notable contribution to the ensuing pamphlet charge which had nothing to gain and everything to lose by the introduction of a Jacobite agenda.[11]

In the eighteenth century Aberdeen was two burghs, each with a university. Old Aberdeen, 'the Aulton', was a distinct burgh which neighboured Aberdeen. It was resoundingly Episcopalian. In 1694, following the death of the incumbent minister at St. Machar Cathedral and his succession by a Presbyterian, the parish nevertheless issued a call for an Episcopalian minister, claiming to reflect the will of the whole parish of some 2,000 people.[12] Hostility to the established church had a broad social consensus. In 1714 the magistrates of Aberdeen imprisoned tradesmen, merchants and even former magistrates of Old Aberdeen for 'disturbing and molesting' St. Machar Cathedral.[13] The council of Old Aberdeen was blatantly Episcopalian. In 1704 two Baillies requested from the Presbyterian minister the communion cup from St. Machar for use in Episcopalian services in the chapel at King's College. King's College may have made a gesture of conformity with the civic authorities in the 1690s when all but one of the staff there acknowledged William as king, but it continued to act as a hub of Episcopacy in the Aulton, maintaining Episcopal church services and an Episcopalian minister. The principal of the college, George Middleton, distributed the English liturgy once its use was officially sanctioned in Scotland.[14]

Although these influential institutions in the Aulton were ostensibly juring, they supported Nonjurors in their midst. The council refused to take action against the Nonjuring minister, Robert Calder, who set up a meeting house in the Aulton in 1702. The university supported James Garden, the professor of divinity deprived of his position for refusing to give allegiance to William, in his several appeals to be reinstated during the reign of Queen Anne. Garden also received tacit support from John Erskine, 22nd Earl of Mar and James Ogilvy, 4th Earl of Findlater and 1st Earl of Seafield. Garden's Jacobitism was well known.[15] It was also alleged that the juring minister at King's College chapel, David Hedderwick, allowed Nonjuring ministers to deliver divine worship in his church, a practice which was not uncommon across the north-east. Hedderwick and George Middleton were identified as Jacobites by their opponents in 1710.[16] We can consider that environments such as that in Old Aberdeen, an environment of deep Episcopalian character, incubated Jacobitism, as was demonstrated by the students at King's. During the '15 students burned an 'effigy' of the 'Duke of Brunswick' in a particularly vitriolic expression of Jacobitism which included the ringing of the bells of King's College and the town drummer calling all residents of the Aulton to participate. After the rising the management of King's was compelled to dismiss several students. Nevertheless, it spread the blame as thinly as possible and at no point was any individual implicated in the actual act of putting George's effigy to the flames. Moreover, an effort was made to defend the elderly town drummer; in court, several defenders testified that he was forced to take his role and did not do so voluntarily. It is also worthy of notice that the principal and two regents of the university declined to participate in the court that expelled students for their Jacobitism. It did not save them. In 1717, the principal and several professors were dismissed.[17]

In Aberdeen, the influence of the university, Marischal College, was only slightly different. There, the town council was opposed to the culture of Episcopacy which prevailed in the college. Like King's, Marischal had a current of Episcopacy running through it. For example, the poet William Meston was appointed Professor of Philosophy by the Earl Marischal, the university's patron. Meston was not merely an instrument of the Earl's policies, he had been the Earl's tutor. The poetry Meston composed in the immediate aftermath of the rising expressed conscientious Jacobitism underpinned by a Nonjuring Episcopalian world-view.[18] The cultivation of Episcopacy in the town was clearly on the Earl Marischal's agenda. In 1711 the Earl established an Episcopalian meeting house in his Aberdeen residence and patronised a minister, Patrick Dunbrack, to read the English liturgy there. This seems to have been a response to the appointment of Thomas Blackwell to the chair of Divinity at Marischal, the only appointment to that college that the council controlled. Dunbrack's flagrant Episcopacy was a source of frustration to the town council. The students of the university were sensible of the tensions between the Earl and the council and in 1714 they, along with their colleagues from King's, broke into the Town House and threatened the magistrates.

Before the '15 Blackwell made an explicit connection between both King's College and Marischal College and the spread of Jacobitism in the town and across the region. During the rising all the staff at Marischal College, with the exception of Blackwell, were implicated in Jacobite activity. Marischal himself led the proclamation of James in Aberdeen and the Aulton; Meston became governor of Dunnottar Castle, the Earl Marischal's fortress near Stonehaven; Patrick Dunbrack prayed for King James VIII in churches in the town.[19] Nevertheless, the value of Marischal College to the town never went unrecognised, even though it was blamed for cultivating Jacobitism in the region. One of the primary acts of the town magistrates, after the Jacobites left the burgh in 1716, was to seek the right of patronage of the university, as well as the resources to rescue and maintain it. The opportunity was not missed to promote such an arrangement as a means of inculcating loyalty in the region.[20]

There was also a contingent of the burgess community which was openly Episcopalian. They belonged to the congregation of Trinity Church, an Episcopalian meeting house owned by the trades guild. The minister there was Andrew Burnet. Burnet had been minister at the West Kirk of St. Nicholas prior to the Revolution; in 1694 he was deprived of his position and imprisoned by an act of parliament, for refusing to take the oaths of allegiance. Burnet felt sufficiently compelled to take the oaths, his Jacobitism was not a sufficient reason to neglect his family. Burnet returned to Aberdeen in 1695 and in 1703 he was ministering at Trinity Church once more. As a qualified minister Burnet repeatedly sought restoration to St. Nicholas, something the council resisted. His congregation, which included several burgesses that would sit on the Jacobite council in 1715, also lobbied the council on his behalf. As a mark of their hostility towards Trinity, the council resurrected old town laws with which to punish the congregation. In 1715 Burnet was restored to St. Nicholas by the Jacobite magistrates, where he prayed for King James. He also addressed James personally at the Earl Marischal's house at Fetteresso during the course of the rising.[21]

Fault-lines can be observed between Episcopalians and Presbyterians of Aberdeen, but that does not mean that the town's internal dynamics were defined by the binary opposites of Episcopalian and Presbyterian, or that the divergences amongst the elite should be viewed through this lens. Although the development of Presbyterianism amongst the ruling elite coincided with a gradual dissipation of Episcopalians on the council, this was not a complete change, for two reasons. First, Jacobites had to retain status for the good of their cause, and if this required compromise then compromise there must be. There is plenty of evidence to show that in rural and urban areas, particularly in the north-east, administrative roles were taken by people who would side with the Jacobites in 1715. After the Union such a decision required giving oaths of loyalty to the queen and her Hanoverian heirs. James Moir of Stonywood and James Catanch provide respective examples of rural and urban Episcopalians and Jacobites of the '15 who, as justices of the peace during Anne's reign, were willing to make this compromise.[22] Secondly, Episcopalians were as inclined to cultivate ambition and business acumen as the next man. As we have seen, Episcopalians practiced patience and discretion when it came to exercising a Jacobite agenda. Meanwhile, the pursuit of wealth and influence was a sensible and natural desire. Even so, such a pragmatic aspect of the Aberdonian Episcopalian mentality can be considered to represent simultaneously Jacobite prudence and subjugation. Prudence, because the Jacobites developed the skills necessary to manage the municipality should the occasion arise; subjugation, because, in the short term, their priorities subordinated Episcopalian and Jacobite endeavour to enterprises which involved and underpinned their Presbyterian, Hanoverian adversaries.

James Catanach provides an excellent exemplar of a member of the urban elite in 1715. He was an Episcopalian and a burgess. He was also an experienced town magistrate; in 1704 he had been a town Baillie. In 1706 Catanach was amongst the most active merchants of the city. That year he again served on the town council. He was a Baillie once more in 1708. Thereafter he no longer appeared on the council, which tallies with the emergence of the council's Presbyterian agenda. But his economic value still gave him significant status in the burgh. He had trading links with the gentry of Aberdeenshire; overseas business interests extending from Gdańsk to New England, and shared financial investments with members of Aberdeen's town council. Catanach is an attractive, but not especially extraordinary, example of the Episcopalian elite. He demonstrates that the elite was broad and that Episcopalians within it enjoyed influence in the town by virtue of their wealth and their connections. Moreover, Catanach shows that within the Episcopal burgess community there were civically responsible folk who had the experience and expertise to manage the urban administration, as well as the willingness to do it for the Jacobites.[23]

The achievement of the union of England and Scotland conflated dynastic and ecclesiastical factors with economic ones. The religious settlement, which favoured Presbyterianism, was counterbalanced by economic opportunity. As well as the short term advantage that Aberdonian merchants made from the accomplishment of union, the town's elite had favoured a commercial concordat with England for years before it actually came to pass. That is not to say that they favoured political incorporation, but the council did instruct their commissioner to Parliament to frustrate the Hanoverian succession if preferable economic terms were not agreed. It would be a stretch to imply this last gesture was Jacobite, as the town's commissioner, John Allardes, firmly supported the Presbyterian settlement.[24] Partisanship, be it religious or political, was engaged with due consideration of economic conditions. When it came to commerce, the trend seems to be that partisan differences were set aside. *The Elizabeth*, a ship that traded between Aberdeen and Cadiz, provides a particularly illustrative example. Year upon year, the largest investments in overseas trade by both contingents of the urban elite made shared use of ships, contacts and networks, and markets. In 1715 *The Elizabeth* departed Cadiz with a cargo bound for Aberdeen. Both the ship and the cargo belonged to several of the town's merchants. Robert Stewart, the sitting (and Hanoverian) provost had just over a quarter share of the cargo and a quarter share of the vessel. John Gordon, a member of the same council, had a third share in the cargo and a quarter share of the ship. James Gellie had a quarter share of the cargo and the ship; he went on to sit on the Jacobite Council. The Jacobite Provost, Patrick Bannerman, had a sixteenth share as did one of the Jacobite Baillies, John Burnet. This particular economic endeavour was undertaken at the same time that several of the interested parties were engaged in hostilities between Trinity Church and the town council. Later on, the matter of the goods on board *The Elizabeth* came before the Harbour court of Aberdeen more than once, and before both Hanoverian and Jacobite magistrates.[25] Even in the midst of the Jacobite rising the Jacobite magistrates endeavoured to protect their commercial interests and those of their political opponents. Moreover, their endeavours demonstrate that they could provide a functioning civic administration competent in managing the town's courts and harbour, as well as the Jacobite war effort.

Unity amongst the divergent groups can be observed in 1708 also. In that year French ships carrying James Stuart were seen off the Aberdeen coast. The town council put up an organised and united defence against hostile forces; specifically, it formed a civic guard, which the town's elite were mustered to lead. Status and investment, rather than political or ecclesiastical opinion, dictated who was given authority. It is fascinating to consider that the guard was comprised of members of the elite who, come 1715, would diverge along Jacobite and Hanoverian lines. Afterwards some were signatories to a laudatory address to Queen Anne, praising her defence of her realm from 'the Frenches'.[26] The most significant thing about the response to the Jacobite threat in 1708 is that it marked a sacrifice of principle and ambition, not just for the security and stability of the town but also for economic prosperity amongst the elite. In 1708 this principle militated against Jacobitism. It is a tentative suggestion, but the coincidence of Episcopacy and Jacobitism coupled with subsequent Jacobite activism in 1715 could suggest that a significant proportion of those standing in arms ready to oppose a Jacobite force represented the leadership of the potential Jacobite activists of Aberdeen. It cannot be said with certainty what was the overriding factor that motivated the united response to the Jacobite threat. Was there enough enthusiasm for union amongst the latent Jacobites that prompted them to eschew the Jacobite chance? There certainly would have been little desire to attract the attention and intervention of central government; swallowing principles to ensure that local authority and civic administration remained in the hands of business colleagues with collective concerns was the sensible thing to do, especially since the Jacobite fleet on the Aberdeen coast did not represent a Jacobite opportunity that was likely to succeed. Unlike the '15 it marked a small intervention with the potential to upset a very tender, but potentially beneficial new political and economic arrangement. By 1715 circumstances were quite different, the Union had come within four votes of dissolution; the House of Hanover had assumed the British throne and the Whigs were in government.

   The developing promise of a Jacobite uprising in 1714/15 imperilled the economic stability and vitality of the town's burgesses. Of course, the urban elite was *au fait* with the looming Jacobite drama and was probably certain that Aberdeen would be involved in it. Thus the leading citizens of Aberdeen were presented with a challenge. How could they follow their own principles, tolerate those of their peers, and preserve the economic and commercial vitality of the town? As the momentum of Jacobitism within Aberdeen picked up, the repeated postulation of the town council was that Jacobitism was not an indigenous problem, it was an external force which the town would defend against if necessary. For example, when James Stuart was proclaimed king at the Mercat cross, surreptitiously and most probably by drunken apprentices and/or students, the town council was content to ignore the scene, rather than bring it to the attention of any higher authority. Nevertheless, rumour will travel. When it reached authority, in the form of the Earl of Mar (still clinging to government), the town reduced the stakes of the alleged crime to some Jacobite song having been sung, rather than a proclamation made. Furthermore, they argued that the crime was perpetrated by folk from outwith the burgh.[27] In May 1715 the council recorded in their minutes that students from both King's and Marischal had 'insulted' the magistrates. Correspondence with government figures painted a different picture; a month later when Robert Stewart, the Provost, wrote to James Graham, 1st Duke of Montrose, he complained that the magistrates' houses had been 'rifled', the prison broken into and most significantly that the bonded warehouse had been burgled. The criminals were identified as Highlanders and Jacobitism was clearly insinuated.[28] In other words, Jacobitism was presented as an external problem which the town magistracy could not do anything about.

In fact, the magistrates were keeping a close eye on how events were unfolding and their intelligence turned out to be particularly sharp. A good month before the Jacobite standard was hoisted at Braemar the council of Aberdeen was aware of the gathering momentum. Once again, the council presented the Jacobites as aliens: 'the Highlanders were in some motion and are lyke to ryse'.[29] Clearly the council's rhetoric and their understanding of the situation on the ground were two different things. In the town things continued to get exciting. James Stuart's birthday was celebrated with bonfires and gunshots on the Castlegate. With the absence of a military presence the situation became volatile. The sense of trepidation among the ruling elite was evident; the Provost, Robert Stewart, chose this moment to reinforce the entrance to his house.[30] But, above all, the ruling elite's approach to the Jacobite threat demonstrates their capacity for organisation. They achieved this through a level of concurrence across the urban elite. They put in place a series of defensive measures, which, in fact, equate to preparations for an orderly Jacobite takeover. Their measures perhaps whisper of a fear of what a Jacobite intrusion might actually have meant to order in the town, and thus explain the burgesses' overriding compulsion to translate authority peacefully, should occasion arise, to known, trusted and, most importantly, unthreatening Jacobites from within. Such an approach is consistent with the council's 'defensive' strategy.

We need to examine these defensive arrangements more closely, in order to discern whether the magistrates' actions tally with their purported understanding. The preparations put in place to withstand an assault from outside were not arrived at by pooling the expertise and experience of a committee of magistrates, but by seeking the advice of urban Jacobites.[31] The precaution of collecting all of the gunpowder within the town into a single stronghold was only taken once the Lord Justice Clerk had compelled the magistrates to see to it. It should be noted, moreover, that they did not do a very thorough job, which may have been deliberate. The magistrates themselves surrendered little. Similarly, other burgesses, who would shortly become the visible Jacobites, did not surrender all of theirs. Throughout the rising, William Simson, a Jacobite councillor, traded gunpowder with rural Jacobites.[32] The magistrates had been instructed to dispatch all that they had to Edinburgh for the use of the government; but they ensured a significant proportion even of the recorded amount, just under a third, was retained in the Tolbooth. This suggests that it was being used as a stockpile for weaponry. It was. The town also procured 'two hundred stand or arms of armes, viz., gunns and bayenotts'. A rational move, when one feels threatened by an insurrection. Except that, in fact, the weapons were not used to defend the town against the Jacobites.

Partisan accounts from both sides conflict only slightly over the amount of force used to take control when the Earl Marischal did enter the town and proclaim James; one claims the magistrates were harried from the Tolbooth, though the records of the Jacobite council merely say the incumbents had 'absented themselves'. They silently concur that no defensive force greeted the Jacobites. It could well be that, as in 1708, the community was (or was expected to be) acting together, in unity, with the primary interest being self-preservation. Days before the Jacobite entry the councillors 'debursed' the town's common good fund. This was only sensible, for it kept the money within the community rather than leaving it vulnerable to either army. It should also be noted that when the Jacobites did take over the municipal administration they quickly showed competence in collecting taxes and little interest in exploiting the town's established material wealth for short term gain.[33]

Significantly, however, the outgoing magistrates did nothing to endorse their successors. The proclamation of James in Aberdeen received no validation in the form of the attendance of the sitting magistrates. They cannot be implicated at all in the nomination of the Jacobite council, as was the established custom for elections. Nevertheless, the council was installed in a ceremonial fashion. Elections were called in which the burgess and trades guilds were invited to participate. They took place in the West Kirk of St. Nicholas, which until then was a Presbyterian stronghold, and the council records make a point of associating this with an older custom, 'to elect and choose Magistrats and Counsellors by poll for the ensueing year as hade been formerly practised', to emphasise its validity.[34] Insofar as custom can validate an action, the council's legitimacy would also have been underpinned by the fact that it was formed at Michaelmas, the usual time for the council to renew itself. Thus, the Hanoverian council dissolved not through force, but through expiration of its term. So too the Jacobite successors followed the practice of limiting their tenure to one year.

A Whig report claims that possession of the Town House, and the keys thereunto, were seized. However, even if they had been retained by the incumbent council, they would have had little customary right to hold them. Patrick Bannerman of Elsick became provost. Bannerman was an eminent merchant with established commercial links to the outgoing magistrates and councillors. The Baillies James Gelly, William Simson and John Leslie had a similar commercial network. John Leslie also had recent council experience, having been a Baillie from 1709 until 1711. James Catanach, a councillor in 1715, also had recent experience of being on the council; he was also one of the town's most connected and energetic merchants. Alexander Bannerman, also a councillor, had been town sergeant since 1713. Of the seventeen burgess councillors, only four were of rural provenance; namely Patrick Bannerman, James Moir of Stonywood, Alexander Moir of Scotstown and James Bisset of Lessendrum. Nevertheless, Alexander Bannerman was usually resident in the town, he owned a house on Guestrow. James Moir of Stonywood, MP for Aberdeenshire, also had established commercial with burgesses in the town.[35]

The Hanoverian magistrates pursued a line of plausible deniability alongside a degree of orchestration with indigenous Jacobites. Thus, the town remained in the trusted control of the urban elite throughout the rising. Should the Jacobites have prevailed Aberdeen would have benefited from its energetic support of the cause, as well as from its administrative continuity throughout. Meanwhile, the Hanoverians maintained a safe distance from Jacobite activity which could sully their reputations, and thus kept themselves in the clear to provide steady and stable administration in the case of a government triumph. It rings of co-operation between the two parties. The Episcopalian ministers were restored to St. Nicholas Kirk, but the Presbyterian ministers were allowed to continue to preach to their own congregations, the only condition being that they did not pray for George by name.[36] Some of the former magistrates were drawn into administrative responsibilities, particularly the collection of taxes. While the council records are careful not to implicate these eminent townsmen in the actual act, the fact that they were even nominated suggests an amount of administrative cohesion between the two supposedly opposed parties. This was emphasised when the Jacobite army began to lean upon Aberdeen disproportionately for financial nourishment. The burgh declined to meet the staggering request for £2,000 sterling on the basis that the collective burgess community could not raise the capital. This decision was informed particularly by advice from three former Provosts of Hanoverian disposition. The Jacobite council accepted the advice, and formed a committee to proceed in the most considerate manner. While appointed to this committee, the eminent Hanoverians tacitly removed themselves.[37] It is unsurprising, however, that these particular burgesses should raise their voices, and be listened to, when the economic competence of the burgh was called upon and challenged.

Discretion was similarly exercised after the prospects of a Jacobite Restoration began to diminish. Following the failure of the Jacobites to consolidate their military advantage with a decisive victory at Sherrifmuir, and the fall of Inverness to Simon Fraser, Lord Lovat, who was acting for the government, overt displays of Jacobitism would have been counterproductive to the town's interest. A process of damage limitation was therefore initiated, rendered all the more difficult by James Stuart's untimely arrival in the north-east. James' tour of the region was probably the highlight of his visit to his family's old kingdom, which otherwise (to James' personal remorse) involved acknowledging the damage to the communities of his estranged subjects in Perthshire before abandoning the rising on a midnight flit from the harbour at Montrose. Nevertheless, James was modestly treated in Aberdeen. Ushered in and ushered out incognito, James received only dinner (perhaps a dram and some stovies – regional culinary delights). There was no ceremonial entrance and there were no pageants, which would hardly have been appropriate after the outcome of Sherrifmuir. The town's magistrates and Episcopal clergy addressed James at the Earl Marischal's house, a safe distance away in Fetteresso. Meanwhile the publicity machine kicked into action. Reports began to leak from the city which remonstrated that the general majority were good subjects of King George. Ostensibly produced by Hanoverian supporters, these reports laid the guilt squarely at the door of the Episcopalian clergy who were credited with a long and laudatory address to 'the Pretender'. The Jacobites among the elite were given a less damaging portrayal. Ascribed to the magistrates was a brief, meaningless salute to James as king, but the corresponding analysis again blamed the clergy for the Jacobite activities in the town.[38]

By and large, the magistrates got off lightly. Patrick Bannerman was imprisoned at Edinburgh Castle and was amongst the prisoners transferred to Carlisle. He escaped once he got there, or perhaps even before. The prisoner lists designate him 'Provost of Aberdeen', the first of many records which lend authenticity to his election to that office.[39] Indeed, the Town House in Aberdeen, a Victorian relic, includes Bannerman to this day amongst the long list of the town's Aldermen and Provosts. Within two years some of the magistrates begin to reappear in the civic annals. James Catanach, testified in the Baillie Court in December 1717, demonstrating he had been conducting overseas trade from Aberdeen in October of that year, which also indicates that he retained his status as a burgess of the burgh.[40] He is just one example. The Jacobite clergy of the city, by and large, also avoided stinging reprisals. George Garden escaped imprisonment and went into exile at Leyden.[41] Six other ministers, including Andrew Burnet and Patrick Dunbrack, appear to have escaped all punishment and they maintained their distinctly Nonjuring presence in the burgh.[42] Nevertheless, by 1720 there was a telling juxtaposition. That year, a group of Aberdonian burgesses established St. Paul's Episcopalian meeting house in the burgh. It was founded in accordance with the law (i.e. according to the Toleration Act it would recognise the sovereignty of the sitting monarch, in this case George I). At the forefront of the organisation, and taking the burden on the financial responsibility were those active on the Jacobite council of 1715/16, most eminently Catanach, Bannerman and William Simson. The burgess community had the resources and skills to orchestrate the congregation's establishment; they along with the local gentry could produce the cash (or at least gain the credit) for it, and, with some regional gentry and the trades guild, they could produce the congregation. It was a clergyman that they were left wanting.[43] Despite the presence of six Episcopalian ministers in the burgh, the congregation of St. Paul's selected the juring Episcopalian Joseph Robertson, of Forfar, to be their minister. Aberdeen's Episcopalian burgesses, unlike the town's clergy, put pragmatism before principle.[44]

There were several classes of Jacobite in Aberdeen around about 1715. Their respective contributions to the '15, and their integration into society before and after it, say some things about their value to the town, the town's priorities, and the realistic engagement the town was willing to make with the rising. The Episcopalian clergy of Aberdeen were blatantly Jacobite. By principle and by institution they were adherents of King James. Disestablished as the national church and largely dissatisfied with toleration, they had little to risk and everything to gain by rising with the Jacobites. Their activism for their church and their impatience with the *status quo* largely overshadowed the intellectual and spiritual contributions they were making to the town. The universities were as effectively Episcopalian, if a little more subtly. Their willingness to maintain Episcopalian academics and clerics effectively incubated Jacobitism between the Revolution and the rising by preserving and delivering Jacobite ideology. The resounding Jacobitism of the colleges prompted the near-closure of Marischal after the rising and led to a purge of King's also.[45] A lot of professionals lost their jobs and their influence. Finally, the merchant class of Jacobites were more modest, more adroit, and altogether more prudent. Their prioritising of the town's stability, their economic value and acumen, their inter-relatedness with the great and the good of regional and civic life made their Episcopacy and their Jacobitism not only more tempered, but more tolerable. It is most probable that they came out for the Jacobites because they believed the established government's position was untenable. The incumbent magistrates gave way with a façade of custom and a defensible display of submission. When one side or the other, Hanoverian or Jacobite, prevailed, the ruling elite protected their interests, the town, and their business colleagues and associates from reprisal so that, after the rising, business could continue as usual. And it did.

What becomes apparent, through a closer investigation of Aberdeen's urban elite in the years between William's usurpation and James' attempt at reclamation, is that Jacobitism was not just a rural phenomenon; Aberdeen's Jacobites were influential and well-organised. But the town's response to national crises was unanimous and guided by instincts of collective self-preservation; partisan initiative was subjugated to considered and co-operative management of civic positioning which, to an extent, diluted the Jacobitism demonstrated in Aberdeen in the vital period of 1715/16.

Although Aberdeen represents a positive exemplar of Jacobite organisation in 1715, it also represents an urban community determined to deal with the uprising and its aftermath on its own terms.

Notes

1 *A Short Memorandum of quhat hath occurred in Aberdeen since xx September M.DCCXV* (Edinburgh, 1837); *Extracts from the Records of the Burgh of Aberdeen*, ed. J. Stuart (Edinburgh, 1872), pp. 349–53.

2 A. Keith, *A Thousand Years of Aberdeen* (Aberdeen, 1972), p. 273; B. Lenman, *The Jacobite Risings in Britain 1689–1746* (London, 1980), p. 137; D. Szechi, *1715: The Great Jacobite Rebellion* (New Haven, 2006), p. 107.

3 A. I. Macinnes, 'Jacobitism in Scotland: Episodic Cause or National Movement?', in *The Scottish Historical Review* [*SHR*], 222 (2007), p. 234; B. Lenman, 'The Scottish Episcopal Clergy and the Ideology of Jacobitism', in E. Cruickshanks (ed.), *Ideology and Conspiracy: Aspects of Jacobitism, 1689–1759* (Edinburgh, 1982), pp. 38–9; Colin Kidd, *British Identities Before Nationalism: Ethnicity and Nationhood in the Atlantic World, 1600–1800* (Cambridge, 1999), p. 135; M. G. H. Pittock, *Scottish Nationality* (Basingstoke, 2001), p. 43; *The address of the episcopal clergy of the dioses of Aberden to the Pretender with remarks upon the said address* (Edinburgh, 1716).

4 M. Lynch and H. M. Dingwall, 'Elite Society in Town and Country', in E. P. Dennison, D. Ditchburn and M. Lynch (eds), *Aberdeen Before 1800: A New History* (East Linton, 2002), p. 186; D. Macniven, 'Merchants and Traders in Early Seventeenth Century Aberdeen', in D. Stevenson (ed.), *From Lairds to Louns Country and Burgh Life in Aberdeen 1600–1800* (Aberdeen, 1986), pp. 57–69; Aberdeen City Archives [ACA], Council Register, vol. 58.

5 *Acts of the Parliament of Scotland* [*APS*] vol. IX, p. 415; Mr R. Langlands to the Reverend James Woodrow, 4 July 1694, reproduced in *Miscellany of the Spalding Club*, vol. II (Aberdeen, 1842), pp. 169–71.

6 *The Register of the Privy Council of Scotland* [*RPCS*] (Edinburgh, 1967), vol. XVI, pp. 347–55; D. Findlay and A. Murdoch, 'Revolution to Reform: Eighteenth-century Politics, c. 1690–1800', in *Aberdeen before 1800*, p. 268; Aberdeen University Library [AUL], MS3320/5/2, [Anon.] *A History of the Diocese of Aberdeen*, [in typescript], untitled, n. d., p. 10; *James Gordon's Diary*, eds. G. D. Henderson and H. H. Porter (Aberdeen, 1949), p. 60, n. 18; ACA, Letters Books (Incoming), viii, no. 16 (the Duke of Argyll to the Magistrates and Town Council of Aberdeen, 30 July 1700).

7 ACA, Council Register, vol. 58, pp. 190, 229; T. Blackwell, *Ratio Sacra or an appeal unto the rational world, about the reasonableness of revealed religion* (Edinburgh, 1710).

8 ACA, Press 18/8/32–34; 'Letters from Professor Blackwell and others, to John Ross of Arnage, Provost of Aberdeen. M.DCC.XI.–M.DCC.XII.' in *Miscellany of the Spalding Club*. vol. I (Aberdeen, 1841), pp. 195–223.

9 ACA, Letters Books (Incoming), viii, no. 149 (A committee in Aberdeen to receive funds for the SSPCK, 30 March 1710) and 227 (Memorandum and querie for the toune of Aberdeen, 17 Feb. 1717).

10 T. Clarke, 'The Williamite Episcopalians and the Glorious Revolution in Scotland', *Records of the Scottish Church History Society* [*RSCHS*], xxiv (1990), p. 43.

11   [George Garden?] *The case of the Episcopal clergy, and of those of the Episcopal perswasion, consider'd; as to the granting them a toleration and indulgence* (1703); George Garden, *A few Brief and modest reflexions perswading a just indulgence to be granted to the Episcopal clergy and people in Scotland* (1703); [John Sage] *A brief examination of some things in Mr. Meldrum's sermon preach'd May 16 against a toleration to those of the Episcopal perswasion. In a letter to a friend* (1703).

12   T. Clarke, 'Nurseries of Sedition?: The Episcopal Congregations after the Revolution of 1689', in J. Porter (ed.), *After Columba – After Calvin, Community and Identity in the Religious Traditions of North East Scotland* (Aberdeen, 1999), p. 63.

13   ACA, Letters Books (Incoming), viii, no. 196 (Warrant to incarcerate in the Tolbooth some that disturbed and molested the established Church of Scotland, July 1714).

14   *Records of Old Aberdeen*, A. M. Munro (ed.), vol. II (Aberdeen, 1909), p. 115; *Mystics of the North-East*, G. D. Henderson (ed.) (Aberdeen, 1934), p. 62; National Archives of Scotland [NAS], CH12/12/8 (Robert Dongworth, James Greenshields and Mr. James Gray, London, to Dr. George Middleton, 24 Jan 1712/13).

15   *Records of Old Aberdeen*, pp. 107–9; G. D. Henderson (ed.) *Mystics of the North-East* (Aberdeen, 1934), pp. 61–5.

16   *James Gordon's Diary*, p. 54; T. Clarke, *Scottish Episcopalians, 1689–1720* (Unpublished PhD thesis, University of Edinburgh, 1989), p. 48; NAS CH12/12/4; *The case of Mr. Greenshields, as it was printed in London, with remarks upon the same; and copies of the original papers relating to that affair, as also a list of the late Episcopal ministers, who enjoy churches or legal benefices in Scotland* (Edinburgh, 1710).

17   *Historical Papers Relating to the Jacobite Period, 1699–1750*, ed. J. Allardyce, 2 vols, (Aberdeen, 1896), II: pp. xliii–xlvi, 585–96; C. A. McLaren, 'The College and the Community, 1660–1860', in J. S. Smith (ed.), *Old Aberdeen: Bishops, Burghers and Buildings* (Aberdeen, 1991), p. 61.

18   William Meston, *The Poetical Works of the Ingenious and Learned William Meston, A. M. Sometime Professor of Philosophy in the Marischall College of Aberdeen. To Which is Prefixed the Author's Life* (Aberdeen, 1802).

19   ACA Press 18/8/32–34; NAS GD220/5/572 (Thomas Blackwell to the Duke of Montrose, 24 June 1715); ACA Council Register, p. 384; *A Short Memorandum*.

20   NAS GD220/5/639/2 (Robert Stewart, Provost of Aberdeen to the Duke of Montrose 23 February 1716); NAS GD220/5/647/2 (Thomas Blackwell to the Duke of Montrose, 24 February 1716).

21   A. E. Smith, 'Register of S. Paul's Episcopal Chapel Aberdeen', *Miscellany of the New Spalding Club*, Aberdeen, 1906; ACA Council Register, p. 385; *The address of the episcopal clergy of the dioses of Aberden*.

22   E. K. Carmichael, 'Jacobitism in the Scottish Commission of the Peace, 1707–1760', *SHR*, 58 (1979), pp. 58–69; ACA, Council Register, vol. 58, p. 303; ACA, Letters Books (Incoming), viii, no. 118 (Magistrates of Aberdeen to the Privy Council of Great Britain, 2 June 1708).

23   ACA, Council Register, vol. 58, p. 53; ACA, Propinquity Books, vol. ii (1706–1730), pp. 125, 127–9; ACA, Transcript of Propinquity Books, vol. i (1706–1722), pp. 84–6.

24   ACA, Letters Books (Incoming), viii, no. 96 (Magistrates to John Allardes, 20 June, 1702); ACA, Letters Books (Incoming), viii, no. 252 (Magistrates to Robert Dundas, 3 March, 1718). D. Findlay and A. Murdoch, 'Revolution to Reform', p. 268.

25   ACA, Propinquity Books, vol. ii (1706–1730), pp. 127–9.

26 ACA, Council Register, vol. 58, p. 93; *A Short Memorandum*; *Extracts from the Records of the Burgh of Aberdeen*, pp. 335–7.

27 *Historical Papers Relating to the Jacobite Period, 1699–1750*, ed. J. Allardyce, vol. I (Aberdeen, 1895), pp. 28–9.

28 Allardyce, *Historical Papers*, vol. II, p. xlvi; NAS GD 220/5/5712 & 3.

29 *Extracts from the Records of the Burgh of Aberdeen*, p. 349.

30 NAS GD220/5/571/1 (Duke of Montrose to Robert Stewart, 23 June 1715); ACA, Council Register, p. 416.

31 *Extracts from the Records of the Burgh of Aberdeen*, p. 349; *A Short Memorandum of quhat hath occurred in Aberdeen*.

32 NAS, CS96/597 (Journal of William Simson, merchant, Aberdeen).

33 *Extracts from the Records of the Burgh of Aberdeen*, pp. 349, 350, 352; *A Short Memorandum of quhat hath occurred in Aberdeen*.

34 ACA, *Council Register*, p. 419.

35 *Extracts from the Records of the Burgh of Aberdeen*, pp. 352–3; *A Short Memorandum of quhat hath occurred in Aberdeen*; ACA, *Council Register*, p. 190; D. Macniven, 'Merchants and Traders', ACA, Transcripts of the Propinquity Books, vol. I (1706–22).

36 *Historical Papers 1699–1750*, vol. I, p. 46.

37 *Historical Papers 1699–1750*, vol. I, p. 47.

38 *The Address of the Majestrates and Town Council of Aberdeen, to the Pretender with Remarks upon the said address* (Edinburgh, 1716); *The Address of the Episcopal Clergy*.

39 *A List of the Scot's Noblemen and Gentlemen Prisoners, that are designed for England* (Edinburgh, 1716); 'Deed of Foundation of S. Paul's, Aberdeen, 2nd August, 1720', reproduced in *Miscellany of the New Spalding Club* (Aberdeen, 1906), p. 86.

40 ACA, Transcripts of the Propinquity Books, vol. I (1706–22), p. 521.

41 AUL MS3320/2/12/9; *Mystics of the North-East*, pp. 31, 131.

42 ACA, Letters Books (Incoming), viii, no. 252 (Magistrates to Robert Dundas, 3 March 1718).

43 'Original Constitution, S. Paul's, 1722', reproduced in A. E. Smith, 'Register of S. Paul's Episcopal Chapel Aberdeen', *Miscellany of the New Spalding Club* (Aberdeen, 1906), pp. 96–8.

44 'Deed of Foundation of St. Paul's, Aberdeen'.

45 NAS, CH12/12/8 (Robert Dongworth, James Greenshields and Mr. James Gray, London, to Dr. George Middleton, 24 Jan 1712/13); NAS, GD220/5/647/3 (Thomas Blackwell to the Duke of Montrose, 2 April 1716); NAS GD220/5/639/2 (Provost of Aberdeen to the Duke of Montrose 23 February 1716).

4

Retrieving Captain Le Cocq's Plunder: Plebeian Scots and the Aftermath of the 1715 Rebellion

Daniel Szechi

Rebellions are *ipso facto* civil wars in the making. However brief and unsuccessful they might be, it is in their very nature to dislocate government and civil society. Hence the condition of Scotland in March 1716. The Jacobite rebellion that had begun in September 1715 was certainly defeated. James Stuart, the Old Pretender, had abandoned his retreating army at Montrose and taken ship for France on 4 February accompanied by the erstwhile leader of the rising, John Erskine, Earl of Mar, and a handful of other senior Jacobite officers.[1] Major-General Thomas Gordon of Auchintoul, left behind with the unhappy task of leading the disintegrating Jacobite army back to the Highlands and negotiating the best terms he could with the pursuing government army and the Whig authorities in London, had disbanded what was left of his demoralised forces at Ruthven in Badenoch on 14 February.[2]

In the Highlands a few clans such as the Mackenzies, Camerons and Macdonalds of Glengarry were harbouring notable Lowland refugees such as George Keith, Earl Marischal and James Carnegie, Earl of Southesk, and a number of officers from the French Irish brigade, who had come to Scotland in January.[3] Technically they were still in rebellion, having as yet refused formally to submit. The firebrands among the clan *fine* still hoped that arms and men might come from France, if only they could hold out a little longer, but all the Jacobite chieftains who were still at liberty were in direct or indirect contact with Lieutenant-General William Cadogan, hoping to negotiate as good a surrender as possible.[4] Cadogan, charged by the government with stamping out the last embers of Jacobite resistance, was preparing the two-pronged invasion of the Jacobite Highlands from Inverness and Perth that was by the end of April finally to end all but the Mackenzies' resistance. The last gasp of the '15 came when Brigadier Colin Campbell of Ormidale gathered a few men on South Uist to resist a landing party led by Colonel Cholmley, 'But upon the approach of our Grenadiers to attack them, they immediately runn away', and Campbell was captured.[5]

Elsewhere in Scotland former soldiers in the Jacobite army were fleeing the country, trying to return home as unobtrusively as possible, or hiding from the retribution threatened by the Whig regime.[6] In the Lowlands north of the Tay in particular, hundreds of heritors were lurking in back country areas, hoping that if they remained out of the way for long enough the government's thirst for revenge would slacken and they could quietly return home.[7] There was as yet, though, little sign that the ministry was losing interest in pursuing former Jacobite rebels.[8] Though its officers in the field, such as Colonel Charles Cathcart, had more than once explained the difficulty in hunting down these fugitives: 'Non of them venture upon being att their oun houses, but ... shift about amongst their tenants, never twoe nights together in one place. This .. [renders].. it difficult to catch any of them by sending out detachments of the regular troopes. They are too much on their guard', the government stubbornly continued to order its forces to find and arrest them.[9] Some of the lurkers duly responded by coalescing into little gangs and launching nocturnal attacks on local Whig notables who were actively hunting their former friends and neighbours. Others, most famous amongst them Rob Roy Macgregor, set about making (or, in Macgregor's case, quite possibly reverting to making) a living permanently outwith the law.[10] Government and society correspondingly remained profoundly dislocated in most of Scotland benorth Tay for many months after the rebellion was officially suppressed.[11]

Even in southern Scotland the regular rhythms of life were not soon reestablished. Many heritors there had also been caught up in the rebellion, and had marched south into England in November 1715. Forced to surrender after the battle of Preston, most of those who had not escaped by March 1716 had been convicted of treason and rebellion and obliged to agree to transportation to the American colonies to save their lives. Their kith and kin were accordingly lobbying, petitioning and expending whatever political capital they had to save their errant friends and relatives from what they feared would be certain death by penal servitude.[12] Equally wrenching were the desperate circumstances of hundreds of plebeian prisoners of war incarcerated in Scotland. Whereas former rebels from the lower orders captured by the authorities in the north were simply disarmed, sometimes required to swear an oath of allegiance to King George, then released to make their own way home, in Glasgow and Edinburgh over 600 plebeian Scots were crammed into every available prison awaiting a decision as to their fate.[13] They were doubly unfortunate in that the great majority of them were deserters from the southern Jacobite army that had marched into England. Many claimed to have been forced out by their landlords and chieftains, and certainly rather than march beyond Scotland they had absconded in October and early November 1715 and tried to make their way home, only to be swept up by local Whig vigilantes as they journeyed north.[14] By March 1716 the foetid gaols into which they were crammed had had their inevitable effect on the health of the prisoners. '[They] are become generally very sickly, and many of them have ulcers, from which ane infection is justly feared, and our people scruple to goe into them or to guard them', complained the magistrates of Glasgow.[15] The municipal authorities were also very unhappy to find themselves stuck with the expense of feeding and guarding these putative felons while Westminster made up its mind how to deal with them. The common prisoners' plight naturally excited considerable sympathy at all levels of society, especially when the government tried to have them moved to England for trial and, very likely, transportation to the colonies, as had been done with the Preston prisoners.[16]

Indeed, the easing of tension within Scotland's Whig community following on the pathetic collapse of the rebellion in the face of John Campbell, Duke of Argyll's, winter offensive at the end of January 1716, coupled with the general groundswell of compassion towards the Jacobite prisoners of war, had by the spring produced a backlash in the Jacobites' favour. Let me be clear: there was no sudden surge of sympathy for the Stuarts among Scotland's Whigs, but there was a growing, ultimately widespread feeling that such a comprehensive failure of a rebellion did not merit swingeing retribution.[17] 'And so there's ane end of this ridicolous story which by artifice of disoblidged and designing knaves has miserably envolved numbers of poor unthinking Gentlemen whose freinds do nou heartilly regrate their delusion', wrote David Graham of Orchill to the Duke of Montrose as early as the beginning of February 1716.[18] By April General Joseph Sabine was warning Secretary of State Charles Townshend, Viscount Townshend:

> ...there are many unwearyed attempts made, by people who pretend to be zealously affected to the Government, for releasing prisoners of note, skreening persons notoriously concerned in the late rebellion. And many persons who have informed against such and were ready to be evidences against them, are either bribed off or menaced and threatened with imprisonment and persecution. So that unless speedy care be taken, and [a] stopp putt to such proceedings, there will, I am persuaded, be very few rebells convicted or forfittures found in this country.[19]

This gathering wave of sympathy within the elite Whig community was eventually to become so strong that it effectively blocked the prosecution of all but a small proportion of the second tier elite Jacobites, persuaded the government to release all the plebeian prisoners without charge and considerably reduced the impact of the government's attempts to punish the rebels at large by confiscating their estates.[20] These effects lay some months in the future in March 1716, but even by that early date Scotland's Whig elite were already showing signs of unease at certain aspects of the military campaign, most notably the wholesale looting of northern Scotland by government forces.

Both sides had levied 'contributions' on the civilian population under their control during the autumn and winter of 1715–16, for which the troops concerned generally issued receipts with promises of payment at some future date.[21] The disintegration of the Jacobite army in the face of Argyll's advance and a change in the composition of his forces, however, dramatically changed the situation. By late January, when Argyll's forces entered Perth, over half his army of 9,000–10,000 consisted of Dutch and Swiss auxiliaries.[22] These were professional soldiers operating, as far as they were concerned, in enemy territory. In the regular course of European warfare at this time invading troops generally regarded the property of enemy civilians as subject to impositions or seizures. European armies, indeed, still regularly employed *Brandmeisters*, i.e. officers charged with extracting a suitable level of 'contributions' from the enemy's civilian population, by negotiation if possible, but otherwise by force.[23] Theoretically, these contributions were supposed simply to come in the form of food, transport and shelter, or their monetary equivalent, in order to facilitate the soldiers prosecuting their business. In reality, the soldiers often helped themselves to little 'extras', and as long as it did not get out of hand senior commanders usually tolerated such pilfering. They sometimes even tacitly encouraged it with a view to keeping the troops happy and reminding the civilian population that they were at the mercy of their military occupiers.[24] What happened after the fall of Perth was, though, a classic case of such looting getting out of hand.

Some of the pillaging done by Argyll's forces could be excused on grounds of military exigency. In contemporary terms his march northwards from Stirling was quite rapid, and this, added to the bitter winter conditions prevailing throughout the British Isles in January and February 1716, made resupplying Argyll's troops from his magazines south of the Forth virtually impossible.[25] Hence his soldiers had to begin taking what they needed from the civilian population even before they reached Perth. They were, of course, paid an allowance to supply themselves with food, drink and shelter as part of their regular wages, but like many professionals were all too inclined to fiddle their expenses; in this case by intimidating their hapless hosts and matter-of-factly helping themselves to free quarter.[26] In due course rural communities and burghs from Jedburgh to Forres were systematically subjected to such extortion.[27] One horrified observer reported:

> The devil a thing dead or alive, eatable or portables do the forreigners leave. And the officeirs of the Brittish say that to see their behaviour dois so make their men's mouths water that faith they cannot but indulge their men a little. The truth is, after passing the bridge of Sterline they imagined themselves to be in ane enemys countrey. Its needles now to

complain, but the poor tennants that belong to me have shoued me what destruction they have made of the barn yards, and the foot burnt whole stacks for fireing.[28]

And as is the way of such things, as the troops found they were being tacitly permitted to take what food, drink and firewood they wanted without consequences, so they began to take other unconsidered trifles from the civilian population.[29] By the time the army reached Montrose the plundering was so out of hand that the commander of the Dutch troops, General Vanderbeck, embarrassedly ordered his men's baggage searched and suspicious items publicly displayed so that their owners might retrieve them.[30] It is not recorded how many victims were brave enough to come forward to reclaim their property.

Nor were the Dutch and Swiss necessarily the worst offenders in this regard. Colin Campbell of Fonab's unit of Argyll's clansmen, attached to the army as light troops during the drive north, quickly became notorious for their wholesale looting of every community they passed through, and Major-General Joseph Wightman had no compunction about helping himself to William Mackenzie, Earl of Seaforth's coach and horses and Alexander Mackenzie of Fraserdale's plate.[31] Cadogan even recruited a force of 1,000 Grants, Frasers and Munros to supplement his offensive against the putative holdouts in the western Highlands with the promise of: 'meal, 3 pence a day and all the plunder they can get.'[32] Nonetheless it was the foreign troops whose depredations were most resented. Scots Whigs could at least argue that they had borne the brunt of the fighting and been subject themselves to Jacobite plundering and were accordingly entitled to pay their enemies back in kind.[33] Bar a couple of minor skirmishes the Dutch and Swiss, by contrast, had fought nobody, only marched from the Forth to the Moray Firth looting as they went.

As the army got further north the pillaging also became more and more indiscriminate and in many places north of the Forth Whigs, Jacobites, neutrals, rich and poor alike were all hard-hit. The loyalist John Murray, Duke of Atholl, for example, suffered at the hands of, 'a party of Swiss and Dutch commanded by one Captain St Amand in their march from Stirling to Perth, who plundered my house of Tullibardine, and took away even the very books out of the library in that house and ruined what was left of the whole barrony.'[34] John Stewart of Grandtully, though bedridden, had sent out his men to fight for the Jacobite cause and duly suffered losses estimated at £3,000 sterling from the depredations of government troops. So sorry was his plight that the Lords of Justiciary recommended that there be no further proceedings against him.[35] Overall, though, it was plebeian Scots who suffered the worst, if for no other reason than their poverty. To lose a house and a library, or have property damage worth £3,000 inflicted upon your estates, is to suffer grievous economic harm, but to lose your only house, your only blanket or your only cow to marauding soldiers is nothing less than a catastrophe. Hence the plight of Jeanet Duncan in Scoolgreen, a minor tenant of Alexander Gordon, Duke of Gordon, who had the misfortune to live near the high road and so was, 'extraordinarily opresed by quartering for my small portion of land. I have had 32 dragoons and 90 foot shouldiers'.[36] Likewise a poor linen weaver encountered by Edmund Burt in the 1720s who was ruined when his home, loom and stock was burned by government troops.[37]

But because they were poor and individually politically weak does not mean that they were ciphers. The notion that plebeian Scots were downtrodden, cowed drudges has been exploded over the last two decades, and there is ample evidence for the new interpretation of Scotland's lower orders as robustly defiant, when they felt the need, to be found lodged in the interstices of the records generated by the '15.[38] Thus, for example, according to Highland tradition at least one Jacobite chieftain (Allan Macdonald, Captain of Clanranald) who forced out unwilling clansmen during the '15 was shot in the back by one of his own men.[39] Many more, to use Lenin's memorable aphorism, 'voted with their feet', by deserting one or other army.[40] And when the miners of Corstophine – legally all serfs and members of a section of Scottish society often presented as the most oppressed and degraded of all their peers – found ammunition wagons laden with explosive shells stopped in their village overnight they showed exemplary initiative and enterprise by promptly stealing twenty of them, the better, 'to break there coals'.[41] When the common folk of eighteenth-century Scotland felt sufficiently moved they were perfectly capable of defending their own interests, expressing their own political views or asserting their collective rights by fair means or foul, and then using the law and the relative obscurity vouchsafed by their poverty to escape detection and/or punishment.[42]

Hence it is interesting to note signs of increasing opposition to government troops and government policies on the part of very humble Scots in a scattering of venues across southern Scotland in the aftermath of the '15. On 4 July, for example, three quartermasters from Stanhope's regiment, who were engaged in purchasing supplies at Haddington market, began loudly to denigrate the quality of the goods on sale. A half pay officer in Dutch service, one Lieutenant Craig, asked them to be more civil and an altercation ensued upon which Quartermaster Grumbleton and Craig drew their swords and fought. Two other officers with Grumbleton intervened, either to aid their comrade or to stop the fight, and in the process impeded Craig's defence so that Grumbleton was able to run him through, mortally wounding him.[43] The local people promptly mobbed all the soldiers in the market, including a number of dragoons who were not involved in the fracas, and, 'miserably beat and bruised them'.[44] In the ensuing melee a local man had his hand cut off by a dragoon, and the burgh magistrates were only able to quell the riot by arresting Grumbleton and the other two quartermasters. General Sabine, commanding in Scotland at the time, was distinctly apprehensive about their prospects of a fair trial and tried to have the three remitted to a military court. The Lords of Justiciary, who had jurisdiction in such cases, absolutely refused to surrender their authority, and only the intervention of the Prince of Wales, acting as Regent on behalf of the absent George I (who had departed to visit Hanover) ultimately saved Grumbleton's life.[45]

Private Thomas Ross of Morrison's regiment of foot was less fortunate. He was one of a batch of replacements recruited in England and sent north to make up the regiment's strength after it suffered severe losses at Sherrifmuir. Near Edinburgh he and another soldier stayed behind to buy some new shoes when their unit moved on, and managed to get lost as they tried to catch up with their comrades. Seeing a local man, James Small, they asked him the way. He was unfriendly, according to Ross, 'having no kindness for their red coats, nor the cause they came upon', and refused to help the two. Ross protested, 'that he being a stranger should be treated after that fashion, seing he was come to the countrey in order to serve King George'. Small replied by, 'bidding both King George and him kiss his arse'. Ross responded that Small, 'was a villan and a rascall for such an undutyfull expression', upon which Small knocked him down, then began beating him with a wooden rod, declaiming that Ross, 'should never go alive out of his hands,' while other locals, 'being mostly women, ...engadged ... by beating him with stones, pulling him by the hair, etc'. Ross's comrade then tried to stop the fight and Ross used the opportunity to stab Small with a knife, mortally wounding him.[46] Arrested by local magistrates, he was promptly haled before the Court of Justiciary, convicted and executed. Ross may have been simply a brutal murderer who got what he deserved, and he certainly confessed to the crime on the scaffold,[47] but the eerily precise unanimity of the depositions against him and the brevity of the proceedings do lend the ring of authenticity to his plea that his red coat gave him, 'a character which is not very gracious with countray people', as does the first statement of his defence, where he claimed, 'great numbers of spectators were present, none of which offered to interpose for the pannel's delivery'.[48]

An unnamed sergeant had a similarly hostile reception in November 1716 at the Hallowfair outside Edinburgh when he intervened to prevent a crowd of locals, 'beating a soldier ... severely'. The sergeant, 'desired them not to kill him', and promised that if he, 'had done any mischeif he would take him prisoner to the guard and have him punisht'. The crowd promptly turned on the sergeant and he laid about him with his sword, wounding one of his attackers, and then fled. Enraged, the crowd pursued him until he escaped down an alley he had reached through the courtyard of Lieutenant-General George Carpenter's house, who just so happened to be the general officer commanding the army in Scotland at the time. Frustrated of their prey, the crowd then began menacing two sentries posted at the entrance and demanding to search the house. The sentries refused to allow this, 'butt numbers presst on, throwing large stones and att last come to handle one of the centinells, who then fired amongst them and killed one.' The crowd promptly retreated and the sentries and Carpenter's servants barred the courtyard gates. Nothing daunted, however, the crowd regrouped at the back of the house, broke all its windows on that side and found some horse sleds which they began rearing up against the back windows to use as ramps to storm the building. At this point the City Guard, summoned by Carpenter, arrived and advanced on the crowd, beating their drum and deploying themselves to fire, at which those involved ran away. Even then the affray was not at an end. The crowd gathered again back in the town, 'gott a drum and beat it formally for more men in order to returne', and were only finally dispersed by John Campbell, the Lord Provost, and another detachment of the City Guard, who made a number of arrests.[49]

Such clashes between the military arm of the Whig regime and plebeian crowds in southern Scotland were also occurring within a notably feverish political atmosphere, which may have disposed those touched by it towards extraordinary actions. Signs and portents such as the unusually bitter winter, but especially the appearance of the Aurora Borealis over Scotland and northern England, concerned many Scots, Whig, Jacobite and neutral, lest they be a warning of coming catastrophe.[50] Indeed, really apprehensive observers like the stalwart Whig and devout Presbyterian Sir John Clerk of Penicuik immediately incorporated the phenomenon into their conviction that they were living at the end of days:

All who formerly wrote on the Revelation, at least many of them, concur in this, that this year 1716 will be fatal to Antichrist. And as forerunners thereof, there appears nothing all Europe over, but wars and rumors of wars, with astonishing phenomena and signs in the firmament, and apparitions in some places, as at Ragusa on 18 February, and as an intestine, cruel war was kindled in Britan, so the like is suspected to be breeding in France.[51]

This general anxiety at the signs of the times, moreover, particularly resonated with those Whigs who feared that a new rebellion might break out or the old one recrudesce.[52]

As is well known, one of the reasons the Jacobites were so resilient as a community was that were incurably optimistic and had a deeply ingrained propensity to talk away their defeats and speculate wildly, yet confidently, about how matters were about to turn their way.[53] Thus Adam Cockburn of Ormiston, the Lord Justice Clerk, wonderingly observed in mid-March, 'there appears most unaccountably a spirrit of disaffection in severall parts, pretending to take encouradgement from transactions both in England and beyond sea, especially in France, and emissarys are very bussy.'[54] Rumours of terrorist Jacobite plots now fed directly on the Jacobites' bravado. One of Robert Wodrow's respondents told him in early April that the fourth Jacobite attempt to set the town of Dumfries alight had just recently been foiled,[55] and in December John Philp wrote to James Ogilvy, Earl of Findlater, graphically describing an attempt allegedly made on the life of the Prince of Wales at a London theatre.[56]

Continued rumours and stories about Jacobite activity were not, however, the only source of alarm. The climate of fear and apprehension was intensified by a drumbeat of reports of cruel and rapacious behaviour by government troops. In an earlier letter to Findlater Philp reported that,

> One of the Dutch regiments at Royston on there way to London fell a quarreling with that town about the payment of there quarters. It chanced to be a mercat day and there happened an engagement. There were 7 or 8 killed on the spott, among whom was the master of the George Inn. The particulars wee have not yet clearly, being only reported by a passenger who came post and made haste, finding them in such confusion.[57]

And around the time of the mobbing of Captain Le Cocq and his men that is the main subject of this essay, one Whig correspondent wrote from Edinburgh that, 'Evry body belived for some days ther was a child killd at Leith. Evrybody belived my Lord Anandal's howse at Cragiehall was rifled, and all by foreners Duch or Swice. Ther are inumberable lies of plunders in the north.'[58] Unlike the reports of alleged Jacobite terrorism, however, reports of brutal behaviour on the part of government forces did actually have a basis in fact, which in turn reinforced the credence given such stories. Ross's killing of James Small (however much he may have been provoked) is one case in point, and even the ultra-Whiggish correspondent from Edinburgh cited above admitted that he knew of at least one authentic case where a denizen of the city had been nearly killed by two Dutch soldiers whom he had challenged about the contents of their baggage.[59] As Robert Key, whose son was killed in a clash with soldiers in December 1716, darkly observed in his information to the Court of Justiciary: 'the insolency of the soldiers is of late gone to a very great height and that they take liberties to act, as if they were above the laws and secure against punishment'.[60]

What is, too, particularly striking about accounts of these incidents is the strong hostility towards the military expressed by the crowd in each case. Early eighteenth-century Scotland was not a nation with a strong, popular anti-military tradition. Indeed, rather the reverse. The Scots had a long-standing tradition of military service within and beyond the British Isles, and while this may have declined from its early seventeenth-century heights, it was still there in 1716.[61] It is, of course, possible that these and other civil-military clashes were all manifestations of popular Jacobitism. And certainly the hostility manifested towards the soldiers at Haddington might well fit into that category. Haddington was at the centre of a notoriously disaffected area which probably supplied William Mackintosh of Borlum's little Jacobite army with several hundred recruits after he crossed the Forth in October 1715, and a year later the Forfeited Estates Commission found that many of George Seton, Earl of Winton's tenants had been complicit in hiding his household goods to prevent their seizure by the government, which suggests they had some sympathy with the earl and his plight.[62] Edinburgh, however, was a different matter. For though, in Leith and the Canongate, it had neighbours who were reputedly Jacobite inclined, the good town had an exemplary record of loyalty during the rebellion.

This is not to suggest that there were no Jacobites in Edinburgh. Wherever there were Episcopalians in any number there were bound to be Jacobites and in 1716 there were at least thirty Episcopal priests ministering in Edinburgh.[63] Yet when the city was threatened by Jacobite forces during the '15, which it was on at least three occasions, the response was overwhelmingly pro-government and there was little sign of substantial support for the Stuart cause. In the first case, the famous Jacobite attempt to capture Edinburgh castle by a surprise escalade on the night of 8 September, the conspirators were able to muster less than forty men, of whom 11–12 were Highlanders infiltrated into the city by James Drummond, Marquess of Drummond, specifically to take part in the attack.[64] On the second occasion, at the end of September, the lineaments of the plot are not so clear, but the Jacobites appear to have aimed at a *coup d'etat* within the city proper with a, if not the, major role to be played by a surreptitiously mustered party of Midlothian gentry.[65] The third occasion, when Borlum's little army appeared before the walls of the city on 14 October, he was confronted by 200 Whig volunteers embodied for the duration under Major James Aikman, c. 400 more Whig volunteers who immediately presented themselves for service with the small force of regulars Argyll rushed to the city from Stirling, plus at least 160 more City Guards, purged and purged again to ensure their loyalty and a further 100 recruited specifically for the defence of the city. In all, Edinburgh raised 860 men in very short order to defend the Whig regime.[66] Borlum undoubtedly received reports from within the city on the state of its defences from local Jacobites, and picked up a few recruits who slipped out of the city before or after he arrived there, but there was no attempt at a rising within its bounds.[67] Very likely the Edinburgh Jacobites were surprised by Borlum's advent, and after two failed attempts to seize control of the city, they were probably in some disarray, yet the contrast between their inactivity and the Whigs' decisive rallying to their cause is quite striking and suggests they were very much a minority at this time.[68]

Which is, in essence, why the events of Monday 26 March 1716 merit closer scrutiny. The day began with John Campbell, the Lord Provost, and the rest of the council happily drafting a loyal address to George I, congratulating him on the success of his armies and the defeat of the rebellion.[69] As far as we can make out, they were completely unaware of any particular tension or problems likely to arise within the city. Meanwhile, on the High Street, two carts and two packhorses were being loaded with baggage left behind for safekeeping by the officers and men of Pallandt's Dutch regiment of foot at the house of John Forrest, the City Treasurer, when the regiment marched north. Forrest had (without authority) taken the precaution of ordering a small detachment of the City Guards to escort the carts and pack horses out of the city, but neither he nor Captain Baron Le Cocq, the officer in charge of moving the baggage, felt it necessary to notify the magistrates of what they were doing or ask for additional protection. Nor was there any apparent reason to do so, as several Dutch regiments had previously moved their baggage through the city without incident, and there was apparently a fair amount of goodwill towards the auxiliaries when they first arrived. As one rather sour observer remarked in January, they were, 'caressed by a sett of people here as in the Bear Garden they do their dogs'.[70] The Edinburgh authorities and the Dutch escort were thus taken completely by surprise as the crisis unfolded.

The trigger for the disorder seems to have been twofold. The carts and packhorses were parked on the High Street outside Forrest's house and were loaded very slowly, the process taking several hours and not being completed until sometime between 10.00 and 11.00 in the morning, during which time a small crowd of onlookers gathered.[71] The reason for this tardiness was very likely the increasingly drunken state of the small party of Dutch soldiers and officers' servants Le Cocq was supposedly commanding. Though he was never directly accused of being drunk himself, he seems to have exercised remarkably little control over his men and was strangely oblivious to the emerging dangers of his situation. He certainly appears to have done nothing to prevent his soldiers misbehaving. Some are noted as having committed, 'atrocious injuries', on the gathering crowd, which may possibly refer to their manhandling, or otherwise physically abusing, some of the women present, but the final straw seems to have been a piece of drunken braggadocio. One of the Dutch soldiers began flourishing a finely decorated targe and waving a Highland broadsword, 'and put himself in a redicolous posture, boasting that these were the spoils of a Hillander whom he had killed with his own hand and cut his head off'.[72] I have been unable to find any surviving account of the event written or dictated by those present in the gathering crowd around the carts that might tell us what they thought of such behaviour. The magistrates acidly observed in their response to a legal instrument taken out against them by Le Cocq, that this 'naturally' drew more onlookers, and further conjectured that, 'knowing the warm reports that were flyeing every where that severalls of the Dutch regements had plundered in the north without measure or distinction', the gathering crowd assumed that the baggage was loot from northern Scotland.[73] What is certain is that it was at that point that the crowd began to attack the Dutch working party.

The soldier brandishing the sword and targe was immediately assaulted and both items taken from him, and a few other pieces of baggage were then grabbed by the crowd. One of the Dutchmen responded by laying about him with a sheathed sword until he was stopped by the sergeant's detail of the City Guard previously summoned by Forrest, which arrived around this time.[74] The crowd was swelling rapidly by this point and the sergeant remonstrated with Le Cocq that he needed to hurry. Under a rain of stones the City Guards then escorted the carts and pack horses as far as the Nether Bow, the entrance to the burgh of the Canongate, which was as far as their jurisdiction extended. There the sergeant deployed his men into a line, blocking the gateway behind the Dutch party and holding the crowd at bay while the baggage train moved down St. Mary's Wynd into the suburb known as the Pleasants.[75] Once in the Canongate Le Cocq could have sent for help from regular troops quartered thereabouts, but seems to have made no effort to do so, which is of a piece with his curiously inept conduct throughout the whole affair.

The crowd, moreover, had not dispersed, but was still growing, joined, doubtless, by the notoriously riotous denizens of the Canongate, and when they found their way blocked at the Netherbow port the crowd streamed off the High Street down Gray's Close to the Cowgate, which allowed them access to the Pleasance and St. Mary's Wynd untrammeled by the City Guard.[76] Le Cocq thus effectively found himself surrounded at the bottom of St. Mary's Wynd by a large crowd drawn from both Edinburgh proper and the Canongate. Eyewitnesses described it as, 'exceeding a thousand in number', 'a great mob', 'a vast number of people', 'a very great mobb of upwards a thousand persons'.[77] The crowd then launched a barrage of missiles at Le Cocq's party, and it was at this stage that one of Le Cocq's men was, 'mortally wounded', trying to defend the carts and horses, and a number of the other members of the escort were hurt.[78] Le Cocq seems to have decided at this point that his life was worth more than the baggage and beat on the door of James Wightman, a cordwainer in the Pleasants, begging for shelter. Wightman's wife admitted the captain and four bruised and bloody Dutch soldiers (the officers' servants appear to have fled by this stage), then bolted the door behind them. The pursuing crowd promptly bombarded the door with, 'vast numbers of stones in order to have broken it open', but it did not give way and so they turned their attention to plundering the abandoned carts and packhorses.[79] Once done, the crowd apparently dispersed, at which point another party of the City Guard, led by Forrest, cautiously ventured down the Wynd to rescue the battered Le Cocq and his men and escort them to safety, though they were apparently so nervous of a renewed attack that they left the Dutchmen's haversacks behind in Wightman's house in order to move more quickly. News of this somehow got about, and part of the crowd reformed and broke down Wightman's door in order to get at the haversacks, which they looted before finally dispersing.[80]

Le Cocq was furious at what had transpired, as well as anxious to retrieve his own and his comrades' property, and was soon demanding the city authorities compensate him for his injuries and the theft of the baggage.[81] The magistrates of Edinburgh responded by blaming him for his, 'indiscretion' and, 'want of due precaution', and forthrightly declared:

> that the magistrates neglected nothing in their power to prevent the disorder, or suppress it when acquainted of it, and were still ready to punish the offenders with due severitie. But that they knew neither reason or law could make them, the magistrates or the community of the city of Edinburgh, whose zeal as well as affection to his Majestie's government there was no place left to doubt of, lyeable to repair a damage done as the Captain said by ane insolent disaffected mob.[82]

The city council nonetheless directed that a search begin forthwith and that rewards be announced by proclamation, 'tuck of drum', and as part of each minister's sermon the following Sunday, for the return of the stolen property with the promise of no questions asked for those who did so.[83] As a consequence just over 548 guilders-worth of Le Cocq's estimated personal loss of over 2,660 guilders (approximately £127 sterling) was retrieved. There is no note of how much, if any, of the property (worth a total of 2,006 guilders) of the nineteen other claimants in Le Cocq's legal proceedings was ever recovered.[84] The Edinburgh magistrates steadfastly continued to refuse to admit liability, and Le Cocq's legal proceedings seem to have became dormant after his regiment marched south into England.[85]

In truth, Lord Provost Campbell and the other magistrates appear to have been far more interested in restoring order than retrieving property. Despite the large numbers involved in the riot few were arrested, and they refused to implicate any of the other rioters, or name any ringleaders.[86] There was, too, a dearth of eyewitnesses with regard to the alleged rioters' personal involvement in the uprising, so that they could only be held on the grounds that they were, 'suspect to have been accessory to the late moab that happened upon the twenty sixth of March last', and as a consequence all of them were released by 6 June.[87] The magistrates could and did make most of those being released sign bonds of caution at the very high rate of £25 sterling, in which they all pledged to answer any further summons, and most were additionally required to, 'keep the peace and quiet of this city and be no disturber thereof, nor ... be accessory to or present att any moabs or tumults within the samen or priviledges thereof'.[88] Nonetheless, the strong impression one gets from the magistrates' response to the riot is that they were doing the minimum they could get away with. They were obviously not happy that a foreigner of elite status had been assaulted on the city's streets, one of his soldiers murdered and a substantial amount of property stolen. On the other hand, they too had heard accounts of the plundering of the north, and while they certainly disapproved of the crowd's methods, they may have had some sympathy with its apparent motive. As our ultra-Whig letter writer darkly observed: 'this is all defended by many and cald a taking from robers.'[89] And thus the anti-Dutch riot was quietly buried.

Which is in and of itself interesting. Public disorder was nothing new or really exceptional in Edinburgh, and the city, unlike much of the rest of the country, did have something of a tradition of being anti-military, or at least of disliking soldiers on its streets.[90] Yet such a big riot, and one involving serious injury and death, was definitely unusual.[91] The city and adjacent suburbs (including the burgh of the Canongate) is generally thought to have had a population of between 25,000 and 30,000 at about this time. Given the population profile of society in the early modern British Isles, about half of these were children, thus the adult population of the city (and in all probability the crowd was overwhelmingly composed of adults) was between 12,500 and 15,000. So if the eyewitnesses were correct and there were at least a thousand people involved, a very significant proportion of the adult population – some 7.2% – participated in the disorder. By way of comparison, modern Edinburgh has a population of about 440,000 people; a modern riot as big as that of 26 March 1716 would bring over 31,000 onto the streets.

The occupational profile of those required to give cautions, and those who stood by them as guarantors is also suggestive, though no definite conclusions can be drawn because of the very limited sample available and the impossibility of knowing how strong the evidence of their involvement was. Of the nine men cautioned, only one, James Ballantyne, seems to have come from a patrician background. Ballantyne was the son of a merchant and his father and fellow-cautioner, also James Ballantyne, correspondingly had to come up with double the usual pledge (£50 as opposed to £25 sterling) to secure his release.[92] Most of the others were solidly plebeian in origin, including 1 gardener, 2 residenters, 1 indweller, 3 fleshers (i.e. butchers)[93] and 2 servants, as were those who co-signed their bonds of caution with them (effectively as guarantors).[94] The only exception was John Robertson, who was a servant to a poulterer but whose father, Peter Robertson, was noted as being a merchant. Robertson *père*, however, was not apparently very well to do. In order to come up with surety enough to get his son out he had to enlist the help of Samuel Livingston, a cooper and apparently a friend or neighbour. Only one of the rioters, Neill Maclean, a gardener, is noted as having been a resident in the Canongate, though two of the fellow cautioners, Alexander Henderson (a tailor) and James Millar (a coppersmith) lived there. All of which, plus one writer's offhand observation that the rioters were all apprentices, suggests a solidly plebeian, youthful event arising primarily from within the bounds of the good town.[95] This contrasts quite sharply with the occupational profile of eleven men arrested and subsequently released on caution after a thoroughly Jacobite event: the tumultuous celebration of James Stuart's birthday in Edinburgh on the night of 10–11 June 1713. Three of the eleven there came from patrician backgrounds, and two of those from outside Edinburgh.[96] To reiterate: no conclusions can be drawn from such small samples of those involved in either riot, but their backgrounds and community connections are certainly thought-provoking.

There were also a number of other incidents in Edinburgh contemporaneous with the attack on Le Cocq's party which, too, suggest the growth of spontaneous, independent plebeian sympathy for the defeated Jacobites. In Leith in March a 'Mr Shirife' broke up the planned ambush of another Dutch party by a group of boys armed with stones. The boys had heard that one of the Dutch soldiers, 'had on a Scots blew bonnet he had taken in the north when he killd a man and robd him', and they intended, 'to revange it', and retrieve the bonnet.[97] When a group of Episcopalian ministers arrested in northern Scotland for publicly supporting the rebellion were paraded through Edinburgh on their way up to the castle in April, the crowds that gathered to watch were noticeably divided in their sympathies. Some clearly celebrated and enjoyed the show, others, 'could hardly be kept from rabbling our guard, at the uncouth and lamentable sight.'[98] In the same vein, in September when Alexander Gordon, Marquess of Huntly, who was widely (but unfairly)[99] believed to have ruined many of his friends and vassals by joining the rebellion and then abandoning them to their fate to save himself, came out of the castle to begin his journey to Carlisle where he was supposed to be tried, 'the people curst and exclaimed against him in his face, saying that he was the cause of the gentlemen's misfortune who were in company with him, by which you see the giddy humour of the populace.'[100] Of course Huntly was a powerful Catholic nobleman, which might have had something to do with it, but the crowd's reaction to the other prisoners, including the Catholics among them, also being brought out to go to Carlisle was not noted as hostile, and one daring plebeian bystander even tripped up a sentry to fling open the door of a coach full of Jacobite prisoners in a mute invitation to escape, as he himself then did by running back through a house while being shot at by the prisoners' military escort.[101]

***

So what conclusions may we draw from an examination of the events of 26 March 1716 in Edinburgh? To be sure, because of the lack of evidence from within the crowd as to their motives we cannot state for certain that they wanted to do anything more than steal. There were ells of cloth, bags of money, a pound of coffee, pots of snuff and doubtless many other tempting items packed onto the carts and packhorses, and the horses themselves were not of inconsiderable value and they, too, vanished into the wynds of Edinburgh and the Canongate. It is also possible that the whole episode was a Jacobite plot. If so, it was a remarkably well concealed one. The Jacobites certainly never claimed it as one of theirs, and frankly, *pace* the understandable apprehensions and even downright paranoia that prevailed within the Scots Whig community after their experiences in 1715,[102] it is highly unlikely the Jacobites were capable of organising something like this so soon after their defeat. The obvious response for the city authorities would have been to blame it all on the Jacobites, but in fact they did not do so. Though one zealous (and notably paranoid) Whig observer declared that the riot proved that Edinburgh was, 'the most disaffected place now in the nation', their responses to Le Cocq make only one tepid claim that the crowd that attacked him was 'disaffected'.[103] They might, of course, have been attempting to conceal the fact that Edinburgh had become a pro-Jacobite city, but in all probability they simply knew the crowd had not been motivated by loyalty to the Stuarts. In all likelihood, then, most of those involved were primarily interested in expressing their anger at the conduct of Le Cocq's soldiers in the heart of Edinburgh and more broadly at the behaviour of government troops north of the Forth.

If the riot did stem from popular anger at the conduct of government troops in the aftermath of the '15, what broader conclusions may we draw? One would certainly be that the government very rapidly compromised its triumph in Scotland by turning a blind eye to the looting carried on by its troops, and particularly the foreign auxiliaries amongst them. Whigs as much as Tories were outraged by the treatment of the north. And in their mutual revulsion the two parties may have found common cause. The gathering mobilisation of the elite Whig community to save their Jacobite kith and kin in the aftermath of the rebellion has already been noted. Human sympathy played a very large part in that development. Mutual disgust at the conduct of government troops provided further cement to hold it together. It also appears that the human sympathy manifested by Scotland's elite may have had a counterpart among the common people. They, too, had a vision of Scotland that embraced more than just their immediate community and they resented the way Scots, *qua* Scots, were being indiscriminately abused in the aftermath of the rebellion, and in Edinburgh at least they were not afraid to take decisive action to demonstrate their displeasure.

Finally, the riot of 26 March 1716 suggests a line needs to be drawn under the still lingering assumption of irreconcilable hostility between Lowlander and Highlander. There were undoubtedly tensions between these two segments of Scottish society, and each was fully capable of being caustic about, and culturally hostile to, the other on an almost reflexive basis. But historians need to keep in mind the counter-pull of other elements in the Scottish identity of the early eighteenth century. The final trigger that set off the riot was a drunken Dutchman's boast that he had murdered a Highlander and cut off his head. Tensions or no, that was too much for the plebeian Lowlanders of Edinburgh to bear, and they paid him back in terrible kind. From sympathy with victims to sympathy with the ideology for which they were victimised is, moreover, a lesser step than the full leap to adoption of a set of principles to which you have hitherto been opposed. The circumstances in which the Jacobites approached, and then captured Edinburgh in 1745 were very different from those of 1715. But it may be that the equally different response of the people of the good town to Charles Edward and his (at that point) predominantly Highland army had roots stretching back to 1716.[104]

Notes

1   Daniel Szechi, *1715. The Great Jacobite Rebellion* (New Haven, 2006), p. 168.
2   National Archives of Scotland (henceforth NAS), RH 2/4/309/96a, 106, 120, 144a: John Campbell, Duke of Argyll to Secretary of State Charles, Viscount Townshend, Aberdeen, 8, 12, 15 and 23 Feb. 1716; Historical Manuscripts Commission, *Calendar of the Stuart Papers Belonging to His Majesty the King Preserved at Windsor Castle* (8 vols, 1902–20), ii. 107–14: Ranald Macdonald, Captain of Clanranald, to Mar, Ormacleit, 11 Apr. 1716.
3   RH 2/4/310/132: Sir Robert Pollock to Townshend, Fort William, 19 Feb. 1716; NAS, GD 220/5/631/5 (Montrose Papers): John Hope to James Graham, Duke of Montrose, Kinross, 18 Feb. 1716.
4   Szechi, *1715*, pp. 194–5; Thomas Constable (ed.), *A Fragment of a Memoir of Field-Marshall James Keith, Written by Himself, 1714–1734* (Edinburgh: Spalding Club, 1843), pp. 31–2.
5   RH 2/4/311/3a, 6: Cadogan to Stanhope, Perth and Edinburgh, 4 and 11 May 1716.
6   Szechi, *1715*, pp. 209–10.
7   RH 2/4/309/96a: Argyll to Townshend, Aberdeen, 8 Feb. 1716; HMC *Stuart Papers*, ii. 70–1: Dr. Patrick Abercromby to Mar, St. Germain, 7 Apr. 1716 ns; Blair Atholl, Atholl Papers, box 45, bundle 12/137: John Murray, Duke of Atholl to Lord James Murray of Garth, Huntingtower, 1 May 1716.
8   RH 2/4/309/120: Argyll to Townshend, Aberdeen, 15 Feb. 1716; RH 2/4/393/112–14: Townshend to Cadogan, Whitehall, 3 Mar. 1716; RH 2/4/393/132–4: Secretary of State James Stanhope to Lord Justice Clerk Adam Cockburn of Ormiston, Whitehall, 14 Mar. 1716; RH 2/4/310/236: Cadogan to Stanhope, Inverness, 24 Apr. 1716.
9   RH 2/4/310/169: Cathcart to Argyll, Edinburgh, 3 Mar. 1716; RH 2/4/393/136–7: Stanhope to Sir Robert Pollock, Whitehall, 21 Mar. 1716.
10 Szechi, *1715*, p. 169; RH 2/4/312/171, 179, 188: General George Carpenter to Townshend, Edinburgh, 11, 13 and 20 Sept. 1716; RH 2/4/312/205b, 261a[2]: Montrose to [Carpenter] and Townshend, Glasgow, 29 Sept. and 21 Nov. 1716.

11 RH 2/4/309/113: Lord Justice Clerk Cockburn to Townshend, Edinburgh, 14 Feb. 1716; RH 2/4/310/194, 202: Cockburn to [Stanhope], Edinburgh, 23 and 29 Mar. 1716; RH 2/4/310/148, 187a, 187b: Provost Campbell of Edinburgh to Townshend and Stanhope, Edinburgh, 25 Feb. and 20 and 22 Mar. 1716.

12 Szechi, *1715*, pp. 170–81; Margaret Sankey, *Jacobite Prisoners of the 1715 Rebellion* (Aldershot, 2005), pp. 17–38, 59–75.

13 RH 2/4/310/194: Lord Justice Clerk Cockurn to [Stanhope], Edinburgh, 23 Mar. 1716; RH 2/4/310/173: General Joseph Wightman to Undersecretary Robert Pringle, Inverness, 10 Mar. 1716; Atholl Papers, box 45, bundle 12/115: procedure for disarming, and oath administered to former Jacobite soldiers [1716]; William Fraser (ed.), *The Chiefs of Grant* (2 vols, Edinburgh, 1883), ii. 98: Wightman to Brigadier Alexander Grant of Grant, Inverness, 10 Mar. 1716.

14 Sankey, *Jacobite Prisoners*, pp. 113–14; Szechi, *1715*, p. 203.

15 RH 2/4/310/229: magistrates of Glasgow, Glasgow, 13 Apr. 1716.

16 Sankey, *Jacobite Prisoners*, pp. 72, 108, 113; RH 2/4/393/132–3: Stanhope to Lord Justice Clerk Cockburn, Whitehall, 14 Mar. 1716; RH 2/4/311/16: magistrates of Glasgow to Stanhope, Glasgow, 23 May 1716.

17 Szechi, *1715*, pp. 241–2.

18 NAS, GD 220/5/635 (Montrose muniments): Perth, 2 Feb. 1716. See also: RH 2/4/310/139: Lord Advocate Sir David Dalrymple of Hailes to [Stanhope?], Edinburgh, 20 Feb. 1716.

19 RH 2/4/311/55a: Perth, 6 July 1716.

20 Sankey, *Jacobite Prisoners*, pp. 114, 118–29, 138–48.

21 Szechi, *1715*, pp. 134–5.

22 Szechi, *1715*, p. 119.

23 Geoffrey Parker, *The Military Revolution. Military Innovation and the Rise of the West, 1500–1800* (Cambridge, 1988), pp. 65–7; Michael S. Anderson, *War and Society in Europe of the Old Regime 1618–1789* 2nd edn (Stroud, 1988), pp. 137–8; John A. Lynn, 'Food, Funds and Fortresses: Resource Mobilization and Positional Warfare', in John A. Lynn (ed.), *Feeding Mars. Logistics in Western Warfare from the Middle Ages to the Present* (Boulder, Colorado, 1993), pp. 143–6.

24 David Chandler, *Robert Parker and Comte de Mérode-Westerloo* (Archon, London, 1968), pp. 120–1; RH 2/4/310/215: Cadogan to Townshend, Inverness, 6 Apr. 1716.

25 Szechi, *1715*, pp. 165, 166.

26 David Chandler, *The Art of Warfare in the Age of Marlborough* (Batsford, London, 1976), pp. 29, 36, 37, 71; RH 2/4/312/211b: representation by Lady Glengarry [Oct. 1716]; Duncan Warrand (ed.), *More Culloden Papers* (5 vols, Inverness, 1923), ii. 92: James Dunbar to John Forbes, Inverness, 6 Mar. 1716.

27 Edinburgh City Archives (henceforth ECA), SL 30/232: petition of Forres to the Convention of Royal Burghs, 1717; petition of Cupar to the Convention of Royal Burghs, 1717; SL 30/233: petition of Jedburgh to the Convention of Royal Burghs, 1718; SL 30/233: petition of Lauder to the Convention of Royal Burghs, 1718.

28 GD 220/5/635: [Grahame of Orchill to Montrose], Perth, 2 Feb. 1716.

29 Szechi, *1715*, p. 254.

30 A. Francis Steuart (ed.), *News Letters of 1715–16* (1910), p. 142.

31 GD 220/1926/10: ? to Montrose, Dundee, 4 Feb. 1716; [H. R. Duff, (ed.)] *Culloden Papers: Comprising an Extensive and Interesting Correspondence From the Year 1625 to 1748* (1815), p. 44: Robert Baillie to John Forbes of Culloden,

Inverness, 30 Mar. 1716; p. 47: Baillie to Duncan Forbes of Culloden, Inverness, 6 Apr. 1716.

32   GD 220/5/631/10a–b: John Hope to Montrose, Inverness, 6 Apr. 1716.

33   RH 2/4/309/108: Captain Robert Munro to Stanhope, Inverness, 13 Feb. 1716; Duncan Warrand (ed.), *More Culloden Papers* (5 vols, Inverness, 1923), ii. 91–3: James Dunbar to John Forbes of Culloden, Inverness, 6 Mar. 1716.

34   Atholl Papers, box 45, bundle 12/140, 147: Atholl to Lord James Murray of Garth, Huntingtower, 8 May and 23 June 1716; 12/175/1–11: Atholl to George I, 1716 (copy). See also: *More Culloden Papers* (5 vols, Inverness, 1923), ii. 92: James Dunbar to John Forbes of Culloden, Inverness, 6 Mar. 1716.

35   RH 2/4/311/32: William Drummond to Undersecretary Robert Pringle, [Edinburgh] 16 June 1716.

36   GD 44/17/11/229: claim by Jeanet Duncan on Gordon, 1716.

37   E. Burt, *Burt's Letters From the North of Scotland. With Facsimiles of the Original Engravings*, intro. by R. Jamieson, 2 vols. (Edinburgh, reprint, 1974 of London, 1754 edn), i. 210–11.

38   Christopher A. Whatley, *Scottish Society 1707–1830. Beyond Jacobitism, Towards Industrialisation* (Manchester, 2000), pp. 142–83; 'The Union of 1707, Integration and the Scottish Burghs: the Case of the 1720 Food Riots', *Scottish Historical Review*, lxxviii (1999) 192–218.

39   Alexander Carmichael, 'Some Unrecorded Incidents of the Jacobite Risings', *Celtic Review*, 6 (1897) 281–3.

40   Szechi, *1715*, pp. 121–2, 123, 125.

41   Steuart, *News Letters of 1715–16* (London, 1910), p. 109: [Edinburgh] 27 Jan. 1716. For a very different view of the serf coalminers than that usually found in treatments of the subject, see: Chris Whatley, 'The fettering bonds of brotherhood': Combination and Labor Relations in the Scottish Coal-Mining industry c. 1690–1775', *Social History*, 12 (1987) 139–54.

42   See for example: Daniel Szechi, *George Lockhart of Carnwath*, (East Linton, 2002), pp. 42–3.

43   RH 2/4/312/170: depositions re: killing of Lieutenant Craig, [Sept.?] 1716.

44   RH 2/4/311/55a, 67: Sabine to Townshend, Perth, 6 and 13 July 1716.

45   RH 2/4/311/67: Sabine to Townshend, Perth, 13 July 1716; RH 2/4/311/97: Lord Justice Clerk Cockburn to Undersecretary Pringle, Edinburgh, 7 Aug. 1716.

46   NAS, JC7/8: information entered by Ross and private Jeffray Roberts, 21 July 1716.

47   NLS, Mf.G.0626(29): 'The Last Speech and Confession of Thomas Ross, Soldier in Brigadier Morison's Regiment of Foot' (Edinburgh, 1716). It is interesting to note that there is a difference here between England and Scotland with respect to the response of the Scottish judiciary to violent acts committed by soldiers off the battlefield. No soldier was punished for assault or murder stemming from violence directed against an alleged or actual Jacobite in England in 1715–16 (I owe this insight to Paul Monod). Not many soldiers were punished for such crimes in Scotland, but some clearly were.

48   JC7/8: information entered by Ross, 17 July 1716; witnesses' depositions against Ross and Roberts, 23 July 1716; trial of Ross and Roberts, 24 July 1716; condemnation of Ross, 30 July 1716.

49   GD 248/562/54/40: [Philp] to Findlater, Edinburgh, 2 Nov. 1716; RH 2/4/312/228: Carpenter to Townshend, Edinburgh, 2 Nov. 1716.

50 John Addy and Peter McNiven (eds), *The Diary of Henry Prescott, LL.B.*, *Deputy Registrar of Chester Diocese* (Record Society of Lancashire and Cheshire, 2 vols, 1992, 1994), ii. 496, 497: 6 and 11 Mar. 1716; *Diary of Mary Countess Cowper, Lady of the Bedchamber to the Princess of Wales 1714–1720* (London, 1864), pp. 90–2; NAS, GD 18/2092/5: Sir John Clerk of Penicuik's spiritual journal for 1716, 20 Jan. 1716.
51 GD 18/2092/5: Sir John Clerk's spiritual journal for 1716: 23 May 1716.
52 GD 220/5/1927/4: [John Dalrymple, Earl of Stair] to Montrose, Paris, 10 Feb. 1716 ns; GD 220/5/615/10: Sir Robert Pollock to Montrose, Fort William, 16 Feb. 1716; RH 2/4/310/186b: Simon Fraser, Lord Lovat, to Cadogan, Inverness, 10 Mar. 1716.
53 Scottish Catholic Archive, Blairs Letters 2/201/11, 2/202/2 and 2/202/5: James Carnegy to Thomas Innes, [Edinburgh?] 24 Apr., 31 July and 21 Aug. 1716; British Library (henceforth BL), Add. MS 29981, ff. 127–8: *On June the 10th 1716*; RH 2/4/312/204: Lord Justice Clerk Cockburn to Townshend, Edinburgh, 29 Sept. 1716; *Diary of Henry Prescott*, ii. 501: 6 Apr. 1716.
54 RH 2/4/310/194: Lord Justice Clerk to [Stanhope], Edinburgh, 23 Mar. 1716.
55 National Library of Scotland, Wodrow Papers, Quarto XI, ep. 95: 'A.P.' to Robert Wodrow, [Glasgow] 9 Apr. 1716.
56 GD 248/562/54/49: Edinburgh, 12 Dec. 1716.
57 GD 248/562/54/15: Edinburgh, 30 Apr. 1716.
58 Steuart, *News Letters of 1715–16*, pp. 143–4.
59 Steuart, *News Letters of 1715–16*, p. 144.
60 JC7/8: information entered by Robert Key, tenant of Pilrig, 28 Feb. 1717.
61 Matthew Glozier, *Scottish Soldiers in France in the Reign of the Sun King* (Leiden, 2004), pp. 24–7; Andrew Mackillop and Steve Murdoch (eds), *Military Governors and Imperial Frontiers c. 1600–1800. A Study of Scotland and Empires* (Leiden, 2003), pp. xlii, xlvi.
62 RH 2/4/305/47, 68: John Sibbit, Mayor of Berwick, to Stanhope, 14 and 21 Oct. 1715; RH 2/4/306/71: Dalrymple to Stanhope, Edinburgh, 22 Oct. 1715; GD 248/562/54/39: [Philp] to Findlater, Edinburgh, 29 Oct. 1716.
63 RH 2/4/312/243b: list of Episcopalian ministers in Edinburgh, Edinburgh, 15 Nov. 1716.
64 SP 54/8/36: depositions taken by the Lord Provost and Baillies of Edinburgh, 9 Sept. 1715; David Laing and Thomas Macknight (eds), *Memoirs of the Insurrection in Scotland in 1715. By John, Master of Sinclair. With Notes by Sir Walter Scott, Bart* (Edinburgh: Abbotsford Club, 1858), p. 30.
65 SP 54/8/115: Lord Justice Clerk Cockburn to Undersecretary Pringle, Edinburgh, 28 Sept. 1715; SP 54/8/120a: Archibald Campbell, Earl of Islay, to Townshend, Edinburgh, 29 Sept. 1715.
66 Alistair and Henrietta Tayler, 'Lord Forfar and the '15', *Journal of the Society for Army Historical Research*, xv (1936), p. 137; RH 2/4/310/203: Provost Campbell to Stanhope, Edinburgh, 31 Mar. 1716.
67 Robert Patten, *The History of the Rebellion in the Year 1715* (James Roberts, London, 1745), pp. 7–9.
68 Szechi, *Lockhart of Carnwath*, p. 120.
69 ECA, SL 1/1/43: Edinburgh Town Council Records, Oct. 1715–Sept. 1716, p. 79: 26 Mar. 1716.
70 RH 2/4/310/217: Edinburgh magistrates' response to instrument, Le Cocq vs magistrates of Edinburgh, [Edinburgh, 30 Mar.] 1716; Henrietta Tayler (ed.), *The Seven Sons of the Provost. A Family Chronicle of the Eighteenth Century*

Compiled From Original Letters 1692–1761 (London, 1949), p. 79: Cornelius Kennedy to Thomas Kennedy, 5 Jan. 1716.

71   RH 2/4/310/217: deposition of James Dobie [Edinburgh, 3 Apr. 1716]; RH 2/4/310/217: Le Cocq's instrument and Edinburgh magistrates' response [Edinburgh, 30 Mar.] 1716.

72   RH 2/4/310/217: Edinburgh magistrates' response [Edinburgh, 30 Mar.] 1716.

73   RH 2/4/310/217: Edinburgh magistrates' response [Edinburgh, 30 Mar.] 1716.

74   Steuart, *News Letters of 1715–16* , p. 145.

75   RH 2/4/310/217: depositions of Patrick Rattray and James Dobie [Edinburgh, 3 Apr. 1716].

76   RH 2/4/310/217: deposition of James Dobie [Edinburgh, 3 Apr. 1716].

77   RH 2/4/310/217: depositions of Patrick Rattray, James Dobie, James Wightman and Andrew Reaburn [Edinburgh, 3 Apr. 1716].

78   RH 2/4/310/217: Le Cocq's instrument [Edinburgh, 30 Mar.] 1716; RH 2/4/310/ 217: deposition of Patrick Rattray [Edinburgh, 3 Apr. 1716].

79   RH 2/4/310/217: deposition of James Wightman [Edinburgh, 3 Apr. 1716].

80   RH 2/4/310/217: depositions of James Wightman and Andrew Reaburn [Edinburgh, 3 Apr. 1716].

81   RH 2/4/310/217: petition from Le Cocq to the Sheriffs of Edinburgh [Edinburgh, 2 Apr.? 1716].

82   RH 2/4/310/217: Edinburgh magistrates' response [Edinburgh, 30 Mar.] 1716.

83   Blairs Letters 2/201/9: Carnegy to [Thomas Innes?], [Edinburgh] 27 March 1716; Helen Armet (ed.), *Extracts from the Records of the Burgh of Edinburgh, 1701 to 1718* (Edinburgh, 1967): pp. 311–12, 31 Mar. 1716.

84   RH 2/4/310/217: statement of losses by officers and men of Pallandt's regiment [Edinburgh?, 7 Apr.? 1716]

85   RH 2/4/310/239: Provost Campbell to [Undersecretary Pringle], Edinburgh, 26 Apr. 1716.

86   Wodrow Papers, Quarto XI, ep. 82: Edinburgh [c. 29 Mar. 1716].

87   ECA, Moses Bundle 154, no. 5968: bonds of caution by Neill Mclean and John Hepburn, 11 Apr. and 6 June 1716.

88   ECA, Moses Bundle 156, no. 5974: bond of caution by William Raffine, 6 June 1716.

89   Steuart, *News Letters of 1715–16* , p. 146.

90   Robert A. Houston, *Social Change in the Age of Enlightenment. Edinburgh, 1660–1760* (Oxford, 1994), pp. 292, 298, 304, 307–8, 310–11, 316–17.

91   Houston, *Social Change*, p. 318.

92   Moses Bundle 154, no. 5968: bond of caution by James Ballantyne, 20 Apr. 1716.

93   Butchers were also involved in a high percentage of English Jacobite riots (I owe this point, and my thanks, to Paul Monod).

94   Moses Bundle 154, no. 5968: bonds of caution by John Hepburn, Neill Mclean and Alexander Work, 11 and 12 Apr. 1716; Moses Bundle 156, no. 5974: bonds of caution by William Raffine, Charles Ramsay, Richard Rankin, William Rankin and John Robertson, 12 Apr. and 6 June 1716.

95   Blairs Letters 2/201/9: Carnegy to [Thomas Innes?], [Edinburgh] 27 March 1716.

96   Moses Bundle 154, no. 5968: bonds of caution by John Abercrombie, Andrew Baird, Alexander Barclay, William Bruce, John Bryce, Walter Hamilton, Hector Mcalister of Loup, Alex. Mclarran, Robert Miller and Robert Willsone, 13, 15 and 16 June and 8 July 1713; Moses Bundle 156, no. 5974: bond of caution by

James Reucastle, 13 June 1713. The three patricians were Mcalister of Loup, Reucastle and Willsone (a merchant from Melrose).
97 Steuart, *News Letters of 1715–16* , pp. 147–8.
98 James Allardyce (ed.), *Historical Papers Relating to the Jacobite Period 1699–1750* (2 vols, Aberdeen: New Spalding Club, 1895–96), i. 127: John Alexander of Kildrummy to his wife, Edinburgh, 14 Apr. 1716.
99 BL, Add. MS. 61632, f. 155v: John Ker, Duke of Roxburgh, to Charles Spencer, Earl of Sunderland, Edinburgh, 8 Sept. 1716; RH 2/4/312/258: Carpenter to Stanhope, Edinburgh, 26 Dec. 1716.
100 GD 248/562/54/32: [Philp] to Findlater, Edinburgh, 5 Sept. 1716.
101 Steuart, *News Letters of 1715–16* , p. 151. There was a good deal of sympathy for the prisoners about to be tried at Carlisle at all levels of society: Tayler, *Seven Sons of the Provost*, p. 84: William Kennedy to Thomas Kennedy, Edinburgh, 25 Aug. 1716.
102 RH 2/4/312/271: Sir Peter Fraser of Durris to [Secretary of State Paul Methuen?] Durris, 30 Nov. 1716.
103 Steuart, *News Letters of 1715–16* , p. 146; RH 2/4/310/217: Edinburgh magistrates' response [Edinburgh, 30 Mar.] 1716.
104 Frank McLynn, *Charles Edward Stuart* (London, 1988), pp. 146–9.

5
Hidden Sympathies: The Hessians in Scotland 1746

Christopher Duffy

The Jacobite Rising of 1745–46 was played for high stakes. On its issue hung the fate of dynasties, and the orders of the British government, church and society. In comparison the forces engaged were tiny. The greatest concentrations brought together at a single place were at the battle of Falkirk (17 January 1746), where Lieutenant General Hawley took the field with about 8,100 troops against probably rather fewer Jacobites. In this context it was reasonable for the government in London to expect great things of the accession of strength which arrived on the theatre of operations in February 1746, in the shape of a substantial corps of hired Hessian auxiliaries. The contingent comprised six regiments or super-large battalions of infantry, a company of elite hussars and a train of twelve 3-pounder cannon, or some 5,100 combatants in all. These made up the best-drilled and turned-out troops now available to the government, and the artillery alone exceeded the number of cannon that the Duke of Cumberland was able to bring to Culloden in April. What the Hessian corps did, or rather did not do, is the subject of the present study.

Hired auxiliary troops were a familiar feature of statecraft in the Europe of the Old Regime, and they were recognised to be entirely distinct from mercenaries, who were individuals or deserters who hawked themselves around for private profit. The loose 'Holy Roman Empire of the German Nation' was a prime source of auxiliary contingents. All parties stood to gain thereby. Thus Britain and the Republic of Venice, as wealthy states with small standing armies, could hire German auxiliaries to meet emergencies as they happened to arise, like the one which faced the British government in 1745. On their side, by hiring out troops to foreign powers, the

The author is grateful to HM the Queen for Gracious Permission to consult copies of the Cumberland Papers at Windsor Castle, and likewise to Dr. Silvia von Hilchen (Murhard'sche Bibliothek der Stadt Kassel), Archivoberrat Dr. Hollenberg (Hessisches Staatsarchiv, Marburg) and Dr. David Brown (National Archives of Scotland, Edinburgh).

German princes could gain useful friends, earn money to apply to constructive purposes at home, and keep up military experiences and values. The troops thus hired out retained the technical status of 'auxiliaries', which kept the princes at a useful distance from the risky quarrels of the full belligerents. The princely entrepreneurs had to hold a difficult balance, between maintaining the value of their contingents as fighting troops, and thus worth hiring in the first place, while keeping this human stock-in-trade in good condition. By the same token it was important to keep a contingent together as a recognisable entity, and not allow the troops to be sent here, there and everywhere in detachments.

From the late seventeenth century the Landgravate of Hesse-Cassel became known as one of the most significant providers of hired troops to the international community. These men were trained, equipped and uniformed in the Prussian style. The officers were responsible professionals of the Protestant German school, reserved, patient and sticklers for order. The Hessian rank and file would have been surprised to learn that they were described by some thinkers as victims of a 'trade in human beings' (*Menschenhandel*). On the contrary, military service was for the Hessians a matter of family pride: boys were keen to learn military skills; the families of serving soldiers enjoyed tax privileges; veterans returned to an honoured place in civil society. Hessian military men of all stations had a strong sense of right conduct. Those who were to serve in North America in the War of Independence formed no high opinion of the American sense of 'liberty', and noted that it did not extend to black slaves.

A long line of subsidy treaties, dating from 1702, established Britain as the most faithful of the Hessian clients. In 1740 this connection was cemented by a dynastic marriage between Prince Frederick, who was the nephew and heir of the reigning Landgrave, and Princess Mary, the eighth child and fourth daughter of George II, the *de facto* king of Britain. Frederick, as one of the victims of this arrangement, was only just entered on his twenties, and although he was an ardent admirer of womankind, the two were to live together for only two months of their fourteen-year marriage. Frederick had absorbed the principles of the Enlightenment and of responsible rule at the University of Geneva, which was amongst other things a finishing school for the teenage sons of German Protestant ruling houses, and he was now bent on forming himself into a soldier-philosopher-prince in the style of his young namesake King Frederick II of Prussia. In retrospect, however, probably the most significant influence upon him is to be traced to the year 1742, when he made the acquaintance of Clemens August, the Catholic Prince Bishop and Elector of Cologne.

Our Hessian Frederick had a brief experience of independent command when in 1744 he led a Hessian corps from Bavaria to the Austrian Netherlands, where a combined army of Austrians, British, Dutch and assorted Germans was facing the French. Here Frederick made his first acquaintance with the British and their ways, most immediately in the person of his brother-in-law, William Augustus Duke of Cumberland. No friendship was formed between the two, and all the evidence suggests that Frederick disliked the duke's company. Among Cumberland's associates Lieutenant General Henry ('Hangman') Hawley made it elaborately clear that Frederick's princely title counted for nothing in the military hierarchy.

In 1745 things were going badly for the common cause. In the Netherlands the allies were pressed back to the neighbourhood of Brussels in the course of the summer, and then in the autumn the whole of the British infantry and a large part of the cavalry were withdrawn to contain the progress of the Jacobite rising. On 13 December Lord Harrington, the Secretary of State of the Northern Department, wrote that the decision had just been taken to invoke the latest subsidy treaty and tap in addition the Hessian contingent in the Netherlands. It was true that the Young Pretender was now retreating towards Scotland, but considerable Jacobite forces were building up in that part of the world, and were receiving substantial support from France by shipments of gold, artillery, military specialists and units of the regular Irish and Scottish troops in the French employ.[1]

On 23 December Prince Frederick reported to Cassel that he had just been ordered to convey a detachment of the Hessians to Britain with all possible speed. The preparations were then delayed by severe weather and the continuing military crisis in the Netherlands, but at last the expedition sailed from the Dutch port of Willemstad on 2 February 1746. Six days later the convoy reached Leith, the port of Edinburgh. The passage had been swift, but the British Admiralty had miscalculated the ration of space to numbers, and the troops reached Scotland in a terrible state. On the 3rd Frederick was received in pomp at Edinburgh, and was described as 'a comely young man off about twenty-five years of age, of a middle stature, and of great benevolence and humanity'.[2]

Frederick's own impressions were not calculated to improve his opinion of the British. The Hanoverian regime had become riddled with corruption, and the prince had to dip into his reserves of cash to provide the customary presents that he now found were due to his British liaison officers and the captain of the sloop who had conveyed him from Holland. Once on shore, he encountered delays and expectant hoverings on the part of the civilian commissaries, and he made progress only after a Hessian diplomat told him that these gentlemen calculated their helpfulness on the size of the bribes that came their way.[3]

Again, Frederick learned that just after he had arrived the active old Jacobite the Dowager Duchess Jean of Perth, with further Jacobite ladies, was conveyed to imprisonment in Edinburgh Castle. It was clear that Cumberland's understanding of 'belligerent' was very wide, and a Whig gentleman conceded that 'this action was deemed a little uncouthly for a young man like the Duke of Cumberland, but there was a necessity for this piece of severity that women might understand that they might be punished for treason as well as others'.[4]

We now have to outline what was expected of the Hessians, and how far they answered those expectations. To begin with they were supposed to do nothing in Scotland at all. On 17 January 1746 the Jacobites had beaten Hawley at Falkirk, upon which his humiliated army fell back on Edinburgh. Thereafter the Jacobites wasted their energies on a technically hopeless siege of Stirling Castle, which gave time for the Duke of Cumberland to take command of Hawley's shaken troops. Cumberland's energy and confidence produced immediate effects, and on 31 January he set out from Edinburgh with his army, at a time when the nerve of the Jacobite high command was giving way.

On 2 February the clan chiefs forced Prince Charles Edward Stuart to order his army to fall back all the way to Inverness. In some places the subsequent retreat resembled an outright flight, and Cumberland jumped to the conclusion that Prince Charles was bent only on escaping to the continent: the Hessians had therefore come to Scotland to no purpose, and Cumberland left it to Prince Frederick whether or not to allow his troops to spend a little time on shore. The men had been suffering terribly, cooped up all this time on the transports at Leith, and the disembarkation was completed on 15 February. They were lodged in Edinburgh and the towns and villages of East Lothian, where their excellent turnout and good behaviour reinforced the fine impression that their prince had already made on the Scots.

As late as 20 February Cumberland was confident that he had ample British troops to deal with the rebels, but four days later, and quite unexpectedly, he assigned the Hessian troops to operations, if only of a precautionary kind, so as to form what he described as a 'a second army at the foot of the mountains'.[5] The regiments left their quarters by instalments, passing on their way by the blackened ruins of the old royal Stuart palace at Linlithgow, which, accidentally or not, had been burned by Cumberland's troops not long before.

By 12 March 1746 all the Hessians were settled in their destinations, at Stirling and Perth, on the edge of the Highlands. Cumberland had meanwhile shifted the axis of his operations to the eastern coastlands, and on 27 February he had planted himself at Aberdeen, where he prepared his army for a final push in the spring against the Jacobite base at Inverness. However, the snowy Cairngorms still separated the redcoat concentration in and about Aberdeen from the axis of General Wade's system of military roads over to the west, which traversed the Highlands from the Great Glen to Dunkeld (the present A9) and to Crieff. The security of this central corridor depended on nothing more than two detachments of regular infantry, of an initial 500 men each, which had been advanced to Castle Menzies and Blair Castle, together with a screen of militia from the great Whig clan of Campbell, holding a multitude of outposts (farmhouses, inns and little castles) that extended all the way from Atholl to the western coast. The Hessians were now destined to provide a rearward support, though separated from the various garrisons by high hills and difficult gorges.

On 14 March Frederick and his staff rode on to Dunkeld, an attractive place, new built after it had been wrecked in a battle between the Jacobites and their enemies in 1689. Dunkeld stood in the region of Atholl, over-hung by Birnham Wood and other bosky eminences, and it brought Frederick to the entrance of the Gaelic Highland Zone. The prince was entertained there by James Murray, the Whig Duke of Atholl, and that night the whole party got beastly drunk on punch.

Frederick had intended to continue his ride by way of Wade's side road to Castle Menzies, but he had to put off his excursion on account of bad weather, and then abandon it completely when the initiative was snatched from him by a bold Jacobite counterstroke. This was the work of one of Duke James's Jacobite brothers, Lord George Murray, who was the dark genius of the Jacobite cause, and the author of some of its most spectacular achievements and disasters. Now Lord George was bent on invading Atholl in a kind of recruiting expedition writ large. On 16 March an advance force of 700 Highlanders surprised the Campbell outposts along a frontage of ten miles, and on the morning of the 17th Lord George invested Blair Castle, where the redcoat garrison had been reduced by detachments to 300 men. In the hands of the Jacobites the place would give them a strongpoint near the Pass of Killiecrankie, valuable to them for both offensive and defensive purposes. The commander was the fierce and cranky old Presbyterian lieu-tenant colonel Sir Andrew Agnew, known to his irreverent young officers as 'the Peerless Knight'. The Jacobite cannon were too light to do any damage to the stout castle walls. Blockade was another matter, for the Peerless Knight had refused to stock up on provisions in advance.

Prince Frederick returned to Perth, and there on the 17th he, his staff and the British liaison officers met in a highly-charged atmosphere. They decided to concentrate all available forces at Crieff, which involved bring-ing across Colonel Rundstedt's two regiments from Perth, and abandoning that town together with its magazines and fearful Whigs. When he wrote to the Duke of Cumberland the senior of the two liaison officers, Major General the Earl of Crawford, described Crieff as 'the most centrical post in the country to prevent the progress of the rebels. To attack them in their strong grounds, as Your Royal Highness judges...is another case, because that must be done after a variety of preparations, and in a proper season'.[6]

In that letter Crawford was referring to the last guidance received from Cumberland, penned at Aberdeen on 8 March, and received on the 11th, by which Frederick was to march directly against the Jacobites if they moved against his quarters, 'I believe however, that you should on no account commit yourself to the mountains, whether before or after that attack, if indeed it does take place'. It was rendered accurately in the Hessian war diary as *'hielten Sie unumgaenglich noetig, sich nicht in die Berge zu engagiren, sey es vor oder nach der attaque'.*[7]

Lieutenant Colonel Webster, the commander at Castle Menzies, reported that the Jacobite force stood at 5,000 men, which was probably an over-estimate; Cumberland on his side downplayed the significance of the Jacobite offensive, and believed that the council of war at Perth had reached its panicky conclusion on the strength of the loss of a post at Bun Rannoch, following 'a ridiculous bagpipe battle'.[8] Cumberland made his displeasure known in a letter which reached Frederick on 23 March, before the intended retreat from Perth could take place. He told the prince that the order to keep out of the Highlands scarcely applied to Blair Castle, which was only two marches distant from Perth. The four Hessian regiments and the British St. George Dragoons must therefore advance without delay. 'I am confident that they [the Jacobites] would never engage in any serious action against your seasoned troops. If they should dare to do so, then your corps would be well placed to deal a decisive and glorious blow against those audacious rebels. As the post at Blair is of the utmost importance, I am assured that you will surmount every difficulty in order to execute that march just as speedily as you can.'[9]

Cumberland's rebuke spurred on Frederick to make a first march from Perth on the 24th. That day's progress took him only as far as Nairn, and was accompanied by skirmishing between the Jacobite outposts on the one side, and the Hessian hussars and the St. George's Dragoons on the other. On the 26th a further bound brought the corps to Dunkeld, a day later than had been stipulated by Cumberland. Meanwhile in the filthy, verminous Blair Castle, the Peerless Knight and his garrison were running low on provisions, firewood and even water, and they were so short of ammunition that they were reduced to taking occasional pot shots at the besiegers. Even now the Hessians were separated by eighteen odd miles from the intervening Pass of Killiecrankie, where Wade's road clung to the side of a deep and heavily-wooded ravine. The skirmishing continued daily, and on 29 March a false report of an imminent attack by 3,000 Highlanders induced Frederick to put his corps in battle array.

Frederick was left completely in the dark as to what Cumberland was doing with his army,[10] but he was reassured when on 30 March he was joined by the greater part of his two regiments from Crieff. The whole of the Hessian corps was now concentrated at Dunkeld, apart from 500 troops under Lieutenant Colonel de la Primaudaye, who had been detached out to the west by way of the side road that ran by way of the Sma' Glen to Taybridge (the present Aberfeldy), 'with orders to make a movement on that side, which might persuade the enemy that he intended to advance on Blair by way of Castle Menzies.'[11]

There was no let-up in the bickering between the rival patrols on the approaches to the Pass of Killiecrankie, and yet no sign of activity on the part of the main force of the Hessian infantry at Dunkeld, for which Frederick offered an explanation of sorts when he wrote to Cumberland on the 31st that, in spite of representations made by Crawford, 'I cannot commit myself to advance the entire corps and thus hazard my 4,000 troops, and just to save about those hundred men who are besieged by the rebels. My dear brother, I would ask you to consider whether it would be reasonable of me to go blundering into those narrows, where my artillery (which must never be separated from my corps) could not venture without great risk. Another obstacle is presented by the lack of provisions and fodder in the country lying ahead, and that alone makes it certain that my corps could not put this movement into effect without being entirely deprived of subsistence. And that is not all. If I abandon my present post, I leave two major routes through the mountains open to the enemy, who would then come here [Dunkeld] and cut us off from our provisions and from our avenue of retreat.'[12]

On 1 April Colonel Rundstedt with 400 Hessian grenadiers, together with Crawford with thirty hussars and 200 British dragoons, reconnoitred to within a mile of the pass. Frederick intended to make a demonstration of goodwill towards Cumberland, and to persuade Lord George Murray that the Jacobites were coming under threat from two directions, over the pass, and by a left-flanking movement via Taybridge and Castle Menzies. On the next morning report after report indicated that the enemy had abandoned the pass and raised their siege of Blair Castle, and on the 3rd Crawford led a first party to the relief. He returned to Dunkeld in the evening, and the Hessian war diary describes him as reporting 'that becoming aware of our general advance, the enemy weighed up the situation and feared that we would send a detachment against Blair by way of Castle Menzies, and thus cut them off and bottle them up in the pass. They thereupon fell back in the greatest haste, and by the current reports they are by this morning already thirty English miles distant.'[13]

On 5 April Frederick in person arrived at Blair with a convoy of ammunition and provisions, which gave him an opportunity to view the pass 'and found it of such a nature that 1,000 men could without the slightest difficulty halt and throw back 5,000.'[14] Back at Dunkeld the prince opened a letter which Cumberland had sent two days earlier. 'I am unable to see how you could consider that you would be putting your 4,000 men at any risk by marching them from Dunkeld to Blair. And the same would apply to your raising the siege. How shameful it would be if you with your powerful corps would let the 300 men in Blair be taken by a handful of rebel wretches, at just one march from you! What a disgrace for your troops to be subjected to such an insult for the first time in their history.'[15] In his defence Frederick replied that he was sorry to think that Cumberland doubted his goodwill, 'but in fact I bore constantly in mind what Your Royal Highness had ordered, namely to raise the siege of Blair Castle. This is what I have so happily achieved by the movements of my troops, and now the rebels have retired in the greatest haste, and the Castle of Blair is entirely free of them and reprovisioned.'[16]

The active participation of the Hessians in the campaign was virtually at an end, and had cost the corps just one or two men killed and a handful of wounded and prisoners. What evidence is available to make sense of the Hessian conduct up to that time? Cumberland had received his first news of the end of the relief of the castle in a roundabout way, and he was 'extremely surprised that neither Prince Frederick nor Lord Crawford should have sent me the least notice of the raising of the siege of Blair. I can in no way account for it, but by supposing and really believing that they know nothing of it, for the terror which seems to be spread among them was so great that they would not allow any of their parties to go further than the entrance of the Pass of Killiecrankie.'[17] Again, Ensign Robert Melville of the 25th Regiment as one of the Peerless Knight's officers at Blair, was given to understand that Crawford had 'spared no pains to prevail with the commander of the Hessians to advance with them against the rebels on Atholl: but without effect, so great was the terror of being attacked in the Pass of Killiecrankie with swords by the wild mountaineers, as they consider them; and who had twice beat the King's troops with firearms as they had heard of.'[18]

The accusations of Hessian pusillanimity are at variance with their reputation as steadfast troops. The same commanders and men acquitted themselves well as part of the allied army in the Netherlands later in the year, and indeed one of the regiments from Scotland, that of Mannsbach, was virtually wiped out when covering the retreat from the field of Rocoux. A wider context is called for.

Prince Frederick was having his first experience of independent command in the field, and in very adverse circumstances. He was operating in an alien land and society, with no support other than that of the Campbell militia, who were thoroughly unreliable, and two regiments of British dragoons, one of which, Naizon's, had been cobbled together from two others (Gardiner's and Hamilton's) which had always run from the Jacobites. The communications from the Duke of Cumberland were rare and uninformative, and no intelligence whatsoever was to be had from the people of Atholl. The region was notoriously Jacobite, and even at Stirling it was found that some of the Hessian muskets had been sabotaged by the natives. Small arms ammunition was short, at twenty-five rounds per man, and provisions could be secured for only a few days at a time, for this was an unproductive land and an unheard-of season for conducting a campaign. Prince Frederick refused to be separated from his artillery, and he was under orders from home not to allow his corps to be split up. The

Hessian officers in general were slow to accommodate themselves to the exigencies of life in Scotland, and the quantities of personal effects and their carriages were the despair of the British liaison officers.

A more fundamental issue related to values. The wars on the continent of Europe were very hard fought, to be sure, but they were conducted within a framework of recognised rules, and the 1740s were the period *par excellence* of 'cartels', which were periodic agreements between the warring parties that regulated the status of prisoners and non-combatants, who were thereby promised good treatment. It so happened that Prince Charles Edward Stuart abided sedulously by the rules of war, whereas the Duke of Cumberland denied the Jacobites all status as lawful belligerents. When he set out for Scotland in January the duke had made it clear that such captured officers as had given their parole to the Jacobites not to escape, were no longer bound by their word, and that they must return to the colours. After the battle of Falkirk rescue parties accordingly went out and virtually kidnapped the officers in question. Many were deeply unhappy at having broken the pledges they had given on their honour as individual gentlemen, and even the ferocious Lieutenant General Hawley was for sending them back.

On 25 February Sir Andrew Fletcher, the Scottish Lord Justice Clerk, warned Cumberland that 'by several whispers among the Hessian officers, which came to me in different channels, I am informed that they will be, at least, unwilling to fight against the rebels till a cartel be settled. I have not heard a word of this from the prince [Frederick] or any about him, nor can I discover who has put this idea in their head, though it is easy to see from what a set of people it must have come.'[19] On 29 March we find a Jacobite officer writing 'Duke William continues still at Aberdeen and the Hessians at Perth and will not join without a cartel.'[20] Matters for the Hessians came to a head on the next day, when one of their volunteer hussars, the Swedish captain Suenson, was captured in a skirmish.

Suenson was bought before Lord George Murray, who returned him with a message for Frederick. 'Our men have taken one of Your Grace's people prisoner. I should be glad to know upon what footing Your Highness intends to conduct war in these kingdoms, and whether you would incline (as we do) to have a cartel settled.' He outlined the difficulties which had arisen concerning what he termed 'the officers of the Elector of Hanover's Army whom we took prisoner,' and he concluded 'as I have the most profound respect for the Illustrious House of Hesse-Cassel and in particular for Your Serene Highness, I have the honour to subscribe myself George Murray.'[21] Frederick sent a copy of the letter to Cumberland, but, as a Hessian officer noted, he did not reply to the Jacobites in person, for 'for it was hoped to speak with this Murray in person.'[22] Cumberland was outraged.

Over the following weeks more evidence emerged concerning the standpoint of the Hessians in the quarrel between the House of Hanover and the

Jacobites. The Hessians were assigned no kind of role, direct or indirect, in Cumberland's final campaign, which opened on 8 April and culminated on the 16th in the battle of Culloden. The corps was earmarked to return to the continent, but meanwhile attended to the security of Atholl, Perth and the lower Tay. The operations were confined to sweeps by the hussars, who gathered up a dozen or so individuals. The prisoners were consigned to Aberdeen, but no other violence was laid to the Hessians' account, and they left in Scotland the memory of 'a gentle race.'[23]

Things were otherwise with the British and their Scottish associates, and the Hessians were angered by reports that reached them of atrocities.[24] One of the first accounts reached them at Perth on 7 April. 'It was there that we learned that a detachment of the king's troops, commanded by a certain Lieutenant Campbell, and therefore called "the Campbells", had irrupted into a district in the north of Scotland had cut down something like forty of the peasants, and solely on a report that they had supported the rebels. Things like that have made a bad impression.'[25]

The Hessian corps sailed from Burntisland on the northern side of the Firth of Forth on 21 June, and reached Willemstad on the 28th. Frederick in person took a long detour by land. In Edinburgh he consorted with known Jacobites, as the Duke of Cumberland noted, and in London, as well as doing his duty by the king, he sought out the company of the Prince of Wales, 'Poor Fred', who was his favourite brother-in-law, and became the figurehead of the 'Country' interest in opposition to the court.

The story does not end there. In 1754 it became known that Prince Frederick of Hesse-Cassel had converted to Catholicism, a process which probably dated back to 1742. Although it might seem a contradiction in terms, he had been drawn by a spirit of Enlightenment enquiry, which led him to a close examination of the authorities and thus to the True Church. This was a period when the Counter Reformation was working in Germany with renewed force, and held a particular attraction among the younger generation of the Protestant princes, who were repelled by the official Calvinism of their courts, and attracted in equal measure by the splendour of the Catholic ceremonial and architecture, and the understanding which Catholic confessors showed towards the failings of hot-blooded young princes. Intellect and emotion alike brought Frederick to a religion in which, in his own words, 'God is celebrated with great magnificence.'[26]

The breach with Princess Mary became total. Frederick was excluded from public affairs, and he and all his Hessian people had to swear to an elaborate legal document (the *Assekurationsackte*) which guaranteed the Protestant religion and put the prince under humiliating personal restrictions. His conditions of life resembled open arrest, and it is probably relevant to our story that his conversion was recognised as having a political dimension. In 1756 we find Empress Maria Theresa working on a rescue mission, and the prince might well have succeeded in escaping to Austria if the plot had not been betrayed. Frederick of Prussia, his former idol, turned against him, and decided that he must be kept under his eye, but in a way that preserved the decencies. Prince Frederick was accordingly promoted in the Prussian service, but consigned to fortress commands away from the field.

Prince Frederick finally succeeded as Landgrave in 1760. Even now he remained under surveillance from Calvinist ministers, the court establishment, the powerful noble Estates and British diplomats, but when he died twenty-five years later this remarkable man had established a reputation as one of the most successful and admired sovereigns of Enlightened Europe.

What are we to make of all of this in relation to the Hessians and the Rising of the 'Forty-Five? It is clear that the Hessians had been unable and unwilling to accommodate themselves to the style of operations as prosecuted by the Duke of Cumberland. Their inhibitions were both of a practical and moral nature, and in the case of Prince Frederick there is cumulative and persuasive, if not finally conclusive evidence to indicate that he was influenced by personal dislike and religious leanings.

German troops returned to the neighbourhood of Crieff almost exactly 200 years after the Hessians had left. Among their number was Heinrich Steinmayer, who had been taken prisoner in Normandy as a Panzer-grenadier of the SS – admittedly not one of the 'gentlest' of races. He became enchanted with the Highlands when he was allowed to go on walks from the camp at Cultybraggan, and made lifelong friends among the local ramblers' group. He might have been speaking for the Hessians when he posed himself the question in 2006, 'why have I been fighting this bloody war?'[27]

Notes

1 Cumberland Papers (CP) 8/73, Lord Harringon to Lord Dunmore, London, 13 December 1745 (Windsor Castle).
2 'Memoirs of Sir John Clerk of Penicuik', *Miscellany of the Scottish History Society* XIII (Edinburgh, 1882), p. 198.
3 *Ibid.*, p. 197.
4 *Feldzug in Schottland* (Hessisches Staatsarchiv, Marburg, Archivband 4 H 2787), Frederick to the Prince Regent Wilhelm, Edinburgh, 27 February 1746.
5 CP 11/104, Cumberland to the Duke of Newcastle, Montrose, 25 February 1746.
6 CP 12/201, Crawford to Cumberland, Perth, 20 March 1746.
7 *Feldzug in Schottland*, Aberdeen, 8 March 1746.
8 National Archives State Papers 54/29, Cumberland to the Duke of Newcastle, Aberdeen, 19 March 1746.
9 CP 12/261, Cumberland to Frederick, Aberdeen, 21 March 1746.
10 *Feldzug in Schottland*, Frederick to the Prince Regent, Dunkeld, 30 March 1746.
11 *Feldzug in Schottland*, Frederick to the Prince Regent, Dunkeld, 3 April 1746.
12 CP 13/67, Frederick to Cumberland, Dunkeld, 31 March 1746.
13 Murhard'sche Bibliothek der Stadt Kassel, 2⁰ Mss. Hass, Gohr, Johann Heinrich, *Journal des General von Gohr (Gohr)*, 497.
14 *Ibid.*

15 CP 13/158, Cumberland to Frederick, Aberdeen, 3 April 1746.

16 CP 13/155, Frederick to Cumberland, 5 April 1746.

17 CP 13/179, Cumberland to the Duke of Newcastle, Aberdeen, 6 or 7 April 1746.

18 National Archives of Scotland (NAS) GD 126/30, Balfour-Melville Papers, General Robert Melville to John Home, 'Heads relating to the Blockade of Blair Castle in 1746', London, 3 August 1801.

19 CP 11/7, the Lord Justice Clerk to Cumberland, Edinburgh, 25 February 1746.

20 NAS, Sheriff Court Records, 'Letter from an Officer in Prince Charles [sic] Army', Inverness, 29 March 1746.

21 *Feldzug in Schottland*, Lord George Murray to Frederick, 30 March 1746.

22 *Gohr*, undated letter, 512.

23 Walter Biggar Blaikie, 'Perthshire in the 'Forty-Five'', in the Marchioness of Tullibardine (ed.), *The Military History of Perthshire 1660–1902* (Perth, Glasgow and Edinburgh, 1908), 330.

24 C. Von Stamford, 'Die Heerfahrt des Prinzen Friedrich von Hessen mit einem Corps hessischer Truppen nach Scottland im Jahre 1746', *Zeitschrift des Vereines für hessische Geschichte und Landeskunde*, new series X (Kassel 1883), 113, 116.

25 *Gohr*, 498–9.

26 Wolf von Both and Hans Vogel, *Landgraf Friedrich von Hessen-Kassel. Ein Fürst der Zopfzeit*, (Munich, 1963), 15.

27 *The Times*, London, 26 January 2006, 'News Section', 23.

6
Thomas Carte, the Druids and British National Identity

Paul Kléber Monod

Was it possible for a convinced Jacobite to imagine an acceptable *British* national identity? Linda Colley raised this question in her book *Britons*, where she argued that Jacobitism was antithetical to the concept of a united Great Britain, as well as to the values for which it stood – namely, anti-Catholicism, anti-French sentiment and a global commercial destiny, shared by Scots and English alike.[1] From a different perspective, Daniel Szechi has depicted Scottish Jacobitism as an ideology fundamentally opposed to the Union of 1707, and strongly imbued with an Anglophobic rhetoric.[2] 'Britishness', in other words, was seen by Jacobites as a curse, an identity imposed by Whigs and their tools. Its rejection was part of the appeal of the Stuart cause. This antipathy may also have nourished the cause's internal weaknesses. Jacobites were seriously divided by national and ethnic allegiances, as contemporary observers often noted. In 1726, the spy John Semple wrote of the exiled Jacobites in Paris that '[t]he Irish, Scotch and English of them seem to have quite different views and ways of thinking, and there are two parties of each Nation, so that I may justly say there are six parties.'[3] None of them could be called a British party, in any sense of the term.

Before we assume that a Jacobite 'Britishness' was impossible, however, we should remember what Colin Kidd has pointed out about national consciousness in early modern Britain: that it was an extremely fluid construction, based on fictions that usually looked back to Biblical or antiquarian sources. We should not expect Jacobites to be rigid in their rejection of British national identity, any more than Hanoverians were united in their promotion of it. Kidd gives some attention to at least one Jacobite writer who advanced what might be called a speculative theology of 'Britishness': the historian and Nonjuror Thomas Carte.[4] To some extent, his views provide a counterpoint to the hard-line Whig nationalism, often tinged with anti-Scottish bias, that flourished in the wake of the '45 rebellion. At the same time, Carte shared with other advocates of 'Britishness' an Anglo-centrism that was in his case determined by religious preoccupations. His writings present an unusual perspective on the varieties of national identity during a period when the concept was still in flux.

Carte was a figure who seemed to pop up whenever the Stuart cause was in question. A Church of England clergyman, he began his long, tempestuous career with a controversial sermon in favour of Charles I. He later refused the oaths to George I and joined the Nonjurors. As secretary to Bishop Atterbury, he was closely involved in the plotting of 1720–22, and was arrested as a consequence. He went into exile in France, where he prepared a seven volume edition of Jacques-Auguste de Thou's history of the late-sixteenth century. Carte returned to England in 1728, spending the next eight years working on a life of the first Duke of Ormonde, father of the Jacobite Duke and the leading politician in Restoration Ireland. No sooner was this work completed than the diligent Nonjuror began planning a *History of England*. He announced it in a letter to Jonathan Swift, dated August 1736, in which he maintained that 'several of our nobility and gentry desire a new history to be wrote', and that they had proposed the project to him.[5] It was to be another eleven years before the first volume was published. During that time, Carte acted as a liaison between the Jacobite court, Tory Members of Parliament and Jacobites in the government of the City of London. He authored a project for a co-ordinated committee to guide the Tory party in elections, and engaged in a pamphlet controversy over the reputation of Charles II. He was imprisoned in the spring of 1744, during a French invasion scare, but was soon released.[6]

Carte's *History of England* appeared in four enormous folio volumes between 1747 and 1755.[7] Never reissued, it might be described as one of the great neglected texts of the eighteenth century. It has the distinction of having been mocked by both Samuel Johnson and Edward Gibbon. Johnson made fun of its immense size, saying of it that '[w]hen a man writes from his own mind, he writes very rapidly.'[8] This was not a fair criticism; if anything, Carte's *History* is overwhelmed with references, and it was certainly not just written off the top of his head. Less unjust was Gibbon's mischievous claim, in a footnote to the *Decline and Fall of the Roman Empire*, that Carte had gullibly accepted Geoffrey of Monmouth as a reliable source for the number of Saxons who entered Britain with Hengist.[9] Carte was in fact sometimes naïve in assuming that controversial evidence could be presented without much explanation.

This characteristic flaw led him into the major blunder that was used to discredit his *History* almost as soon as the first volume appeared in December 1747: the retelling in a footnote of the story of Christopher Lovel, a labourer of Bristol who in 1716 was supposedly cured of scrofula after being touched by the Pretender, James III, in France.[10] The tale was immediately decried as both fallacious and treasonable in a pamphlet ostensibly written by a Jacobite Highlander, 'Duncan MacCarte'. It was further pilloried by Josiah Tucker in *The London Evening Post* and by Henry

Fielding himself, writing as 'John Trot-Plaid', in the *The Jacobite Journal*.[11] Carte tried to defend himself by offering a rather weak reply, published in *The General Evening Post* in February 1748, but Fielding continued to attack him with gusto for 'perverting the Intent of History, and applying it to the sordid and paltry Use of a Party.'[12] The Whig attacks were ferocious, and the damage was quickly done. The reputation of Carte's *History* has never recovered.

This is a pity, because Carte's work deserves to be remembered. It was the first successful attempt by an English-born scholar to produce a comprehensive, multi-volume narrative history of his country, based on original materials, from antiquity to recent times (Carte's work broke off in 1653, due to his death, but it was supposed to continue down to 1688). Its only rival, the *History of England* by Paul de Rapin de Thoyras, published in 1723–5, was written by a Huguenot exile, in French. Carte was contemptuous of the Whig Rapin, dismissing him as 'a Foreigner and utterly unacquainted with our Constitution, Laws, and Customs, any farther than he could learn in conversation, or pick up in Coffee-houses.'[13] This was a prejudiced view of Rapin's remarkable literary achievement; but Carte was not wrong in pointing out his rival's failure to consult archival sources. The only predecessor Carte would acknowledge as worthy was Robert Brady, the Tory physician whose *Complete History of England* appeared in 1685–1690, largely to vindicate James II against Whig constitutional attacks. Brady's unfinished work, however, was really a collection of documents, not a narrative. Moreover, the second volume of the *Complete History*, published after the Glorious Revolution, lacked commentary, perhaps because it would have been dangerous for the author to have publicised his pro-Stuart opinions.[14] Carte had fewer inhibitions.

While he was not a critical historian in the mould of Voltaire, who was willing to question Biblical chronology, Carte followed Brady in wanting to test received historical notions against original sources. As the notes for his *History* now found in the Bodleian Library attest, he was remarkably diligent in seeking out and copying unpublished materials.[15] In this sense, Carte's research methods were more 'modern' than Rapin, or even than David Hume, whose famous *History of England* (1754–61) relied mainly on published sources. Carte was a duller writer than Hume, but arguably a more careful scholar in amassing information. Although, like Hume, he was highly opinionated, his opinions were coloured by a number of factors – critical reading, personal temperament or religious beliefs, for example – and were not simply the result of partisan bias. The notorious Christopher Lovel footnote, for example, was preceded by a passage in which the author questioned whether anointment with oil at a coronation could account for the Royal Touch. Carte was suggesting that any miracles wrought by touching were the products of divine intervention rather than of a special power vested in the person of the monarch. This had been the accepted Anglican position before 1714. Unfortunately, the evidence Carte presented to defend this religiously orthodox opinion was Lovel's highly questionable and politically charged story.

Carte was a remarkably innovative and forward-thinking writer in another major respect. He funded his research on a level that was not matched by any eighteenth century historian. Realising that such a vast project would be costly, he attempted to raise money, not just by one-time personal subscriptions, but through annual donations from wealthy individuals, Oxford colleges (notably, New, Magdalen, Brasenose and Lincoln colleges), the Dean and Chapter of Westminster, the Cathedral Chapter at Durham, City companies (the Goldsmiths, Grocers and Vintners) and the Corporation of London, which contained a powerful Jacobite element in the early 1740s. Carte estimated as early as 1738 that he had been pledged the enormous sum of £600 per annum in research funds. Not all of the private donors were Jacobites or Tories; in fact, they included Whigs like the Speaker of the House of Commons, Arthur Onslow, as well as the Duke of Rutland and the Earl of Burlington.[16] His attempts to solicit money from Whigs show that Carte did not regard his *History* as purely Jacobite, and that he took seriously its appeal to a diverse public. He was not always successful in conveying this message to others, however. The Whig Earl of Egmont initially promised him an unspecified sum, but changed his mind during the '45 rebellion, observing in his diary that 'there is reason to believe that his [Carte's] history will be wrote to support the doctrine of indefeasible hereditary right, in order to serve the Pretender.'[17] By contrast, in a 1743 letter to Carte, the Reverend Edward Collins of St. Erth in Cornwall, who was presumably a Tory, expressed 'a great desire to see a History of England from such a stand.'[18]

A tireless organiser, Carte enlisted the subscribers to his work into a 'Society for encouraging the writing of an History of England', whose members would pay either 10 or 20 guineas a year towards the project, depending on whether they were gentlemen or peers. The Society was to supervise Carte's expenses, to order the transcription of papers from the archives, and to delegate a 'learned Committee' to which he would report his progress. The Society existed at least up to the publication of the first volume. Thomas Coxeter, a minor literary figure and friend of Samuel Johnson, was elected as its Secretary in February 1747, a position he held for two months before his death. The Society probably disbanded after April 1748, when the London Court of Common Council unanimously resolved to withdraw its subscription as a result of embarrassment over the Christopher Lovel affair.[19] As late as 1750, however, Carte successfully petitioned the Common Council for £50 that was still owing to him from the City government, and he was pursuing individual subscribers for money until a few months before his death.[20]

The parallel between the organisation of Carte's *History* and his efforts to co-ordinate Tory electoral support through steering committees is telling. Both were broad-based, participatory efforts that avoided the normal hierarchy of aristocratic patronage. They reveal an imagination that was keenly attuned to the wide commercial audience that existed in England for both culture and politics. The stated political intention of Carte's *History* was in keeping with this attitude. The work was intended to build national consciousness or patriotism. 'No Country in *Europe* affords such a quantity and variety of materials for its History, as *England* does', he claimed in his first proposal for the project, published in 1738. Echoing the patriotic sentiments of the period, which were soon to lead Britain into war with Spain, Carte argued that '[b]y such a History the people of *England* will see upon what foundations their Civil Rights, Privileges and Liberties stand, and be better enabled to support them.'[21] The author's name appeared on the title page of each volume of the *History* as 'Thomas Carte, an Englishman', as if to announce his patriotic allegiance and set him apart from the Frenchman Rapin. Only in the first volume, however, did he offer a picture of *British* rather than *English* nationalism. That volume contained a long, admiring disquisition on the ancient Britons, particularly extolling the priesthood known as the Druids. In depicting the priests of ancient Britain, Carte revealed his own vision of a modern British national identity that went beyond Englishness.

The Druids were loaded with patriotic potential, in part because so little was known about them. Their history was built on a few fragmentary Greek texts, notably Posidonius, as well as on the more complete Latin writings of Diodorus Siculus, Julius Caesar and Tacitus. The many gaps in these sources could be supplemented by observation of Celtic artifacts and monuments, on which the most fanciful speculations were built.[22] Although the Druids had fascinated antiquarians for two centuries, they had become newly fashionable in the patriotic atmosphere of the 1740s, as the supposed forerunners of British uniqueness and greatness.[23] Echoing an opinion first expressed by John Aubrey, Reverend William Stukeley had argued that the Druids were the builders of Stonehenge and Avebury, which he saw as the remains of a great architectural tradition. Stukeley dressed up the Druidic priesthood as proto-Christians who had maintained the purity of the original religion of Noah. He also pictured them as the possessors of remarkable practical wisdom, which allowed them to become great mathematicians and builders. As David Haycock has pointed out, Stukeley's interpretation of the Druids implied that the English nation had been specially chosen by God for the preservation of true religion.[24] In the rest of Europe, according to Stukeley, 'they had not the Druid religion so pure, as with us; which not a little favoured Christianity; as being the remains of the old patriarchal religion, of which Christianity is but a republication.'[25] Stukeley's glorification of the Druids was further informed by ardent

Freemasonry. He saw the mysterious rituals of the ancient Britons as prefiguring those of the Freemasons, whose purpose was the unveiling to initiates of the eternal secrets of nature.[26]

An even wilder fantasy about the Druids was proposed in 1742 by John Wood, the famous architect of Bath, in a popular guide to the spa town. Wood asserted that Bladud, the mythical Druidic founder of Bath, was none other than Abaris, a Hyperborean priest who had visited ancient Greece and purportedly introduced the philosophical principles that were later linked with Pythagoras, notably the transmigration of souls. Wood also made Bladud into the creator of a Druidic 'university' at Stanton Drew in Somerset. Like Stukeley, Wood attached Masonic as well as patriotic purposes to his fabulous evocation of the Druids. His admiring image of them was also cleverly designed to publicise the city of Bath as the latter-day home of Druidic architectural principles, which he imitated in designing the famous Circus.[27]

Thomas Carte may have appreciated Wood's association of Bath with the Druids, as he had been a reader at Bath Abbey in the reign of Queen Anne. He certainly regarded the Druids as a priesthood of wise men, and Druidism as a forerunner to Christian revelation. Moreover, like Wood and Stukeley, Carte was apparently a Freemason. His correspondence with the Chevalier Andrew Ramsay attests to his knowledge of Masonic rituals. Ramsay, a former tutor to Prince Charles Edward Stuart, was the originator of the myth that Freemasonry had its origins in the chivalric orders of the Middle Ages. An avid student of ancient religions, Ramsay argued in his celebrated work *The Voyages of Cyrus* that the ethical systems of the Egyptians and Persians had prefigured Christianity. Ramsay wrote regularly to Carte in the 1730s, on historical and theological as well as Masonic matters.[28] Although his mystical, elitist brand of Masonry differed considerably from that of Stukeley or Wood, Ramsay shared their preoccupation with finding the roots of the brotherhood in ancient religions that had preserved the remnants of the *prisca theologia*, the original, monotheistic faith of humanity.

However similar their intentions may have been, Carte's *History* did not cite Ramsay at all. Its account of the Druids does not seem to owe very much to William Stukeley either. Rather, it drew inspiration from an earlier (and much more unlikely) source, namely the plan for a history of the Druids written in 1718–19 by the anti-clerical Whig radical and pantheist philosopher, John Toland. An Irishman, fluent in Gaelic, Toland had argued that Celtic antiquities were worth recording, not because they were admirable, but because they provided evidence of ancient 'superstitions', of which Toland was just as contemptuous as he was of modern ones. He summed up the history of the Druids as '*the complete History of Priestcraft*', which damned it in his eyes, but may of course have recommended it to a High Churchman like Carte.[29] In spite of his disapproval of the Druidic order, Toland was nonetheless intrigued by aspects of Druidic history. He was particularly fascinated by the Hyperborean traveller Abaris, possibly because he perceived a parallel between the teachings of Pythagoras, which Abaris supposedly inspired, and his own unorthodox religious views. Toland believed that Abaris was a Druid from the Hebrides, and was 'already sufficiently prepared' to understand the transmigration of souls before he became a pupil of Pythagoras.[30] Carte would later duplicate these assertions in his *History*, and he even included a footnote acknowledging his debt to Toland. He further borrowed from Toland the assumption that Irish Druids had the same roles as their British counterparts, although the classical sources, as well as old Irish texts, indicated that Druids did not have the same high status in Irish society as they did in Britain.

Carte was able to appropriate Toland's views partly because the Whig writer's work had already been 'sanitised' by an orthodox Anglican historian, the Welsh clergyman Henry Rowlands. In a study of the antiquities of Anglesey, Rowlands duplicated Toland's claims about Abaris and Pythagoras. As might be expected from an Anglican minister, however, Rowlands did not repeat the vilification heaped by his freethinking predecessor on 'Priestcraft'. On the contrary, he was elegiac and rapturous in his Druidic fantasy, going so far as to present ancient Britain as 'a wish'd Elyzium' for the Greeks. In one particularly striking passage, Rowlands lyrically evoked a British landscape of 'Woods resounding with nature's Musick; curiously cut into pleasant Walks, and Theatres and Temples: … And above all, walking and meditating *here* a Company of divinely inspir'd Souls, abounding with instructive Documents of Virtue, and profound Discoveries of Nature.'[31] Apparently, the ancient Greek philosophers did not mind the cold rain of North Wales.

Rowlands further claimed that the ancient British language, ancestor of Welsh, was the original tongue of Adam. Carte did not mention this view in his *History*, but he was certainly fascinated by British languages. He tried to collect the vanishing remnants of Cornish, relying heavily on the 'Glossography' contained in Edward Lhwyd's *Archaeologia Britannica*, and he made a long list of Welsh words.[32] He also consulted the Welsh-speaking poet and antiquarian, Lewis Morris, as an expert on early British sources. Morris was at first delighted to provide Carte with information: 'I am glad', he wrote, 'to find such a sinewy advocate as you are for our ancient Britons, who have been so shamefully abused in their graves, by our modern wits.'[33] He became dissatisfied, however, with the results of Carte's efforts. Morris accused the historian of publishing sections from his letters without attribution, and was particularly annoyed that Carte 'doth not allow that our British Druids had the use of any letters.'[34] That the Druids possessed a distinctive script was one of the few achievements Carte was *not* willing to grant them.

By contrast, he had a lofty estimation of their impact on European culture, which he derived from the writings of the Abbé Paul-Yves Pezron, a late-seventeenth century Breton cleric. Pezron's fantastic account of the ancient Celts was judged by John Toland to be 'tolerably done', a grudging assessment, but noteworthy as it was bestowed by a freethinker on a Roman Catholic clergyman.[35] For his part, Carte admired Pezron unreservedly. He repeated the Abbé's claim that the Celts were direct descendants of Noah's grandson Gomer, which accounted for their clear understanding of the original religion. Like Pezron, Carte described the Celts as the founders of an empire that had once stretched throughout Europe. Its powerful rulers – Uranus, Saturn, Jupiter and Mercury – would later give their names to the gods of Greek mythology. Pezron had tied together Biblical and classical chronology, boldly suggesting that the 'Gomerian' Celts were the actual originators of European civilisation.[36] Consequently, the ancient Britons, however peripheral they may have been in the writings of classical authors, could be regarded as central not only to secular history but to the preservation of the true faith of Noah, the *prisca theologia*, amidst the errors of paganism. Pezron's sweeping and audacious theory made a deep impression on Carte, who used it as the basis for advancing his own version of British Druidic identity.

Drawing on Pezron, Rowlands and Toland, Carte represented the ancient Celts not as contemptible barbarians, but as a people of impressive accomplishments, who had developed an encyclopedic knowledge of the natural world, and who believed, like later Christians, in the eternity of the soul. They were transmitters of wisdom to the Greeks and Romans, not *vice-versa*, and were vital to the development of classical civilisation. Equally important, they were British. They had populated Ireland, Wales and Scotland as well as England, and were the common ancestors of all the peoples of the British Isles. They might therefore provide a model for contemporary Britons.

For Carte, the most captivating aspect of Celtic society was its priesthood, the Druids. While his description of the Druids and their rituals may have been slightly less fanciful than those of Stukeley or Wood or Rowlands, it was equally enthusiastic. Carte's Druids were magistrates as well as priests, 'who, besides a mighty influence in all civil affairs, had in sacred matters an authority, full as absolute, as ever the *Magi* enjoyed in Persia.'[37] Although their religious beliefs were tainted by magic, they became proficient in the natural sciences of astronomy, medicine and mathematics. In spite of these innovative pursuits, Carte made the Druids resemble Nonjurors or conservative clergymen of the Church of England. He described them as 'men of a retired life; ... stiff and uncomplying in respect of the new fashions of the world, and... tenacious of their own customs.'[38] They formed a secretive yet enlightened brotherhood of initiates that might remind readers of the Freemasons, although Carte never made the parallel explicit.

These strict Druidic traditionalists ruled over a kind of utopia. Carte praised 'the happy situation of these islands: Happy in being divided from the rest of the world, and free from the calamities of war, and the inundations of barbarous nations.'[39] According to Carte, the Druids were the first to teach the immortality of the soul, making them forerunners to Christianity. Their rites were practiced either in groves of oak, which had provided the first temples before the Deluge, or in simple structures of unwrought pillars, like Stonehenge and Avebury. That these sacred buildings prefigured the Temple of Solomon, the mythic model for the lodges of Freemasons, might be inferred. On the negative side, Carte admitted that the Druidic practice of human sacrifice was deplorable, although it was common enough among ancient peoples, so he did not dwell much on it.

In their governance, the Druids were wise and effective patriarchs. Carte did not imagine, however, that they adhered to uniform laws. 'Nations must be formed before they can make laws', Carte wrote, and the ancient Britons did not constitute a nation – rather, they comprised up to 400 self-governing communities.[40] Nonetheless, the legal judgements of the Druids were based on common principles of ethics that were spread among the whole people. While they governed through councils, including an annual general council for all Britain, each Druidic community also named a 'dictator' who might assume complete authority in case of an emergency. Moreover, the Druids scorned democracy. A separate noble order of *Equites* or knights existed in ancient British society, but '[p]lebeians had no manner of power, nor were admitted to any of the councils for ordering public affairs.'[41] The Druids, in other words, ruled alone, a race of philosopher kings as well as the heads of families or clans. 'They were an order of the first quality'; Carte concluded about them, 'endowed with all that greatness of mind, which a noble birth, uncorrupted by vice and luxury, naturally inspires;... collected out of all the various nations spread through the wide extent of that country, and related to all the princely and noble families.'[42] To pass their values on to future generations, they maintained seminaries of instruction, similar to the universities of modern times. Entrance into these seminaries was reserved for the male offspring of their order.

Like previous chroniclers of the Druids, Carte was captivated by the story of the Hyperborean traveller Abaris. He insisted, even more strongly than John Toland, that the homeland of Abaris was located in the Hebrides. The 'grove of Apollo' that once stood among those Scottish islands, according to Carte, provided direct inspiration for the Apollonian rites of Delos. Regular embassies were exchanged between the Hebrides and Greece. Here Carte hinted at another link to Freemasonry, because the rites practiced in Masonic lodges were often compared to the ancient mysteries of the

Greeks. Carte further praised the pristine culture of the island peoples in terms that foreshadowed Adam Ferguson or even Jean-Jacques Rousseau. 'As for the genius, customs, and manners of the *Hyperborei*, [ie. the Hebrideans]', he wrote, '... all antiquity agrees in representing them, as an harmless, innocent, religious and happy people; living a simple life according to nature, ... which is well known to be the case of the inhabitants of the *Hebrides*, even in this age.'[43]

The main weakness in this otherwise perfect Druidic social structure appears to have been disunity, both among the clans and within them. Carte noted that the individual clan polities, 'when the country grew too much crowded with numbers, and every one was tempted to encroach on his neighbour's territory, were too weak to defend themselves alone'.[44] Agreements among the clans could not prevent internal factions, within communities and even individual households. Ultimately, disunity made the Britons vulnerable to attack by the power of imperial Rome. Carte did not specify whether or not a strong monarchy might have addressed this problem.

In his glowing account of ancient Britons, Carte hardly mentioned the Picts, the inhabitants of the Scottish mainland, who had long resisted Roman attacks. In particular, he made no reference to the recent study of Pictish kingship by the Scottish Jacobite historian Father Thomas Innes. Innes argued that the Picts had instituted a powerful Scottish monarchy, an innovation usually dated to a later period, and ascribed to the Scots who lived in the northern islands.[45] Carte avoided the knotty issue of the genesis of Scottish monarchy. He sought to glorify the northern islanders as British, and seems not to have been quite sure how to fit the Picts, who were usually seen as 'Gothic' or German, into his conception of Celtic Britain.

In any case, if the early sections of Carte's *History* had heroes, they were not kings, but priests, and they headed what resembled a Church, divided into dioceses, rather than a centralised polity. Carte pictured a successful, localised and ecclesiastical form of government, without the unifying presence of a powerful national monarch. The ancient Britons might have been better off united under a king, Carte suggests, but apparently, they did not do so badly without one. It may seem remarkable that a Tory and Jacobite would make such an argument, but it is less of a paradox than it appears to be. While Tories exalted the monarchy, they also wanted it to be a distant, god-like institution whose power was seldom felt in daily life. For the purposes of practical administration, they preferred local government based on the wise patriarchal judgement of members of 'ancient families', serving as parish ministers and justices of the peace. The near-anarchy of ancient Britain, in which 400 tiny polities coexisted, may well have seemed utopian from this viewpoint.

To a large extent, Carte's evocation of ancient British society was a High Church clergyman's consoling vision of a mythical past, in which an educated and benign clerisy held absolute sway over the whole British archipelago. While this vision may appear unconnected to contemporary events, in fact it had direct political implications for Carte's own day. In the late summer of 1745, what seemed to be the last remnant of ancient British clan society, the Highlanders of Scotland, rose up in rebellion against the modern British state, and in support of the exiled Stuarts. Always ready to play the role of *agent provocateur*, Carte rushed into print a 'Specimen' of his *History*, comprising the central sections of his chapter on the Druids. It appeared in London on 22 February 1746, about a month after the unexpected Jacobite victory at Falkirk, and before the final collapse at Culloden. Read in the context of the '45 rebellion, the ancient Celtic society of Carte's 'Specimen' deliberately reflected what he thought to be that of the contemporary Highlands, and the Druids surely would have made English readers think of the Jacobite chiefs of Scotland.[46]

This treasonous parallel did not go unnoticed by the defenders of the Hanoverian state. The most sustained response to it came from the Archdeacon of Bath, Samuel Squire, himself a noted antiquarian. Writing early in 1748, when the threat of the rebellion had passed and shortly after the first volume of the *History* had appeared in print, Squire accused Carte of exalting 'the absolute Power of the ancient *Pagan* Priesthood', as a means of 'recommending Church Authority in general.'[47] Far from being hereditary legislators, Squire asserted, the Druids had 'the same *Right* that every other native free-born *Gaul*, or *Briton*, had, to be present in the general and sovereign Assembly of the nation, and there, together with the rest of their independent Brethren, to examine into the Necessities of the Public.'[48] Ancient Britain, according to Squires, was governed by both of the 'free-born' orders, the Druids and the *Equites*. The Plebeians below them could not participate in councils, but they were not vassals or slaves of the aristocracy. Indeed, according to Squire, '[s]lavery was the original Product of Asiatic Warmth and Luxury. – Our Ancestors, neither the *Britons*, *Gauls*, nor *Germans* knew any Thing of it.'[49] Ultimately, in Squire's opinion, the Jacobite Carte was recommending 'the *paramount Power* of the Pope and his Cardinals to bind your Kings in Chains and your Nobles in Links of Iron.'[50] As usual in Whig polemics, the whiff of Jacobitism was identified with the stronger odours of 'Popery' and slavery.

Squire was also setting up an old debate, between those who saw the pre-feudal constitution as based on the consent of free-born men, and those who argued that it was dominated by the authority of monarchs, or of a governing caste. In a recently published *Enquiry into the Foundation of the English Constitution*, Squire had praised Anglo-Saxon government as 'excellently well adapted in every respect to obtain all the true ends of government, the public peace and safety, the defense of private property, and the preservation of the natural liberty of individuals.'[51] The Saxon constitution, according to Squire, stood for liberty, against the feudalism and absolutism of the Normans. Carte rejected this view, picturing the Saxons as barbarians. We should not, however, imagine the debate as one between Celtic and Anglo-Saxon apologists, since Squire believed that the Celts, like all 'Germanic' tribes, shared the same constitution as the Anglo-Saxons. Britons and Saxons were simply pawns in a rhetorical argument that had more to do with contemporary politics than with the particular histories of those peoples.

The disagreement between Carte and Squire reflected differences of national identification as well. While Squire's work can be read as the glorification of an *English* constitution, the first chapter of Carte's *History* is more broadly a celebration of the *British* past, drawing in important elements of Welsh, Scottish and even Irish history. Carte's desire for inclusiveness is well illustrated in his treatment of the ancient inhabitants of Ireland. He was careful to note that the ancient Greek geographer Strabo did not credit reports that the Irish '*are more savage than the Brittains*', since his informants were unreliable.[52] Carte suggests that we should not believe such stories either, which was a considerable concession for an English historian to make towards the Irish. Throughout his *History*, Carte was careful not to insult the Irish in the gratuitous manner that was common among English observers. This attitude may have been shaped by the time he spent in Ireland in the mid-1730s, when he raised subscriptions among Irish Catholic landowners for his *Life of Ormonde*. His emphasis on the resemblance of Ireland to Britain served to advance Carte's position that the British Isles were once part of a single society, and might be again.[53]

Of course, Carte's inclusive 'Britishness' was a fiction, just as much as Samuel Squire's Anglo-Saxon 'Englishness'. Using scanty evidence, it merged ancient British and Irish societies into a single Druidic model, implicitly denying the importance of national or regional distinctions, and casting doubt on cultural divisions between the English, Welsh, Scots and Irish. Carte's conception of British identity was based firmly on a belief in the orthodoxy of the Church of England, which in his view had roots that preceded even the conversion of the British archipelago to Christianity. This belief did not leave much room for Roman Catholic or Presbyterian claims. In fact, Carte's 'Britishness', while it may have been influenced by modern or 'enlightened' notions of Masonic brotherhood, was ultimately derived from an older, ecclesiological definition of Englishness, founded on the supposed primacy of the English Church. It was not without reason that he called himself an Englishman on the title page of his book: it meant, above all, that he was a defender of the English ecclesiastical settlement.

Carte's patriotic exaltation of Anglicanism may have been widespread among his orthodox coreligionists, but it was not likely to win

broad acceptance among those who were outside the Church's communion, or who did not happen to be English or Welsh. This may have
been true even of those who shared the historian's Jacobitism. Exhibiting,
perhaps, his own inspired but somewhat impractical approach to contemporary politics, Carte proposed an embracing, transnational British
identity, at a moment when most active Jacobites were far more concerned
with defending the rights of their own nations. To some extent, this
reflected the historian's lack of sensitivity to the conflicting national elements within Jacobitism. Like most English Jacobites, Carte had little
contact with Gaelic-speaking cultures. He knew nothing about the bards
who had fervently composed reams of Jacobite poetry in the native
languages of Scotland and Ireland. He seems not to have read the Scottish history of his fellow Jacobite Thomas Innes, and he was apparently
unacquainted with the Abbé Macgeoghegan, another Jacobite exile who
between 1758 and 1762 would publish an important history of Ireland.[54]
Just as Carte's writings failed to fulfil the aspirations of a Welsh patriot
like Lewis Morris, who happened to be a Whig, so too they probably dis-
appointed Scots or Irish patriots whose political persuasions were closer to
his own.

Carte might have replied that he was not interested in stirring up a Celtic
cultural revival; rather, he sought to merge individual national identities
into a 'Britishness' that was fundamentally spiritual and had deep religious
connotations. His goal was to illuminate Britain's place in divine as well as
secular history. He was addressing himself to those who, whether they
might be Tories or Whigs, Nonjurors or Freemasons, suspected that Britain
enjoyed a privileged status in God's cosmic plan. Carte's British Druids,
therefore, were not Celtic patriots. They were only distantly related to
the mythical bard Ossian, whose epic works, partly reconstructed, partly
invented by James Macpherson, did so much to stimulate Scottish national
culture in the 1760s. On the other hand, Carte's Druids had much in common with the learned priests, possessors of ancient theological wisdom, who inspired the Welsh poet Edward Williams (Iolo Morganwg),
the founder of the *Gorsedd* or festival of bards. More unexpectedly, they
resembled the mystical patriarchs imagined by later radical prophets like
William Blake or Richard Brothers. These visionaries continued to regard
the Druids as figures of universal importance, the inheritors of the *prisca
theologia* and the heralds of a future British Jerusalem, a sacred city that
might be reestablished in the Holy Land itself.[55]

Like those later conceptions, Carte's Druidic 'Britishness' was somewhat
out of step with the times because it was non-expansionist. It focused on a
self-sustaining, inward-looking, non-belligerent 'little Britain', at peace
with its neighbours and willing to separate itself from the world, because it
basked in divine approval. By contrast, the Union of 1707 with Scotland, as
John Robertson has indicated, was a commercial 'Union for Empire', that

opened up vast imperial vistas to the new British state.[56] For newly forged Britons, patriotism translated easily into imperialism. The great historian of that first British imperial moment was the Scottish Presbyterian, Principal of Edinburgh University and staunch Whig, William Robertson, who held the Celts, like most ancient peoples, to be 'savages'.[57] A stronger contrast to Carte could hardly be imagined.

Now that the British Empire is gone, however, Carte's vision may seem more in tune than Principal Robertson's with current debates over the future of British identity. The once-dominant ideology of 'Britishness', shaped by early eighteenth century Whigs, is fast unraveling, raising new possibilities: a decentralised Britain, a federal state or even Scottish independence. About these options, however, Thomas Carte was silent. His writings did not consider any constitutional alternatives to the centralised British state of his own time. While he was certainly a critic of the 'despotism' that he identified with the rule of the Commonwealth (and later, of the Whigs), Carte never discussed a reduction in the authority of a unitary Parliament. If he espoused the dissolution of the Union, he was careful not to mention it openly. At the same time, by providing a counternarrative to the teleological Whig history of his own day, which was obsessed with the triumphs of 1688 and 1714, Carte repeatedly suggested that the rise of the British state was not determined by an inexorable Providence. Rather, it had come about through a series of unfortunate historical accidents, dating from the Civil Wars of the 1640s. However tedious and pedantic its tone may be, therefore, Carte's massive work contained a potentially subversive political message. Did the author himself realise its full implications? Would he have been delighted or disconcerted to think that his mythic treatment of the ancient Britons had exposed the artificiality and fragility of modern British national consciousness? Like a good Freemason, Carte has kept some secrets from us, and ultimately, the hidden intentions of his *History* may be accessible only through the magical science of the Druids.

Notes

1 Linda Colley, *Britons: Forging the Nation 1707–1837* (New Haven, 1992), pp. 71–85. Colley's book was followed by a stream of essay collections debating British national identity, including Steven G. Ellis and Sarah Barber (eds), *Conquest and Union: Fashioning a British State* (London, 1995); Alexander Grant and Keith Stringer (eds), *Uniting the Kingdom? The Making of British History* (London, 1995); Brendan Bradshaw and John Morrill (eds), *The British Problem, c. 1534–1707: State Formation in the Atlantic Archipelago* (London, 1996); Tony Claydon and Ian MacBride (eds), *Protestantism and National Identity: Britain and Ireland, c. 1650–c. 1850* (Cambridge, 1998); S. J. Connolly (ed.), *Kingdoms United? Great Britain and Ireland since 1500* (Dublin, 1999); Julian Hoppitt (ed.), *Parliaments, Nations and identities in Britain and Ireland, 1660–1850* (Manchester, 2003).

2   Daniel Szechi, *George Lockhart of Carnwath, 1689–1727: A Study in Jacobitism* (East Linton, 2002), pp. 205–11; also, Daniel Szechi and Margaret Sankey, 'Elite Culture and the Decline of Scottish Jacobitism, 1716–1745', *Past and Present*, 173 (2002), pp. 90–128.

3   Quoted in Edward Gregg, 'The Politics of Paranoia', in Eveline Cruickshanks and Jeremy Black (eds), *The Jacobite Challenge* (Edinburgh, 1988), p. 43.

4   Colin Kidd, *British Identities Before Nationalism: Ethnicity and Nationhood in the Atlantic World, 1600–1800* (Cambridge, 2002), pp. 68, 197, 206.

5   Harold Williams (ed.), *The Correspondence of Jonathan Swift* (5 vols., Oxford, 1963–5), vol. 4, pp. 523–4. Carte was not close to Swift, but they were both friends of the Irish Nonjuror Reverend Thomas Sheridan.

6   For his life, see the biography by Stuart Handley in *Oxford Dictionary of National Biography* (Oxford, 2004; henceforth *ODNB*), as well as John Nichols, *Literary Anecdotes of the Eighteenth Century* (6 vols., London, 1812), vol. 2, pp. 471–518, and Eveline Cruickshanks and Howard Erskine-Hill, *The Atterbury Plot* (London, 2004), p. 157. For the edition of de Thou, see Samuel Kinser, *The Works of Jacques-Auguste de Thou* (The Hague, 1966), as well as Alfred Soman, 'The London Edition of De Thou's *History*: A Critique of Some Well-Documented Legends', *Renaissance Quarterly* 24, 1 (1971), pp. 1–12. The value of Carte's biography of Ormonde was upheld by J. C. Beckett, *The Cavalier Duke: A Life of James Butler, First Duke of Ormond* (Belfast, 1990), but was put in question by Toby Barnard and Jane Fenlon (eds), *The Dukes of Ormonde 1610–1745* (Woodbridge, Suffolk, 2000). Carte's electoral plan is found in R. W. Greaves, 'A Scheme for the Counties', *English Historical Review*, 48, 192 (Oct. 1933), pp. 630–8.

7   It has been most recently disparaged for not measuring up to the 'detached' standards of 'neoclassical' history by Philip Hicks in *Neoclassical History and English Culture: From Clarendon to Hume* (London, 1996).

8   James Boswell, *The Life of Samuel Johnson, LLD.* (2 vols., London, 1791), I, p. 476 (1775).

9   Edward Gibbon, *The History of the Decline and Fall of the Roman Empire* (3 vols., London, 1789), III, ch. 38, p. 621, note 146.

10 Thomas Carte, *A General History of England* (4 vols., London, 1747–55), I, pp. 291–2, note 4. Originally, this story was included in the text, but either Carte or his printer thought better of it and relegated it to a note. See Bodleian Library, Carte Ms. 184, gathering inserted between ff. 249–50.

11 'Duncan MacCarte', *A Letter to John Trot-Plaid, Esq; Author of the Jacobite Journal, Concerning Mr. Carte's General History of England* (London, 1748); Nichols, *Literary Anecdotes*, II, pp. 491–9; Henry Fielding, *The Jacobite's Journal and Related Writings*, ed. W. B. Coley (Oxford, 1975), pp. 145–6.

12 *The Gentleman's Magazine*, XVIII (London, 1748), pp. 13–14; Fielding, *Jacobite's Journal*, p. 169, as well as pp. 165, 168–71, 177–9, 195–7, 249–50, 298.

13 Thomas Carte, *A Collection of The Several Papers Published by Mr. Thomas Carte in relation to his History of England* (London, 1744), p. 3.

14 Robert Brady, *A Complete History of England* (London, 1685) and *A Continuation of the Complete History of England* (London, 1700). See also J. G. A. Pocock, *The Ancient Constitution and the Feudal Law* (2nd ed., New York, 1967).

15 See in particular Carte Ms. 139–41, 228, 230–1, 234–5, 240, 261, 263, 266–7, containing extracts and notes for the *History*. Draft copies of the work are found in Carte Ms. 184–9.

16 Carte, *Collection of Several Papers*, pp. 16, 38; Nichols, *Literary Anecdotes*, vol. 2, pp. 480, 487–97, 504; British Library, Additional Manuscripts 215800, ff. 12, 115–16, 117–18; Carte Ms. 240, ff. 341–5.

17 Historical Manuscripts Commission, *Manuscripts of the Earl of Egmont: Diary of Viscount Percival, Afterwards First Earl of Egmont* (3 vols., London, 1920–23), III, p. 312.
18 Carte Ms. 240, f. 346.
19 *The British Magazine, or, The London and Edinburgh Intelligencer* (Edinburgh, 1747), p. 401, for Coxeter, along with Coxeter's entry in *ODNB*; *Gentleman's Magazine*, XVIII (1748), p. 185; and for Jacobites in the London Corporation, Eveline Cruickshanks, *Political Untouchables: The Tories and the '45* (London, 1979).
20 Somerset Record Office, DD/TB 15/8, Thomas Carte to Thomas Carew, June 9, 1753. There are four letters from Carte to Carew in the Somerset Record Office, dated 1748–54.
21 Carte, *Collection of Several Papers*, pp. 1, 9.
22 The classic study of the Druids in history and myth is Stuart Piggott, *The Druids* (London, 1968), which appeared in many editions down to 1985. See also A. L. Owen, *The Famous Druids: A Survey of Three Centuries of English Literature on the Druids* (Oxford, 1962); Sam Smiles, *The Image of Antiquity: Ancient Britain and the Romantic Imagination* (New Haven, 1994); Rosemary Sweet, *Antiquaries: The Discovery of the British Past in 18th-Century Britain* (London, 2004), ch. 4.
23 For political and literary uses of the Druids in this period, see Christine Gerrard, *The Patriot Opposition to Walpole: Politics, Poetry and National Myth, 1725–42* (Oxford, 1994), pp. 136–45.
24 William Stukeley, *Stonehenge: A Temple Restor'd to the British Druids* (London, 1740); William Stukeley, *Abury: A Temple of the British Druids* (London, 1743); Aubrey Burl and Neil Mortimer (eds), *Stukeley's 'Stonehenge': An Unpublished Manuscript 1721–1724* (New Haven, 2005), esp. 124–5, 128; Stuart Pigott, *William Stukeley: An Eighteenth-Century Antiquary* (revised edn., London, 1985), ch. 4; David Boyd Haycock, *William Stukeley: Science, Religion and Archaeology in Eighteenth-Century England* (Woodbridge, Suffolk, 2002), chs. 5–8.
25 William Stukeley, *Palaeographia Britannica: or Discourses on Antiquities that relate to the History of Britain. Number III* (London, 1752), p. 55.
26 Haycock, *William Stukeley*, pp. 174–80.
27 John Wood, *An Essay Towards a Description of Bath* (2nd ed., London and Bath, 1747), pp. 1–180; see also Tim Mowl and Brian Earnshaw, *John Wood: Architect of Obsession* (Taunton, 1988).
28 Carte Ms. 227, ff. 62–3, 65–6, 163–4; Carte Ms. 246, ff. 395–8, 415–20; see also G. D. Henderson, *Chevalier Ramsay* (London, 1952).
29 John Toland, *A New Edition of Toland's History of the Druids*, ed. R. Huddleston (Montrose, 1814), p. 56. For Toland's views, see Justin Champion, *Republican Learning: John Toland and the Crisis of Christian Culture, 1689–1722* (Manchester, 2003).
30 Toland, *History of the Druids*, pp. 207–10, 226–8.
31 Henry Rowlands, *Mona Antiqua Restaurata: An Archaeological Discourse on the Antiquities, Natural and Historical, of the Isle of Anglesey, the Antient Seat of the British Druids* (Dublin, 1723: reprinted, Macclesfield, 1993), p. 73.
32 Carte Ms. 240, ff. 346–7, 375–6; Carte Ms. 267; Edward Lhwyd, *Archaeologia Britannica,… vol. 1: Glossography* (Oxford, [1707]).
33 Carte, *History*, I, p. 33; Hugh Owen (ed.), *Additional Letters of the Morrises of Anglesey* (2 vols., London, 1947–9), I, p. 141, and see pp. 154–8, 174.
34 *Additional Letters*, II, p. 514, and see pp. 471, 518. For the similar reactions of Morris's brother William to Carte's work, see John Davies (ed.), *The Letters of Lewis, Richard, William and John Morris of Anglesey* (2 vols., Oxford, 1907),

I, pp. 86, 129. I am grateful to David L. Jones for translating the original Welsh in William Morris's letters.

35   Toland, *History*, p. 106.

36   Paul-Yves Pezron, *The Antiquities of Nations; More particularly of the Celtae or Gauls, Taken to be Originally the same People as our Ancient Britains*, trans. D. Jones (London, 1706).

37   Carte, *History*, I, p. 27.

38   *Ibid.*, I, p. 34.

39   *Ibid.*, I, p. 37.

40   *Ibid.*, I, p. 45.

41   *Ibid.*, I, p. 77 .

42   *Ibid.*, I, p. 51.

43   *Ibid.*, I, p. 59.

44   *Ibid.*, I, p. 78.

45   Thomas Innes, *A Critical Essay on the Ancient Inhabitants of the Northern Parts of Britain, or Scotland* (2 vols., London, 1729); Colin Kidd, 'The Ideological Uses of the Picts, c. 1707–c. 1990', in Edward J. Cowan and Richard J. Finlay (eds), *Scottish History: The Power of the Past* (Edinburgh, 2002), pp. 169–90; Colin Kidd, *Subverting Scotland's Past* (Cambridge, 1993), pp. 101–7.

46   I have not been able to find an original copy of Carte's 'Specimen', but the full text, along with revisions that appeared in the *History*, is appended to [Samuel Squires], *Remarks upon Mr. Carte's Specimen of his General History of England* (London, 1748), pp. 50–62.

47   *Ibid.*, p. 13.

48   *Ibid.*, p. 26.

49   *Ibid.*, p. 37.

50   *Ibid.*, p. 44.

51   Samuel Squire, *An Enquiry into the Foundation of the English Constitution; or, An Historical Essay upon the Anglo-Saxon Government both in Germany and England* (London, 1745), p. 80.

52   Carte, *History*, I, p. 72. The manuscript version of this passage, in Carte Ms. 184, f. 53v, shows that it was a later addition.

53   Carte Ms. 103, f. 545; see also Carte Ms. 103, ff. 537–8, 541, and Carte Ms. 227, ff. 30–1, 83, as well as transcripts in British Library, Additional Ms. 39, 268.

54   Vincent Geoghegan, 'A Jacobite History: The Abbé Macgeoghegan's *History of Ireland*', *Eighteenth-Century Ireland*, 6 (1991), pp. 37–55; and for Irish Jacobitism in general, Éamonn Ó Ciardha, *Ireland and the Jacobite Cause, 1685–1766: A Fatal Attachment* (Dublin, 2004).

55   Owen, *The Famous Druids*, chs. 10–11; Prys Morgan, 'From a Death to a View: The Hunt for the Welsh Past in the Romantic Period', in Eric Hobsbawm and Terence Ranger (eds.), *The Invention of Tradition* (Cambridge, 1983, 1992), pp. 43–100; Eitan Bar-Yosef, '"Green and Pleasant Lands": England and the Holy Land in Plebeian Millenarian Culture, c. 1790–1820', in Kathleen Wilson (ed.), *A New Imperial History: Culture, Identity and Modernity in Britain and the Empire, 1660–1840* (Cambridge, 2004), pp. 155–75.

56   John Robertson, 'Empire and Union: Two Concepts of the Early Modern Political Order', in John Robertson (ed.), *A Union for Empire: Political Thought and the British Union of 1707* (Cambridge, 1995), pp. 3–37.

57   See Stewart J. Brown (ed.), *William Robertson and the Expansion of Empire* (Cambridge, 1997).

7
Jonathan Swift and Charles Leslie

Ian Higgins

This essay examines literary relations between two famous and important propagandists, the juring High Churchman Jonathan Swift (1667–1745) and the Nonjuror Charles Leslie (1650–1722). It will draw attention to the evidence of Swift's elective affinities with Leslie in political theology and rhetorical strategy despite the official political distance between them. Leslie was not just another pious Nonjuror. He was an incendiary Jacobite polemicist whose explosive rhetoric ignited paper wars. Reviled by the Whigs, Leslie was *outré* for the Tories. To quote or be associated with so polemical a figure as Leslie was to be tainted with treason. In print Tory writers kept their distance from him, even when essentially taking Leslie's side, as is well illustrated in one of Mary Astell's pamphlets published in 1704, the full title of which is: *A Fair Way with the Dissenters and their Patrons. Not Writ by Mr. L[esle]y, or any other Furious Jacobite, whether Clergyman or Layman; but by a very Moderate Person and Dutiful Subject to the Queen.*[1] It seems incredible that Swift, while protesting that he was not a Jacobite, should be prepared to cite Leslie favourably in print. In his willingness to record his respect for Leslie, Swift was perhaps unique among literary figures of his time. This essay will indicate that Swift drew upon Leslie's polemical arsenal in his own polemic and satire.

Leslie and Swift were of different generations, and although they had mutual friends, such as the Nonjuror Robert Nelson, the two Church of Ireland clergymen and graduates of Trinity College Dublin seem not to have been personally acquainted. In the late 1720s Swift would become friendly with Charles Leslie's sons, Robert and Henry, former exiles like their father, whom Swift met on visits to the north of Ireland where they were then living. They figure in two of Swift's outspoken political poems, 'The Revolution at Market Hill' (c. 1729) and 'Traulus' (1730).[2] 'Robin' and 'Harry' Leslie received the ultimate Swiftian token of esteem, having a poem of affectionate abuse addressed to them. The raillery in the poem 'Robin and Harry' (1729) attests to Swift's intimacy with the brothers and their circumstances.[3] The literary appearance of Leslie's sons in Swift's poetry can be rapidly sketched.

Like his father, Robert Leslie had been a Jacobite activist at the Stuart court in exile and had been involved in producing propaganda for distribution in Britain during George I's reign. He had literary interests, and appears to have facilitated Swift's contact and literary exchanges with Charles Wogan, Andrew Michael Ramsay and other Jacobites on the continent.[4] The raillery of Robin in 'Robin and Harry' presents the character of Robert Leslie that we find in the Stuart papers: the 'confident, positive, notional spark', talkative, self-important, extravagant and heavily indebted.[5] Swift's poem reports how 'Robin from noon to night will prate,/Runs out in tongue, as in estate', and refers to his 'broken fortunes' and 'courtly style'.[6] The Oxford Jacobite Dr. William King thought Swift's humorous portrait of Robin an accurate likeness.[7] At the exiled Stuart court, Robert Leslie was looked upon as a mercurial political projector, 'not far from being ripe for B[edla]m' and James III had called him 'mad'.[8] Swift gives 'mad' Robin (if it is him) a speaking part in 'Traulus. The First Part. In a Dialogue Between Tom and Robin', a virulent satire on the Whig politician Joshua, Viscount Allen. 'Tom' and 'Robin' in the poem may have been meant to signify Tory madmen, but they turn out to be sane and sage compared to Viscount Allen, with 'Robin' in the poem diagnosing 'Traulus' (Viscount Allen) as mad.[9]

The younger brother, Henry Leslie had served as an officer in the Spanish army. He was an essayist and part of Swift's regular circle in Ireland sharing literary interests with Swift, especially in relation to Cervantes.[10] In 'The Revolution at Market Hill', the 'Dean and Spaniard' are allies, fellow 'sufferers in a ruined cause'. The poem boasts of their active service in the Tory cause: of 'their two fames the world enough rings', of their 'services and sufferings'. They 'ventured to be hanged'.[11]

While Charles Leslie has always figured in ecclesiastical histories of the Nonjurors, the work of political historians over the last thirty years has seen his restoration to the canon of early modern and eighteenth-century political thought, redressing that neglect or lack of acknowledgement of his theological and political writings complained of by Leslie's nineteenth century biographer.[12] Specialist studies have been published devoted to Leslie and necessary work done on the bibliography of his writings.[13] I think, however, that this Jacobite High Churchman, a high-profile author of some eighty-five works, remains a relatively neglected and unnoticed figure as far as literary history is concerned. He was certainly underrepresented in one of the standard reference works of the second half of the twentieth century, the *New Cambridge Bibliography of English Literature*, where he does not appear in the index, or under 'Essayists and Pamphleteers'. He did gain an entry under 'Philosophy', where he is mentioned for *The Snake in the Grass*, *A Short and Easie Method with the Deists*, and his

Theological Works. His *Cassandra* and *The Rehearsal* appear under 'Periodical Publications' and under 'Scottish Literature: Prose, Jacobite Literature' Leslie's *Galienus Redivivus* is listed.[14] There has been some interest in Leslie's political-theological literary criticism of Milton's *Paradise Lost* expressed in works such as *The History of Sin and Heresie* (1698).[15] But Leslie's own writings, particularly the pamphlets, have an intrinsic literary interest and deserve more attention in their own right.

Leslie is one of the pamphleteering genre's great masters and the most visible, vitriolic and vilified of all Jacobite writers. His pamphlets display an array of rhetorical resources: arresting titles, diatribe and exaggeration, violent imagery and sardonic jokerie, irony, parody, obliquity and innu-endo, ambiguity and paradox. He is a memorable polemical phrase maker, capable of delivering the epigrammatic finishing stroke. On the subject of the episcopal church's plight, its rights invaded by the Pope's supremacy and by the Erastian state, Leslie writes: 'the *Western Church* was (like her *Master*) Crucify'd betwixt the *Usurpations* of the *Pontificat* on the One side, and the *Regale* on the Other'. On the interconnection of politics and theo-logy and the church's danger he observes: '*Republican* and *Whigg* are *Jack Presbyters Lay-Elders*; *Rebellion* is his *Lay-Face*, as *Schism* his *Ecclesiastical*'; 'A *Whigg* is a *State Enthusiast*, as a *Dissenter* is an *Ecclesiastical*'. King William, 'educated under the *Geneva* Model, made *Erastian* in *Holland*', is a tyrant, a '*Gallienus redivivus*'. Several theories justifying the transfer of allegiance in 1689 (conquest, abdication, desertion and possession) are summarily satirised in a sardonic domestic allegory bringing home to readers the Jacobite view of the illegality of the transfer of the crown:

Because a Wife may be Ravished, and forc'd from her Husband, therefore it is Lawful for her to yield to an *Adulterer*, Nay, to invite him to come, and Drive away her *Husband*, to Intrigue with this *Gallant* under-hand, Contrive and Assist him to Frighten her *Husband* out of his House to save his Life, and then to make a Present of it, together with her self, to her *Deliverer*. And then it is Justly and Legally their own, for, *What made him Run away and leave his House*? And his Wife holds still Faithful to her Matrimonial Vow; she only *Changes the Object*, she is for *Matrimony* still: And Therefore, by her Vow to her *First* Husband, she is Bound to the *Second*. She only Transferrs her Allegiance: And therefore it is the same Allegiance still ... We are still Faithful to our Oath of *Allegiance*; we only *Change the Object*; we are for *Monarchy* still; and therefore by our Oath of Allegiance to K. *James*, we are Bound to K. *William* ....

The Jacobite elision of William of Orange with Cromwell, and of the Revolution against James II with the Rebellion against Charles I, appear in satirical epitome in a rhetorical query put by Leslie to his opponents in 1694: 'Whether Dame *Britannia* were not less culpable in being forc'd to endure a Thirteen Years Rape from *Oliver* and the *Rump*, than by living a Five Years Adulteress now by Consent?' In answer to William Higden's argument that the authority to coin money entitled a government to the allegiance of the subject, Leslie, in a later pamphlet, offered this short summation of Higden's case: '*Allegiance* must follow the *Coin*. It generally do's indeed –'.[16]

Leslie's pamphlets also display (a now rather fashionable) attention to the paratexts of books and pamphlets. In answering Whig works, he is alert to the effect and significance of titles, dedications, mottos, epigraphs, prefaces, postscripts, notes, typography, italics, publisher's name and lists, the price of a work and where it is sold or read, citations and reprints, and its reception in different communities of political allegiance. If there had been dust-jackets, Leslie would have commented on the Whig ones. Leslie also looked for what a text does not say; its silences and omissions. In his examination of Archbishop Tillotson's sermons and Bishop Burnet's discourses on the Trinity and divinity of Christ, Leslie sought to expose a heretical episcopate elevated by the Erastian usurpation of 1690. In *The Charge of Socinianism against Dr. Tillotson Considered* (1695), Leslie explains that it is not the words on the page but what is meant by the words in context that is important: 'for the Dispute is not about the words *Trinity*, or *Person*, but as to the *Sense* of these words, in which they are used by *Divines*. The *Socinians* own a *Trinity* ... But all the matter is in what Sense the word *Trinity* is us'd by our *Divines*, and by the *Socinians*.'[17] Leslie found ambiguities, and positions that seemed susceptible to Socinian inflection in Tillotson's sermons, and noted that Socinians (or Unitarians) certainly approved the doctrine they found in Tillotson's sermons. Socinians rejected the Athanasian Creed on the Trinity. Leslie's reading of Tillotson seems to have been successful in pointing out what was not said on the printed page. In his 'Life' of Gilbert Burnet, affixed to Burnet's *History of His Own Time*, Thomas Burnet quoted a letter from Tillotson to Gilbert Burnet in 1694 about Burnet's *Exposition of the Thirty Nine Articles* in which the Archbishop commented: 'The Account given of *Athanasius's* Creed, seems to me no-wise satisfactory; I wish we were well rid of it.' Against this sentence in the margin of his friend John Lyon's copy of Burnet's *History* Jonathan Swift drew a pointing finger.[18]

Some of Swift's more famous satiric passages and satiric strategies were anticipated in Leslie's writings and may owe particular debts to him. There appears to be tacit awareness, assimilation or appropriation of Leslie's polemical writing in Swift: evidence of Swift's undeclared allusion to and borrowing from him. Swift's satires such as *A Tale of a Tub*, *An Argument Against Abolishing Christianity*, and the 'Isaac Bickerstaff' pamphlets attacking John Partridge, were interventions in paper wars in which Leslie was a major combatant as High Church champion.

Leslie's polemic against the Quakers in the 1690s and his accounts of Scots Presbyterian activities are important sources for the satire on Dissent in Swift's great early satiric volume of 1704 containing *A Tale of a Tub*, with its religious allegory of Peter (Popery), Martin (the Church of England), and Jack (Protestant Dissent), and *The Mechanical Operation of the Spirit* with its 'History of Fanaticism'. General and particular details about 'Knocking Jack of the North' in Swift's satire: Jack's appearance, tailoring, pranks and antics, quackery, ideas and idiom, heretical ancestry, links with Peter (Popery), Islam and Socinianism, can be annotated precisely from Leslie's polemic or from the anti-sectarian sources to which Leslie gives prominence, such as Ephraim Pagitt's *Heresiography: or, A Description of the Hereticks and Sectaries of these Latter Times* (1645), Thomas Edwards's *Gangræna* (1645), and Richard Blome's *The Fanatick History: Or, An Exact Relation and Account of The Old Anabaptists and New Quakers* (1660).[19]

The great literary work to emerge out of the Socinian controversy of the late seventeenth and early eighteenth centuries is Swift's *An Argument to prove, That the Abolishing of Christianity in England, May, as Things now Stand, be attended with some Inconveniencies, and perhaps, not produce those many good Effects proposed thereby*, written in 1708, and first published in 1711. Swift's satire may have had a topical occasion in a flare up of the Socinian controversy in 1707–1708 in which the high-profile polemicists were Leslie, the former Dublin-based Socinian celebrity Thomas Emlyn, and the Irish High Churchman Francis Higgins who had been taken into custody in March 1707 for insinuating that the 'Church was in danger'. In the *Argument Against Abolishing Christianity* Swift is mock-anxious about offending the Whig government with any hint that 'the Church is in Danger':

> NOR do I think it wholly groundless, or my Fears altogether imaginary; that the Abolishing of Christianity may perhaps bring the Church in Danger; or at least put the Senate to the Trouble of another Securing Vote. I desire, I may not be mistaken; I am far from presuming to affirm or think, that the Church is in Danger at present, or as Things now stand; but we know not how soon it may be so, when the Christian Religion is repealed.[20]

Swift's much-remarked paradox that the Church is not in danger, but that it might be if Christianity is abolished, had been anticipated by Leslie in a pamphlet supporting Higgins and his concerns about anti-Trinitarianism. Leslie sardonically wrote: 'As to the Churches being in Danger, that's over, and out of the Question: But it is too evident that Christianity is in Danger, from the many virulent Pamphlets and Books that daily come out against its Fundamental Principles'.[21] Swift's satire of 1708 specifies the anti-Trinitarians as the principal writers who want to abolish Christianity. On the heretical threat and the Church in danger, Swift was in agreement with Leslie, whose massive *The Socinian Controversy Discuss'd* was published in 1708.[22]

In his first book of 1692, and later in his *Rehearsals*, Leslie anathematised the Whig astrologer John Partridge, deploring his almanacs with their Whig commentary, chronologies, martyrology, and festival days. In '*Partridge*'s Almanack for the Year 1692', Leslie notes, the anniversary of the Battle of Naseby is regarded as a festival day and he leaves out 'the 30th. of *January*', the anniversary of the execution of Charles I, 'with *Good-friday*, *Ashwednesday*, and other Superstitious Days' from his list of solemn dates.[23] Moonlighting as an astrologer called Isaac Bickerstaff, Swift went further than Leslie and killed Partridge. Operating anonymously and pseudonymously in a sequence of premeditated mock-astrological pamphlets in 1708, Swift predicted and then reported Partridge's death in circumstantial detail, and then vindicated his report of Partridge's death when the Whig astrologer claimed in print that he was alive and had been alive on the night he was said to have died. A Whig response to Swift's pamphlets took the form of a mock-astrological sequel in which it is predicted that '*Les[le]y*, the *Rehearser*…will infallibly be hanged' later in the year, followed by the 'Exit of several Eminent' Jacobite High Churchmen, '*A-la-mode de Lesley*'.[24]

Leslie's polemic against the Dutch, and against the Hanoverian regime, provide close analogues for passages in Swift's great later satire, *Gulliver's Travels*, a work which was recommended to James III and which he was pleased to receive.[25] Gulliver's disquisition, in Part IV of Swift's satire, on a corrupt legal system in Hanoverian Britain where hereditary title to property seems no longer recognised, reprises the contemporary Jacobite insinuation that all Hanoverian property was theft. As Chevalier Ramsay put it in a work of 1722, if 'there is no difference between a lawful King and an Usurper, there is none betwixt a natural Heir and an unjust Possessor; betwixt a true Proprietor, and a Robber'.[26] This claim and the satiric *topos* equating political leaders with highwaymen and robbers made famous in literary works such as John Gay's *The Beggar's Opera* and Henry Fielding's *Jonathan Wild* had been anticipated in Leslie's polemic against the 'Elector of Brunswick': 'The great Thief that gives our Subject, Hangs those that have not stole a Shilling, where he has stolen Millions; and the Law that Hangs them, pleads a greater necessity for his being brought to the same Justice; because his continuing in the Throne of another warrants all the Robberies that Men can commit.'[27] Swift's satiric strategy of contrasting European corruption with a mythical ideal state of nature used in Part IV of *Gulliver's Travels* has, among several antecedents, a polemical precursor in a fictional dialogue between 'Higden', 'Hoadly' and 'Hottentote' appended to Leslie's *The Finishing Stroke* of 1711 in which there are some fifteen pages of misanthropic satire directed at militarism, luxury and pride. The mythic state of nature described by Leslie's Hottentot, like the state of nature embodied in Swift's Houyhnhnms, affords a powerful moral contrast to the corruption of civilised European society.[28]

Swift did not subscribe to Leslie's Filmerian patriarchalist political philosophy, expounded in works such as *The Finishing Stroke*, though Swift shared a Biblical literalism with Leslie.[29] But both High Churchmen were often, and were perceived to be, saying the same things in the area of political theology. The intertextual relation between Swift and Leslie has never been considered in detail in the literary criticism on Swift where the usual move among biographers and critics is to look the other way and associate Swift with John Locke.

There are nine explicit references to Leslie in Swift's prose works. By comparison there are six explicit references to Locke: three which date from 1707 are mocking and hostile, identifying Locke's paternity of Matthew Tindal's execrable ideas and language, one is neutral, one is complimentary in an apolitical context, and one occurs in the fourth *Drapier's Letter* of 1724 where Swift is quoting Whig ideologues against the English Whig government in support of Irish legislative independence from the English parliament. Leslie also used radical Whig theory against the Whigs in his Irish writings when he argued that Acts of an English Parliament are not binding on Ireland, thus asserting Irish legislative independence.[30] Leslie was a proscribed man when Swift was referring to him in the last years of Anne's reign. *The Rehearsal* had been closed down in March 1709 and Leslie was outlawed in 1710 for writing *The Good Old Cause, or, lying in truth, being a Second Defence of the Lord Bishop of Sarum, from a Second Speech. And also, the Dissection of a Sermon it is said His Lordship Preached in the Cathedral Church of Salisbury last 29th of May* (1710), and he was in exile at the Jacobite court in 1711. Leslie's work attacking Whigs and Dissenters also impales the conforming Tories as time-serving apostates from true Church principles of hereditary right monarchy and passive obedience. Swift was the apologist and propagandist for the Harley Tory government which shunned Leslie, and as Tory Examiner Swift dissociated the government from 'an open *Nonjuror*, whose Character and Person, as well as good Learning and Sense, discovered upon other Subjects, do indeed deserve Respect and Esteem; but his *Rehearsal*, and the rest of his Political Papers' have a pernicious effect because of their influence.[31] Swift's explicit references to Leslie are cautious but respectful. Leslie is both a formidable ally and opponent.

Swift's first references to Leslie, chronologically, occur in Swift's unpublished 'Remarks' upon Tindal's *Rights of the Christian Church* of 1706, and were written in 1707. Tindal's sensational book drew on Hobbes's Erastianism and Locke's political theory, as Leslie and Swift noticed. Tindal particularly targets Leslie's formulation of the doctrine of the two societies and claims for ecclesiastical authority. In *The Case of the Regale and of the Pontificate Stated* Leslie accepts that a Christian king's authority extends over all subjects, ecclesiastical and lay, but that regal authority does not have a spiritual character. The Church was wholly independent from the State in its purely spiritual power and authority. Church and State 'ought to Assist the other, without *Incroaching* upon one another's Province. The *State* may *Protect* and *Honour* the *Church*, without Invading any Part of her *Office*: As the *Church* ought to Enforce *Obedience* to the *Civil Magistrate*, in all *Lawful* Things, without assuming any *Temporal* Power over him.'[32] The '*State* cannot Deprive *Bishops* of their *Episcopal Character*'. For the Nonjuror this means that the state cannot legally deprive bishops of the exercise of their episcopal function within their dominions or sees or substitute others in their places.[33] Leslie adduces the whole verse of Isaiah 49.23 as Scriptural authority on the true relation between Church and Crown: '*Kings shall be thy Nursing Fathers, and Queens thy Nursing-Mothers: They shall Bow down to thee with their Face toward the Earth, and Lick up the Dust of thy Feet.* Hence it Appear'd, That the *Office* here Ascrib'd to *Kings* and *Queens*, was an *Office* of *Servitude*, and not of *Authority*'.[34]

Tindal quotes Leslie to the effect that the Mitre has always stood next to the Crown in the civil constitution, that the office ascribed to kings was an office of servitude in relation to the Church, and that it is a sign of God's judgement on the Crown for the sacrilegious lay impropriation of Church lands that the Crown has 'become an Honourable Beggar for its daily Bread.'[35] Although Swift affects at the start of his 'Remarks' not to know if 'the Author of the *Regale*' has carried any points further than Scripture or reason will allow, his remark on Tindal's attack on Leslie at this point is: 'Mr. *Lesly* may carry Things too far, as it is natural, because the other Extreme is so great. But what he says of the King's Losses, since the Church Lands were given away, is too great a Truth'.[36] Swift's 'Remarks' on Tindal's *Rights* may have drawn upon Leslie's *The Second Part of The Wolf Stript of His Shepherds Cloathing: In Answer to a Late Celebrated Book Intituled The Rights of the Christian Church Asserted*, published in 1707, in its substantive argument and in its *ad hominem* satire. There are similarities. Leslie sees Tindal as a follower of 'Mr. *Lock*' who 'has *stumbled*' on more absurd notions. Swift finds that Tindal 'limpeth' after 'Mr. *Locke*'.[37] Swift's much commented upon distinction in his 'Remarks' between the establishment and the being of the Church, is found in Leslie, who points out that Tindal, by saying the Church of England, being established by Acts of Parliament, is a perfect creature of the civil power, 'confounds the *Constitution* of the *Church* and her *Establishment* by Law; the *Establishment* by *Law* may be *alter'd* or taken away, as of *Episcopacy* in *Scotland*: but the *Constitution* of the *Church* she must receive from her *Founder*'[38] and 'Christ most certainly *Founded*' the Church '*Independant* of all *Powers* upon *Earth*.'[39] Swift writes that 'the Church of *England* is no Creature of the Civil Power, either as to its Polity or Doctrines. The Fundamentals of both were deduced from Christ and his Apostles, and the instructions of the purest and earliest Ages'.[40] Swift writes that 'Our Saviour telleth us, *His Kingdom is not of this World*; and therefore, to be sure, the World is not of his Kingdom, nor can ever please him by interfering in the Administration of it'.[41] The civil power might hinder the Church from consecrating bishops or refuse those that are consecrated or go even further. Swift puts the case 'that walking on the slack Rope were the only Talent required by Act of Parliament for making a Man a Bishop; no Doubt, when a Man had done his Feat of Activity in Form, he might sit in the House of Lords, put on his Robes and his Rotchet, go down to his Palace, receive and spend his Rents; but it requireth very little Christianity to believe this Tumbler to be one whit more a Bishop than he was before; because the Law of God hath otherwise decreed; which Law, although a Nation may refuse to receive it, cannot alter in its own Nature'.[42] (Rope dancing is the qualification for high office under the Emperor of Lilliput, Swift's fictional image of a Whig King in Part I of *Gulliver's Travels*).[43] Like Leslie, Swift writes that the Church's power is from Christ, the liberty of exercising that power depends upon the permission, connivance or authority of the civil government. The ecclesiastical constitution of the episcopal Church is by divine law. Its Being remains although its Establishment may be taken away.[44] In ecclesiology there is substantial agreement between the juring High Churchman and the Nonjuror.[45]

In a letter of February 1704 Swift refers to 'Lesley' as having written several pamphlets 'of late, violent against Presbyterians and Low Churchmen'.[46] In *The Sentiments of a Church of England Man*, written in 1708 and published in 1711, Swift refers to such pamphlets when he comments that if 'Mr. *Lesly*' 'could make the Nation see his Adversaries, under the Colours he paints them in; we had nothing else to do, but rise as one Man, and destroy such Wretches from the Face of the Earth'.[47] The allusion to Genesis 7.6 ('destroy from off the face of the earth') was a favourite of both Swift and Leslie. In *The Shortest-Way with the Dissenters* Defoe had shown that the violent tropes in pamphlets by Leslie were being understood precisely as literal incitement. In the 'Sentiments' Swift alludes obliquely to the controversy surrounding *The Shortest-Way with the Dissenters* and to one of its sequels, *The Experiment: or, The Shortest Way with the Dissenters Exemplified* (1705). Swift comes to Leslie's defence: 'But, I suppose it is presumed, the common People understand *Raillery*, or at least *Rhetorick*; and will not take *Hyperboles* in too literal a Sense; which, however, in some Junctures might prove a desperate Experiment'.[48] The most extended of Swift's explicit references to Leslie occurs in his *A Preface to the Bishop of Sarum's Introduction to the Third Volume of the History of the Reformation of the Church of England* (1713), where he alludes to Leslie's *The Case Stated between the Church of Rome and the Church of England* (1713), a work which was part of Leslie's attempt to convert James III. Burnet thought Leslie 'the violentest Jacobite in the nation'[49] and

Leslie personifies the Jacobite counter-revolution and counter-reformation in Burnet's *Introduction*. Swift responds to Burnet as follows:

> Without doubt, Mr. *Lesly* is most unhappily misled in his Politicks; but if he be the Author of the late Tract against Popery, he hath given the World such a Proof of his Soundness in Religion, as *many a Bishop* ought to be proud of. I never saw the Gentleman in my Life: I know he is the Son of a great and excellent Prelate, who, upon several Accounts, was one of the most extraordinary Men of his Age. Mr. *Lesly* hath written many useful Discourses upon several Subjects, and hath so well deserved of the Christian Religion, and the Church of *England* in particular, that to accuse him of *Impudence for proposing an Union* in two very different Faiths, is a Stile which I hope few will imitate. I detest Mr. *Lesly*'s Political Principles as much as his Lordship can do for his Heart; but I verily believe he acts from a mistaken Conscience, and therefore I distinguish between the Principles and the Person. However, it is some Mortification to me, when I see an *avowed Nonjuror* contribute more to the confounding of *Popery*, than could ever be done by a hundred thousand such *Introductions* as this.[50]

Leslie is a political untouchable for Harley's propagandist, but there is elective affinity with the High Churchman here.

Leslie took notice of Swift's writings. In 1701 Swift produced a high-brow pamphlet of parallel classical history entitled *A Discourse of the Contests and Dissensions between the Nobles and Commons in Athens and Rome*. Ostensibly it was a defence of Whig Lords (Somers, Orford and Portland, as well as Halifax) threatened with impeachment by the Tory House of Commons over the partition treaties.[51] The work bore the imprint of a trade publisher, John Nutt, who was identified with the Tory interest,[52] but it was rumoured to be the work of Bishop Gilbert Burnet. Leslie interrogated it in the *New Association* of 1702 and in the Supplement of the *New Association Part II* in 1703, believing it to be the work of Burnet as rumoured. Leslie expresses astonishment at Burnet's changed views. Leslie approves the work's indictment of popular power and notes appreciatively its attack on the Puritan faction.[53] Leslie must have found the pamphlet's imagery rather familiar. Swift's most graphic anti-populist imagery in the *Discourse* derives from Psalms 65.7, comparing the madness of the people and the raging of the sea. It was one of Leslie's favourite allusions, quoted in his first book of 1692, answering William King's *The State of the Protestants in Ireland Under the Late King James's Government*, and the imagery appears afterwards in *The Rehearsal* and in political pamphlets such as *Best of All*.[54] After Leslie's critique of his *Discourse*, Swift also came to feel it was a Tory work, and he reprinted it in his *Miscellanies in Prose and Verse* of 1711, when he was now editor of the Tory *Examiner*. (In the reprint Swift removed a defence of bribing members of parliament, a compromising passage that Leslie had exposed in the original edition). There is an oblique glance at Leslie's answer to his *Discourse* in Swift's *Sentiments of a Church of England Man*, published in the *Miscellanies*. Swift hints that he is one of those good men, mentioned by Leslie in a postscript to *The New Association Part II*, who had found themselves associated with the wrong party by circumstances of early friendships and patronage.[55]

There may be undeclared but approving allusion to *A Tale of a Tub*, the publishing sensation of May 1704, in Leslie's *Rehearsal* later in that year. For instance, the *Rehearsal* of 9 December 1704 presents the Countryman's allegory of his house (the Church) and his servants (the Dissenters). The Dissenters find fault with the clothes they are required to wear and proceed to schismatic violence, which is imagined as coat tearing. This allegorical *Rehearsal* seems to recall the *Tale*'s sartorial allegory, where Dissenting Jack tears the coat (Christian doctrine and faith) that his father requires him to wear and preserve. In *A Tale of a Tub* Swift found satiric potential in that origin myth, advanced in the work of Edmund Spenser and Sir William Temple among others, which claimed that the Scots and the 'Irish Scots' had a Scythian ancestry. There is much insistence on the barbaric Scythian ancestry of the sectarian targets of Swift's satire in *A Tale of a Tub*. The fanatic writers have '*Scythian* Ancestors',[56] as do sectarian, especially Quaker preachers.[57] The Puritan Roundheads are the posterity of the Scythian Long-Heads,[58] and so on. Leslie's virulent attack on Scots Presbyterians in the *Rehearsal* of 30 December 1704, deploys the Scythian simile: 'You must know that at the beginning of the *revolution*, in *Decem.* 1688, our *Cameronian* ZEALOTS had the *wink* tipp'd to them, and took *arms*, and shew'd their *moderation* to the *clergy*, like the *Scythians*, O, most CURIOUSLY! plundering, tearing, and murdering....'

There are similarities in the way Swift and Leslie negotiated the conditions of censorship and answered Whig charges of Jacobitism in print. For the first five years following the Hanoverian accession, Swift practised the genre of silence.[59] Swift's poetic obituary for himself, *Verses on the Death of Dr. Swift, D.S.P.D.* (published in 1739), has this to note about his silent years: 'Upon the Queen's death, the Dean returned to live in Dublin, at his deanery house: numberless libels were writ against him in England, as a Jacobite; he was insulted in the street, and at nights was forced to be attended by his servants armed.'[60] Swift ended his silence in 1720, resuming normal pamphleteering service in the Irish political theatre with *A Proposal for the Universal Use of Irish Manufacture*. The printer, Edward Waters, was tried for sedition and the anonymous author was alleged to be for the Pretender. The Waters trial may have prompted Swift to produce his self-justificatory political position statement, which took the form of a pamphlet 'Letter to Alexander Pope' dated 10 January 1721. The last ten paragraphs of the 'Letter' set out Swift's political tenets. Swift admits that 'I have passed for a disaffected person', but declares: 'I have neither been so ill a Subject nor so stupid an Author, as I have been represented by the virulence of Libellers, ... I am too much a politician to expose my own safety by offensive words'.[61] It was, of course, Swift's printers who exposed their safety. Swift used Tory printers in Ireland who had some Jacobite form, that is, the political risk-takers: Edward Waters, John Hyde, John and Sarah Harding.[62] Swift's 'Political Catechism' is cast in the past tense, 'what my Political principles were in the time of her late glorious Majesty, which I never contradicted by any action, writing, or discourse'.[63] The 'Letter to Pope' presents itself as an apologia, but most of his political principles, such as antipathy to standing armies, adoration of the Gothic and ancient law of annual, freely-elected parliaments, opposition to corruption and to the suspension of the Habeas Corpus Act, for instance, are consonant with the current Jacobite and Opposition critique of the Hanoverian Whig regime.

The way Swift casts his 'Political Catechism' in the past tense, in my view, introduces a note of ambiguity on the question of his current allegiance, leaving residual doubt about what his sentiments are 'at present' on the dynastic question. The first of Swift's political principles in the time of Queen Anne was: 'I always declared my self against a Popish Successor to the Crown, whatever Title he might have by the proximity of blood: Neither did I ever regard the right line except upon two accounts, first as it was establish'd by law; and secondly, as it hath much weight in the opinions of the people.' Whiggish revolution principles perhaps, but a Jacobite application seems calculated when he adds that 'necessity may abolish any Law' and 'Right of inheritance' is 'perhaps the most popular of all topicks'. A popular rising for the right line and revocation of the Act of Settlement was being plotted by Bishop Atterbury in the year Swift penned this apologia.[64] Swift's declaration against a popish successor in Queen Anne's time is not quite the unequivocal anti-Jacobitism that it may appear to be. In Queen Anne's reign, Leslie, answering his Whig antagonists in the *Rehearsal* and in his political pamphlets, declared himself in favour of a Protestant succession, as he put it in a pamphlet of 1712: '*Lesley* ... wishes a *Protestant Succession* as much as you, or any man in *Britain*'. As Swift was well aware, Leslie had sought to bring a Protestant succession about by attempting to convert James.[65]

Leslie's pamphlets in 1710 such as *Now or Never: Or, A Project under God, To Secure the Church [and Monarchy] of England ... By a well-meaning Tory, who is willing to clear the Church of England from Jacobitism* and *Beaucoup de Bruit pour une Aumelette, or Much a Do about Nothing, being a Tryall of Skill Betwixt the Jacobite's Hopes Reviv'd, and The Good Old Cause, By a True Trojan* are masterpieces of multiple irony. They offer a model of how to ridicule paranoid Whig Jacobite-spotting and scaremongering, acquit the Tories of treason, yet through innuendo and double meaning appeal to the Jacobite

Tory constituency. Leslie's pamphlets anticipate Swift's achievements in this polemical enterprise. Answering Benjamin Hoadly's *The Jacobite's Hopes Reviv'd*, which claimed to have discovered Jacobitism in Leslie's *The Good Old Cause*, Leslie writes: 'But pray, Sir, What has *High-Church* to do with a profess'd *Jacobite*, as you Represent Mr. *Leslie*? Tho' it will Puzzle you to shew where he has so *Professed* himself.' It is the reader, Hoadly, not the pamphlet's author, Leslie, upon whom 'must be Charged all the *Jacobitism* you have *Innuendo'd* in the *Good Old Cause*.' Leslie responds ingenuously: 'I *Innuendo* not whom you Mean ... I only Repeat your own *Words*'.[66] As Tory 'Examiner' in 1710–1711, Swift rejected Whig claims of Tory Pretenderism: '*Dodwell*, *Hicks*, and *Lesley*, are gravely quoted, to prove that the *Tories* design to bring in the *Pretender*; and if I should quote them to prove that the same Thing is intended by the *Whigs*, it would be full as reasonable; since I am sure they have at least as much to do with *Nonjurors* as we'.[67]

In pamphlets written in Hanoverian Ireland, such as *A Vindication of his Excellency John, Lord Carteret, From The Charge of favouring none but Tories, High-Churchmen and Jacobites* (1730) and *An Examination of Certain Abuses, Corruptions, and Enormities in the City of Dublin* (1732) Swift mocked Whig Jacobite-spotting, while enabling readers to see the just grounds for Tory disaffection, and reanimating and inventing Jacobite slanders against George II.[68] In a 'Letter' prefacing a new edition of *Gulliver's Travels* in 1735, Lemuel Gulliver says that he has been told 'that People in Power were very watchful over the Press; and apt not only to interpret, but to punish every thing which looked like an *Inuendo*'. Gulliver wonders how his south-seas voyages written in another reign could 'be applied to any of the *Yahoos*, who are now said to govern the Herd'. But Swift's Tory or Country opposition rhetoric in the *Travels* was readily construed as seditious by contemporaries. In Part II of the *Travels*, for example, the King of Brobdingnag's critique of England's taxes and national debt, its foreign deployment of the fleet and mercenary standing army, looked like 'a common *Jacobite* Insinuation'.[69]

Operating under conditions of censorship throughout his writing life, Leslie used various strategies of ironic indirection. Jacobite meanings are insinuated by innuendo, or they are purveyed while their presence is ostensibly denied, disavowed, or imputed to wild Whig paranoid reading. Leslie's second political work, and his first in an ironic mode, was *The Anatomy of a Jacobite. Or, The Jacobites Heart Laid Open, With a Sure & Certain Method for their Cure*. It was addressed to the apostate Nonjuror William Sherlock and published in 1692. It opens with 'the Words of King *Lemuel*', applied to Sherlock as the Revolution government's best writer: 'I Congratulate your Good Success in the Words of King *Lemuel. Many have done Nobly*, to this Theam, *but thou Excellest* them all.' Leslie then ingenuously lists the principal Jacobite objections to the Revolution settlement, for

Sherlock's convenience, so that Sherlock might attempt to refute them, and thus help Sherlock to retain his reputation and reclaim the Jacobites. Perhaps it is just a coincidence, an accidental homage, that Swift's master-piece of political satire in this ironic idiom, *Gulliver's Travels*, should also use the words of a Lemuel.[70] Whether or not Swift was always against a popish successor after 1715 is debatable. He did say, in another letter to Pope (of 20 September 1723) that: 'I have often made the same remark with you of my Infelicity in being so strongly attached to Traytors (as they call them) and Exiles, and state Criminalls'.[71] However, it is the case that Swift found much that was useful in the writings of the most prominent and most polemical of all Jacobite pamphleteers, a writer denounced as an extremist by Whig and Tory alike. It is a sign of Swift's independence as a writer he was prepared to refer to Leslie favourably and to cite him. Such citation was probably unique for someone who claimed not to be a Jacobite. Swift's writings disclose real sympathies with Leslie's hard-line High Church positions and an affinity with the pamphleteer's sardonic ridicule and rhetorical violence.

Notes

1 On Astell dissociating herself from Leslie, see Ruth Perry, *The Celebrated Mary Astell: An Early English Feminist* (Chicago and London: University of Chicago Press, 1986), pp. 186–8.
2 Jonathan Swift, 'The Revolution at Market Hill' and 'Traulus' in Jonathan Swift, *The Complete Poems*, ed. Pat Rogers (Harmondsworth, 1983), pp. 396–8, 422–7. For traces of Swift's friendship with the Leslies, see *The Correspondence of Jonathan Swift* (hereafter *CW*), ed. David Woolley (5 vols , Frankfurt am Main, 1999), IV, pp. 186, 222. Robert lived at the family estate, which he had inher-ited, at Glaslough, County Monaghan close to the Armagh border. Henry lived at Markethill, in County Armagh.
3 'Robin and Harry', in *The Complete Poems*, pp. 379–80.
4 See Ian Higgins, 'Jonathan Swift and the Jacobite Diaspora', in Hermann J. Real and Helgard Stöver-Leidig (eds), *Reading Swift: Papers from The Fourth Münster Symposium on Jonathan Swift* (Munich, 2003), pp. 87–103 (pp. 87, 97); Marsha Keith Schuchard, 'Ramsay, Swift, and the Jacobite-Masonic Version of the Stuart Restoration', in Richard Caron et al. (eds), *Ésotérisme, Gnoses & Imaginaire Symbolique* (Leuven, 2001), pp. 491–505 (p. 505). On Robert's literary interests, see Historical Manuscripts Commission (henceforth HMC), *Calendar of the Stuart Papers Belonging to His Majesty the King Preserved at Windsor Castle* (8 vols, London, 1902–20) II, pp. 102–3.
5 *Calendar of the Stuart Papers*, III, p. 379. The debts were accumulated while in exile, for the circumstances of which see the letter of the Jacobite banker William Gordon on the debts owed by Charles and his son in 1716, in *Calendar of the Stuart Papers*, II, p. 452.
6 'Robin and Harry', lines 9–10, 31, 50; *The Complete Poems*, pp. 379–80.
7 William King, *Political and Literary Anecdotes of His Own Times* (2nd edn, London, 1819), pp. 137–40.

8   *Calendar of the Stuart Papers*, III, p. 350; *Calendar of the Stuart Papers*, VI, p. 408.
9   *The Complete Poems*, pp. 422–5, and notes pp. 816–17.
10 See A. C. Elias, Jr., 'Swift's *Don Quixote*, Dunkin's *Virgil Travesty*, and Other New Intelligence: John Lyon's "Materials for a Life of Dr. Swift", 1765', *Swift Studies*, 13 (1998), 27–104 (pp. 49–50).
11 'The Revolution at Market Hill', lines 30, 6, 31–2, 40; *The Complete Poems*, pp. 396, 397.
12 R. J. Leslie, *Life and Writings of Charles Leslie, M.A., Nonjuring Divine* (London, 1885), Ch.1, pp. 1–2. Leslie receives important attention, for example, in Jonathan Clark, *English Society 1660–1832: Religion, Ideology and Politics During the Ancien Regime* (2nd edn, Cambridge, 2000).
13 Bruce Frank, '"The Excellent Rehearser": Charles Leslie and the Tory Party, 1688–1714', in J. D. Browning (ed.), *Biography in the 18th Century* (London, 1980), pp. 43–68; William Kolbrener, 'The Charge of Socinianism: Charles Leslie's High Church Defense of "True Religion"', *Journal of the Historical Society*, 3 (2003), 1–23; Robert Cornwall, 'Charles Leslie and the Political Implications of Theology', in William Gibson and Robert C. Ingram (eds), *Religious Identities in Britain, 1660–1832* (Aldershot, 2005), pp. 27–42 and see his entry on Leslie in the *Oxford Dictionary of National Biography*. For Leslie's bibliography, see F. J. M. Blom, 'The Publications of Charles Leslie', *Edinburgh Bibliographical Society Transactions*, VI, Part 1 (1990), 10–36.
14 George Watson (ed.), *The New Cambridge Bibliography of English Literature, Vol. 2: 1660–1800* (Cambridge, 1971), cols. 1847, 1293, 1344, 2075. Leslie's curious neglect has been remarked upon, see John Valdimir Price, introduction, Humphrey Prideaux, *A Letter to the Deists/Charles Leslie, A Short and Easie Method with the Deists* (London, 1995), p. xii.
15 William Kolbrener, 'The Jacobite Milton: Strategies of Literary Appropriation and Historiography', *Clio*, 32, 2 (Winter, 2003), 153–76 (162–4), and Abraham Stoll, 'Discontinuous Wound: Milton and Deism', *Milton Studies*, 44 (2005), 179–202 (183–7).
16 *The Case of the Regale and of the Pontificat Stated* (n.p. 1700), p. 161; *The Wolf Stript of his Shepherd's Cloathing* (London, 1704), pp. 51, 65; *Querela Temporum: Or, The Danger of the Church of England* [London, 1694], p. 18; *Gallienus Redivivus, or Murder Will Out, etc. Being a True Account of the De-Witting of Glencoe, Gaffney* etc. (Edinburgh, 1695), *passim*; *The Anatomy of a Jacobite* (Cambridge, 1692), p. 67; *A Catalogue of Books of the Newest Fashion* [London, 1694], p. 8; *The Constitution, Laws and Government of England, Vindicated. In a Letter to the Reverend Mr. William Higden* (London, 1709), p. 23. For the rhetorical and ideological contexts of Leslie's arguments and tropes see Howard Erskine-Hill, 'Literature and the Jacobite Cause: was there a Rhetoric of Jacobitism?', in Eveline Cruickshanks (ed.), *Ideology and Conspiracy: Aspects of Jacobitism, 1689–1759* (Edinburgh, 1982), pp. 49–69 (esp. pp. 49–53).
17 *The Charge of Socinianism Against Dr. Tillotson Considered. In Examination of some Sermons He has lately Published on purpose to clear Himself from that Imputation … To which is Added Some Reflections upon the Second of Dr. Burnet's Four Discourses concerning the Divinity and Death of Christ. Printed 1694 …* (Edinburgh, 1695), p. 13.
18 Herbert Davis *et al.* (eds), *The Prose Writings of Jonathan Swift* (hereafter PW; 16 vols, Oxford, 1939–1974), V, 294.
19 PW, I, 89. The forthcoming edition of *A Tale of a Tub*, edited by Marcus Walsh, in *The Cambridge Edition of the Works of Jonathan Swift*, will indicate Swift's debts

to Leslie. See also, Ian Higgins, *Swift's Politics: A Study in Disaffection* (Cambridge, 1994), pp. 105–8.

20 *PW*, II, 36.

21 *A Postscript to Mr Higgins's Sermon* ... (Dublin, 1707), p. 1 and *passim*.

22 For a detailed study of Swift's satire in relation to the Socinian controversy, see Ian Higgins, '*An Argument against Abolishing Christianity* and its Contexts', in Hermann J. Real (ed.), *Reading Swift: Papers from The Fifth Münster Symposium on Jonathan Swift* (Munich, 2008), pp. 203–23.

23 *An Answer to a Book, Intituled, The State of the Protestants in Ireland Under the Late King James's Government* (London, 1692), pp. 40–1; *The Rehearsal* (Saturday 30 March and Wednesday 24 July 1706).

24 *Bickerstaffe's Prediction Confirm'd ... With farther Predictions for the Months of October, November, and December, 1708* (London, 1708), in *PW*, II, 269–72 (p. 270). For Swift's pamphlets satirising Partridge, see *PW*, II, 139–64.

25 For some of these analogues see the annotation in Jonathan Swift, *Gulliver's Travels*, eds Claude Rawson and Ian Higgins (Oxford, 2005), pp. 313, 319, 339–40; Patrick Fagan (ed.), *Ireland in the Stuart Papers. Correspondence and Documents of Irish interest from the Stuart Papers in the Royal Archives, Windsor Castle* (2 vols, Blackrock, Co. Dublin, 1995) I, 109, 120–1, see also I, 83.

26 *PW*, XI, 249–50; [Andrew Ramsay], *An Essay upon Civil Government* (London, 1722), pp. 65–6. See Frank McLynn, *Crime and Punishment in Eighteenth-Century England* (London, 1989), p. 57; Murray Pittock, *Inventing and Resisting Britain: Cultural Identities in Britain and Ireland, 1685–1789* (Basingstoke, 1997), pp. 91–5; Ian Higgins, *Jonathan Swift* (Horndon, Tavistock, 2004), pp. 60–1.

27 Charles Leslie, *The Church of England's Advice to her Children, and to all Kings, Princes, and Potentates* (1715), in John Somers, *A Fourth Collection of Scarce and Valuable Tracts*, (4 vols, London, 1751), IV, pp. 223–59 (p. 254).

28 *The Finishing Stroke. Being a Vindication of the Patriarchal Scheme of Government, In Defence of the Rehearsals, Best Answer, and Best of All ...To which are Added, Remarks on Dr. Higden's late Defence, In a Dialogue between Three H — 's* (London, 1711). The appended dialogue pamphlet on pp. 125–39 is entitled *A Battle Royal Between Three Cocks of the Game. Mr. Higden, Hoadly, Hottentote. As to the State of Nature and of Government*, see pp. 145–60. Some of the similarities between Swift's satiric fable and Leslie's pamphlet are noticed in Daniel Eilon, 'Swift's Yahoo and Leslie's Hottentot', *Notes and Queries*, 228 (1983), 510–12.

29 See Swift's 'Further Thoughts on Religion', *PW*, IX, 264.

30 *An Answer to a Book, Intituled, The State of the Protestants in Ireland Under the Late King James's Government* (London, 1692), pp. 46–7; *Considerations of Importance to Ireland* ... (n.p., 1698), *passim*.

31 *PW*, III, 13–14.

32 *The Case of the Regale*, p. 18.

33 *The Case of the Regale*, pp. 1–2.

34 *The Case of the Regale*, p. 26.

35 [Matthew Tindal] *The Rights of the Christian Church Asserted* ... (3rd edn, London, 1707), pp. lxiv, lxv.

36 *PW*, II, 74, 87.

37 *The Second Part of The Wolf Stript of His Shepherd's Cloathing: In Answer to a Late Celebrated Book Intituled The Rights of the Christian Church Asserted* (London, 1707), p. 19; *PW*, II, 80.

38 *The Second Part of The Wolf Stript*, p. 27.

39 *The Second Part of The Wolf Stript*, p. 23.

40 *PW*, II, 79.

41 *PW*, II, 77.

42 *PW*, II, 75.

43 *PW*, XI, 38–9, 60. On the images of Whig and Tory monarchy in *Gulliver's Travels*, see Howard Erskine-Hill, *Poetry of Opposition and Revolution: Dryden to Wordsworth* (Oxford, 1996), p. 99.

44 *PW*, II, 77.

45 An instance of a consonance witnessed in Mark Goldie, 'The Nonjurors, Episcopacy, and the Origins of the Convocation Controversy', in *Ideology and Conspiracy*, pp. 15–35; Robert D. Cornwall, *Visible and Apostolic: The Constitution of the Church in High Church Anglican and Non-Juror Thought* (Newark, 1983).

46 *CW*, I, 150.

47 *PW*, II, 13.

48 *PW*, II, 13.

49 Gilbert Burnet and Sir Thomas Burnet (eds, vols 1 and 2 respectively), *Bishop Burnet's History of His Own Time* (4 vols, London, 1753), IV, 278.

50 *PW*, IV, 79–80.

51 For this work, see Jonathan Swift, *A Discourse of the Contests and Dissentions Between the Nobles and the Commons in Athens and Rome With the Consequences they had upon both those States*, ed. Frank H. Ellis (Oxford, 1967).

52 Michael Treadwell, 'London Trade Publishers 1675–1750', *The Library*, 6th ser., 4, no. 2 (1982), 99–134 (p. 108). For Nutt in trouble for Tory publications, see William Cobbett (ed.), *Cobbett's Parliamentary History of England from the Earliest Period to 1803* (36 vols, London, 1810), VI (1702–1714) col. 21.

53 For a detailed analysis of Swift's *Discourse* highlighting the actual Tory nature of Swift's political thought and historical analysis in the tract and Leslie's response, see F. P. Lock, *Swift's Tory Politics* (London, 1983), pp. 146–61.

54 *An Answer to a Book* (1692), p. 32; *The Rehearsal* (no. 51, 21 July 1705); *Best of All* (London, 1709), p. 29. See also Lock, *Swift's Tory Politics*, pp. 155, 159.

55 *PW*, II, 2; *The New Association Part II* [London, 1703], p. 62.

56 Jonathan Swift, *A Tale of a Tub, The Battle of the Books, The Mechanical Operation of the Spirit*, ed. Frank H. Ellis (Frankfurt am Main, 2006), pp. 41, 65, 66.

57 *A Tale of a Tub*, p. 129.

58 *A Tale of a Tub*, pp. 127–8.

59 During the Stalinist purges, the Russian Jewish writer Isaac Babel famously called himself 'a great master of the genre' of 'silence'. See Nathalie Babel (ed.), *The Complete Works of Isaac Babel*, trans. Peter Constantine, intro. Cynthia Ozick (New York, pbk edn 2005), p. 1055.

60 *The Complete Poems*, p. 855.

61 *CW*, II, 361, 362.

62 M. Pollard, 'Who's for Prison? Publishing Swift in Dublin', *Swift Studies*, 14 (1999), 37–49. See also Éamonn Ó Ciardha, *Ireland and the Jacobite Cause, 1685–1766: A Fatal Attachment* (Dublin, 2001, reprint 2004), pp. 165–6, 171.

63 *CW*, II, 361, 359.

64 *CW*, II, 359. For the Jacobite plot of 1721–23, see Eveline Cruickshanks and Howard Erskine-Hill, *The Atterbury Plot* (London, 2004).

65 *Salt for the Leach* (1712), p. 14; *PW*, VIII, 91.

66 *Beaucoup de Bruit pour une Aumelette or, Much a Do about Nothing* ... (London, 1710), pp. 13, 9, 10.

67 *The Examiner*, 22 March 1711, *PW*, III, 115.

68   *PW*, XII, 153–69; 217–32.
69   *PW*, XI, 6, 130–1; *Gulliver Decypher'd: or, Remarks on a Late Book, Intitled, Travels into Several Remote Nations of the World. By Capt. Lemuel Gulliver. Vindicating the Reverend Dean on whom it is Maliciously Father'd* (London, n.d.), p. 38.
70   For an investigation into the possible origins of Gulliver's first name, see Hermann J. Real, 'Gullible Lemuel Gulliver's *Banbury Relatives*', *The Eighteenth-Century Intelligencer*, n.s. vol. 21, no. 3 (September 2007), 3–16.
71   *CW*, II, 468.

8

'Our Common Mother, the Church of England': Nonjurors, High Churchmen, and the Evidence of Subscription Lists

Richard Sharp

> *It seems, Sir, that the writing of Nonjurors is grievous to you...You might have remembered the zeal they have shown for our common mother, the Church of England, and how they have been her constant champions against her adversaries of all sorts since the Revolution...They have all along show'd this zeal and affection for her, tho' since the Revolution they have neither eat of her bread, nor enjoy'd her possessions.*[1]

More than twenty years had passed since the Revolution of 1688–9 when an anonymous Nonjuring sympathiser published what the diarist, Thomas Hearne, described as this 'excellent paper' against Dr. Thomas Wise, a 'muddy whigg Writer'.[2] It was an eloquent reminder that differences over the political question of dynastic allegiance had failed to eclipse the identity of theological purpose that continued to exist between Nonjuring and conforming High Churchmen. This sense of common cause was manifested, above all, by a joint endeavour to publish and promote books and pamphlets in support of orthodox doctrine and devotional and liturgical practice. By examining in detail the lists of subscribers to two even later, but still substantial, works, both edited by Nonjuring clergymen, this essay will show how the spirit of co-operation between Nonjurors and other High Churchmen remained strong for the space of at least another generation and how it was by no means confined to the professional ranks of the clergy, but was widely diffused amongst the laity of both communions.

By the late 1720s, forty years after the origins of the Nonjuring schism in England, the number of separated clergy and laity had dwindled. Many of those who had accepted deprivation or gone into retirement after 1690 had either died or become reconciled to the new order, while the Nonjuring church had recently suffered bitter internal division as a result of disagreements over liturgical uses, particularly with regard to Eucharistic celebration and the practical question of whether or not to re-unite with the main body of the Church of England. However, at least part of this loss had been offset by the reception of other clergy and laity who had been unable to reconcile their consciences with the progressively harsher terms required for allegiance to the post-1688 political order.[3] A regular, though increasingly shadowy, line of episcopal succession had been maintained and Nonjuring congregations continued to meet, not only in London, where there were several acknowledged chapels and oratories, but also in various provincial centres. One of the largest of these congregations was in Newcastle upon Tyne, while other groups gathered wherever a Nonjuring clergyman was available to officiate, often under the patronage of a sympathetic lay patron. Centres of Nonjuring activity were also to be found in both the ancient English Universities, and particularly at St. John's College, Cambridge, while Oxford's ancient loyalty to the Stuart cause had found new vigour in the aftermath of the 1715 Jacobite Rising.[4] Like their separated brethren in the conforming Church of England, many Nonjuring clergy at this time continued to be university-educated, even though scruples over the oaths prevented most new recruits from taking their degrees. Unsurprisingly, therefore, some, like Thomas Brett and Richard Rawlinson, took advantage of the leisure afforded by relative freedom from pastoral responsibility to continue to make important contributions to liturgical and antiquarian studies, while others, such as Nathaniel Spinckes and William Law, made distinguished contributions to a common Anglican store of devotional and controversial writing.

The first of the two books to be considered in this essay, *A Vindication of the Church of England and of the Lawful Ministry thereof: that is to say, Of the Succession, Election, Confirmation and Consecration of Bishops; as also of the Ordination of Priests and Deacons*, was a translation, extension and commentary on a work first published by Francis Mason in 1613. It was re-published in 1728, edited and updated by John Lindsay (1686–1768) who, in a manner common amongst Nonjurors, styled himself on the title page simply as 'a Priest of the *Church of England*.' Mason's original work had long been regarded as the most effective and substantial refutation of the so-called 'Nag's Head Fable',[5] deployed to damaging effect by Catholic apologists to cast doubt on the validity of Matthew Parker's consecration to the episcopate in 1559, but in Lindsay's updated version it served also to undermine claims that a regular and valid ministry could be found amongst English dissenters and other non-episcopal churches. A native of Cheshire, Lindsay probably attended St Mary Hall in Oxford, but took no degree before being ordained deacon and priest in 1717 by the Nonjuring bishop Henry Gandy (1649–1734) at Trinity Chapel, Aldersgate, London. In 1741, on the death of Bishop John Blackbourne, he went on to assume responsibility for the Nonjuring congregation at Blackbourne's oratory in Gray's Inn. Although Lindsay's Jacobitism was plainly attested in his anonymously-published but widely-circulated *Short History of the Regal Succession* (1731), this is said not to have prevented him from attaining eminence in 1750, as chaplain to the Tory-Jacobite Lord Mayor, John Blachford. In 1768, at the time of his death, he was one of the last Nonjuring clergymen in London.

The second work, published in 1732, is a text of the history of the Church of Durham by the twelfth-century monk, Symeon, edited by Thomas Bedford (1707–1773), a Nonjuror, with a prefatory essay by Thomas Rudd (1668–1733), an antiquary who held preferment in the conforming Church of England as a Prebendary of Ripon and Rector of the wealthy living of Washington in County Durham. Thomas Bedford was the son of Hilkiah Bedford, a Nonjuring bishop. Although an outstanding student, he left St. John's College, Cambridge, without taking a degree, on account of the Oaths.[6] Immediately after finishing work on this book, in 1731, he received Orders in the Nonjuring Church, as Lindsay had done, at the hands of Bishop Henry Gandy. He then spent five years at Angers in France, as chaplain to the exiled Jacobite family of Sir Robert Cotton, before returning to England, where he stayed, first, at Burnhall near Durham with his brother-in-law, the Nonjuring bishop George Smith, before moving in 1741 to Ashbourne in Derbyshire, where he remained for more than thirty years until his death, travelling to minister to scattered and dwindling Nonjuring congregations as far away as Chester and York.

The two works are, in some ways, very different. Bedford's volume is a scholarly edition of an academic text, while Lindsay's book, which asserts the claim of the clergy of the Church of England to the inheritance of the Levitical priesthood as incorporated into the Christian Church at its foundation and then transmitted through the bishops by regular succession, was a topical contribution to a long-running debate. It provided a substantial defence of the English model of reformed episcopacy at a time when the old arguments of Roman and dissenting critics were reviving, notably in response to the renegade French Catholic Fr. Pierre Francois le Courayer, whose *Dissertation on the Validity of the Ordinations of the English* (1723) had argued in defence of the regularity of the English episcopal succession and the validity of Anglican orders. However, by building on Mason's original arguments and drawing on subsequent writers, including John Barwick, John Bramhall, Jeremy Collier, John Cosin, Henry Hammond and Peter Heylyn, Lindsay evoked an inheritance that was common to Nonjuring and conforming clergy alike, in much the same way that Bedford's book appealed to a shared sense of local identity in the north-east and particularly at Durham.

Although the tone of Lindsay's work is conciliatory, his treatment of post-Reformation English Church history reveals a distinctively Nonjuring perspective. Politically-aware contemporaries would have noted many deliberate resonances, particularly in Lindsay's treatment of the experience of the English Church under Mary Tudor and during the Great Rebellion. In the first case, he declared, the bishops deprived by Queen Mary

'...continued...the true and lawful Bishops of their respective Sees till their death and those who were put into their full sees during their lives were...*Intruders* and *Usurpers*' (p. xxviii). Later, in Oliver Cromwell's time, '...the Pulpits and Revenues of the Church being usurp'd by *Schismaticks*, who had consciences large enough to comply with those pretended Higher Powers, in opposition to the known rights both of the Church and the Crown, the Bishops were driven into the *Wilderness,* and the Orthodox Clergy in general reduc'd to a necessity of feeding their Flocks in Corners and Secret Places; where they religiously dispens'd the word and sacraments of God, at all hazards...in *private Oratories*, or *upper-rooms*, as the *Primitive Christians* did in times of the like persecution for the benefit of such Orthodox Persons as were steady in their adherence to the principles of *true Religion and Loyalty*' (pp. lxix–lxx). Lindsay offered an indignant defence of the Church before the Revolution, commenting that it was doubtful '...whether (there was) ever...a greater Freedom of Religion, or...Bishops who better deserv'd...to be call'd *good* ones, than...those...who were promoted by that secret Papist (as they call King Charles II); not to say the same likewise of those who were promoted by his Brother King James II, who was, indeed, a *profess'd* one' (p. lxxxi). Significantly, though, he eschewed later polemic, and declined to engage with a writer like Thomas Bennet, who in 1716 had accused the Nonjurors of making a schism, on the grounds that '...this would open a way to a new Controversy...therefore, to waive that which I can't do justice to without giving offence to one side or the other of them, I shall pursue the Succession of Bishops no further, but shall without ceasing...pray for the peace of our Jerusalem...That, when the Happy Time of Healing shall come, we may all be disposed to reconcile our Dissensions, and repair our Breaches, and to become one Fold under one Shepherd, Jesus Christ the Righteous...' (pp. lxxxv–vi).

The subscription lists to both works are extensive and reveal much about patterns of association amongst Nonjuring clergy and laity, besides showing their ability to share in common endeavour with those for whom issues of dynastic allegiance were less urgent. Four hundred and twenty eight individuals and one institutional library are listed as subscribing to Lindsay's volume, while 260 individuals and two libraries took copies of Bedford's book. Lindsay's subscribers ranged geographically through most parts of England, with concentrations in London and in the editor's native locality of Cheshire and its surrounding areas of South Lancashire, Denbigh and Flint, while Bedford's subscribers came mostly from North East England, with particularly strong support in Durham and York, especially in those two cathedral chapters, and in the town of Newcastle.

Unsurprisingly, the largest single group of subscribers to both volumes was the clergy. Lindsay's list identifies 147 clerical subscribers (34.3% of the total), of whom eighteen were Nonjurors (including eight Nonjuring bishops). Bedford's work lists 101 clergy (38.8% of the total), including sixteen Nonjurors, six of whom were bishops. Strongly represented amongst the clergy were past and present members of St. John's College, Cambridge, twenty one of whom (14.3%) including six Fellows, subscribed to Lindsay's book, while thirty two (31.7%) including nineteen Fellows, supported Bedford's volume. In the latter case, this high proportion was no doubt explained by the traditional association of that College with the North East. A similar regional association probably accounts for the presence in Lindsay's list of eighteen former members (twelve clergy and six laymen) of Brasenose College, Oxford, which traditionally recruited from South Lancashire and Cheshire. It is also noticeable that Lindsay secured three subscribers from St. Mary Hall, Oxford, a small community, well-known for its Jacobite sympathies: the Principal, William King (1685–1763), the late Vice-Principal, Thomas Bromwich (d. 1724) and John Leake (1682–1745).[7] Seventeen noblemen and women, and eleven past, current or future Members of Parliament appeared on Lindsay's list, while Bedford's subscribers included seven noblemen and eleven current, former or future MPs. Lindsay's subscribers, interestingly, included thirty eight women (8.9% of the total), but there were no women on Bedford's list. For his publisher, Bedford selected James Bettenham of St. John's Lane, London.

Bettenham was a Nonjuring layman, identified as such in Negus's analysis[8] of the affiliations of London publishers in 1724, and son-in-law to William Bowyer the elder, the senior Nonjuring member of the book trade. Bettenham's output had a marked Jacobite emphasis and included works by Thomas Carte and the Nonjuring bishop, Thomas Brett. In 1718 he had published *A Hymn to the Holy and Undivided Trinity*, ostensibly composed by James Shepheard, a young Jacobite apprentice who had been executed at Tyburn in March of that year.[9] Lindsay, by contrast, engaged not one publisher, but a conger of seven: James Crokat, Fletcher Gyles, Robert Gosling, John Hooke, George Strahan, Richard Wilkin and Richard Williamson, most of whom were also noted for High Church and Tory sympathies.[10] Williamson, of Gray's Inn Gate, Holborn, had taken over the business of Richard Sare, an intimate of the elder Bowyer, on the former's death in 1724 and in 1730 he published an edition of the Greek *Devotions* of bishop Lancelot Andrewes, translated by George Stanhope, the Dean of Canterbury and a High Churchman, who had preached the sermon at Sare's funeral. Crokat's first recorded production, in 1726, had been *The Clergy's Right of Maintenance*, by William Webster, a prominent High Church propagandist. Wilkin, of the King's Head in St. Paul's Church Yard, was noted as '...devout at Prayers...not only a True Son of the Church, but also a Resolute Champion in behalf of the Hierarchy...(who)...to convince us of the great Respect he bears to the Pious Memory of King Charles I has lately publish'd several Evidences which have not yet appear'd in the

Controversie, concerning *Eikon Basilike*...'[11] Most notable of all was George Strahan, of the Golden Ball in Cornhill, who for more than half a century sustained a consistent Jacobite and Nonjuring output, steadily republishing works by Jeremy Collier, Charles Leslie and Robert Nelson and regularly running foul of the authorities. Arrested in 1706, for complicity in publishing *The Memorial of the Church of England*,[12] and again in 1715, when his correspondence with the exiled Charles Leslie was intercepted,[13] Strahan continued to communicate with the Stuart Court in exile and in 1727, the year before Lindsay's book appeared, he received personal thanks for his loyalty from King James III.[14] Amongst publishers subscribing to Lindsay's book, it is striking to find Nathaniel Mist, the prominent Jacobite, and Robert Freebairn of Edinburgh, who in earlier life had taken an active part in the 'Fifteen.[15]

Not all who were involved in the publication of these books or whose names appear on the subscription lists shared the Nonjuring convictions of their editors or held Jacobite principles. Academic or local interests might also provide sufficient reason for subscribing. Conyers Middleton, for example, University Librarian at Cambridge from 1721–1750 and noted for his pro-Hanoverian and heterodox opinions, subscribed to both volumes, while Thomas Rundle, a Canon of Durham whose Arianism would in 1734 cost him promotion to the see of Gloucester, subscribed to Bedford's book, as did Roger Gale, Vice-President of the Society of Antiquaries, who, as a Whig MP in 1710, had voted against the High Church champion, Dr Sacheverell. Yet, in general, investigation confirms a preponderance of High Tory and Jacobite sympathisers, exemplified by many of those who subscribed to both volumes, including not only Nonjurors like the bishops Thomas Brett, Henry Gandy and Richard Rawlinson; the priests John Creyk, William Law and Thomas Wagstaffe and laymen like Thomas Bowdler, but also the conforming High Churchman, Zachary Grey, editor of *Hudibras* (1744), and the Tory-Jacobite Parliamentary leader, Sir Watkin Williams Wynn.

Like Wynn, who 'audaciously burnt' an image of the Hanoverian King George I in public when campaigning during the election of 1722,[16] many of the subscribers to Lindsay's volume had been identified as likely Jacobite supporters in the list compiled for King James III in 1721.[17] They included, among the peerage, the Dukes of Beaufort and Wharton, the Earls of Plymouth and Winchelsea, Viscount Bulkeley and the Lords Digby and Middleton, together with several Tory Members of Parliament: Charles Cholmondeley, from the old Cavalier and Nonjuring family of Vale Royal, MP for Cheshire since 1722; Sir Richard Grosvenor of Eaton, MP for Chester since 1715; Sir John Pakington of Westwood, long-serving MP for Worcestershire until his death in 1727, and Borlase Warren of Stapleford, MP for Nottingham from 1713–15 and again from 1727. Other gentlemen whose names had appeared on the list included the former MPs Peter Legh of Lyme, Cheshire (1669–1744), a veteran Jacobite who, having withdrawn from public life after the Revolution, had been imprisoned on suspicion of conspiracy in 1694 and again in 1696, and Sir George Warburton of Arley, MP for Cheshire until 1722; together with William Massey of Coddington, Cheshire; Holland Egerton of Heaton and Alexander Ratcliffe of Fox Denton (both Lancashire); Richard Mostyn of Penbedw, Flint; Edward Repington of Ammington, Warwickshire, and Sir Philip Sydenham, Bt., of Brimpton, Somerset.

Lindsay's subscribers included other MPs with High Tory and Jacobite sympathies. Francis Annesley, who sat for Westbury, had served as a trustee for Lord Bolingbroke's estates in 1716; the Hon. James Bertie (Middlesex) had opposed the attainder on Sir John Fenwick and had refused the Association in 1696, and his brother, the Hon. Henry Bertie (Beaumaris) had been Register of the Board of Brothers during the last Parliament of Queen Anne. Seven former members of the October Club subscribed: six already mentioned above (the Bertie brothers, Francis Annesley, Charles Cholmondeley, Sir John Pakington and Sir George Warburton), together with the first Lord Middleton, who, as Thomas Willoughby, had sat as MP for Nottinghamshire from 1698–1710 and for Newark from 1710 until his ennoblement in 1712.[18] In the case of several of these, subscription to Lindsay's volume can be recognised as the manifestation of a strong Anglican churchmanship that had already found earlier expression. James Bertie, Sir George Warburton and Sir John Pakington had been promoters of the Tack in 1704, and Pakington, the grandson of a Cavalier and a former ward of the Nonjuring Viscount Weymouth, had been one of the most assiduous supporters of Dr Sacheverell, organising support during his trial in 1710 and arranging for him to deliver a characteristically high-flying Restoration Day sermon before the House of Commons in 1713.[19] Similarly, Francis Annesley had served from 1711 until 1715 as one of the Commissioners for building fifty new churches and had previously been active on behalf of Thomas Sheridan, the deprived and impoverished Nonjuring bishop of Kilmore.[20]

The subscription lists to both works reveal much about how the Nonjuring movement was sustained by personal associations and friendships. In the case of Lindsay's volume, many of the subscribers were, like him, resident in London and identified with those who had rejected the liturgical innovations of the so-called 'usager' party.[21] All but one of the eight subscribing bishops (here listed as 'Reverend', rather than 'Right Reverend') were 'Non-Usagers', the one exception being the liturgical scholar, Thomas Brett (1667–1743). Nathaniel Spinckes (1653–1727), consecrated in 1713, was the greatly-respected author of an important devotional work, *The Sick Man Visited* (1712; 5th edition 1744) and had taken an energetic leading part against liturgical innovation throughout the Usages controversy. Henry Gandy (1649–1734), who had ordained John Lindsay as deacon and priest in 1717, had been consecrated in 1716. Originally a Fellow of Oriel College, Oxford, he had served as Proctor in 1683, when the University promulgated its famous *Judgment and Decree...Against certain Pernicious Books and Damnable Doctrines, Destructive to the Sacred Persons of Princes, their State and Government, and of all Humane Society*. Hilkiah Bedford (d.1724), a graduate of St. John's College, Cambridge, had been consecrated by Spinckes and Gandy in 1721, together with Samuel Hawes (d.1722). Henry Doughty (1664–1730), another St. John's graduate, who had received Episcopal orders at the hands of four Scottish bishops in Edinburgh in 1725, assisted Spinckes and Gandy later that year in consecrating John Blackbourne (1681–1741) and, shortly afterwards, these four together consecrated Henry Hall (1677–1731), who had matriculated at St. John's in 1692 and served towards the end of his life as chaplain to the Duke of Ormonde at Madrid. The final bishop on Lindsay's list was the anti-quary Richard Rawlinson (1690–1755), whose consecration in 1728 by Gandy, Blackbourne and Doughty, was witnessed by Lindsay. Interestingly, Rawlinson was styled neither 'Reverend' nor 'Right Reverend', but simply 'L.L.D.'

Most of the remaining Nonjuring clergy who subscribed to Lindsay's volume were also based in London. The elderly Robert Orme was well known to Lindsay, who took over from him as priest in charge of the Nonjuring Aldersgate chapel after Orme's death in 1733. John Creyk of Westminster (1688–1747) had matriculated at St. John's College, Cambridge, in 1705 but, like most later Nonjurors, he had never taken a degree. He attended George Kelly in the Tower, after the Atterbury Plot, and served as chaplain to the Duchess of Ormonde and to Heneage Finch, 4th Earl of Winchelsea (d.1726), an antiquary whose close involvement with the Nonjuring cause was attested by his frequent attendance as a witness to episcopal consecrations, including those of Hilkiah Bedford, John Black-bourne and Nathaniel Spinckes. Creyk was also literary executor to the Countess of Winchelsea, Anne Finch (d.1720). In 1725 his name appeared as a witness to the consecration of bishops Blackbourne and Hall, and in 1730 he took charge of Doughty's congregation, following that bishop's death. In Westminster, he lived near to other subscribers, including the scholarly Richard Russell and Alexander Smith (d.1747), one of several Scottish Nonjuring Episcopalian clergy residing in London at this time. Another subscriber was William Law (1686–1761), who, having received priest's orders from bishop Gandy in 1728, was living in Putney, as chap-lain to the family of Edward Gibbon. Already famous for his leading part in the Bangorian controversy, Law was about to publish his best-known work, the *Serious Call to a Devout and Holy Life* (1729). Thomas Wagstaffe (1692–1770), son of a distinguished father of the same name, had been ordained deacon in 1718 and priest in 1719 by the Nonjuring Primus, Jeremy Collier, whose Usager principles he adopted. He later served for many years as a chaplain to members of the exiled Stuart Court in Rome.

Among the lay subscribers, several can be identified with certainty as Nonjurors. These included noblemen and gentlemen who maintained Nonjuring chaplains, such as Lord Digby, of Sherborne and Coleshill (the former parish of John Kettlewell), who offered patronage to Thomas Carte; Lord Winchelsea, protector of John Creyk and Samuel Hawes, and Charles Cholmondeley of Vale Royal, where the deprived Vicar of Whitegate, John Oakes, had continued to serve after the Revolution. The Hon. Lady Fanshaw (d.1729), who had employed Lindsay himself as a chaplain, was the widow of Sir Thomas Fanshaw (1628–1708), sometime Tory MP for Essex, who had withdrawn from public life after the Revolution. Another subscriber, Sir Jemmatt Raymond (1663–1754) of Harwell, Oxfordshire, had incurred the displeasure of Thomas Hearne for his equivocation over the Oaths in 1724, but later went on to receive a significant obituary notice in the Tory *London Evening Post* as '...an excellent Scholar and Patron of learned Men, particularly such as were in Distress on Account of unfashionable Principles...steady and loyal to his Obligations in Politicks and (who) retiring from the World lived privately.'[22] Mrs Port, of Ilam in Staffordshire, was the widow of John Port, a wealthy Nonjuring layman and founder of one of the more important charities for the relief of Nonjuring clergy.[23] 'Mr Jennings', of Gopsal, Leicestershire, was father to Charles Jennens, Handel's librettist, noted for his Nonjuring and Jacobite sympathies. Another subscriber, 'Mr Cotton', cannot be identified for certain, but was very probably Robert Cotton, of Stratton and Steeple Gidding, a committed Jacobite who had been 'out' in 1715. In 1721 he had witnessed the consecration of the Nonjuring bishops Ralph Taylor and Hilkiah Bedford, and in 1723 he had been memorably acquitted on a charge of asserting in public that a picture of the Princess Clementina Sobieska was a portrait of 'the Queen of England'.[24] Taken into custody in 1722, at the time of the Atterbury Plot, his surety had been found by Thomas Bowdler (1661–1738), another prominent lay Nonjuror and subscriber to Lindsay's volume, who had witnessed the consecrations of bishops Gandy and Brett and who died in exile at Boulogne. Another subscriber was a friend of Bowdler's, Thomas Martyn, a London merchant who had served with him as a witness at the consecration of bishops Gandy and Brett and stood as godfather to his son. Martyn also witnessed the consecration of John Blackbourne and Henry Hall in 1725 and of Richard Rawlinson in 1728. A further witness of Hall's consecration, the apothecary George Bewe, also subscribed to Lindsay's book.[25]

The subscription lists to Bedford's volume reflected that work's antiquarian interest and regional appeal, with a distinguished roll call of antiquaries, including Thomas Baker, Browne Willis, Thomas Carte, Francis Drake, Thomas Hearne, Roger Gale, Samuel Pegge and Richard Rawlinson.

At Durham, the bishop, dean and sixteen prebendaries subscribed, together with the Episcopal and chapter libraries. At York, the dean and seven prebendaries subscribed. Nineteen Fellows, a high proportion of the total, testified to the regional associations of St John's College, Cambridge. Although regarded as Whig independents, both Members of Parliament for the County of Durham (George Bowes and John Hedworth) subscribed, along with Members for the City of Durham (John Shaftoe), Newcastle (Nicholas Fenwick) and Northumberland (Ralph Jenison). However, as with Lindsay's volume, notable support came also from the editor's fellow Nonjurors and Jacobites, and three of the Nonjuring bishops on Bedford's list (Henry Gandy – identified as 'the very Reverend' – Thomas Brett and Richard Rawlinson) had also subscribed to Lindsay's work, along with three priests (John Creyk, William Law and Thomas Wagstaffe). A fourth bishop, George Smith (1693–1756), a distinguished Anglo-Saxon scholar who had been consecrated as a non-usager in 1728, owned an estate at Burnhall near Durham and was brother-in-law both to Thomas Bedford, who was living at Burnhall at this time, and to Robert Gordoun (1704–79), who in 1741 was to become the last regularly consecrated bishop in the English Non-juring succession. A native of Wolsingham in Weardale, Gordoun passed through St John's College, Cambridge,[26] before being ordained into the Nonjuring ministry by Bishop Gandy in 1727, in the presence of his College contemporary, William Bowyer the younger (1700–77), who also subscribed to Bedford's book. Most of the other Nonjuring clergy in the North East at this time also appeared on Bedford's list: Rowland Burdon (1681–1750) of Sedgefield, who had been received into communion by bishop Spinckes in 1717; Timothy Mawman (1683–1763) of Stockton, who would himself become a bishop in 1737, and William Fothergill (d.1759), ordained priest in 1731 by George Smith to take charge of the Nonjuring congregation in Newcastle.

Other Nonjuring clergy subscribing to Bedford's book included George Harbin (c. 1665–1744), author of *The Hereditary Right of the Crown of England Asserted* (1713); Thomas Carte (1686–1754), the Jacobite historian; Thomas Browne (1655–1741), a sometime Fellow of St John's, who had taken an active part in the allegiance controversy during the early 1690s, and Samuel Jebb (1694–1772). After leaving Cambridge, Browne had found security in the household of Sir Francis Leycester (d.1742), of Nether Tabley in Cheshire. Leycester, who also subscribed to Bedford's book, had been a close associate of Peter Legh of Lyme, a Jacobite, for whose borough of Newton he sat in Parliament from 1715–27. Samuel Jebb had been ordained deacon in 1716 and priest in 1718 by the usager Bishop Jeremy Collier, for whom he also worked as a librarian. He later served as a chaplain to the Cotton family, two members of which (Sir Robert Cotton and John Cotton of Gidding) joined him as subscribers to Bedford's book.

In Newcastle, it is striking to see how subscribers for Bedford's book included not only members of the Nonjuring congregation (the priest, William Fothergill, with leading laymen such as George Bulman, a goldsmith, and William Hanby, a surgeon), but also a wider cross-section of local society, including one current and one future MP for the town (Nicholas Fenwick and Walter Calverley Blackett); the headmaster of the Grammar School (Edmund Lodge) and the Vicar (Thomas Turner), together with other prominent clergy (including the antiquary Henry Bourne), and other doctors, lawyers and gentry. Reasons for this are not hard to discover. Blackett, for example, was the son of Sir Walter Calverley (d.1749), an active Jacobite, who had gone into exile after the Rising in 1715.[27] Bourne's *History of Newcastle* was first published in 1732, the same year as Bedford's book. Thomas Turner was another graduate of St John's, as were other Newcastle subscribers, including Adam Askew, a doctor, and Thomas Clennel, a lawyer.

Discoveries like these are not without value. Although it is not unusual in this period to find large subscription lists for theological works, testifying to the substantial enduring influence of traditional religious learning and orthodox belief, it is striking to see such clear evidence for the full and equal contribution made to this endeavour by Nonjurors, as well as by conforming High Churchmen. It is also instructive to observe how, particularly in the case of Lindsay's volume, these lists show the continuing contribution made by well-informed orthodox religious conviction to the formation and definition of Tory political identity, even as the Nonjuring movement was shrinking, in the space of less than two generations, from a nationwide crisis of conscience to a network of local associations, entirely reliant upon individual contacts and friendships.[28]

Notes

1 *A Seasonable and Modest Apology on behalf of the Rev. Dr. George Hickes and other Nonjurors, in a Letter to T. Wise, D.D., on occasion of his Visitation at Canterbury, June 1, 1710*, cited in John Henry Overton, *The Nonjurors, their Lives, Principles and Writings* (London, 1902), p. 392.

2 Charles Edward Doble, *et al.* (eds), *Remarks and Collections of Thomas Hearne*, (11 vols, Oxford, 1885–1921), iii. 69. (21 October 1710).

3 Oaths of Allegiance and Supremacy were imposed by Acts of 1 William & Mary, s.1, c.8 and 1 George I, s.2, c.13. An oath explicitly abjuring the right of James Francis Edward Stuart was imposed by the Act of 13 William III, c.6 and re-imposed by 1 George I, s.2, c.13. For discussion of the impact of state oaths on the intelligentsia in general see J. C. D. Clark, *Samuel Johnson: Literature, Religion and English Cultural Politics from the Restoration to Romanticism* (Cambridge, 1994), especially ch. 4 'Johnson's career and the question of the oaths 1709–58' and ch. 5 'Johnson and the Nonjurors' and *ibid.*, 'Religion and Political Identity: Samuel Johnson as a Nonjuror' in Jonathan Clark and Howard Erskine-Hill (eds), *Samuel Johnson in Historical Context* (Basingstoke, 2002), pp. 79–145. Professor

Clark's work has been particularly valuable in serving to demonstrate that, although the traditional view of the Nonjuring movement as essentially clerical was not wrong, it may be said to have been too narrow, by overlooking the extent to which Nonjuring convictions were shared by members of the laity. For the Usages controversy see Henry Broxap, *The Later Nonjurors* (Cambridge, 1924), pp. 35–65; William Jardine Grisbrooke, *Anglican Liturgies of the Seventeenth and Eighteenth Centuries* (London, 1958), pp. 71–112 and 273–96; and James David Smith, *The Eucharistic Doctrine of the Later Nonjurors: A Revisionist View of the Eighteenth-Century Usages Controversy* (Cambridge, 2000). For Samuel Johnson's detailed knowledge of the issues at stake in this controversy, and particularly of the four liturgical details (Prayer for the Dead, Mixture of water and wine in the eucharistic Cup, and Invocation of the Holy Spirit upon, and Oblation of, the Eucharistic Elements), as restored in the new Communion Office drawn up by Thomas Brett and adopted by a section of the Nonjurors in 1718, see Matthew M. Davies, '"Ask for the Old Paths": Johnson and the Usages Controversy', *The Age of Johnson*, 17 (2006), pp. 17–68.

4 An adequate new study of the Nonjuring movement is badly needed. At present, the best works on the subject are still Thomas Lathbury, *A History of the Nonjurors. Their Controversies and Writings with Remarks on Some of the Rubrics in the Book of Common Prayer* (London, 1845); Overton, *Nonjurors* and Broxap, *Later Nonjurors*. See also J. Findon, 'The Nonjurors and the Church of England 1689–1716' (unpublished D.Phil. dissertation, University of Oxford, 1977). On the Newcastle congregation see Richard Sharp, '100 Years of a Lost Cause: Nonjuring Principles in Newcastle from the Revolution to the Death of Prince Charles Edward Stuart', *Archaeologia Aeliana*, 5th series, viii (1980), pp. 35–55.

5 A story first put forward in 1604 by the Jesuit, Christopher Holywood, in order to cast doubt on the validity of the consecration of Matthew Parker as Archbishop of Canterbury, together with other Anglican bishops, in 1559. By claiming that one of the principal participants in this ceremony, John Scory, the deprived Bishop of Chichester, had himself never been duly consecrated, Holywood effectively undermined the validity of all subsequent Anglican Episcopal orders.

6 (Thomas Bedford) '...of St John's Coll., Camb.,...left...upon Principle, as his Brother had done before him, tho' they had a full Propriety to Fellowships, and had the immediate enjoyment of Scholarships and Exhibitions' (*Remarks and Collections of Thomas Hearne*, x.166).

7 See David Greenwood, *William King: Tory and Jacobite* (Oxford, 1969).

8 'A List of London Printers, classified by their political parties, drawn up by Samuel Negus in 1724', reproduced in John Nichols, *Literary Anecdotes of the Eighteenth Century* (9 vols, London, 1812–15), i. 288–312.

9 This publication was advertised in the *Weekly Journal*, 22 March 1718.

10 For publishers, see Henry R. Plomer *et al.*, *A Dictionary of the Printers and Booksellers who were at work in England Scotland and Ireland from 1641–1775* (3 vols, London, 1907–32; reprinted by the Bibliographical Society, 1968).

11 *The Life and Errors of John Dunton* (1705), p. 314.

12 *Remarks and Collections of Thomas Hearne*, i. 169, 184.

13 *Remarks and Collections of Thomas Hearne*, v. 99.

14 Sir Charles Petrie, *The Jacobite Movement* (3rd, revised, edn, London, 1959), pp. 326–7. It should be noted that, although King James III maintained an interest in the nomination of Catholic bishops for service in Ireland and occasionally exercised his Royal prerogative to influence the appointment of Cardinals, he

had no involvement with the episcopal succession in the English Nonjuring church.

15 Plomer, *Dictionary of...Printers and Booksellers*, ii. 121–2.

16 See the recent summary biography of Sir Watkin Williams Wynn by Peter Thomas in the *Oxford Dictionary of National Biography* (61 vols, Oxford, 2004).

17 'A State of England' (RASP 65/16), reproduced as Appendix B in Eveline Cruickshanks and Howard Erskine-Hill, *The Atterbury Plot* (Basingstoke and New York, 2004), pp. 246–54.

18 For MPs see Eveline Cruickshanks, Stuart Handley and David W. Hayton, *The History of Parliament: The House of Commons 1690–1715* (5 vols, Cambridge, 2002).

19 Geoffrey Holmes, *The Trial of Dr Sacheverell* (London, 1973), p. 263n.

20 *House of Commons 1690–1715*, iii. 37.

21 For the Usages see note 1 above.

22 *Remarks and Collections of Thomas Hearne*, viii. 248–9; *London Evening Post*, 31 December 1754–2 January 1755.

23 P. Mottram, 'A Village Nonjuror', *Staffordshire History*, 38 (Autumn, 2003), pp. 3–19. I am also grateful to Mr. Mottram for kindly allowing me to read a pre-publication draft of his complementary study: 'Charitable Support for Nonjuring clergy deprived of their livings 1689–1808', which contains further important information about the Port charity.

24 A report of this case is given in Abel Boyer, *Quadriennium Anne Postremum; Or, the Political State of Great Britain During the Four Last Years of the Late Queens Reign* (2nd edn, 38 vols, London, 1718), xxv. 184–6.

25 Copies of the documents attesting to this and other Nonjuring consecrations are reproduced in Broxap, *Later Nonjurors*.

26 John and John Archibald Venn, *Alumni Cantabrigienses. A Biographical List of All Known Students, Graduates and Holders of Office at the University of Cambridge, from the Earliest Times to 1900* (10 vols, Cambridge, 1922–54), ii. 241.

27 Eveline Cruickshanks and R. Sedgwick, *The History of Parliament: The House of Commons 1715–54* (2 vols, London, 1970), i. 464.

28 There is substantial scope for further work on this topic. The enormous subscription lists to Jeremy Collier's, *An Ecclesiastical History of Great Britain, Chiefly of England: from the First Planting of Christianity, to the End of the Reign of King Charles the Second. With a Brief Account of the Affairs of Religion in Ireland, Etc* (2 vols, London, 1708, 1714) and to Peter Barwick's, *Vita Johannis Barwick, S.T.P. … Adjicitur Appendix Epistolarum tam ab ipso Rege Carolo II. quam a suo Cancellario exulantibus, aliarumq; Chartarum ad eandem Historiam pertinentium, etc.* [ed. Hilkiah Bedford] (London, 1721), would be particularly worth investigating.

9
The Location of the Stuart Court in Rome: The Palazzo Del Re

Edward Corp

At the beginning of 1719 the exiled Stuart court, which had recently arrived in Rome, moved into a building rented for it by the Pope. That building, which James III was to occupy until his death in 1766, and which his son Prince Charles would then occupy for several years until his own death in 1788, has always been called – incorrectly – the Palazzo Muti. Every book on Jacobitism, and all the biographies of James III and his two sons, call it by that name. In fact, its correct name after 1719 was the Palazzo del Re, and it was known to contemporaries as such.

The building is situated at the north end of the Piazza dei Santi Apostoli, where it can still be seen today. Yet a biography of 'Bonnie Prince Charlie', published in 1988, contained a photograph of a completely different building, which it called the Palazzo Muti and described – incorrectly – as the location of the Stuart court.[1] Since then other books on Jacobitism, one of my own included, have repeated this mistake, using contemporary engravings to illustrate the appearance of the second building, which in reality was never occupied by the Stuart court.[2]

This article will briefly examine the history of these two buildings, and show why and how the confusion has come about. It will argue that their names and functions should now be properly identified and described in all future works on Jacobitism and the exiled Stuarts. Briefly stated, in the years after 1719 King James III and the Stuart court occupied the Palazzo del Re (*Palais Royal* or Royal Palace) at the north end of the Piazza dei Santi Apostoli, while an Italian nobleman called the Marchese Muti occupied the other building, which was called the Palazzo Muti, on the west side of the adjacent Piazza Pilotta.

Correctly distinguishing between these two buildings is not simply a question of historical accuracy. It also has implications for our understanding of the exiled Stuart court, and thus of the role it played in the Jacobite movement. Unless we can identify and describe the Palazzo in which the court was located, we cannot understand how it was used by the Stuarts and their household, nor can we estimate the influence that its architecture had on court ceremonial. Without this, we cannot appreciate the impact it made on Roman society and on the many British and Irish Grand Tourists who visited the Papal city during the eighteenth century. The great majority of these Grand Tourists, whether Jacobite or Hanoverian in their political sympathies, took lodgings in and around the nearby Piazza di Spagna. Anyone wanting to walk from the Piazza di Spagna to visit the Roman Forum was obliged to go near or even directly past the Stuart court. The British and Irish visitors to Rome knew exactly where the Palazzo del Re was situated, what it looked like, and how and where to enter it secretly without being seen. This is something which we also need to know.

Moreover, the name given to the building occupied by the Stuart court was important because it reflected the status given to James III by the Pope, the cardinals and the Roman aristocracy. James was always treated in Rome as the King of England, and given full royal honours. Therefore, his home was naturally called the Palazzo del Re. If it had really been called the Palazzo Muti after 1719, that name would have implied that James did not enjoy royal status. Contemporaries were well aware of this, and knew that the name given to the building was politically significant.

Despite this, Jacobite historians have called the palazzo by the wrong name, have minimised the impact which it would have made, and have even ascribed to it some of the problems encountered by the exiled royal family. It has been variously described as a 'drab little palazzo',[3] 'dark and gloomy',[4] and 'an insignificant building of moderate size which stood at the end of a small cul-de-sac'.[5] This is not the way it was regarded by people who walked through the Piazza dei Santi Apostoli, or by the people who visited the royal apartments, furnished and decorated at great expense by the *Camera Apostolica* (the Papal Chamber). Alice Shield and Andrew Lang, in their biography of James III, described the palazzo as 'a very dreary little Court', and added that 'it was just as it had been at St. Germains'.[6] Now that we have a much greater understanding of what the Stuart court had been like at Saint-Germain, this comment is bound to provoke an immediate riposte. The Château de Saint-Germain was a large and impressive royal palace; and the Jacobite court there was far from dreary.[7] The location and significance of the Stuart court in Rome is in need of reassessment.

During the seventeenth century the Muti family, which had risen to prominence by holding both municipal and papal offices, had divided into two branches, which owned distinct but adjacent buildings, on either side of a street which is now called the Via dell'Archetto. The plots on which these buildings stood were described for convenience in the parish registers in Latin as the 'Insula Maior de Mutis' and the 'Insula Minor de Mutis', or in Italian as the 'Isola Maggiore' and the 'Isola Minore.' By 1719, the former was occupied by Marchese Giovanni Battista Muti, the latter by his third cousin, Marchese Girolamo Muti. The residences of these two men,

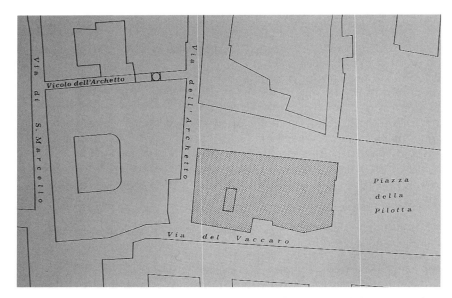

Plate 1   A plan showing the *isola maggiore*, the *isola minore* and the surrounding streets.

Source: Adapted from Giuseppe Marinelli, *L'architettura palaziale romana tra Seicento e Settecento* (doctoral thesis, Universita Sapienza di Roma, *circa* 1990).

although totally distinct buildings, were at that time both confusingly referred to as the Palazzo Muti. When the Pope rented the one on the 'isola maggiore' for King James III and the Stuart court, it was only natural that the name should be changed, no doubt to the relief of the local inhabitants, to become the Palazzo del Re. Thereafter there was only one Palazzo Muti, in the Piazza Pilotta, occupied by Marchese Girolamo Muti.[8]

There is no need to give here the history of the building on the 'isola minore' which continued to be called the Palazzo Muti, but one point needs to be made. It had recently been expanded, with a completely new east façade and entrance. Much admired at the time, the architecture of this new east side became the subject of two contemporary engravings – and these are the ones which have been erroneously reproduced since 1988 as showing the Stuart court.[9] These engravings, however, are of great interest because they both show, in the background on the right hand side, part of the building on the adjacent 'isola maggiore' which became the Palazzo del Re, and which therefore really did house the Stuart court.

The palazzo on the 'isola maggiore' needs to be considered in rather more detail. In reality this building, regarded then and now as a single palazzo, contained several distinct residences. This was partly because the north side of the 'isola' was actually split into two parts by a little alley, known as the Vicolo

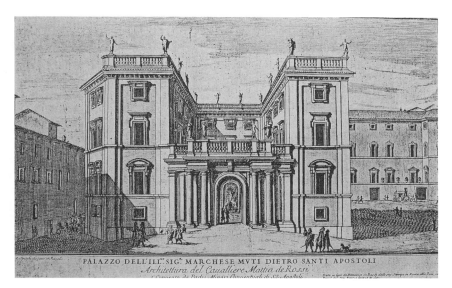

Plate 2 Alessandro Specchi, the east façade of the Palazzo Muti, with the Palazzo del Re visible in the background on the right, engraving (1699).

Source: Author's own photo, in the public domain.

Plate 3 Giambattista De Rossi, the *palazzo grande* seen from the Piazza dei Santi Apostoli, engraving (1638).

Source: Author's own photo, in the public domain.

dell'Archetto, which ran through the property beneath a connecting covered bridge (the *Archetto*). It was partly also because the entire west side, running along the Via di San Marcello from the Piazza dei Santi Apostoli in the south to the Vicolo dell'Archetto in the north, had been rebuilt in a different architectural style and with rooms on a different level. The new building, called the *palazzo grande*, was finished at the beginning of 1638, and can be seen in an engraving published that year by Giambattista De Rossi.[10] The most important rooms had ceilings painted by Charles Mellin,[11] although Giuseppe Passeri and Claude Lorraine were said to have contributed to the decoration.[12] This prestigious west side was regarded as sep-

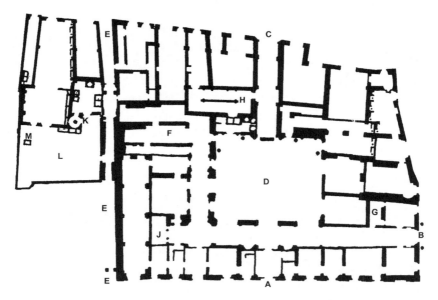

Plate 4 A plan of the ground floor of the Palazzo del Re. Based on plans in the *Archivio di Stato di Roma*.

KEY TO GROUND FLOOR PLAN.

A Front Entrance from the Via di San Marcello
B Side Entrance from the Piazza dei Santi Apostoli
C Back Entrance from the Via dell' Archetto (opposite the back of the Palazzo Muti)
D Courtyard (*Cortile*)
E Vicolo dell' Archetto
F Grand Staircase
G Secret Staircase, from 1724
H Princes' Staircase
J Chapel Staircase, from 1724
K Spiral Staircase
L Garden
M Fountain

arate, but was nevertheless joined to the east side of the building around a spacious central courtyard. The east side was then itself divided into two parts, described as *palazzetti* or small palaces, each with its own separate principal staircase. One was situated in the north-east corner, on the angle of the Vicolo and the Via dell'Archetto, the other in the south-east corner, on the angle of the Via dell'Archetto and a street called the Via del Vaccaro (which led from the Piazza Pilotta to the Piazza dei Santi Apostoli).[13] These two *palazzetti* were separated on the ground floor by an entrance which was situated opposite the back of the adjacent Palazzo Muti on the 'isola minore'.

After 1660 the *palazzo grande* was rented out by the Muti family, which itself only occupied one of the two *palazzetti*.[14] The principal entrance to the *palazzo grande* was situated between two Ionic columns and beneath a balcony on the narrow south side of the building, on the Piazza dei Santi Apostoli, but there was a second entrance in the middle of the long façade running along the Via di San Marcello.[15]

Conscious that their property had now effectively been divided into two main parts (the *palazzo grande* in the west and the *palazzetti* in the east), the successive Muti owners did what they could to improve the appearance of the east side of the 'isola maggiore'. Because the north-east corner projected further into the Via dell'Archetto than the rest of the building, the façade was straightened at ground level in 1661, with a spacious *loggietta* or balcony above, which extended outside the two *palazzetti* on the first floor or *piano nobile*.[16] It can be seen in the background of the engravings of the other Palazzo Muti on the 'isola minore', which have already been referred to. In 1685 two columns were placed on either side of what had originally been the back entrance on the east side beneath the *loggietta*, to reflect its enhanced status as the only entrance to the two *palazzetti*.[17]

The legal agreement between the *Camera Apostolica* and Giovanni Battista Muti, whereby the entire 'isola maggiore' was to be rented on behalf of James III and the exiled Stuart court, is dated 22 December 1718.[18] It refers specifically both to 'the palace of Marchese Giovanni Battista Muti in the Piazza dei Santi Apostoli' (the *palazzo grande*) and 'the two other small palaces (*palazzetti*) adjoining it.'[19] It states that the *palazzetta* in the south-east corner was then occupied by Conte Musignani, and that the one in the north-east corner was occupied by both Giovanni Battista Muti himself and his nephew, Abate (later Cardinal) Mario Mellini. Muti (with his wife and daughter, Ginevra) occupied the 'lower part' (presumably the ground and first floors, which gave access via the *Archetto* to an enclosed garden), and Mellini the 'upper part' (presumably the second and third floors). When the Stuart court moved in during 1719 the *palazzo grande* and the two *palazzetti* were joined up to form a single large residence. James III and Queen Maria Clementina occupied what had been the *palazzo grande*. When their children were born they were given apartments in what had previously been the *palazzetto* in the north-east corner.

The rental agreement, however, also refers to two 'adjoining small houses with their appurtenances' which Giovanni Battista Muti had previously been renting for his own use, both of which were 'included in the lease'. One of these houses was rented from Giovanni Battista Muti's cousin, Marchese Girolamo Muti, the other from a relation called Giacinto Manni. It is not possible to identify with any certitude where these two houses were located, although there are certain clues.[20]

The property belonging to Giovanni Battista Muti was chosen by James III to be the new residence of his court because the *palazzo grande* happened to be available in December 1718, and because Muti and his two tenants (Musignani and Mellini) were prepared to vacate the *palazzetti*. It was never intended, or even expected, to become a permanent residence. Nevertheless, it was well situated and perfectly suitable in the short term.

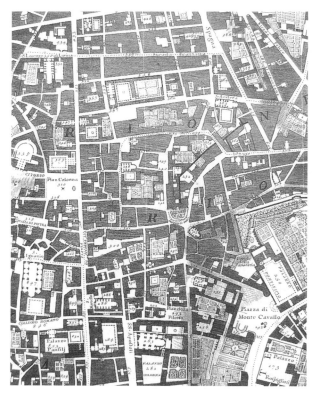

Plate 5 A detail from the Nolli map of Rome, showing the general position of the Palazzo del Re in relation to the Quirinale and the Corso (1748).

Source: Author's own photo, in the public domain.

The Piazza dei Santi Apostoli was also the location of the Palazzo Colonna, the home of James III's cousins, and was conveniently close both to the Quirinale (where the Popes normally lived during the eighteenth century), and to the Corso, where Cardinal Gualterio, the Protector of England, had his palazzo.[21] The entire building was cleaned, painted, decorated and furnished during 1719, under the supervision of the architect Alessandro Specchi.[22] In particular, an entirely new ceiling was painted, in what was to become the king's gallery on the first floor, by Giovanni Angelo Soccorsi.[23]

There were three entrances to the Palazzo del Re. The main one was in the Via di San Marcello, in the centre of the *palazzo grande*,[24] but the narrowness of the street made it easier for carriages to enter through the decorated entrance from the Piazza dei Santi Apostoli on the south side. Passing under the king's apartment, they turned right into the central courtyard, dropped off their passengers, and then departed through the entrance on the east side, between the two former *palazzetti*, towards the Palazzo Muti.

The façade of the *palazzo grande*, running along the Via di San Marcello, contained thirteen windows on the first and second floors. These windows, however, were not regularly spaced. The four on the left were separated by a wider gap from the nine on the right. This was significant because the nine on the right provided light for the royal apartments, whereas the four on the left illuminated rooms used for other purposes.

There was another irregular feature, this time on the first floor only: a row of smaller windows between the first and the second floors. The six

Plate 6   A nineteenth century drawing of the west façade of the Palazzo del Re in the Via di San Marcello. *Su conessione del Ministero per i Beni e le Attività Culturali, Archivio di Stato di Rome*, ASR 18, 2009.

on the left were taller than the seven on the right. This is because there was a mezzanine floor on the left, whereas the rooms on the right had much higher ceilings. Given that the king's apartment on the first floor contained nine windows overlooking the Via di San Marcello, and that two of these nine were taller than the other seven, it meant that the apartment had some rooms with, and others without, mezzanines above.[25]

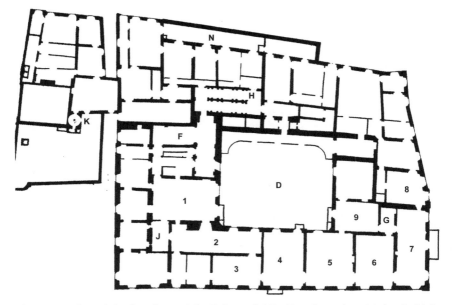

Plate 7   A plan of the first floor of the Palazzo del Re. Based on plans in the *Archivio di Stato di Roma*.

KEY TO FIRST FLOOR PLAN

D   Courtyard (*Cortile*)
F   Grand Staircase
G   Secret Staircase, from 1724; Back Staircase (connecting the Bedchambers)
H   Princes' Staircase
J   Chapel Staircase, from 1724
K   Spiral Staircase
N   Balcony (*Loggietta*)

The King's Apartment

1   Guard Chamber
2   First Antechamber
3   Second Antechamber
4   Third Antechamber
5   Fourth Antechamber
6   Bedchamber
7   Gallery
8   Closet
9   Private Secretary's Room

The grand staircase was situated in the middle of the north wing and led directly up to the king's guard chamber overlooking the central courtyard. Beyond the guard chamber, extending around the courtyard on the inside, and along the Via di San Marcello on the outside, the apartment then consisted of four antechambers, a bedchamber and a gallery. The first two antechambers had low ceilings because of the mezzanines above, and led to the other rooms through a sequence of doors placed *enfilade* on the San Marcello side. The third and fourth antechambers and the bedchamber had impressive high painted ceilings. The gallery had the high ceiling painted by Giovanni Angelo Soccorsi. Beyond the gallery there was a cabinet, situated in what had been the south-eastern *palazzetto*. It was on a different level, and probably not decorated until after 1719.

These rooms are all in very bad condition today, and only small parts of their ceilings have survived. The third antechamber, which had a little balcony immediately above the entrance, had a large painting within a heavy gilded frame, showing an angel appearing before a kneeling Virgin Mary and sleeping child. The fourth antechamber had a frescoed ceiling by Charles Mellin showing *La Fama* blowing a trumpet, between a pair of sphinxes on either side (placed above the interior walls). Above the windows overlooking the courtyard Mellin had also painted some large seated male nudes on top of an antique bas relief. The bedchamber contained a framed painting by Mellin showing the legendary hero Marcus Curtius, fully armed and on horseback, leaping down into the chasm (effectively formed by the bedchamber itself) which had opened in the Forum.[26] These three rooms all overlooked the Via di San Marcello, and were therefore shaded from the sun, but the bedchamber had a view down the Via dei Santi Apostoli, across the Corso, towards the Collegio Romano.[27]

The king's gallery, which had a balcony above the entrance for carriages, looked due south down the Piazza dei Santi Apostoli towards the Palazzo Bonelli (which, from 1732 to 1740, was the French embassy).[28] The church of Santi Apostoli and the Palazzo Colonna were on the left, and the Palazzo Chigi and the Palazzo Cibò on the right. Only part of the ceiling of the gallery has survived, but the papal archives contain a brief description of Soccorsi's overall design. In the centre there was a framed oval painting containing two *putti* (cupids), one holding a sceptre, the other the royal crown of England. At the west end of the gallery there was a seated lady, dressed in white, who represented *la Religione Cattolica*, and at the east end, beneath a white dove, there was another seated lady, also dressed in white but with a yellow cloak, representing *la Fede*. Although it probably did not reflect James III's own opinion, the message conveyed in the design chosen by the Papal court was perfectly clear: the eventual triumph of the exiled King of England would be brought about with the help of the Catholic religion and faith. The ceiling also contained, in small round painted frames, more references to Marcus Curtius, whom the Muti family regarded as an ancestor. The only painting from that series which has survived happens to be the one in which the mounted hero is shown leaping on his horse into the chasm. It was placed at the east end of the gallery, near the picture representing *la Fede*.[29]

The king's cabinet, beyond the east end, was in the adjacent *palazzetto* rather than the *palazzo grande*, and consequently on a different (higher) level. An opening had to be made in the connecting wall, with a short flight of four steps, in order to reach it. This cabinet, which was probably decorated for James III a little later, was a delightful room. The rounded ceiling, which is in surprisingly good condition, was painted to be open to the sky, and showed several birds fluttering above. *Putti* could be seen within a delicate floral design, supported by a wooden rococo trellis frame.[30] It was beneath this attractive ceiling that James III conducted his business, receiving and despatching the Stuart Papers which are now preserved at Windsor Castle.

The queen's apartment was situated on the second floor, immediately above the king's, with a small inner staircase connecting the two bed-chambers. It was accessed by continuing further up the grand staircase, and contained exactly the same sequence of rooms. Unfortunately, no details of its decoration have survived. When Prince Charles was born in December 1720 he was also given an apartment on the second floor, on the north side of the *palazzetto* overlooking the Vicolo dell'Archetto.[31] Once again, no details of the decoration have survived.

There is no need to identify here the location of the apartments and rooms of all the more important household servants – though that can be done from a close study of the papal archives and the Stuart Papers. But the position of the Chapel Royal is of some interest, because it was inconveniently placed above the *archetto* which connected the main part of the 'isola maggiore' with the smaller part (including the garden) on the other side of the Vicolo dell'Archetto.

Beneath the *archetto*, in the little lane outside but protected by the bridge, the Muti family had created a small shrine dedicated to the Virgin Mary. It was properly called the shrine of 'La Madonna dell'Archetto', and contained a picture of the Virgin, painted in oil on stone by Domenico Muratori in 1690.[32] Because of its small size, it was referred to as *la Madonella*. When the 'isola maggiore' was rented by the *Camera Apostolica* for James III, this shrine was specifically excluded from the lease. Muti wrote that 'one dark room is reserved to the lessor, which is under the Arch of the Madonna in the lane under the house at present inhabited by him, which room is used for the furniture of the said sacred image, to which his family have a particular devotion'.[33]

Muti had had his own chapel built on the second floor directly above the arch, accessible from both sides of the 'isola maggiore', and this was the chapel which was used by the Stuart court after 1719. Situated immediately beside the apartment destined for the king's first child, it was the place where Prince Charles was baptised at the end of 1720.

The chapel contained a painting given to the king by Pope Clement XI in 1719. It showed *La navicella di san Pietro con la virtù Teologali*, and had been painted the previous year by Giuseppe Chiari. The painting, which is now at Frascati, measures 170 × 122 centimetres. It shows St. Peter steering a small boat during a storm at sea, accompanied by Faith, Hope and Charity (the theological virtues), observed and protected from above by the Holy Trinity.[34] At the end of 1722, in front of this picture, James III gave the orders of the Garter and the Thistle to the little Prince of Wales.[35] Six months later, in the summer of 1723, the chapel was used for two important social occasions involving the Roman aristocracy: the marriage of one of the daughters of James's close friend the Principessa di Piombino,[36] and the baptism of the son of another friend, Don Carlo Albani (one of the nephews of Clement XI).[37]

In the autumn of that year, James ordered that the six large gold candlesticks in the little chapel at Saint-Germain-en-Laye, which had remained there after the death of Mary of Modena, should be sent to Rome and placed on the altar of the Chapel Royal in the Palazzo del Re.[38] He also purchased another (but unknown) painting to be placed above the altar, possibly because the candlesticks obscured the bottom of the large one by Chiari.[39]

Unfortunately this chapel posed a major problem for the Stuart court. There was no direct communication between the first floor of the Palazzo del Re and the private garden on the north side of the arch. In order to reach the garden, without going out into the street, one had to go up to the second floor and through the chapel, and then down a spiral staircase. The chapel therefore presented an obstacle to free circulation within the palazzo, and must, at least to some extent, have been used as a kind of connecting corridor.

By 1724, after the failure of the Atterbury Plot, it had become clear that James III would have to remain in Rome for much longer than originally expected. This prompted him to reconsider the suitability of the Palazzo del Re as the location of the exiled court. It certainly had some positive advantages: it was well situated, it had a private garden, and it did not contain any shops running around the outside of the ground floor. Yet by 1724 James was perhaps more conscious of its disadvantages. The chapel was inconveniently positioned; it was not possible to go for long walks, as had been the case at Saint-Germain, without travelling out to the Borghese gardens, or those of some other villa on the edge of the city; and there was no secret staircase. This last point was significant. A steady stream of British visitors to Rome wanted to see the king without being observed, but could not easily do so because of the need to go up the grand staircase, and then

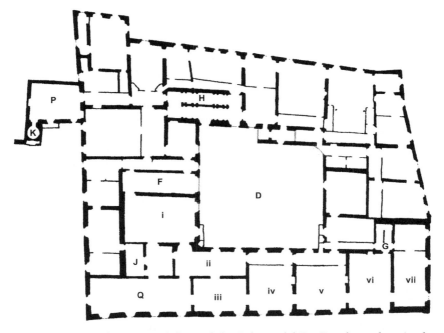

Plate 8 A plan of the second floor of the Palazzo del Re. Based on plans in the *Archivio di Stato di Roma*.

KEY TO SECOND FLOOR PLAN

D Courtyard (*Cortile*)
F Grand Staircase
G Back Staircase (connecting the Bedchambers)
H Princes' Staircase
J Chapel Staircase, from 1724
K Spiral Staircase
P First Chapel, 1719–24
Q Second Chapel, from 1724

The King and Queen's Apartment

i   Guard Chamber
ii   First Antechamber
iii Second Antechamber
iv   Third Antechamber
v   Fourth Antechamber
vi   Bedchamber
vii Gallery

through the four antechambers. There was no other convenient way of reaching the gallery or the cabinet of the king's apartment.[40]

Perhaps the most important problem was the growing shortage of space. At first the palazzo contained enough accommodation for all the members of the royal household, but the birth of Prince Charles resulted in an increase in the number of servants employed, and it was obvious that as he grew older more would have to be taken on. Then, in the summer of 1724, the queen became pregnant for a second time. The birth of another child would eventually increase the size of the household even more.[41] It was this that prompted James to ask for an alternative, larger residence.

He cannot have been very optimistic about obtaining one. Nevertheless, the timing seemed propitious. A new Pope, Benedict XIII, had been elected in May 1724, and had already shown himself to be particularly well-disposed towards James and Maria Clementina. One of his first acts was to give to the king a present of 10,000 *scudi*, which amounted to an entire year's pension, and to the queen all the rich furnishings which had been recently purchased for the private apartments of his predecessor, Innocent XIII.[42] The latter were said to be worth 12,000 *scudi*, the equivalent of seven and a half times the annual rent paid by the *Camera Apostolica* for the Palazzo del Re.[43]

In June 1724, a few weeks after the papal election, James III asked Benedict XIII to let him move to the Palazzo Riario in Trastevere.[44] It had once been occupied by Queen Christina of Sweden, and had more accommodation to house his expanding household. Although it was inconveniently situated on the other side of the river Tiber, it had a large and spacious garden, with the possibility of easy access to agreeable walks. It also offered the important advantage, because of its location away from the centre of the city, of making it easier for Jacobites and other British Grand Tourists to visit him discreetly.

Benedict XIII considered the matter during that summer, but eventually decided (probably because of pressure from the Imperial ambassador) that the Stuart court should remain where it was. He did, however, come up with a compromise proposal. James III should go away for several months to Albano, where he had the permanent use of the *palazzo apostolico*, so that the entire Palazzo del Re could be refurbished and made more suitable.[45] James accepted this offer, and the building works were carried out during a period of a little over three months, from September to November.[46] When the court returned from Albano one of the Jacobites observed that 'our Palazzo is quite an other thing than it was.'[47]

The changes cannot be analysed here, but two points might conveniently be made. A new secret staircase was created, giving direct access from beside the south entrance to the king's gallery and cabinet. A visitor could thus enter discreetly on foot through one of the other entrances, leaving the one for carriages closed, and could see the king without the need to go up the grand staircase and pass through the guard chamber and ante-chambers.[48] The second important change concerned the chapel. The old one was suppressed and replaced by an entirely new one in a much more convenient position.

The new chapel is the only part of the interior of the Palazzo del Re which can be seen today in a contemporary painting. It was situated on the second floor, overlooking the Via di San Marcello, behind the four windows on the left hand side. It was adjacent to the apartment of the queen, and was provided with its own staircase, which enabled people to reach it without having to pass through her apartment. It contained the six great gold candlesticks, and probably the two paintings, which had been in the previous chapel, and some additional rich furnishings which were given as a present by Benedict XIII.[49]

Three months later, in March 1725, the queen gave birth to her second son, Henry, created Duke of York. As the Pope had not yet seen the new chapel, where the little prince was to be baptised, he decided to visit the palazzo and perform the ceremony himself.[50] Benedict also increased James's annual pension from 10,000 *scudi* to 16,000 *scudi*.[51] The king then commissioned his principal painter, Antonio David, to produce a large picture showing the interior of his new chapel. James decided, however, that the picture should not show the baptism of his second son, but rather the baptism of his heir, the Prince of Wales. That ceremony had in reality taken place four years earlier in the previous chapel, but David was ordered to show it in the new one.[52] The six large gold candlesticks from Saint-Germain can be seen on the altar, with the rich red damask hangings decorated with gold, the gift of Benedict XIII, in the background. Neither of the two paintings is visible, so if they were retained for the new chapel, as was probably the case, they were no doubt displayed on one of the other walls. In addition to the cardinals in attendance, the group includes both the Principessa di Piombino and Don Carlo Albani, who had been allowed to use the previous chapel for their family ceremonies.[53]

It was thus the decision of Pope Benedict XIII to refurbish the entire Palazzo del Re, rather than let James III move elsewhere, which ensured that it became the permanent residence of the Stuart court in Rome. Although James moved his court to Bologna in October 1726, following Maria Clementina's retirement into the convent of Santa Cecilia in Trastevere, the palazzo was still rented for him by the *Camera Apostolica*, and therefore remained available whenever he chose to go back.[54] It was in the Palazzo del Re that the Stuart court was re-established when the king and queen returned to Rome in the spring of 1729, following their reconciliation.

In the years which followed, the *Camera Apostolica* continued to maintain and furnish the building for James III and his court. The papal archives show that it was thoroughly cleaned and refurnished in 1729,[55] and that a great deal of money was spent on it during the early 1730s.[56] The queen continued to live on the second floor of the *palazzo grande* until her death in January 1735. Prince Charles, as already stated, was brought up on the north side of the *palazzetto* overlooking the Vicolo dell'Archetto, and Prince Henry on the east side of the same *palazzetto* overlooking the Piazza Pilotta.[57] This last point is important, and will be referred to again at the end of this essay.

Let us then examine the causes of two misunderstandings. Why have historians consistently referred to the Palazzo del Re as the Palazzo Muti? And why has the real Palazzo Muti been wrongly described in recent years as the building which housed the Stuart court?

The first misunderstanding becomes more surprising if we consider the correspondence of Baron von Stosch, the Hanoverian spy employed first by Lord Carteret and then by the Duke of Newcastle. The reports which Stosch sent back to London were written in French, and have been used by many historians. They are particularly instructive because they never once refer to the building in which the Stuart court was situated as the Palazzo Muti.[58] Stosch regarded James III as the 'Pretender', not as the legitimate king, so he always referred to the building as the 'Palais du Prétendant' which was, in effect, a direct translation of Palazzo del Re. If even a pro-Hanoverian called it that, it seems unlikely that people who were pro-Jacobite or dynastically neutral would have called it the Palazzo Muti.

The reason for calling it the Palazzo Muti becomes even more difficult to understand if we consider who actually owned the building during the eighteenth century. Marchese Giovanni Battista Muti died in 1730, and left all his property to his daughter Ginevra, who had married Marchese Giovanni Battista Sacchetti.[59] From that point onwards, the alternative name would have been the Palazzo Sacchetti, or perhaps Sacchetti-Muti. When Marchesa Ginevra Sacchetti died in 1779, thirteen years after the death of James III, she left the palazzo to a relation named Giuseppe Casali.[60] By then the building was being occupied by Prince Charles, who had not been recognised by the Pope as King Charles III. Nevertheless it was still called the Palazzo del Re (rather than the Palazzo Stuart) until his death in 1788.[61] At that point the *Camera Apostolica* finally stopped renting the building, and returned it to its owner.[62] It immediately became the Palazzo Casali.[63]

So why have Jacobite historians consistently called it the Palazzo Muti? The reason seems to be connected with the publication in the middle of the eighteenth century of two important engravings, both of which show views of the Piazza dei Santi Apostoli, looking north. The first, by Giovanni Battista Piranesi, shows the Palazzo Odescalchi on the west side of the piazza, and was published in 1753.[64] The second, by Giuseppe Vasi, shows the Palazzo Colonna on the east side, and was published in 1754.[65] Both engravings include the Palazzo del Re in the distance at the north end of the piazza, and both call it the Palazzo Muti. As both Piranesi and Vasi would have been perfectly well aware that the building was occupied by the exiled Stuart court, and that by then the only Palazzo Muti was actually

Plate 9   Giuseppe Vasi, a detail showing the Palazzo del Re at the north end of the Piazza dei Santi Apostoli, engraving (1754).

Source: Author's own photo, in the public domain.

a different building, in the Piazza Pilotta, we need to consider what motives they might have had for giving the Palazzo del Re a name which was no longer correct – and had not been correct for over thirty-five years.[66] It is not difficult to identify them.

By the 1750s, hundreds of Grand Tourists were visiting Rome each year, providing a lucrative market for the sale of engravings which showed views of the principal buildings in the city. The British and Irish constituted the largest, and generally the wealthiest, national groups among these foreigners, and were therefore Piranesi's and Vasi's most important clients.[67] The engravings which these artists produced were intended to provide a visual record or souvenir of what the Grand Tourists had seen and admired in Rome.

The British and Irish were naturally curious to see the Palazzo del Re, regardless of their political sympathies. They also knew that their relations and friends would be interested to see what the building looked like when they returned home. Yet it was politically sensitive, even dangerous, to possess and publicly display engravings which referred to James III as the king, or to his residence as the royal palace. Just as many Stuart portraits were given deliberately incorrect identifications, so the engraved views of the Stuart court were given a deliberately incorrect name.[68] Of course, the name chosen was one which had, originally, been correct. This seems likely to be the reason why people in Great Britain and Ireland, including all Jacobite historians and Stuart biographers, have been misled into calling the building by the wrong name.

The time has surely come, in the interests of historical accuracy, to refer to the building as the Palazzo del Re, and to restrict usage of the name Palazzo Muti (after 1719) to the completely different building on the 'isola minore' which was never occupied by the Stuart court. Distinguishing between the two buildings in this way will also help us to understand why the real Palazzo Muti has been wrongly described in recent years as the building which housed the exiled court.

This second misunderstanding was the result of something which happened in 1747. In that year, Pope Benedict XIV decided that a decorated false façade, or *facciata*, should be erected for forty days on the outside of the palazzo of each newly created cardinal.[69] The first new cardinal to be affected by this ruling was Prince Henry, Duke of York, who was obliged to select the most suitable part of the Palazzo del Re against which to erect his *facciata*.[70] He needed a position which would not obstruct the traffic in the adjacent streets, and which was sufficiently wide to be impressive. Above all, he needed a position which could be seen and appreciated from a distance.

There were in fact only two possible locations, because most of the palazzo was situated in narrow streets (the Via di San Marcello, the Via del Vaccaro and the Vicolo dell'Archetto). The first was on the south side of the *palazzo grande*, overlooking the Piazza dei Santi Apostoli. But that would have meant erecting the *facciata* against part of the king's apartment (his gallery), which would have been inappropriate. The second was on the side of the north-east *palazzetto*, on the corner of the Via dell'Archetto and the Vicolo dell'Archetto, overlooking the Piazza Pilotta. That, as we have seen, was precisely where Prince Henry's own apartment was situated, which made it particularly appropriate.

To understand what followed, we need to recall what has already been said about that part of the Palazzo del Re. On the ground floor, the building had a straight façade which stretched from the Vicolo dell'Archetto to beyond the east entrance, situated behind the Palazzo Muti. On the first floor, however, the façade was recessed because of the balcony, or *loggietta*, which had been added in 1661. Thus, as one looked at the building, the right hand side of the façade, above ground level, projected further forward than all the rest – as can be seen in the two contemporary engravings. The problem confronting the architect, Clemente

Orlandi, was therefore how to incorporate these irregular features into a satisfactorily balanced design, and to do so without covering over the east entrance and rendering it unusable.

Orlandi's solution was to divide the *facciata* into three separate parts, the one in the centre flanked by two identical ones on either side. The middle part rested against the building, with the upper part (above the balcony) recessed. The right part was brought a little forward, and rested on some scaffolding behind. To balance that, the left part was then brought further forward, with deeper scaffolding behind. The left hand side had to include a real opening, to allow access through the east entrance into the courtyard of the palazzo, so the one on the right was given a pretended opening, backed by *trompe l'oeil*, leading nowhere. Beyond the *facciata* to the right, the little Vicolo dell'Archetto remained open to traffic as usual. And beyond the *facciata* to the left, completely behind the Palazzo Muti, the building remained uncovered.

Orlandi commissioned Claude-Olivier Gallimard, then a *pensionnaire* at the nearby Académie de France on the Corso,[71] to make an engraving of the *facciata*, to be dedicated to the new cardinal. Gallimard's engraving managed to show the entire *facciata* from a distance, by pushing back the Palazzo Muti on the left and the building adjoining the monastery of

Plate 10   Claude-Olivier Gallimard, the *facciata* erected against the east façade of the Palazzo del Re, engraving (1747). Private Collection.

the Humiltà on the right, thus creating an image which could not in reality have been seen from his vantage point. His engraving is valuable because it enables us to situate the precise location of the *facciata*. The continuation of the Palazzo del Re can be seen on the left, and the entrance to the Vicolo dell'Archetto on the right.[72]

Gallimard's engraving is also of great interest because it shows that the overall shape of the *facciata* was similar to the east façade of the Palazzo Muti: a recessed central part with a balcony above, between two sides which projected further forward into the street. If, therefore, one were mistakenly to call both buildings by the same name, it would be easy to conclude that the *facciata* had been erected on the real Palazzo Muti rather than on the Palazzo del Re. And that is precisely what has happened.[73]

The *Diario Ordinario*, the weekly newspaper published in Rome, reporting the construction of the *facciata*, states that it was on the Palazzo del Re, opposite (*'dirimpetto'*) the Palazzo Muti. There are two announcements, both of which make this perfectly clear. The first one informs its readers that the *facciata* was to be erected 'al Portone del Palazzo di Sua Altezza Reale Eminentissima il Sig. Card. Duca di Yorck, a SS. Apostoli dirimpetto al Palazzo Muti'.[74] The second one records that the *facciata* had been finished, and could be seen 'apposta al su Regio Palazzo, e propriamente dalla parte dirimpetto al Palazzo Muti'.[75] And there we have in a single sentence, written for people living in Rome at the time, a clear distinction between the Palazzo del Re, occupied by the Stuart court, and the completely distinct and separate Palazzo Muti.

Identifying and naming the building in which James III and Maria Clementina lived and brought up their two sons should be regarded as the first step in an overdue reassessment of the Stuart court in Rome. In the past generalisations have been made, and various assumptions adopted, based on inadequate or partial information, and on the know-ledge that the Jacobite movement ended – eventually – in failure at home and dishonour abroad. Now we need to discover more about the relations between the Stuarts, the papal court and Roman society between 1719 and the 1750s, a period when many people there anticipated an eventual Stuart restoration. How was the court organised during those years, and how did its ceremonial compare with what it had been at Saint-Germain and Whitehall? Why was it regarded as one of the most important musical centres in Rome? To what extent did its patron-age of portrait painters influence the British and Irish Grand Tourists who visited the city? Why and to what extent did those Grand Tourists, Hanoverian Whigs as well as Tories and Jacobites, use it as a sur-rogate British embassy? These are just some of the things which are wait-ing to be discovered and analysed in a full-scale study of the Stuart court in Rome.

Notes

1 Rosalind Marshall, *Bonnie Prince Charlie* (Edinburgh, 1988), p. 47.
2 Hugh Douglas, *Bonnie Prince Charlie in Love* (Stroud, 1995), p. 29; Peter Pininski, *The Stuarts Last Secret* (East Linton, 2002), pp. 70–1, illustration 2; Edward Corp, *The Stuart Court in Rome: The Legacy of Exile* (Aldershot, 2003), p. 15.
3 Douglas, *Bonnie Prince Charlie*, p. 30.
4 Frank McLynn, *Charles Edward Stuart: A Tragedy in Many Acts* (London, 1988), p. 4.
5 Flora Maxwell Stuart, *Lady Nithsdale and the Jacobites* (Traquair House, 1995), p. 125.
6 Alice Shield and Andrew Lang, *The King over the Water* (London, 1907), p. 402.
7 Edward Corp, *A Court in Exile: The Stuarts in France, 1689–1718* (Cambridge University Press, 2004).
8 For the history of the 'isola minore' in the Piazza Pilotta, see Giuseppe Marinelli, *L'architettura palaziale romana tra Seicento e Settecento. Problemi di linguaggio. Un approccio filologico: la testimonianza delle incisioni dello 'Studio d'Architettura Civile'; una verifica sistematica: il palazzo Muti Papazzurri alla Pilotta* (Universita Sapienza di Roma, doctoral thesis, no date shown but after 1990), particularly pp. 146–7, 152–3 (notes 11 and 12), 157–61 and 250–3. For the history of the 'isola maggiore' in the Piazza dei Santi Apostoli, see Aloisio Antinori, 'Il Palazzo Muti Papazzurri ai Santi Apostoli nel Secoli XVI e XVII: Notizie sull'attività di Giovanni Antonio de Rossi, Carlo Fontana e Carlo Francesco Bizzaccheri', in *Architettura: Processualità e Trasformazione*, proceedings of the international conference, Rome, Castel Sant'Angelo, 24–27 November 1999, eds. Maurizio Caperna and Gianfranco Spagnesi (Rome, Bonsignori Editore, 2002), pp. 439–46.
9 The better known engraving was published in Alessandro Specchi, *Il Nuovo Teatro delle Fabbriche et Edifici in prospettiva di Roma Moderna* (Rome, 1699), as plate no. 45 'nel disegno et intaglio'. It is the one reproduced by Hugh Douglas (see note 2). The other engraving, by Freicenet after a drawing by Barbault, was published separately in the 1750s, and is reproduced by both Pininski and Corp (see note 2). There is also an engraving by Giovanni Carlo Alet, which shows the entrance only, which was published in Domenico De Rossi, *Studio d'Architettura Civile, Libro Primo: sopra gli Ornamenti di Porte e Finestre* (Rome, 1702), illustration 142.
10 Giambattista De Rossi, *Palazzi diversi nel'alma città di Roma* (Rome, 1638), plate 30. This engraving, despite the fact that it has an inscription on it, was accidentally published by De Rossi in reverse, and therefore gives a completely misleading impression of the palazzo as it was at that time. It was reproduced as illustration no.3 in McLynn, *Charles Edward Stuart*, pp. 320–1, and described as the prince's 'prison'. In fact the prince lived in one of the *palazzetti* on the other side. It also shows a row of shops on the ground floor which were no longer there after 1719.
11 Rossella Pantanella, 'Palazzo Muti a piazza SS. Apostoli residenza degli Stuart a Roma', *Storia dell'arte*, 84 (1995), pp. 307–15.
12 Lione Pascoli, *Vite de' Pittori, Scultori, ed Architetti Moderni* (Roma, 1730, facsimile edition, 1933), p. 220: 'In casa Muti a Santiapostoli [Giuseppe Passeri painted] la soffita della sala, ed un gran quadro, ed in una stanza la soffita d'un alcova'. The involvement of Claudio Gellée [Claude Lorraine] is referred to on p. 25.
13 Antinori, 'Il Palazzo Muti Papazzurri ai Santi Apostoli', p. 444.
14 *Ibid.*, pp. 443–4.

15 Paul-Marie Letarouilly, *Les Edifices de Rome Moderne* (Paris, 1860, revised edition, Novara, 1992), plate 28.

16 Archivio di Stato di Roma (henceforth ASR.), Presidentze delle Strade b.45, f.174, has a drawing dated 7 October 1661 showing the new *loggietta* on the east façade of the Palazzo Muti on the 'isola maggiore', with the Vicolo dell'Archetto on the right hand side.

17 Antinori, 'Il Palazzo Muti Papazzurri ai Santi Apostoli', p. 444.

18 ASR. Camerale I, Giustificazione di Tesoreria (henceforth Cam I: GT), b.444, f.9, *istromento rogito*, 22 December 1718.

19 Marchese Giovanni Battista Muti's letter of 22 December 1718 to the *Camera Apostolica*, in which he confirmed the details of the rental agreement, was published in English translation by the Historical Manuscripts Commission in volume 7 of the *Stuart Papers ... at Windsor Castle* (London, 1923), p. 662.

20 In 1683 Giovanni Battista Muti was said to have owned two houses in the Piazza Pilotta, one beside a palazzo which occupied part of the north side of the piazza, described as a 'casino posto incontro la Casa delli Sig.ri Ciogni', the other beside a monastery which occupied the rest of the north side, described as a 'casino posto incontro il Muro di fianco del Monastero dell'humiltà' (Antinori, 'Il Palazzo Muti Papazzurri ai Santi Apostoli', p. 444). It is possible that Giovanni Battista Muti had sold these two properties, and subsequently rented them. A document of 1724, referring to building works carried out for the Stuart court, includes the 'Stalla incontro al Palazzo de Sig.r Cionni [sic]', which might be the house by then owned by Giacinto Manni (Archivio Segreto Vaticano, Palazzo Apostolica Computisteria (henceforth ASV. PAC) 983, no.63/10, payments made by the *Camera Apostolica* for King James III, 15 October 1724). An inventory drawn up in 1713 after the death of the father of Girolamo Muti refers to a 'casa incontro il Monastero del l'Humiltà', which might well be the house rented for the Stuart court from him (Marinelli, *il palazzo Muti Papazzurri alla Pilotta*, p. 241). Although there are other possibilities, these seem the most likely. The nineteenth century *Catasto Gregoriano* of Rome (reproduced between pp. 164–5 in Marinelli, *Il palazzo Muti Papazzurri alla Pilotta*) shows two properties (on the corners of the monastery of the Humiltà and the former Palazzo Ciogni), which might well have been the two houses used by the Stuart court.

21 James III originally hoped to be lent the Palazzo Cibò, on the west side of the Piazza dei Santi Apostoli, immediately opposite the Palazzo Colonna: see Edward Corp, *The Jacobites at Urbino: An Exiled Court in Transition* (Basingstoke, Palgrave, 2009), chapter 11. The Palazzo Gualterio was on the west side of the Corso, immediately to the south of the Palazzo Ruspoli, and was rented by Gualterio from the family of Cardinal Ottoboni.

22 James III would have been familiar with the work of Alessandro Specchi because the architect had previously worked for the Albani family at Urbino (Anna Fucili Bartolucci, 'Urbino e gli Albani', pp. 441–8, in *Arte e Cultura nella Provincia di Pesaro e Urbino dalle Origini a Oggi*, ed. Franco Battistelli (Venice, Marsilio Editori, 1986), p. 443).

23 ASV. PAC 982 (mainly but not completely reproduced in Pantanella, 'Palazzo Muti a piazza SS. Apostoli', pp. 317–28); ASR. Camerale I, Conti della Depositeria Generale (henceforth Cam I: CDG) b.2017 bis/f.13/7 (partly reproduced in Pantanella, pp. 316–17) and f.13/8/pp. 1–11 (not reproduced). The previous ceiling, painted by Charles Mellin, presumably included the arms of the Muti family, and would have been inappropriate for the residence of the Stuart court. The redecoration of the gallery in the king's apartment therefore symbolised the

change in the building's status from the Palazzo Muti to the Palazzo del Re. The total cost of preparing the palazzo for the Stuart court during 1719 was 14,559 *scudi* (ASR. Cam I: CDG b.2017 bis/f.13/8/pp. 1–2).

24 This was the entrance guarded by the head of the Swiss Guards, known as the *Guarda Portone*. From 1719 to 1746 this position was held by Bernard Nieriker.

25 These windows can easily be seen today, because the façade has not been significantly changed above the ground floor. The appearance of the façade as it was in the nineteenth century can be seen in ASR. Collezione Disegni e piante I, c.87, n.562, 'Palazzo Muti-Pappazzuri', tipo VII.

26 When a deep chasm opened in the Forum in 362 BC it was believed that it would not close until Rome's most valued possession had been thrown into it. Marcus Curtius, believing this to be a brave citizen, leaped fully armed on horseback into the chasm, which immediately closed.

27 There are no existing ground plans showing how the floors of the palazzo were arranged during the eighteenth century. The ones in the Archivio di Stato di Roma (see note 25, tipi I–VII), which show how it was arranged in the second half of the nineteenth century, need to be corrected by careful comparison both with the inventories in the Stuart Papers and with the descriptions in the papal archives of the building works carried out by the *Camera Apostolica* for James III. Parts of the ceilings are shown in Pantanella, 'Palazzo Muti a piazza SS. Apostoli', pp. 311–14. Restoration work was in progress when I inspected and photographed the king's apartment in July 2005.

28 It was used as the French embassy by the duc de Saint-Aignan, the younger half-brother of the duc de Beauvilliers.

29 ASV. PAC 982, reproduced in Pantanella, 'Palazzo Muti a piazza SS. Apostoli', pp. 319–20. The gallery was decorated by Soccorsi in 1719 while James III was in Spain, and it is unlikely that he had anything to do with its design.

30 Notes and photographs taken during my visit to the palazzo in July 2005.

31 ASV. PAC 983, no.63/10, payments made by the *Camera Apostolica* for King James III, 15 October 1724.

32 Information taken from the notice displayed (in 2005) on the wall of the Madonna dell'Archetto.

33 HMC *Stuart* VII, p. 662, G. B. Muti to *Camera Apostolica*, 22 December 1718.

34 ASV. PAC 982, reproduced in Pantanella, 'Palazzo Muti a piazza SS. Apostoli', p. 317. The painting itself is reproduced in colour in *Il Settecento a Roma*, catalogue of the exhibition in the Palazzo di Venezia, edited by Anna Lo Bianco and Angelo Negro (Rome, Silvana Editoriale, 2005), no.91, pp. 206–7.

35 National Archives, State Papers (henceforth NA. SP) 85/14/f.207, Stosch to Carteret, 26 December 1722.

36 NA. SP 85/14/f.388 and f.394, Stosch to Carteret, 3 and 10 July 1723; *Diario Ordinario* (Rome, Chracas), no.926, 10 July 1723, pp. 6–7.

37 NA. SP 85/14/f.374, Stosch to Carteret, 19 June 1723.

38 Corp, *A Court in Exile*, p. 102; NA. SP 85/14/f.498, Stosch to Carteret, 30 October 1723.

39 Royal Archives, Stuart Papers (henceforth RA SP) Misc 34, 'To Father Brown for a picture for ye altar in ye Ma.ties Chappel ...: 131 livres', November 1723. It is possible that the king had his own small chapel, or oratory, on the first floor and that this painting was purchased to be placed there rather than in the Chapel Royal.

40 In the absence of contemporary ground plans, it is very hard to be absolutely sure about the distribution of space within the Palazzo del Re. It seems that there

was a 'scaletta segreta' which led up to the apartment with the *loggietta* on the east side of the palazzo, within one of the *palazzetti*: 'la Scaletta segreta, dove ... è ... la Loggia'. That apartment was occupied during the early 1720s by Lord and Lady Inverness: 'App[artamen]to di Monsu Ess [Hay] dove stà la Loggia' (ASV. PAC 983, no.63/10 and no.64/9, payments made by the *Camera Apostolica* for King James III, 15 and 20 October 1724). Stosch referred to it in a letter dated 6 April 1723 which reported that it had been used by William Bromley (NA. SP 85/14/f.318, to Carteret).

41 In 1720, before the birth of Prince Charles, the household contained 109 people. By the middle of the 1720s it contained 135 people.

42 ASR. Camerale I, Registro de' Mandati Camerale (henceforth Cam I: RMC) b.1070/f.21, 30 June 1724. James III's annual pension from the Pope from 1716 to 1724 was 10,000 *scudi* (ASR. Cam I: RMC, various references in b.1066, b.1069, and b.1070). It was paid out of 'li frutti de Luoghi de Monte Camerale' (ASR. Cam I: RMC b.1066, f.46), an arrangement formalised by Clement XI in 1717 and renewed by his successors (ASV. Segretario di Stato: Inghilterra 21, pp. 245–53).

43 NA. SP 85/15/f.149 and f.151, Stosch to Newcastle, 24 June and 1 July 1724. The annual rent for the Palazzo del Re was 1632 *scudi* (ASR. Cam I: CDG b.2017 bis/f.13/10/pp. 1–4 and p. 19).

44 NA. SP 85/15/ff.137, 161, 163 and 171, Stosch to Newcastle, 10 June, 22 and 25 July, and 5 August 1724.

45 NA. SP 85/15/ff.194, 210, 212, Stosch to Newcastle, 16 September, 4 and 11 November 1724. The *palazzo apostolico* at Albano (incorrectly referred to in most books as the Palazzo Savelli) had been lent to James III since 1721 (ASR. Cam I: GT b.449, 457–60).

46 ASV. PAC 983, payments made by the *Camera Apostolica* for King James III. The principal references are nos.63/10, 64/9, 62/6 and 64/10, respectively 15 October, 20 October, 30 November and 15 December 1724. The total cost of the building works was 5,064 *scudi* (ASR. Cam I: CDG 2017 bis/f.13/12/pp. 1–2).

47 NA. SP 85/13/f.118, Edgar to Clephane, 28 November 1724.

48 Stosch reported on 30 December 1724 that two masked men (believed to be John Guise, MP, and Christopher Milles) had been brought up 'l'Escalier secret' into the king's bedchamber by Lord Inverness (NA. SP 85/15/f.237, to Newcastle). If Stosch is to be believed, a secret door was later made which gave direct access to the secret staircase from the Via del Vaccaro: 'Mes Emissaires m'assurent que plusieurs nuits consecutives, ils ont vû entrer dans une maison contigue a celle du Prétendant des Etrangers. J'ay decouvert depuis que dite maison a été loues expres et que au travers de la Muraille on a ouvert le passage, par où on peut commodement passer, jusques dans l'Apartement du Prétandant par un escalier derobé' (NA. SP 85/16/f.104, Stosch to Newcastle, 6 July 1726). Protestant visitors who used the secret staircase were received in the king's cabinet, which they reached by passing through one end of the gallery. Whether they would have had time to examine the overtly Catholic allegory painted on the ceiling by Soccorsi is unclear.

49 NA. SP 85/15/f.233, Stosch to Newcastle, 23 December 1724.

50 NA. SP 85/15/f.310 and f.314, Stosch to Newcastle, 6 and 10 March 1725.

51 ASR. Cam I: RMC b.1070/f.133. Because Benedict XIII supported Maria Clementina against her husband during their separation, he later reduced it to 12,000 *scudi* in March 1726, and to 10,000 *scudi* in April 1728 (ASR. Cam I: RMC b.1070/f.290 and b.1074/f.198).

52 David was paid 603 *livres* (approximately 120 *scudi*) for the picture in November 1725 (RA. SP Misc 34). The picture, now in the Scottish National Portrait Gallery (no.2511), measures 243.9 × 350.3 cm.

53 The Principessa di Piombino is shown standing with her daughters to the right of the middle of the picture. Don Carlo Albani is standing in front of the group of cardinals on the right hand side. The presence of the cardinals on both sides of the picture gives the ceremony an unmistakably Catholic appearance, but otherwise the painting merely presents a richly decorated Chapel Royal. The Anglican chapel in the Palazzo del Re was of course rather different. It 'had neither Confessional, Crucifix, nor Picture except an Altar-piece, nor any one thing to distinguish it from an English Chapel, as indeed it was in effect' (Anon., *Genuine Memoirs of John Murray, Esq., late Secretary to the Young Pretender ... in a Letter to a Friend* (London, 1747), p. 5). I am grateful to Richard Sharp for giving me this reference.

54 ASR. Cam I: CDG b.2017 bis/f.13/12; ASV. PAC 5044, 'Rincontro del Banco in conte a parte delle spese che p. ordine di N.tro Sig.re si fanno p. la Maestà di Giacomo 3° Rè d'Inghilterra', 1719–33.

55 ASV. PAC 983, payments made by the *Camera Apostolica* for King James III. The principal references are nos.110/10, 111/11, 113/16 and 135/14, 2 February to 31 March 1729, and no.124/11, 24 November 1729. The payments amounted to 4,379 *scudi*.

56 ASV. PAC 983 and 984, payments made by the *Camera Apostolica* for King James III, 1724–36. Stosch wrote to the Duke of Newcastle on 17 September 1735 that 'le Pape Clement XII plus splendide de ses Predecesseurs vient de donner ordre a la Chambre Apostolique, de luy [James III] payer hors en avant tout ce qu'il demandera, et autre besoin pour le maintien de sa Maison et Famille sans luy avoir fixé la somme precise de la Depense' (NA. SP 98/37/f.271). The money spent by the *Camera Apostolica* on the Palazzo del Re (excluding rent) during the papacy of Clement XII averaged 1,780 *scudi* per annum between 1730 and 1734, but thereafter (after the death of the queen) went down between 1735 and 1740 to 667 *scudi* per annum. During the first four years of the papacy of Benedict XIV the average was 792 *scudi*. Throughout this period the bills for maintenance work and new furniture for the Palazzo del Re were sent to the *Camera Apostolica* for payment. Then in 1745, by which time both Prince Charles and Prince Henry had gone to France, Benedict XIV decided to give James III a lump sum of 600 *scudi* per annum to spend as he wished, with any money left over added to the amount of his annual pension. This arrangement continued until the death of James III, after which Prince Charles was expected to pay for the maintenance and furnishing of the palazzo out of his own pocket. These details are all taken from ASV. PAC 5044 (1719–33), PAC 5045 (1734–42), PAC 5220 (1743–70), and PAC 5223 (1775–89). The volume covering 1770–75 is missing.

57 Numerous references in ASV. PAC 983–7, payments made by the *Camera Apostolica*, 1724–43.

58 NA. SP 85/14, 15 and 16 (1722–29); NA. SP 98/32, 37, 41, 43, 46, 49, 53, 58 and 61 (1730–57). When Stosch described the precise location of the Stuart court for the Duke of Newcastle, he specified that it was not in the Palazzo Muti, but in a building beside the Palazzo Muti (NA. SP 98/37/f.16, 2 January 1734).

59 ASR. Cam I: CDG b.2017 bis/f.13/14/p. 1, p. 3 and pp. 9–10.

60 ASV. PAC 5223, 'Registro de Mandati per ... che so fanno per il Palazzo e sui annessi gia abitati dalla glor. me. di Giacomo III Rè d'Inghilterra dall anno 1775', pp. 40–6.

61 Archivio Storico Vicariato di Roma, Santi Apostoli vol. 78, pp. 25^r, 61^r, 126, 134, *Stati d'Anime* for 1767, 1768, 1770 and 1771.

62 ASV. PAC 5223, pp. 111–16.

63 Archivio Storico Vicariato di Roma, Santi Apostoli vol. 81, pp. 18^r, 16, 14, *Stati d'Anime* for 1788, 1789 and 1790; and vol. 82, no.524, *Stati d'Anime* for 1792.

64 It was published by Piranesi separately in his series entitled *Vedute di Roma*. The Palazzo Odescalchi had previously been known as the Palazzo Chigi.

65 It was published by Vasi in the fourth volume of his *Delle Magnificenze di Roma Antica e Moderna.*

66 It is probably not a coincidence that the second of the engravings of the real Palazzo Muti (see note 9) was published shortly after the publication of these engravings by Piranesi and Vasi. It is dedicated 'All'Illustrissimo Signore Il Sig. Marchese Curzio Muti de' Papazzurri, Da Suoi Umiliss. obbligatiss. servitori Bouchard e Gravier' (private collection). Curzio Muti (1712–97) had succeeded his father Marchese Girolamo Muti in 1750.

67 John Ingamells, *A Dictionary of British and Irish Travellers in Italy, 1701–1800* (Yale University Press, 1997).

68 Richard Sharp, *The Engraved Record of the Jacobite Movement* (Aldershot, 1996). Good examples can be seen on p. 67 and p. 97.

69 RA. SP 285/187, James III to Cardinal de Tencin, 25 July 1747.

70 Marcello Fagiolo, ed., *Corpus delle feste a Roma. Vol. 2, Il settecento e l'ottocento* (Rome, Edizione De Luca, 1997), pp. 138–9.

71 *Subleyras, 1699–1749*, eds. Olivier Michel and Pierre Rosenberg, exhibition catalogue (Paris, Réunion des Musées Nationaux, 1987), p. 117.

72 Gallimard's engraving is extremely rare, and has apparently never been reproduced. I am very grateful to Richard Sharp for drawing it to my attention, and for giving me a facsimile. The first person to identify the location of the *facciata* on the Palazzo del Re was Dr. David Marshall, during the conference 'Roma-Britannica', held at the British School at Rome in February 2006.

73 At some point Cardinal York commissioned an unidentified artist to paint a large picture based on the engraving by Gallimard. It is now in the Scottish National Portrait Gallery. The details are all similar, but the painting also shows the new cardinal greeting his father and showing him the *facciata*. Rosalind Marshall, then a curator at the Portrait Gallery, reproduced it in 1988, in her biography of 'Bonnie Prince Charlie', with a modern photograph of the Palazzo Muti in the Piazza Pilotta. She drew the perfectly reasonable, although erroneous, conclusion that the shape of the *facciata* shown in the painting demonstrated that the Palazzo Muti in the Piazza Pilotta must have been occupied by the exiled Stuart court. As it was known that the Stuart court had definitely occupied the adjacent building at the north end of the Piazza dei Santi Apostoli, this implied that it had occupied both buildings. Adopting Rosalind Marshall's conclusion, this was the interpretation wrongly given in Corp, ed., *Stuart Court in Rome*, p. 15 and pp. 21–2 (note 33). See also above, note 2. In fact the Palazzo Muti was occupied throughout the eighteenth century by the Muti family (Archivio Storico Vicariato di Roma, Santi Apostoli, the annual lists of *Stati d'anime*; Marinelli, *Il palazzo Muti Papazzurri alla Pilotta*, pp. 262–3).

74 *Diario Ordinario*, no.4674, 8 July 1747, p. 17.

75 *Diario Ordinario*, no.4683, 29 July 1747, p. 20. The *facciata* was created between 6 and 25 July 1747, and would have remained in position until September.

10
The Irish Jacobite Regiments and the French Army: A Way to Integration

Nathalie Genet-Rouffiac

> Our dutie to our King will make us serve the French King with all zeale and faithfulness that he can expect.[1]

So wrote Captain Rutherford to Henry Browne, secretary of Mary of Modena, from Lille, on 21 August 1691. This quotation is a rather good illustration of the nature of the presence of the Jacobite Irish regiments – or perhaps we should say the Irish Jacobite regiments – in the French army after 1690. This presence was a clear proof of their commitment to the Jacobite cause, but it also led to their integration into French society. Yet the whole process never questioned their 'Irishness', which was always loudly proclaimed. The point here is not to describe the life of these regiments, or even their social integration throughout the eighteenth century, but to underline the subtle balance and game of influence that was involved, from the first generation of exile, between Versailles, Saint-Germain and the Irish themselves.

The wild geese in France

It is very significant that the Irish Jacobite exile in France was part of a broader movement of Jacobite exile, and that the 'flight of the Wild Geese' also gave a new dimension to an old phenomenon, the presence in France of Irish soldiers. For as much as the exile of the Jacobites in France was entangled in the long-term relationship between France and Great Britain, there was also a new reality, specifically linked to Jacobite history. Soon after 1603, some Irish soldiers had entered the service of Spain and France, and this continued throughout the seventeenth century. The French armies always attracted the poor from economically backward countries like Ireland. Louis Cullen has already noted a constant flood, averaging 900 Irishmen each year, between 1601 and 1701, that rose to perhaps 1,000 annually between 1701 and 1750.[2]

Of course, the 'flight of the Wild Geese' occurred on a much bigger scale, but their number is difficult to establish from the seventeenth century archives, and has been at the centre of many scholarly debates.[3] The Irish researcher J. C. O'Callaghan and the French historian Guy Chaussinand-Nogaret[4] estimate their numbers at 19,000 men, but Guy Rowlands, the English specialist on Louis XIV's military administration, thinks that no more than 14,000 Wild Geese, with 4,000 women and children, came over to Brittany.[5] When it comes to the Irish in Louis XIV's army, it is also important to keep in mind that they were spread between two different kinds of regiment: the Irish regiments *of* the French army (the Mountcashel brigade) and the Jacobite Irish regiments *in* the French army (the Wild Geese themselves).

The Mountcashel brigade was created at an early stage of the war in Ireland. In May 1690, James II's situation had been weakened by William of Orange's landing. Louis XIV agreed to send more French troops, but only if Irish infantry regiments were integrated with his army. The French king had been warned by his agent the comte d'Avaux to be extremely demanding with regard to the quality of these troops, because most regiments in Ireland had been recruited by 'gentlemen who know nothing of war... the companies are made of tailors, butchers or shoe-makers, who keep them at their own expense and are the captains.' The statement was not purely rhetorical, for the registers of the Hôtel des Invalides, from 1689 to 1715, show that one-third of the Irish who had a professional occupation before entering a regiment were actually clothes-makers or tailors![6] Louis XIV made his requirements very clear: he wanted men of experience and noble birth. The negotiations between the two cousins were rather tense, and the comte d'Avaux often found himself in an uncomfortable position,[7] but eventually James II had to give in to the French king's demands.[8]

Once they had arrived in France, these troops were sent to Bourges and organised into three regiments: Mountcashel, O'Brien and Dillon, known jointly as the Mountcashel brigade. They were given a red uniform with white socks and the hat known as the 'chapeau lampion'.[9] All the officers were commissioned by Louis XIV as *his* officers, and the regiments were paid like French foreign regiments, one *sol* more a day than the French troops. In all respect, the regiments were French regiments composed of Irish soldiers. In fact, this feature was not unusual in the French army, where 13.8% of the *maréchaux de France* were foreigners.[10]

The arrival in France of the Mountcashel brigade did not put an end to the military transactions between the two courts. The war on the Continent made France more and more demanding. On 30 July 1690, the marquis of Louvois, *secrétaire d'état de la guerre*, let the duke of Lauzun know the new demands of the king of France for Irish recruits.[11] James II needed persuading, and the French minister had to become more insistent with the duke of Tyrconnel in May 1691: 'I'm very surprised to see that, in spite of your promises, you are very cold in the sending of new recruits.'[12] When James persisted in ignoring his cousin's demand, the French became far more explicit. 'I order you,' wrote Louvois to the *commissaire* Fumeron, 'to tell the duke of Tyrconnel in a private discussion, that if he fails me in the matter of recruits, he will find me failing in all matters concerning Ireland.'[13] The message was clear enough. By 21 May Louvois could thank Tyrconnel for having sent 1,200 more men to the Mountcashel brigade, 'which is a small present in comparison with all the expenses the King incurs for the sake of Ireland.'[14]

The situation was rather different for the 'Wild Geese' that Patrick Sarsfield had brought over with him. After the fall of Limerick, and even before the Treaty was signed in February 1692, three quarters of the Jacobite army in Ireland was persuaded to follow its officers to the Continent, at the expense of the Prince of Orange. It was a free decision, for the Treaty would have allowed them to stay, and the Williamite anti-Catholic legislation had not yet been introduced. A retreat to the Continent, however, seemed to be the best way to defend James II's interests.

The upkeep of such a large number of troops was a very big expense for the French. It also represented a foreign army on French territory. Louis XIV seems to have accepted this situation for four main reasons: a feeling of moral obligation toward his cousin, the demands of James II, the need for the French army to acquire spare troops and the need to make sure the Irish would enter French service before they could be recruited by an opposing Catholic country.[15] All the Irish troops were gathered in Brest, under the command of Dominick Sheldon. James II visited them with Berwick and declared himself satisfied with their fidelity. In fact, they were in very poor condition. The voyage had finished the dislocation of the Irish army. At least 1,500 men were sick, and the French had to supply them with hats, shoes, shirts and socks.

Until the battle of La Hougue, on 24 May 1692, they all expected to re-embark soon for Ireland. The defeat sealed the fate of the Irish regiments. In the second week of June, Louis XIV unilaterally decided to break some of them up and spread them between his armies. The officers were given their travel warrants to join the French forces. The reorganisation of the regiments was extremely painful (see Appendix 10.1). James II had to reduce his army to two regiments of horse guards, two cavalry regiments, two dragoon regiments, eight infantry regiments and three independent companies. Many regiments that had fought in Ireland were abolished and many officers were reduced in rank, but they all continued to be commissioned by James II.[16]

The 1692 reorganisation lasted until the peace of Ryswick in 1697. In addition to his political failure, the king of France had to undertake a reform of the Irish troops (see Appendix 10.2), which would have major repercussions for the economic situation of the Wild Geese and their families.[17]

Of the three-fifths of the Irish soldiers who were disbanded (amounting to about 5,000 men), many turned to Saint-Germain for help and charity. The Scot Walter Innes offered a striking description to his friend Charles Leslie on 24 March 1698:

> It would pitie a heart of stone to see the Court of Saint-Germain at present, especially now that all the ... Irish troups are disbanded, so that there are now at Saint-Germains not only many hundred of shouldiery starving, but also many gentlemen and officers that have not cloathes to putt on their backs or shoes to putt on their feet or meat, etc.[18]

The other option for the Irish was to enter the Hôtel des Invalides in Paris. The number of Wild Geese to be admitted at the Invalides increased by 150% between 1697 and 1698![19] This stark choice, Saint-Germain or the Invalides, symbolises the situation of the Wild Geese in France.

Versailles, Saint-Germain and the Irish

To understand the situation of the Wild Geese, it is important to start with their position in the first generation of the Jacobite Diaspora in France (Appendix 10.3). The first wave of arrivals from 1688 to 1691 consisted almost exclusively of English people and was the immediate consequence of political events in England. In 1692, there was a spectacular increase in the number of exiles (more than 230%), easily traced to the arrival of the Wild Geese. The numbers swelled until 1698, particularly in the years 1696–1697, then slowed down, although it continued at a steady rate until 1701. This phenomenon of continuing growth was especially noticeable among the Irish and may be explained by the regrouping of army families close to Saint-Germain after the disbanding of the troops. After 1701, the exiled population decreased. The process was identical for the English as for the Irish and was accompanied by a decrease in the number of mar-riages and baptisms, a sign that the population that had arrived between 1688 and 1692 was then getting older. In addition, younger people had 'escaped', mainly because disbanded soldiers had left for other Catholic countries with their families.

The composition of the exiled community (Appendix 10.4) stabilised after 1692 and remained the same until 1715, a date which saw the second wave of arrivals and coincided with the second generation of exiles. The Irish formed the majority, around 60% of the exiles, as against 35% who were English and only 5% Scots, even though the political influence of this last group was in inverse proportion to its numbers.

The links between Saint-Germain and the regiments were maintained by the frequent presence of officers at the Stuart court, especially in winter times. Some of them, and even more of their relatives, were members of the king's household. Dominick Sheldon, colonel of the regiment of the same name, was one of the main figures at the court of Saint-Germain, where he was vice-chamberlain and under-preceptor to the Prince after 1697. His brothers Ralph and Edward were esquires to the king and to the queen. The French courtier Saint-Simon, usually sparing with compliments, declared Sheldon to be 'one of the rarest, finest and largest minds in Britain.'[20] In his youth, he had served with the troops Charles II had lent to Louis XIV, before coming back to England in 1675. He became brigadier in 1693, *maréchal de camp* in 1694, and served as *aide de camp* of the duke of Vendôme in 1708.

The connection between the regiments and Versailles was maintained specifically by a small number of representatives, called 'the agent of the Irish troops in the service of France', as Morgan Scully, captain in Lee's regiment, was called in a 1695 document.[21] A letter of the duke of Berwick is more explicit: 'the habit has always been, for the 18 years the Irish troops have been in France, to have someone at court to take care and manage the interests of the regiments of this nation, for the expense of a single agent is infinitely lower than that of many officers we should have to send.'[22] This agent was in charge of their interests both at Versailles and at Saint-Germain. At the same time, the English king maintained written relationships with the regiments, usually with the colonel. In 1691, while at Lille, his correspondents were the captains Knighteley and Rutherford. The responsibility was so heavy that on December 31, 1691, Knighteley asked the court to send him help for he was overwhelmed by his task, '*to that degree that I am harassed to death.*'[23]

Yet the relationship between the Wild Geese and the Jacobite court ended up in a double failure: first of all, because the Irish failed politically at Saint-Germain. There, the persons of the king and his family were the focal points for the exiles. The importance of any exile could be determined according to his social distance from the monarch. The whole community in exile can be likened to four concentric circles around the Stuart sovereign (Appendix 10.5), to which all those living in Paris and Saint-Germain can be assigned. The first circle consisted of the aristocrats with political power and social leverage. Around sixty-five nobles can be placed in this first circle, composing a narrow political elite. To the second circle belonged the gentry and all the nobles who had an office in the royal household, totalling about 200. Beyond this, in the third group, were the servants and all those who lived on grants and pensions: perhaps 300 Jacobites in all. Finally, in the fourth circle, were found those who did not live at the court but were occasionally linked to it. Seventy-seven percent of the Jacobite community in exile occupied this outer circle, and 85% of Irish families belonged to it.

The closer to the centre, the more Scots and English are to be found; the more distant the circle, the more Irish it was. The outermost circle was in fact composed mainly of Irish Jacobites. Since political influence was determined by social status and proximity to the king, the Irish, despite their numbers and fidelity, exerted little influence. The main problem was the weakness of Irish patronage. At Saint-Germain as at all courts, patronage was very important. Receiving grants from the king could determine ranking and sometimes simply ensure survival. It was essential in the exiled Jacobite world to rely on patrons, naturally the leading aristocrats of each national group. The Scots were extremely well protected by the duke of Perth, but Irish patronage soon appeared to be too weak for their needs. The deaths first of Tyrconnell and then, at the battle of Neerwinden, of Patrick Sarsfield, deprived them of any prominent patron at the court. Protection was given by Tyrconnell's and Sarsfield's widows, and by Francis Plowden, but he was never more than a second-rank courtier to James II. Another patron was the duke of Berwick, who had married Sarsfield's widow.[24] The duke is known to have been very fond of his Irish soldiers, and his private clerk, Patrick Farelly, was Irish. But the duke was more successful in the French army than at the court of Saint-Germain, and after his second marriage to Lady Bulkeley, he seems to have been closer to the English community than to the Irish.

Another problem was the social distinction between the Irish members of the courts, including the officers, and the rank and file of the Irish regiments. Most of the soldiers belonged to 'Old Irish' or Gaelic families, while the officers were more often 'Old English', descended from medieval English settlers. A very simple, but striking, evidence of this difference is to be found in their names. The Irish on the parochial registers of Saint-Germain, and the Irish soldiers in the registers of the Invalides during the same period, simply do not have the same first names. You can find names like 'Oine' and 'Oile', 'Darby', 'Mortagh', 'Dawson' or even 'Eoghan' among the soldiers, names that cannot be found at Saint-Germain.

The second failure was due to the fact that Saint-Germain lost control of the Irish regiments. When it came to the 1697 disbanding, for example, the decision was taken by the court of Versailles, although the consequences fell on the court of Saint-Germain. From their first landing in Brittany, the fate of the Irish regiments had been a matter of hard bargaining between the French and the Jacobite court. The stakes were high. For the French king, the Irish regiments were a weapon against England that he never found wanting. For the Irish, service in the French regiments was the only way left to fight for their king and their country. For James II, however, they were proof not only of loyalty to his person, but also that he was still a sovereign.

It is important to stress that Louis XIV made a major political concession to his cousin when he left him the right to commission the officers of the Irish regiments. For keeping an army was the prerogative of a sovereign, and it is a sign of the depth of Louis's commitment to James that he let him do so in his own kingdom. The fact that the Irish regiments were *de facto* parts of the French army does not diminish the importance of his gesture, for no one was more aware of the political significance of such a measure than the Sun King himself. The Irish regiments, as the army of James II, were a proof that he was still a king. They gave James and his son a different status from all the other exiled princes protected by the court of Versailles. 'As long as there is a body of Irish Roman Catholiks troops abroad', Charles Forman was still writing to the Walpole government in 1720, 'the chevalier will always make some figure in Europe by the credit they give him.'[25]

At the court of Saint-Germain, the two kings had agreed that James could keep a military administration proportional to the size of the Irish regiments, under the direction of Sir Richard Nagle, James's Secretary of State for Ireland and his Attorney-General, who became secretary for war until his death in April 1699. James II appointed the officers; he could also suspend them and decide on their replacement amongst his colonels. He supervised the court martial sessions and reviewed them several times. Most of the administrative questions were managed at the court of Saint-Germain or in the regiments. Nagle often had to settle quarrels between Irish colonels, and he created the loan system which made them able to pay their troops. But Saint-Germain's authority and control over the regiments were weakened by the early deaths of Tyrconnel and Sarsfield, in spite of the many disagreements between the two men.

Guy Rowlands, in his study of the *Bureau de la Guerre*, the military administration created by Louvois, has shown that the management of the Irish regiments was an issue between Saint-Germain and Versailles that has often been underestimated. Until the death of Nagle and the peace of Utrecht, a regular correspondence and cooperation were settled with the French minister, and James II gave several audiences to Louvois' son and successor, the marquis de Barbezieux.[26] From the very beginning, however, it was the French minister who gave the officers their travel warrants and the regiments their leave to move. His commissaries could inspect the Irish regiments, even though Dominick Sheldon had been made controller-general. Above the rank of brigadier, the Irish officers ceased to be given their commission by James II, and were promoted by Louis XIV alone.[27] It was a good way to settle the French King's patronage on the Irish officers, whose careers ultimately depended on Versailles, not on their relationship with Saint-Germain.

James II was very eager to display the image of a royal court at St. Germain, but he never fully understood that keeping up a royal military administration could also have been a proof of his royalty.[28] In fact, when it came to managing the regiments, the Jacobites were mere amateurs compared to the French professionals of the *Bureau de la Guerre*. Beyond the boundaries of official reverence to James II, the professionals clearly took over from Saint-Germain.

Links with France

But taking absolute control over the Irish regiments was another matter! In fact, the French never quite succeeded in doing so. The first decision of the French administration was to try to teach them order and discipline. Already at Brest, Louis XIV had sent officers of the *gardes françaises* to form the Irish into 100-man companies, and to teach them French drill. M. de Famechon, French *brigadier* in Ireland, had warned the marquis of Louvois about the difficulty of the task: 'I have no doubt that in other places and under the command of other officers, they could become good troops, for the Irish have good dispositions for war, but they first have to be taught how to be soldiers.'[29]

The temperament of the Irish and their lack of discipline had already surprised Louis XIV's agent in Ireland. In France, they provoked the indignation of the French *commissaires des guerres*. The *commissaire* Bouridal complained to minister Barbezieux: 'I would never have believed old troops could lack discipline so badly, and the officers are even worse than the soldiers.'[30] Barbezieux had strong convictions about the best way to deal with the Irish temperament: 'the only way to avoid the disturbances committed by Irish soldiers, horsemen and dragoons is to have the most guilty of them hanged, as I've already told you. That should put an end to the troubles and the troops will get used to French discipline.'[31]

Even after Barbezieux was put in charge of the inspection of the Irish regiments in 1696, his agents found it difficult to understand the way the Irish officers were managing their regiments, especially with respect to wages. The Irish kept 'their own way', which often led to financial problems or extortion. In 1695, 100,000 French *livres*, seven months wages for a battalion, were stolen, and four regiments were almost driven to bankruptcy.[32] The payment of Irish troops remained an exception in the French military administration, and kept the Irish regiments in a very ambiguous position.

This was exacerbated by the question of Irish identity. First and foremost, the Irish regiments were a kind of 'little Ireland on the Continent'. For these men who at first had thought they would be back soon in Ireland, and who often knew nothing of life in France, the regiments offered a reassuring milieu. The colonels of the regiments were the landowners they had known at home, and usually the men served with others from the area they came from originally. The regiments were also worlds to themselves because they included families. Very often, the families of the poorest soldiers could not afford to stay away from their relatives and followed them during the military campaigns. They can be traced in the records of French archives. On 6th October 1712, John Gernon, one of Mary of Modena's chaplains, gave to a lawyer in Paris a 'leave,' written in favour of Catherine Sloakes, widow of a captain in Berwick's regiment. She was said to be with her children at the regiment's winter quarters at Manosque in Provence, and the letter had been written by a local lawyer. Two years later, Geron gave the Parisian lawyer a second letter from the same woman, written by 'Diego Garcia Calderon, lawyer in Malaga' in Spain, where the regiment was then stationed.[33]

The French carefully kept the Irish apart from the rest of the French army and made it very clear that all the Irishmen in French service had to join the Irish regiments. The *ordonnance* of 29 November 1694, and even more that of 12 February 1702, made it a strict obligation 'for all the English, Scottish and Irish that are in France to enter the Irish regiments on the King's service' on pain of being prosecuted for vagrancy, which meant being sentenced to the galleys.[34] We know that these measures enforcing centralised control on the Irish were effective, for after 1694, all the Irish soldiers at the Invalides belonged to Irish regiments.[35] In March 1702, the *intendant* of Franche-Comté wrote to Michel Chamillart, the minister of War, that the magistrates and sub-delegates had been looking for Irish, Scots and English in his area, and had found none.[36] The actual purpose of such searches was less to find new soldiers – in fact, it had been necessary to disband troops in 1697 – than to try to keep control of these troublesome foreigners in the century of the 'great confinement'. This could explain the threat of charging them with vagrancy and the penalty of the galleys. In the same way, the minister of War ordered in 1702 that Irish, Scottish and English soldiers should be looked for in the other French regiments, so that they could be sent to the Irish regiments.[38]

The connection with Ireland was still strong and recruitment vigorous. Éamonn Ó Ciardha has underlined the major part that the Catholic clergy and the Catholic gentry played in eighteenth century enlistments. They created rituals and gave a strong religious significance to departure for the Continent, which became a main theme in Jacobite literature in Ireland. Enlistment provided the main form of public commitment to Jacobitism in the eighteenth century. The owners of the Irish regiments kept agents on their previous estates, maintaining a network of local patronage. But the French also kept recruiting officers in Ireland, before and after 1692. A pamphlet of 1693, entitled *Mémoire touchant des moyens pour avoir des recrues d'Irlande*, stipulated that 'an agent was to be established at Dublin, who was to have agents to act, according to his directions, in the several Counties. They were to enlist recruits and to facilitate their escape to France.'[38] The danger of being discovered by the Irish authorities was real. Sir Nicholas Dempster, Marie of Modena's secretary, could complain to Cardinal Gualterio about 'the severity with which are persecuted recruits and recruiting staff of our Irish regiments. It is most unlikely that the English government should tolerate this enlistment for it's a deadly crime to enlist people in a Prince's estates without his leave.'[39] After the failure of the '45 in Scotland, a register of Jacobite prisoners shows that most of the rank and file Irish prisoners were native-born, and a *registre de contrôle de troupe* for FitzJames cavalry in 1737 records that 80% of the men were actually born in Ireland.[40]

The individuality of the Irish was certainly reinforced by the strong animosity that existed between the three national groups of the Jacobite diaspora. It seems that suspicions between the three groups were very intense – indeed, they hated each other. D'Avaux, Louis XIV's agent in Ireland, had already discovered before 1692 that 'the Irish love the French and are the enemies of the English so that if they were let loose, it would not take them long to slaughter them.'[41] Animosity was particularly strong in the army where the Irish at first refused to serve under officers who were not their own countrymen. Even in Paris and Saint-Germain, the tensions were in evidence. To quote the passionate Lord Lovat, a Scot, 'there's a lethal hate between Scotland and England because they have kept us for so long in slavery; in the same way there's such hate between the Irish and the English that the three nations have totally different and irreconcilable interests'.[42] The princess Palatine summarized the French point of view by complaining that the exiles were all living like dogs and cats.[43]

The French parochial records reveal the extreme rarity of marriages between members of the three national groups. Only a very few can be traced in the Saint-Germain registers during the first generation. The phenomenon may seem very obvious, but actually it was something new for the 'Old English' gentry. Before their exile, they had been used to looking for suitable alliances among the daughters of the English Catholic gentry, rather than among the 'Old Irish'. It was as if the restrictions they were exposed to at the court of Saint-Germain made them more Irish than they had been before their exile. When it came to matrimonial alliances, the two options, once again, were Ireland… or France.

The way to integration in French society

Except for the aristocrats, whose French was often fluent, the first difficulty for the Wild Geese in France must have been the language. When the exiles were involved in a judicial action, the French authorities had to ask for translations. They turned to British exiles who could speak French, most of them Irish bankers (Richard Cantillon, Daniel Arthur) or priests of the Irish college.

Gaelic is totally absent in the French archives. As in Brittany, where the names of the wealthy were spelled in French, while humbler folk used Breton spellings, the richest Irish exiles seem to have used an English way of spelling their names; but the names of the poorest seem to have been spelled by the French from an Irish pronunciation.[44] James 'Foyalaine', buried in Saint-Germain in 1695, aged 22, is closer to 'Faoláin' than a more English 'Phelan'; and the name of James 'Frenaghty,' witness at a wedding the same year, seems to come from the Irish 'Finnachta.' Amongst the soldiers in the Invalides can be found several 'Eamons' but no 'Edmond'. Bad spelling and misunderstandings on the part of the French military administrators were the first steps to the francisation of Irish names. Swinton became 'Sainton', Forbes 'Forbois', Blackwood 'Blaquehut'. When Edme Keand, an Irishman, was sent to the hospital de la Charité, rue Jacob, after a violent fight, he said he was the son of Daniel Keand and Helene 'Pleine de grace' (Full of grace), which is most likely 'Prendergast' in the original version.[45]

To make their names sound more noble in France, some Irish started to wear the French 'de' at the beginning of their names. The *Dictionnaires de la langue bretonne* records two Irish brothers in Brest called O'Brien who turned their names into D'obrien![46]

Strange animals they were indeed to the French people. Strangers, but foreigners too, they were what the French called *aubains*, which means born elsewhere. Indeed, under the *ancien régime*, only people born in France, or granted the privilege of naturalisation, had full legal rights. All others had the rights that every human soul should be given, the *jus gentium*, but only people born in France or naturalised could be allowed the *jus civile*, the rights of civil law. Foreigners were allowed to get married, to own property and to go to court, but they had no right to civil parenthood. This meant that they could not inherit or bequeath their properties to relatives, unless these relatives were French. All properties of a foreigner dying in France belonged to the king of France, as his *droit d'aubaine*. Only the rents on the Hotel de Ville de Paris were not subject to this, which is why they soon became the Jacobites' favourite way of saving money, and the king of France's favourite way to tax them.[47] The average tax was 200 *livres*. Both the lowest and the highest taxes on foreigners were paid by Irishmen: Patrice Montcolif had to pay '38 livres 3 sous et 9 deniers', and the Irish banker Sir Daniel Arthur, 18,000 livres.[48]

There were only two ways to escape the *droit d'aubaine*. First, the king could give the inheritance to the children of the deceased by a letter of 'don d'aubaine'. Louis XIV seems never to have refused it to any Jacobite, but it never became an automatic gift. The second way to escape the *droit d'aubaine* was to ask for a 'letter of naturalisation' and to become French. The Jacobites sought to obtain a general measure of naturalisation for the whole exiled community. In November 1715, Louis XV naturalised all foreigners who had served in the French army for more than ten years, rank and file as well as officers. As late as 1749, the main aristocratic families of Irish origin or with Irish connections (Tyrconnel, Lally, Dunkell, FitzJames) were promoting a project to make all the Irish Catholics living in France true French *naturels*.[49] Such a privilege, however, was never granted. Unlike Spain, where Philip V in 1701 and 1718 gave all the Wild Geese the same rights as the native Spanish,[50] naturalisation in France was still a personal personnel request and an individual grant.

From 1689 to 1715, 508 Jacobites were naturalized as French (Appendix 6), which makes an average of almost nineteen a year. They numbered 309 between 1697 and 1703, or forty-four a year. Of these, 56% were Irish and 39% English, which is very close to the general distribution of the Jacobite community, but they do not seem to have been reacting to the same circumstances. The number of Irish naturalisations rose after 1697, following the treaty of Utrecht and the disbanding of the Irish regiments, while the English asked for naturalisation mainly after 1701 and the death of James II.

Some of them, starting with the duke of Berwick, found it necessary to ask for James II's leave to become French.[51] In many ways, however, naturalisation was more a convenience than a real change. In the French archives, the new subjects of the king of France are never called 'French,' but 'naturalised French'. For the Wild Geese, service to France and loyalty to Ireland were never confused. In 1745, François Sarsfield declared that 'letters of naturalisation give us a right that we had not yet... but they can't break the old link to the homeland for this bond can't be destroyed.'[52]

One of the main concerns of the Jacobite exiles was to have their nobility acknowledged by the French. To do so, they had to ask for a certificate from the herald of arms of their nation at the court of Saint-Germain (James Tiry for the Irish), which allowed them to request a letter of recommendation from the English king's secretary which could be used to obtain a letter of nobility from the French authorities. In 1700, no less than fifteen of these requests were granted at St. Germain. Amongst them was Nicolas Lukes, the son of Etienne Lukes of Waterford and Elizabeth Linch, both of noble birth.[53] He came to France with his brother John and their cousins (the Commerfords of Waterford) and enlisted in the Irish regiments.[54] In Ireland, their rights were forfeited, their lands confiscated and their father sent to jail. John was killed in Catalonia, but Nicolas was part of an infantry regiment from 1688 to 1693. Sent to Guadeloupe in the West Indies, he was saved from drowning by his Irish temperament, for he refused to get back on board the *Ville de Nantes*, which sank a few days later on the return journey to France, with a loss of 220 men. He then became *cornette de cavalerie* under the command of governor d'Amblemont, and settled on the island. He married the daughter of a French nobleman and became French himself.

The Irish regiments also turned out to be spearheads in the process of assimilation and in the success of exiled families in French society. An example of this is Arthur Dillon, who commanded the regiment that bore his name. He had come over to France after several of his estates had been confiscated (2,800 acres in Mayo, 825 in Roscommon and 1,042 in Westmeath). He was made a brigadier after the victory of Cremona in 1702, became lieutenant-general in 1706 and distinguished himself at the side of the duke of Berwick in the campaign of 1714, which was his last. When he retired from active service in 1730, he handed the regiment over to his eldest son, thus permanently establishing the Dillons as one of the great officer families of *ancien régime* France. His youngest son, Arthur, became abbot of St. Etienne de Caen, then archbishop of Evreux, archbishop of Toulouse and finally archbishop of Narbonne, which made him a leading cleric in the French church. Yet the elder Dillon's career at the heart of the Mountcashel brigade never lessened his links with the court of Saint-Germain, where his wife, Catherine Sheldon, was maid of honour to Mary of Modena. This link lasted after the departure of James-Edward in 1713, and even after the death of Marie of Modena in 1718, for Dillon was still lodged at the castle of Saint-Germain when he died, on 5 February 1733.

The case of the Dillon family is also very revealing, because the French Revolution tore apart, on the one hand, those who simply could not make peace with England, and on the other, those like the archbishop, whose social behaviour was now the same as the French native upper class. Feeling betrayed by revolutionary France, he came over to die and be buried in England. In many ways, it was the French Revolution that put an end to the Jacobite episode in France.

In conclusion, we have to return to the triangular relationships between Saint-Germain, Versailles and the Wild Geese. In the long term, the most natural connection, linking the Irish Jacobites and their king, turned out to be the weakest. Not that the emotional bond was shallow, or that any notion of republicanism affected it: on the contrary, the Wild Geese were strong Jacobites, and one has to remember what they had been prepared to lose for their king, not knowing in advance what exile would bring them. Nevertheless, it simply happened that for the court of Saint-Germain, an invasion of Ireland ceased to be a viable option, and the Irish exiles began to look more like a burden than an effective weapon. The French got the point. If Louis XIV protected his cousin, the professionals of the *Bureau de la Guerre*, without of course ever breaching the official policy of support for the Jacobites, tried to make sure that they took it over, at least as much as was possible with the Irish regiments.

For the Irish Jacobites, exile had been chosen out of loyalty to the Stuart cause, but when the centre of Jacobite activity left France after 1714, they did not follow. Eventually, the conditions of exile had prevailed over the sentiment of Jacobitism. The army gave them an extremely successful way of becoming integrated into French society, not by assimilation or acculturation, but by maintaining the symbols of their identity, which is very revealing of the French *ancien régime*. The Wild Geese gave officers to the French army throughout the eighteenth century, and even provided some of Napoleon's generals. The Irish themselves, in spite of the privations of the early years, found larger opportunities for profitable careers, first in

France, then on the whole continent. With increasing confidence, they ranged across Europe and even into expanding European overseas empires.

Appendix 10.1 Irish Regiments in French Army between 1692 and 1697[55]

Regiments	Battalions	Officers and Rank and file	
INFANTRY			
By commission of Louis XIV:			
Mountcashel Brigade:			
Lee	3	2013	
Clare	3	2013	6 039
Dillon	3	2013	
By commission of James II:			
Royal Irlandais	2	1342	
Regiment de la reine	2	1342	
Regiment de Marine	2	1342	
Limerick	2	1342	
Charlemont	2	1342	17 220
Dublin	2	1342	
Athlone	2	1342	
Clancarthy	1	671	
Dragons du Roi	1	558	
Dragons de la Reine	1	558	
Three independent companies		201	
Total Infantry		=	**17 421**
CAVALRY			
Gardes du corps:	1re troupe		100
	2e troupe		100
Régiment du Roi	2 escadrons		372
Régiment de la Reine	2 escadrons		372
Total cavalry		=	**944**
TOTAL		=	**18 365**

Appendix 10.2　Irish Regiments after 1697[56]

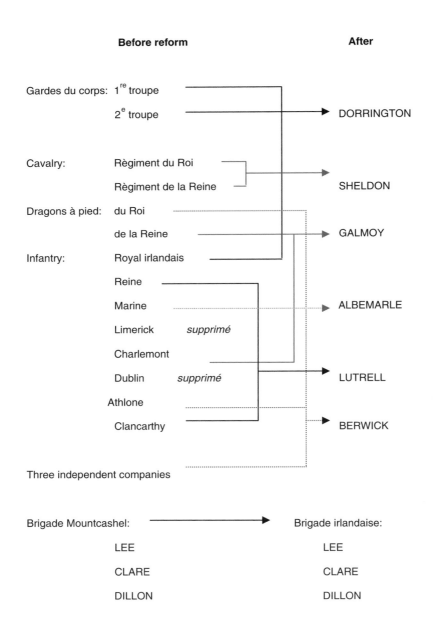

Appendix 10.3   Demographic Evolution of the Irish Diaspora in Paris and Saint-Germain-en-Laye, 1688–1714[57]

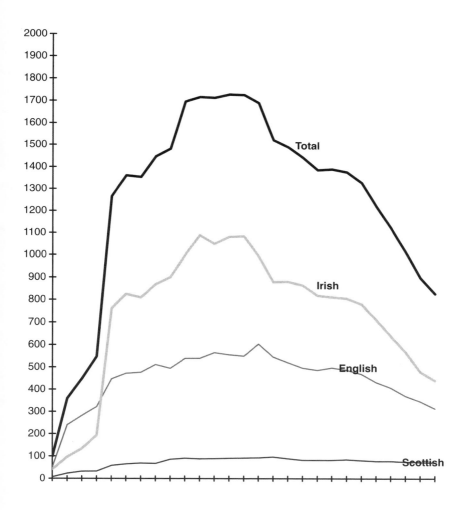

Appendix 10.4   Percentage of English, Scots and Irish in the Jacobite Diaspora in Paris and Saint-Germain, 1688–1714[58]

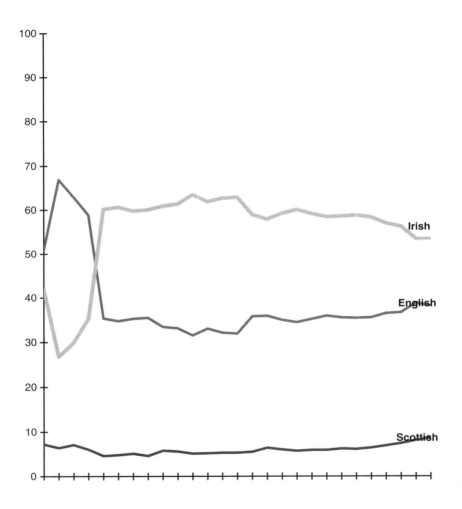

Appendix 10.5 Social Organisation of the Jacobite Diaspora in Paris and Saint-Germain-en-Laye[59]

Degree of Proximity to the Royal Family

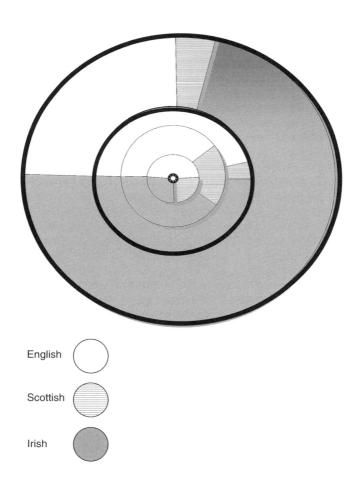

English

Scottish

Irish

Appendix 10.6   English, Scottish and Irish Naturalisations from 1689 to 1715[60]

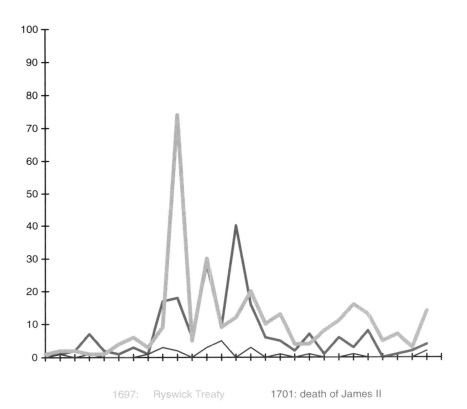

1697:   Ryswick Treaty   1701: death of James II

Irish

English

Scottish

Notes

1 British Library, Add. Ms. 37662, fol. 244.
2 L. Cullen, 'The Irish Diaspora of the Seventeenth and Eighteenth Centuries' in Nicholas Canny, ed., *Europeans on the Move. Studies on European Migration, 1500–1800* (Oxford, 1994), pp. 139–140.
3 A useful summary is given by Eamonn Ó Ciardha, *Ireland and the Jacobite cause, 1685–1766: A Fatal Attachment* (Dublin, 2004), p. 32
4 J. C. O'Callagahan, *History of the Irish Brigade in the Service of France* (Dublin, 1854), p. 29; G. Chaussinand-Nogaret, 'Les Jacobites au XVIIe siècle : une élite insulaire au service de l'Europe', *Annales E. S. C.*, 28 (1973), p. 1098.
5 Guy Rowlands, *An Army in Exile, Louis XIV and the Irish Forces of James II in France, 1691–1698*, Royal Stuart Society Papers, LX (2001), p. 5.
6 Service historique de la Défense, Vincennes, Archives de la Guerre, 2Xy 10–19.
7 'Better regiments could have been given, Milord. The truth is that we find here some bad will, and the fear of missing troops, but even more the wish to make Milord D'avaux's negotiations fail, for he is not well loved in this court.' Letter from the *commissaire* Fumeron to the marquis of Louvois, Cork, 28 March 1690: Service historique de la Défense, Vincennes, Archives de la Guerre, A¹ 894, f. 174.
8 'One has to consider that the king of France had demanded four regiments of 1,600 men each, but the ambassador has said that five regiments of 1,000 men would be enough, that colonels from the Service were not necessary if they were of good condition. On this, King James has designated the regiments of Mountcashel, O'Brien, Butler, Dillon and Fielding, that should make 5,000 men of the best kind the country can give.' *Mémoire sur les troupes irlandaises*, July 1690: Service historique de la Défense, Vincennes, Archives de la Guerre, A¹ 1082, f. 74.
9 According to Arthur Dillon, the brigade counted 5,371 officers at its creation, 6,039 in 1697.
10 A. Corvisier, *L'armée française de la fin du XVIIᵉ siècle au ministère de Choiseul* (Paris, 1964), p. 951. The percentage grew with the rank: 5 % of the *maréchaux de camp*, 12.6% of the *lieutenants généraux* and 13.8% of the *maréchaux de France* were foreigners.
11 'Her Majesty would be very pleased and expect from Milord Tyrconnel's affection that you may embark three, four or even five thousands Irishmen in four or five regiments and that you embark at least eight hundred, and even one thousand or twelve hundred men as new recruits for the Irish regiments that are already here.' Service historique de la Défense, Archives de la Guerre, A¹ 960, f. 325.
12 Letter from Louvois to Tyrconnel, 12 March 1691: Service historique de la Défense, Archives de la Guerre, A¹ 1065, f. 65.
13 Letter of Louvois to the *commissaire* Fumeron, 27 March 1691: Service historique de la Défense, Archives de la Guerre, A¹ 1065, f. 71.
14 Service historique de la Défense, Archives de la Guerre, A¹ 1065, f. 85. These troops left Limerick on July 18 (A¹ 1065, fol. 116). Only in December 1691 did Barbezieux let M. d'Usson know that 'there is little evidence now that more troops can be expected from Ireland' (Service historique de la Défense, Archives de la Guerre, A¹ 1065, f. 153). Still, in January 1692, when the Irish Jacobite regiments arrived on the continent, six hundred men were detached to reinforce the Irish regiments of the French army (Service historique de la Défense, Archives de la Guerre, A¹ 1065, ff. 178 et 184).

15 Rowlands, *An Army in Exile*, p. 5.

16 As foreign soldiers in the French army, they should have received higher wages than the French troops, but it was agreed that they would be paid the same: 50,000 french livres each month. James II promised them he would pay back the difference as soon as he had recovered his throne (Historical Manuscript Commission, *Calendar of the Stuart Papers* (6 vols., London, 1902–16), vol. 1, p. 66). No doubt the measure was very unpopular. An Irish officer complained to his son: 'No sooner had we arrived in France that King James made an arrangement with Louis XIV by which he had put us on a French footing, reserving for himself the difference in our pay for his own upkeep and that of his house' (Bibliothèque Nationale, Paris, Mss. Français 1261).

17 As early as September 1697, the 25 battalions had to reduce the number of their companies from 16 to 14, and each of them had to disband half their men. A broader revision occurred in February 1698. Only the three regiments of the Mountcashel brigade, who were already French, and the Marine regiment, now Albemarle's, were totally spared. The two regiments of Limerick and Dublin were totally suppressed, the others merged into five new ones (Sheldon, Dorrington, Galmoy, Lutrell then Bourke and Berwick). The two cavalry regiments were made one in Dorrington's new regiment (Bibliothèque municipale, Nancy: Ms 305 (423): *Notes concernant les régiments irlandois depuis leur arrivée en France en may 1690 recueillies par milord Clare, maréchal de France*. Quoted by Yves Poutet, 'Jacques II, MacMahon et Kennedy', *Revue d'histoire de l'Amérique française*, 21, 3 (1968), p. 432, note 8).

18 Scottish Catholic Archives, Blair Letters BL 2/38.

19 Thirty-three men were admitted in 1696, 48 in 1697 and no fewer than 107 in 1698. The worst year was 1700, with 147 soldiers admitted (Service historique de la Défense, Vincennes, Archives de la Guerre, 2Xy 12). The 1696 disbanding was the end of the pre-Wild Geese generation, which had merged into the new 'Jacobite regiments.' The oldest men were not kept in the regiments, but sent to the Invalides. The percentage of soldiers who had been in the service of France before 1690 was at its highest between 1698 and 1700, before collapsing.

20 *Mémoires de Saint-Simon*, quoted by Jacques Dulon, *Jacques II Stuart et sa famille* (Paris, 1897), p. 142.

21 Leave from colonel Talbot, 30 January 1695 (Archives Nationales, Minutier central, étude LIII/ 112).

22 Letter of the duke of Berwick, 9 February 1710 (Archives de la guerre, Vincennes, Archives de la Guerre: A¹ 2262, f. 109).

23 Letter to Henry Browne, Westminster Diocesan Archives, Browne Papers: B7 n. 106.

24 Lady Honora Bourke, daughter of William, earl of Clanricarde, married Berwick on 26 March 1695. The duke acted as the guardian of Sarsfield's son. The French courtier, Saint-Simon, admired the duchess as 'une très belle femme, touchante et faite à peindre, et qui réussit très bien à la cour de Saint-Germain.' Quoted by A. Rohan-Chabot, *Le Maréchal de Berwick* (Paris, 1990), p. 57.

25 C. Forman, *A letter to the right Honourable Sir Robert Sutton for Disbanding the Irish Regiments in the Service of France and Spain* (Dublin, 1728), quoted in Rowlands, *An Army in Exile*, p. 1.

26 Richard Nagle stayed in charge of the war department for James II until his death in April 1699, but the Versailles correspondence was given to the Secretaries of State Melfort and Middleton.

27   On these matters, Louis XIV did not always give satisfaction to James II: see Rowlands, *An Army in Exile*, p. 8.

28   *Ibid.*, p. 13.

29   Letter of Ignace de Belvalet de Famechon to the marquis de Louvois, Limerick, 9 August 1690 (Service historique de la Défense, Vincennes, Archives de la Guerre, A[1] 1082, f. 80).

30   Letter of 28 December 1691 (Service historique de la Défense, Vincennes, Archives de la Guerre, A[1] 1082, f. 145).

31   Letter of the marquis de Barbezieux to the maréchal d'Estrées, Versailles, 14 February 1692 (Service historique de la Défense, Vincennes, Archives de la Guerre, A[1] 1065, f. 191).

32   *Ibid.*, p. 15.

33   Archives Nationales, minutier central des notaires, étude LIII/152 and 163.

34   François-André Isambert *et al.*, *Recueil général des anciennes lois françaises* (29 vols., Paris, 1821–33), vol. 20, p. 405.

35   This remained the case until 1697. After the disbanding, some officers tried to stay in French service by hiding in French regiments.

36   Letter of 26 March 1702 (Service historique de la Défense, Vincennes, Archives de la Guerre, A[1] 1581, f. 48).

37   None could be found in the cavalry regiments 'where they have already been taken, so that it prevented the colonels from taking others' (Letter from de Courtebourne to Chamillart, 9 March 1702, Service historique de la Défense, Vincennes, Archives de la Guerre, A[1] 1561, f. 92). But the Irish officers in charge of this inspection could find eighty-seven men in Flanders, 120 in Artois, ninety-six in Alsace and six in hospitals (Service historique de la Défense, Vincennes, Archives de la Guerre, A[1] 1561, f. 260 ; A[1] 1581, f. 52 and f. 46*). They were first granted an amnesty for not having transferred voluntarily, and were then spread between the Irish regiments.

38   O'Callaghan, *History of the Irish Brigade*, p. 160.

39   Letter of 12 August 1714 : British Library, Add. Ms 46495, f. 140.

40   Eoghan Ó hAnnrachain, 'An Analysis of the FitzJames Cavalry Regiment, 1737', *The Irish Sword*, 19 (1993–5), p. 254.

41   James Hogan, ed., *Négociations de Monsieur le comte d'Avaux en Irlande, 1689–90* (Dublin, 1934), pp. 50–1.

42   Copy of a letter written to M. de Calliéres, most likely in 1704, according to its place in the correspondence register (British Library, Add Ms 31250, f. 48: Papers of Simon Fraser, Lord Lovat; also found in the Archives des Affaires étrangères, Paris, Correspondance politique, Angleterre, 217, f. 22).

43   A. Joly, *Un converti de Bossuet: James Drummond, duc de Perth* (Lille, 1934), p. 317.

44   Eamon O'Ciosain, 'La langue irlandaise et les irlandais dans le *Dictionnaire de la langue bretonne* de Dom Le Pelletier', in G. le Menn, ed., *Bretagne et pays celtiques : Langues, histoires, civilisations. Mélanges offerts à la mémoire de Léon Fleuriot* (St. Brieuc and Rennes, 1992), p. 58.

45   Register of admissions, 1702–1707, Archives de l'assistance publique, Paris, La Charité: 1Q2, 3, p. 166.

46   Eamon O'Ciosain, p. 57.

47   See J. F. Dubost and P. Sahlins's work, *Et si on faisait payer les étrangers* (Paris, 1999).

48   'Rôles d'imposition sur les naturalisés', Archives Nationales, Paris, E 3706/11 et 12.

49 Archives des Affaires étrangères, Paris, Correspondance politique, Angleterre, 425, pp. 336–60.
50 Micheline Kearney-Walsh, 'Irish-Spanish Links: a Case Study', paper delivered to *The Place of the Irish in British and European History*, seminar at Trinity College, Dublin, 14–17 September 1988, pp. 27, 33.
51 Bodleian Library, Oxford, Carte Papers 209, f. 6.
52 Chaussinand-Nogaret, note 7, p. 1102.
53 Archives Nationales, Paris, O^1 221, f. 102.
54 His cousin Joseph Commerford was given in January 1717 a certificate of nobility (Archives Nationales, Paris, PP^1 46bis, f. 54). Joseph's son, Luc Commerford, had received his on 2 January 1700 (HMC, *Stuart*, vol. 1, p. 145).
55 According to O'Callaghan, *History of the Irish Brigade*, p. 142.
56 Nathalie Genet-Rouffiac, *Le Grand Exil: Les Jacobites en France, 1688–1715* (Vincennes, 2007), p. 413.
57 Genet-Rouffiac, *Le Grand Exil*, p. 430.
58 Genet-Rouffiac, *Le Grand Exil*, p. 431
59 Genet-Rouffiac, *Le Grand Exil*, p. 440.
60 Genet-Rouffiac, *Le Grand Exil*, p. 426.

11
The Influence of the Jacobites on the Economic Development of France in the Era of the Enlightenment

Patrick Clarke de Dromantin

When King James II was forced to seek refuge in France after the Dutch Stadtholder, William of Orange, had defeated him at the Battle of the Boyne in 1690, tens of thousands of his followers and their families, known to history as the Jacobites, also had to flee their unfortunate country to seek refuge in Louis XIV's kingdom. About half of them joined the Irish regiments in French service, and greatly distinguished themselves, while others followed civil careers in the higher reaches of the civil administration, in the Church and, most of all, in different sectors of the French economy. This essay will focus particularly on their industrial and commercial ventures, as well as their impact on the economic development of the kingdom of France and on the outlook of the French nobility.

The arrival of people persecuted for their faith could inspire nothing but sympathy in a kingdom seeking to be the champion of Catholicism. No doubt this explains why these exiles, who often arrived denuded of money, mostly succeeded in stabilising their financial situation. With all their troubles, the Jacobites had the luck to arrive in the most prosperous country in Europe, or at any rate, the most populous, with nearly twenty-eight million inhabitants, as many as Russia at that time. However, unlike in Great Britain, the nobility in France had taken little interest in economic ventures, and it was not until the end of the seventeenth and above all the start of the eighteenth century that the embryonic beginnings of a French 'business nobility' emerged. There was a long tradition in France that the nobility should not be involved in industry and commerce, although a few had not waited until the arrival of the Jacobites to invest in new inventions. The contribution of the Jacobites was to give France the benefit of their technological knowledge, and to pull in their wake the most dynamic portion of the French Second Estate, whose mentality and actions they helped to change, bringing them to invest personally in industrial and commercial activities that were until then little to the taste of the nobility. The French nobility's reluctance to become involved in economic acti-vities was due in part to the idea that it was a derogation of their status, a particularly sensitive point for the French noble mentality. We will first have to examine the change in this notion of derogation (*dérogeance*) before assessing the role of the Jacobites in the economic development of France in the eighteenth century and the evolution of the state of mind of the French nobility.

French noble elites and the economy of the kingdom

The image of the French nobility spread by French school textbooks is unfortunately always the same: a lazy, frivolous, debauched and even noxious social group. The historical reality is fortunately different and somewhat reassuring. First, we have to examine the alleged laziness of the noble elites, for this was most often not chosen but imposed on them. An American historian, David D. Bien, has undermined this legend by stating that 'idleness on the part of the nobles, in most cases, was not voluntary, and a substantial part of the nobility had a profession.'[1] He estimates that out of 40,000 adult men of second rank nobility, at least a quarter served in the army or navy, while others exercised their talents as magistrates, as members of the clergy, in municipal administration, finance and even in commerce and industry, despite the reticence imposed from above by the notion of derogation.

Derogation, which has not always been understood, largely explains the exclusion of the nobility from the development of industry and commerce. It should be pointed out that the idea of derogation suited everyone. It flattered the nobility, who from time immemorial had paid taxes in their blood, and because of this were at least partially exempt from monetary taxation. We often forget to add that this partial fiscal exemption had another consequence: it prevented the nobility from engaging in certain lucrative activities without derogation and losing their fiscal advantages. On the other hand, the bourgeoisie resented the possible disappearance of derogation, as its suppression would enable the nobility to engage in professional activities that the bourgeoisie considered its own domain, and to exercise a form of unjust competition, due to the preservation of the nobility's fiscal exemption. Of the three Estates that composed French society, it was the Third Estate which showed the greatest vigilance in the strict application of the concept of derogation. Thus, in the 1576 Estates General at Blois, the representatives of the Third did not hesitate to remind the assembly of the functions devolving upon each Estate, which denied any possibility for the nobility 'to undertake trade in any manner.'[2] Professor Jean Meyer summed it up perfectly when he wrote: 'Derogation was, in a way, the refusal of the bourgeoisie to allow the nobility to become too interested in economic ventures.'[3]

The first persons who tried to limit the effects of derogation on industry and commerce were none other than the kings of France. In fact, they grasped quite early the benefits that would accrue for the economy of the kingdom if the nobility were allowed to pursue such activities. They intervened in this field on two levels: first, by drawing the nobility into commerce by declaring laws that exempted a certain number of specific cases from derogation, and second, by raising the prestige of trade by ennobling wealthy merchants.

The exceptions to derogation

From the fourteenth century onward, the kings of France took measures, often on an individual basis, to incite one noble or another to interest himself in the kingdom's economy. For instance, in 1318 Philip the Tall granted to Gerard Gueite, a royal counsellor, permission to trade without derogation, while Jacques le Flamand, master in ordinary in the *Chambre des Comptes*, obtained in 1357 permission to 'make and promote trade in cloth and other goods just as he did before he was named and instituted into the said office.'[4] A century later, in 1462, an edict of Louis XI authorised nobles to practice commerce by giving them permission 'to sell merchandise without prejudice to their reputation and status', while in 1492 Charles VIII ennobled Jacques de Bézu and allowed him to trade without loss of status.[5] For his part, Charles IX in 1566 allowed 'the inhabitants of Marseille to call themselves both nobles and merchants provided it was in wholesale and on the sea.'[6] From the beginning of the eighteenth century, however, French royal power was not content to grant individual permissions only, but decided instead to adopt general measures applicable to the whole of the Second Estate. On 23 January 1629, doubtless prompted by Richelieu, Louis XIII published an ordinance to invite gentlemen to take part in wholesale trade, but it had little effect as it was not registered by the Paris Parlement and was opposed by the majority of the nobility.[7]

Louis XIV and Colbert actively pursued the same policy, notably to encourage maritime commerce which was experiencing great difficulty. For this reason, they promulgated a new ordinance on 13 August 1669, which met with little success. The provisions of this ordinance were extended in 1681 to shipbuilding and army supplies and in May 1686 to marine insurance, there again without much impact. This new setback did not discourage the government, which issued an edict in March 1696 renewing former proposals, but noble gentlemen mostly ignored the offers made to them. This led Louis XIV in December 1701 to set out once again the contents of previous measures. Here again the government's appeal fell on deaf ears, as a new edict which came out in March 1765 had to summarise, explain and complete that of 1701. It is obvious that the multiplicity of royal decrees surveyed here had little impact on those targeted, even though some families from the old nobility had benefited from the edicts by launching into commercial or industrial activities. Among the best known was René Auguste de Chateaubriand of Saint-Malo, father of the celebrated writer, who had made his fortune in Saint-Domingue, then went into maritime trade, privateering, the Newfoundland fishery and, of course, the slave trade. Rare indeed were those who, like the comte d'Hennezel in Beaujeux or the marquis de Toulongeon in Crochot, personally took charge of their iron forges. While royal attempts to incite the nobility to play their part in the economic life of the country had not failed completely, we may wonder whether more had come of the efforts to raise the prestige of commerce by ennobling people who had made a significant contribution to the economic prosperity of the country.

Ennobling merchants and manufacturers

Here again, the results, while not fulfilling the hopes of the government, were far from negligible. In 1708 René Moreau de Mautertuis, a ship-owner in Saint-Malo trading with Spain and the Indies and a deputy for commerce, was raised to the nobility because 'he had known how to combine the skill and prudence of a good trader with the valour of a military man'. In fact, as a good inhabitant of Saint-Malo, Mautertuis had taken up with enthusiasm the part played by the privateers in the *guerre de course*. The two Trouin brothers, well-known ship-owners and corsairs, had been ennobled in 1709 for the same reason. This was the case too for Jean-Yves de Garnier du Fougeray, merchant and corsair, who became a noble in 1723, and for Pierre Jacques Meslée de Grandclos, who was admitted to the second order of nobility in 1768 as 'one of the most worthy merchants in the kingdom'. The case of another merchant from Saint-Malo deserves mention, because the reason for his being made a noble was one that applied to many merchants. The man in question was Robert de La Mennais, who asked for letters of nobility in 1786 because 'single-handed, he had enabled the town of Saint-Malo to survive for eight month by supplying grain and flour from abroad and selling them at a fixed price'. About fifteen families settled in Morlaix, Lorient and mainly in Nantes benefited from ennoblement in the course of the eighteenth century. In Normandy too, this was the case for Michel-Joseph Dubocage de Bléville, ship owner from Le Havre, and in 1749 for Jacques Lestorey de Boulongue, an alderman (*échevin*) and ship-owner, also from Le Havre. Pierre Feray and his cousin Jean-Baptiste Feray, both ship-owners in Rouen, were ennobled in 1769 and 1775 respectively for their services to commerce. It is interesting to note in passing that their belonging to the reformed (Protestant) religion did not prevent their social ascent. This list is not at all inclusive, and others were ennobled in Atlantic ports such as La Rochelle, Bordeaux and Bayonne. Moreover, many merchants preferred to attain nobility by buying the office of King's secretary, which was a surer path, but also a much more expensive one.

Although the ancient nobility may have been poorly represented in the ranks of industry, they allowed some manufacturers, and not the least among them, to become nobles. One of the most famous was Jean Dietrich (1715–1795), ennobled in 1761 and a member of a remarkable dynasty of bankers and captains of industry. Another no less famous captain of industry was Jean-Martin Wendel, who had joined the noble Estate in 1711 by purchasing the office of King's secretary. The textile industry also saw some remarkable cases of social promotion. Among the names worthy of mention are those of Christophe-Philippe Oberkampf, who was naturalised in 1770 and ennobled in 1787; of Jean-Abraham Poupart, director of a huge cloth manufacture in Sedan, who received letters patent of nobility in 1769; and of Charles-Antoine Elie-Lefebvre, the owner of a cotton manufacture in Rouen, who was admitted to the Second Estate in 1788.[8]

If at the end of the seventeenth and even more in the eighteenth century, a nobility involved in business was in fact emerging, it is equally undeniable that it greatly increased in scope as a result of the settlement of Jacobite exiles in France.

Technical innovations introduced by the Jacobites

In numerical terms, the Jacobites were not so important, but the quality of their contribution was otherwise, as they introduced hitherto unknown or little used techniques in the kingdom of the Bourbons, along with a brand new mentality. In fact, the new technology they brought to France aroused great interest among many French nobles, who did not hesitate to launch into industrial and commercial activities. In other words, what the kings of France could never really attain became a reality, in great part through the influence of the Jacobite refugees.

Although the industrialisation of France may already have begun by the beginning of the eighteenth century, English entrepreneurs possessed greater knowledge in several areas of technology, such as mining, textiles, manufacturing that required continuous combustion, metallurgy and even chemistry. It is in these fields that the Jacobites made their greatest contribution. However, we should note that Britain's industrial primacy diminished in the course of the century and that by the time the French Revolution was set in motion, France had reached technological parity with its rival.[9]

Numerous Jacobites were involved in the mining industry. Among the most eminent were Sir Patrick d'Arcy in the lead mines of Poullaouen in Britanny, David Floyd, an Englishman, in the copper and lead mines of Planché-aux-Mines in Burgundy, William Brett, another Englishman, in the mines of Alsace and Martin O'Connor, an Irishman, in the copper, lead and silver mines of La Garde-Freinet in Provence. We will pause to consider the mines of Poullaouen in detail, as they were the model of their kind. With over 600 workmen, a capital of two million livres and a turnover of over 400,000 livres, the Mining Company of Lower Britanny, managed by

Sir Patrick d'Arcy, was one of the most remarkable enterprises in the eighteenth century.[10] D'Arcy was an extraordinary man, *maréchal de camp* in the King's armies, resident geometrician at the Royal Academy of Sciences, and a true pioneer of ballistics. To this end, he pursued long researches to improve the performance of the artillery, and in 1777 invented a new and remarkable model of infantry musket. The famous Jean-Baptiste Gribeauval turned down d'Arcy's proposal, which greatly humiliated the inventor. D'Arcy took part in Prince Charles Edward's 1745 rising and was taken prisoner in Scotland. As at that time he had not yet acquired French nationality, he could have been considered a rebel, and treated as such, but in this instance the British government was lenient and exchanged him for other prisoners.

With such a man in charge, the mines of Poullaouen became a centre for experiments to find new techniques of treating minerals. Among its successes was the introduction of a reverberatory furnace, a purely British invention and hitherto unknown in France. This involved putting the materials to be treated in contact with combustion gases, while the heat of a hearth reverberated from the arched roof of the furnace, allowing separation without damage to the different minerals being treated. The most important role of the Company, without a doubt, lay in spreading the new techniques. The renown of its director was such that the mines of Poulaouen soon had an uncommon fame and became a sort of fashionable phenomenon. It was imperative for the leading lights at the time to have visited them, first among them the inspectors of mines, but also celebrities such as Etienne Mignot de Montigny, Caze de La Bove, intendant of Britanny, the duc de Chartres, the duc de La Rochefoucauld, and Bertier de Sauvigny, the intendant of Paris, to mention only the best known.

In manufactures needing continuous combustion such as glass-making, the technological contribution of the Jacobites was even more striking, because it took place on two levels: the use of a new method of combustion on the one hand, and a new glass-making technique on the other. The use of coal instead of wood to feed the furnaces was revolutionary in itself. Until then, continuous combustion furnaces used in glassworks and other manufactures used only wood, which was a source of concern for the intendants, who worried about the excessive consumption of wood in French industries. One exemplary advocate of conversion to coal was Peter Mitchell, an Irish Jacobite refugee, who obtained in 1723 'permission to build in the suburbs of Bordeaux an oven suitable for making bottles in the English way.' The intendant of Guyenne had made it clear that this manufacture was conditional on the use of the new fuel, 'as wood is scarce and very expensive in this province and as new works using wood would greatly raise its price and would be detrimental to the public.'[11] The coal used by Mitchell came mostly from England, as was the case for the majority of manufacturers. The superior quality of English coal justified this preference, as it was recognised by industrialists that French coal, and that of Quercy particularly, 'was of poor quality, grimy, burnt too quickly and did not keep an even heat and thus was not suitable for glass works which need a fierce fire such as is produced by English coal.'[12] In addition, English coal was cheaper than French coal, as its transport by sea was much easier, whereas coal from the Massif Central had to be carried on hazardous roads and rivers. It was less expensive than French coal too because about a third less of it was consumed, due to its higher degree of combustibility. Besides, French methods of coal extraction were less efficient than those in England.

An English glassworks was totally different from the French variety. Volume XXXV of the *Encyclopédie* gives a very good description of the superior methods of English glassworks. In simple terms, the English had perfected an ingenious draught furnace which enabled them to get an exceptionally hot fire and thus a quicker fusion, which saved a lot of time. 'Experience showed that melting took a third less time than in French works … English works burn a fifth less coal than a French glass works.'[13] To get a better draught, there was only one ventilation point through the grill and a large chimney which opened wide at the bottom and narrowly at the top, giving the appearance of a beehive to English glassworks and making them easy to spot. French glassworks, by contrast, were large rectangular buildings, open to the winds, with defective ventilation and full of smoke.

The Mitchell glassworks, with an annual production of 200,000 to 300,000 bottles, was an outstanding success, and it stayed in the hands of the same family until the twentieth century. This achievement was all the more remarkable as Peter Mitchell had no money when he arrived in Bordeaux to start his career as a mere barrel maker. Not content with industrial success, Peter Mitchell managed to acquire, at Arsac in the Médoc, a wine-growing property in the midst of which he built a magnificent chateau, known as the chateau du Tertre, now classed as a *Cinquième Grand Cru* in the *Appellation Contrôlée* for the wines of Margaux!

The use of coal instead of wood also spread to earthenware crockery, but with many more difficulties. It was not until the end of the eighteenth century that William Sturgeon, an Irishman from Rouen, managed to make the new fuel widespread after a struggle lasting several years with his competitors, who were determined to preserve the old ways. William Sturgeon ruined himself completely in this fight, which he waged on two fronts, to preserve French forests and to withstand English competition by using a cheaper fuel. Sturgeon's will, energy and determination presented a fine example for all captains of industry wishing to ensure, come hell or high water, the technical progress of their country.

Without doubt, the most wide-ranging technical innovations were made in the textile industry by an extraordinary English Jacobite, John Holker

(1719–1786). After working for about a half-dozen years in the Manchester cotton industry, he took an officer's commission in the Jacobite Manchester regiment in 1745 and sought refuge in Paris in the aftermath of the failed rising. He then enlisted in the Scottish Ogilvy regiment in the service of France. Some years later, he met Trudaine, the *Directeur du Commerce*, whom he impressed with his knowledge of textiles. He founded at Rouen a royal manufacture of textiles, using the latest British technological inventions, and became a highly regarded adviser to the French government. Soon after, he was named inspector general of manufactures, and became the founder of mechanised production in France, thanks especially to a perilous mission of industrial espionage conducted in England at the end of 1751. He brought back across the Channel, not only an impressive quantity of material, but also a precious team of highly skilled workmen.[14] He thus made known in France all the latest technical processes in the textile industry: carding with special combs which did not tear the wool; silk-throwing frames; the reeling or spinning of silk thread from a large wheel onto spindles; hot dyeing of silk; and finishing of cloth through the technique of calendering, which gives a lustre or shine to the material.

In the last of these cases, the innovation was twofold. First of all, the concept of mechanical calendering was changed. The machines utilised in France up to this time were slow, heavy, difficult to operate and very bulky. In fact, 'on a table, wooden rollers were placed around which the cloth was rolled; on the rollers were placed a mobile wooden case, full of large stones, which strongly compressed the rollers and was drawn alternatively back and forth by a horse.'[15] The innovation consisted of a sort of laminator which enabled the cloth to be laid flat between two rollers, with the degree of pressure regulated by a system of screws or levers. The second major invention concerned the use of hot calendering. Hitherto French workmen did this cold, with mediocre results. The breakthrough came with a new machine combining a wooden roller with a copper roller which could be heated. From then on, it became possible to obtain a lustre of much higher quality, and most important, longer lasting. General use of the technique using heat brought great gains in productivity as well as decisive advances in spinning, washing, pressing and dying the cloth.[16]

The influence of John Holker was great because of his persistent and well-informed prodding of manufacturers, but also because of the many British technicians he was able to bring to France. Among them should be mentioned Thomas Le Clere, who in 1764 founded at Brive a justly famous cloth manufacture on the English model, then started a large-scale cotton mill which carried on until the middle of the nineteenth century. His works used, of course, all the techniques developed by John Holker, such as spinning wheels operated by foot levers, and the spinning jenny, which enabled cotton to be spun with huge gains in productivity. From 1780 onwards, Thomas Le Clere speeded up cotton spinning by the general introduction of the spinning jenny, the carding machine and the 'rowing-billy' which did large-scale spinning and paved the way for the jenny. He also introduced some of Arkwright's machines, and finally the spinning mule. In fact, we owe to John Holker and his disciples the amazing rise of the French textile industry at the end of the eighteenth century. Other Jacobites who distinguished themselves in this branch of manufacture were John MacAuliffe and James Macarty, but lack of space make it impossible to say more of their contribution.[17]

Not content with being the creator of the French textile industry in France, John Holker became interested in agriculture, notably the breeding of sheep, and the chemical industry. In this last area, he played with his son a leading part in the manufacture of vitriol, thus freeing France from the British monopoly of sulphuric acid. This took ten years to achieve, in the course of which Holker was able to build at Saint-Sever in the suburbs of Rouen a manufacture of vitriol that not only supplied French needs, but soon made France into an exporting country. The procedure was always the same: bring in the tools as well as a competent staff.

The story of John Holker, who joined a Scottish Jacobite regiment in French service before taking part in the textile industry, is very remarkable and confirms Nathalie Genet-Rouffiac's findings on the role of the army as a way of integrating foreigners into the population. In fact, Holker was aware of this point himself, and suggested it to the French government in a well-known memorandum which amounted to a whole programme of industrial policy:

> There is another way, a fairly straightforward one, to provide English workmen for factories who may need them. This is to send Mr. Holker to go round the towns where the Irish or Scottish regiments in the service of France are quartered; one could draw from them a fairly large number of good workmen that the sergeants of these regiments would engage by surprise, when they go to England to find recruits, by persuading them that they were engaging for the French factories. The government would reimburse each captain for the price of each soldier suitable for working in new or old manufactures, and might even give a little more. This manner of filling our factories with good English workmen would be the least costly of all.[18]

Finally, in the field of metallurgical industry, we must emphasise the part played by Count William Stuart, who in association with other manufacturers, took part in the first French enterprise able to produce coke from coal so as to smelt iron. Other Jacobites included William Hide, who was concerned in the making of machine tools for the ironmongers of Burgundy, Edward Warren who made powder and saltpetre in Lorraine, and the Sutton de Clonard and MacCarthy families, processors of potassium in the Bordeaux region. What is remarkable is that nearly all these industrial enterprises were set up in collaboration with representatives of the French nobility, showing the primordial influence of the Jacobites in changing the state of mind of the Second Estate by persuading it to participate actively in the economic life of the kingdom.

Synergy between the French business nobility and the Jacobite refugees

As was underlined at the start of this paper, the hesitant emergence of a 'business nobility' began before the eighteenth century, with repeated encouragement from the monarchy. A few examples will suffice to show that this tendency developed considerably under the influence of Jacobite refugees.

Sir Patrick d'Arcy was able to attract into the Company of Mines of Lower Britanny a large number of nobles such as the baron Guiguer de Frangins, the comtesse de Monteclerc, the comte de Blangy, and the chevalier du Guer, a member of the Breton Parlement. For his part, François de Rothe, former Commander of the Port of Lorient and the owner of the coal mines of Montrelais, was in partnership in the management of these mines with Madame de Sauvigny, wife of the *premier président* of the Paris Parlement, Monsieur de Marolles, *premier président des enquêtes* in the same Parlement, and the Chevalier de Borda.

In the copper and lead mines of Burgundy and Alsace, already mentioned, the partners David Floyd and William Brett were both English gentlemen, as were Thomas Tyrwhitt and George Robinson. Other partners included Alexandre Alexander, a Scottish banker, William Domville, an Irishman, and Henry Alexandre de Lieuray, baron d'Anthenay, who belonged to a Norman family of knightly extraction that had been received at court. In other words, this was a typical Jacobite enterprise, joining the three components of the diaspora with a representative of the old French nobility.

Although Provence is not especially known for the importance of its mines, the mountain range of the Maures has always aroused the interest of entrepreneurs. This was why in 1732 Martin O'Connor obtained a claim in perpetuity to search for copper, lead and silver at La Garde-Freinet. The owner was a Provencal gentleman, Jean Giraud, lord of Agay, who took a close interest in the working of these mines. As usually happened, Martin O'Connor went to England to seek the skilled labour that he needed. At first his partners were Erasmus Philips, a banker brought back from across the Channel, and two French aristocrats, the comte de La Saunière d'Ameysin and the baron d'Anthenay, the same person we have already met in Burgundy. The skill and experience of the English workmen made a very good impression on the owner of the sites, so that Jean d'Agay began talks with Martin O'Connor to form the Minerals Company of Provence and managed to persuade many gentlemen to join the new Society. After several months the Company's capital was in the hands of the following shareholders:

Main Shareholders[19]

Martin O'Connor. Irish gentleman, holder of claim and director of Mines of Provence. 6 shares: no money deposited as he had spent 20,000 livres already.
Erasmus Philips. English banker. 6 shares.
Baron d'Anthenay. 6 shares, no money deposited.
Comte de Saunière d'Ameysin. 3 shares, worth 1,200 livres.

Holders of 1,200 livres worth of shares.

Jean de Giraud, lord of Agay (1684–1769). 3 shares.
Henri de Laurens, lord of Peyrolles and of Saletes. 2 shares.
François Antoine d'Augery, King's attorney in Draguignan (1685–1769). 2 shares.
Melchior de Raimondis, lord of Canaux, Combaux and Allons (1698–1746). Captain in the cavalry regiment of Blaisois. 1 share.
Henri de Lyle, lord of Callian. Lieutenant-general in the *sénéchauseé*, mayor and 1st consul of Grasse. 1 share. Cousin of M. d'Agay.
Joseph de Rasque, lord of Taradeau. Mayor and 1st consul of Draguignan (1723, 1729, 1730). 1 share.
Joseph Chapman. Equerry, receiver of tobacco in Draguignan (1687–).

Holders of 1,000 livres worth of shares

André-Georges du Grou, lord of Sulauze (1682–). Receiver-general of the domains of Provence. 2 shares. Cousin of M. d'Agay.
Antoine de Laugier. Subdelegate-general of the Intendancy, Knight of St-Michel. 1 share.
M. Varlon. Father-in-law of M. de Laugier. 1 share.
M. Légay. Secretary to the Intendancy of Provence. 1 share.
Jean-Joseph de Laugier, lord of Beaurecueil and Roques-Hautes (1705–1780). *Conseiller* in the Parlement of Provence. 1 share.
Bruno-Louis Lenfant de La Platrière, baron de Bormes. Provincial Commissioner for War, governor of Brégançon. 1 share. Son of Louis, Planning Commissioner for War, by Anne de Berlier.
Jacques de Laurens, lord of Peyrolles and Seranon. *Lieutenant des Maréchaux de France*, Knight of St. Lazare and N.D. du Mont Carmel. 1 share. Second cousin of M. de Peyrolles.

Joseph-Barthélémy de Rafelis, lord of Broves and Clamagnan (1696–1758). 1 share. Husband of Anne-Marie de Glandévès.

Charles-François de Glandévès, lord of St. Cassien, Amirat, Vergons and Entrevaux (1688–1776). 1 share

Jean-Baptiste Joseph du Grou de Sulauze (1707–1763). French Consul-general in Tunis. 1 share Brother of M. du Grou.

Pierre du Grou de Castel (1690–1775). Army officer. 1 share.

Jean-Joseph de Perrot, lord of Avaye. 1 share.

Marie-Anne de Rippert. Widow of M. de Raimondis. 1 share. Mother-in-law of M. de Peyrolles.

Joseph de Croze. Governor of La Garde Fort. 1 share. Married to Claire de Laurens.

M. de Laurens. From Lorgues. 1 share.

Mlle de Nolin. From Luc. 1 share.

M. Meilhe. 1 share.

About thirty Provencal nobles were persuaded by Martin O'Connor to invest in these new industrial activities. In the course of the first years of the Company, all had been impressed by the skills of the English technicians in charge of the sinking of wells and the art of extracting the silver while preserving the lead, thanks to the technology of the reverberating furnaces. Despite its outstanding technical success, however, Martin O'Connor's enterprise ended in failure in the long term owing to under-capitalisation or, more accurately, because of the disproportion between its stated aims and the available financial means.

Other partnerships deserve a mention such as that of William Sturgeon, the famous earthenware manufacturer from Rouen, with Bartholemew Macnemara and Pierre Abraham Simon de Suzay, whose factory was opened in 1780; that of John Holker with Pierre d'Haristoy, a Basque gentleman, who together formed the cotton mills at Darnétal in the suburbs of Rouen in 1752; that of Abdon Frédéric Victor Hély with Messrs Le Vaillant des Marest and de Caqueray de Fossencourt in the glassworks of Lihut in Normandy in 1756; and that of Thomas Le Clere, the manufacturer from Brive, with the duc de La Rochefoucauld Liancourt in 1791. The last-named of these partnerships founded a company to manufacture in France the carding combs which the textile industry needed. The Le Cleres, father and son, obtained from England the machines to make the carding combs, while the duke supplied the raw materials and the necessary tools. This is a good example of the dynamism of partnerships between the Jacobite diaspora and the French nobility. Unfortunately, the advent of the French Revolution interrupted this fruitful interchange.

This brief account shows that the Jacobites had a great influence over the outlook and behaviour of the Second Estate, in persuading them to take, without reservation, a greater part in the most diverse and innovative spheres of development of the French economy in the eighteenth century. The partnerships between the Jacobite nobles and the French nobles surveyed in the preceding pages bear testimony to the fact that part of the French nobility became a socially dynamic and entrepreneurial group, contrary to the backwards image too often projected by a hostile historiography. Moreover, these partnerships show that the contribution of nobles in the industrial development of the kingdom was not limited to the high nobility, but comprised equally the lesser nobility as defined by Laurent Bourquin.[20] The outstanding success of the Jacobites may be surprising, but it is easily explained by several concurrent factors: widespread sympathy for them, as they had been persecuted for their faith; their business sense, with no fear of derogation; their perfect knowledge of British technology; their unique personal network; and, lastly, their need to succeed when faced with the fate of refugees. As Guy Chaussinand-Nogaret has stressed: 'The qualities and defects shown by the Jacobites, through the vicissitudes of an exile endured with courage, result in large measure from the constraints under which they were placed.'[21]

Translated by Eveline Cruickshanks

Notes

1 David D. Bien, 'Aristocratie', article in François Furet and Mona Ozouf, eds, *Dictionnaire critique de la Révolution Française* (Paris, 1988), pp. 639–52.
2 Guy Richard, *Noblesse d'affaires au XVIIIᵉ siècle* (Paris, 1974), p. 30.
3 Jean Meyer, *La noblesse bretonne au XVIIIᵉ siècle* (Paris, 1985), p. 1043.
4 Marcel de La Bigne de Villeneuve, *La dérogeance de la noblesse* (Rennes, 1918, reprinted Paris, 1977), p. 92.
5 Richard, *Noblesse d'affaires*, p. 28.
6 Gilles André de La Roque, *Traité de la noblesse* (1678), chapitre 88.
7 De La Bigne de Villeneuve, *La dérogeance*, pp. 93–7.
8 Richard, *Noblesse d'affaires au XVIIIᵉ siècle*. Basic information concerning the commercial nobility has been derived from this work.
9 P. Bairoch and J.-P. Poussou, cited by P. Delsalle, *La France industrielle aux XVIᵉ–XVIIᵉ–XVIIIᵉ siècles* (Paris, 1993), p. 174.
10 Edmond Monange, *Une entreprise industrielle au XVIIIᵉ siècle: les mines de Poullaouen et du Helgouat* (thèse de 3e cycle, Rennes, 1972), pp. 237–42.
11 Archives Départementales Gironde C 1594, letter of Dodun, *contrôleur général des finances* to the intendant of Bordeaux, 7 September 1723.
12 Archives Départementales Gironde C 4401, memorial of Mitchell to the duc de Choiseul, *ministre de la guerre et de la marine*, 15 December 1763.
13 *Encyclopédie ou dictionnaire raisonné des sciences, des arts et métiers*, vol. XXXV (Genève, 1778), pp. 145–6, subject 'Verrerie'.
14 [*Translator's Note*: John Kay, inventor of the flying-shuttle, was one of the Englishmen brought to France by Holker. A year before his 1751 trip, Holker had accompanied Charles Edward Stuart on a secret visit to London.]
15 Charles Ballot, *L'introduction du machinisme dans la grande industrie* (Paris, 1923), p. 294.

16 A. Rémond, *John Holker, manufacturier et grand fonctionnaire en France au XVIIIᵉ siècle* (Paris, 1946), pp. 55–6.

17 For more information, see Patrick Clarke de Dromantin, *Les réfugiés jacobites dans la France du XVIIIᵉ siècle* (Presses Universitaires de Bordeaux, 2005).

18 John Holker, 'Mémoire tendant à multiplier et perfectionner les fabriques de France, 1754', Bibliothèque Sainte Geneviève Ms 2810, 'de Montigny, de l'Académie des Sciences'.

19 Frédéric d'Agay, *Une entreprise économique nobiliaire au XVIIIᵉ siècle: la compagnie des mines de Provence* (mémoire de maîtrise, Université de Paris-Sorbonne, 1979–1980), and *Annales du Sud-Est Varois*, vol. 5 (1980), pp. 15–16.

20 Laurent Bourquin, *La noblesse dans la France moderne (XVIᵉ–XVIIIᵉ siècles)* (Paris, 2002), p. 187.

21 Guy Chaussinand-Nogaret, 'Une élite insulaire au service de l'Europe: les Jacobites au XVIIIᵉ siècle', *Annales E.S.C.* (Sept.–Oct. 1973), pp. 1097–2.

12

Tilting at Windmills: The Order del Toboso as a Jacobite Social Network[1]

Steve Murdoch

> Do not grudge me my vanity, if I allow yours; or rather, let us laugh at both indifferently, and at ourselves, and at each other [...] 'But Dulcinea del Toboso is peerless, eh?' says the other. 'Well, honest Harry, go and attack windmills—perhaps thou are not more mad than other people,' St John added, with a sigh.[2]

This quote, from an 1852 novel by William Thackeray, is an imaginative dialogue between two gentlemen of conflicting opinions on a variety of subjects. On this occasion, one encourages the other to pursue a particular woman with whom he is preoccupied. While wholly fictitious, the commentary represents pretty accurately an attitude apparently enshrined in one esoteric Jacobite organisation that appears to have taken its inspiration from the characters of Miguel de Cervantes Saavedra's novel, *Don Quixote*.[3] Among the distinguished membership of this organisation were such prominent Jacobites as George Keith, last Earl Marischal of Scotland.

It has long been known that George Keith acted as Grand Master of the Jacobite-oriented Order of Saint Thomas of Acre, and that he was also a member of a Masonic Lodge in Berlin (along with Frederick the Great) after he moved to Prussia in 1747.[4] Other Jacobite associations are said to have included the Realm of Sion, the Order of Sangreal and the Scots Club of Boulogne.[5] In Paris, Alexander Montgomerie, 10th Earl of Eglinton, operated a Jacobite lodge under his title as 'Knight of the Red Feather' in 1742–1743 and had an attachment to the arch-Jacobite Mason, Chevalier Andrew Ramsay (Grand Chancellor of French Masons 1734–1743) through the latter's cousin Michael Ramsay, the earl's tutor.[6] The number of 'Orders' to which Jacobite membership has been attributed is actually quite staggering. The Masonic historian John Hamill has noted the evolution of some 1,000 new degrees attached to the extra-Craft system, arising out of the 'marriage of Freemasonry and Christian Knighthood', although he concluded that there is no evidence to support the idea that any of these can be considered as 'Jacobite cells'.[7] That claim can be contested, at least to some degree. 'The Most Ancient, the Most Illustrious and Most Noble Order del Toboso' is one association we can be sure Jacobites were exclusively involved with, if not so certain as to what it actually represented.

Despite the potential significance of the group, only fleeting reference is made to the Order del Toboso in secondary sources. Some authors pass it off as simply a trivial, self-parodying organisation, or 'mock order'. Henrietta Tayler was among the first to publish that description, with other scholars repeating it by rote thereafter.[8] For example, Rebecca Wills argued that they were simply a body dedicated to the entertainment of the Jacobite princes in Rome.[9] However, turning potential generals into court jesters does not seem the best way to maintain loyalty, while the distribution of Toboso across Europe would also challenge the hypothesis of it being a simple, Roman-based comedy club.[10] Indeed, from the sources available we know there were certainly members of Toboso in Spain, Russia, Prussia, the Dutch Republic, Flanders, France, England and Rome. The big questions that need to be answered are these: what was the Order del Toboso, who were its members, and just what did they seek to achieve?

The origins of the Order are obscure. D. F. Allen, among others, has asserted that Toboso was founded in Rome in 1732.[11] However, there are indications from one of the Grand Masters that the society had been around since at least 1726, and certainly we have evidence of letters written by members supporting the existence of the Order before 1732. For example, Captain William Hay in Rome told Admiral Thomas Gordon in St. Petersburg that he had presented rings of the Order to the Stuart princes in the summer of 1731, while senior members certainly addressed each other with Tobosan titles before 1732.[12] That said, 1732 was an active year for the Order. In one letter Hay invited Gordon to:

[Find enclosed] a small wooden box containing two rings of the order of Toboso, such as all the knights wears; one for yourself, the other for my Dear Sir Henry [Stirling] ... we knights daily after drinking the health's of the Royal Family, a fair meeting on the green follows: our two young Princes are protectors of the order and wear the rings.[13]

This quote comes from the small corpus of Hay-Gordon letters, and is actually quite revealing, telling us that the Stuart royal family was aware of the society, while simultaneously giving us clues to at least some of the membership.[14] We learn that Admiral Gordon and Sir Henry Stirling received their rings of Toboso in February of that year, but whether this was enough to be considered an initiation is not made clear.[15]

From the *Journal de la Négociation de M [Thomas] Carte avec M. Robert Walpole* we are informed of one of the uses the Toboso rings were put to.[16] In this document, written in Paris in 1739, we learn that Walpole allegedly:

> told Carte of a new mode he had heard of drinking healths: putting a ring into a glass which they 'drank about'. Carte said that this was new to him also, but privately he supposed this must be the ring of the Knights of Toboso with the inscription 'To a Fair Meeting on the Green'.[17]

The inscription on the ring referring to a 'Fair Meeting' matches the motto noted by William Hay in his 1732 letter to Admiral Gordon. The confirmation of the expression as a Toboso slogan corroborates one Alexander Hay in Spa as a member of the Order. In 1737 Hamilton wrote to him about three men on their Grand Tour:

> The three gentlemen to whom I desired you to shew my Broad Sword are members of ye University of Oxford. They are Torys but I know not whether They would be for a Fair Meeting.[18]

The exact context of 'Fair Meeting on the Green' as used by the Order del Toboso remains to be firmly established through archival evidence. However a likely origin for the maxim can be found in a scene from Cervantes' novel where Don Quixote and Sancho Panza, finding themselves somewhat impecunious after their adventures, met with the 'Fair Huntress' on the 'Green Meadow'.[19] In this chapter, the colour green features abundantly; at the meeting place, in the lady's clothes, and even the colour of the tack on her horse. The Fair Huntress, a duchess, welcomed Don Quixote and made it plain she and her husband had enjoyed reading about his quest. They invited Quixote back to their castle where they hilariously indulged his fantasy as a Knight Errant over an extended period of time, with uproarious consequences. They staged numerous situations which allowed the duo plentiful opportunities to play out their fantasy. For the duration of their stay at the castle, the duke and duchess became protectors of the wayward pair, providing them with shelter, sustenance and entertainment. However, they did so from the vantage point of clarity, setting ever more fantastic trials for the pair to see if they would continue in their delirium or snap out of it. In a Tobosan sense, 'To a Fair Meeting on the Green' might well refer to a meeting of the Order under the protection of those of clear vision, particularly those who enjoyed being entertained but who could also provide succour for those who required it, deluded or otherwise.

Thus, in the context of the Oxford Tories, we can reasonably assume that Hamilton simply did not know them well enough to be sure if they were ready for a humorous 'Fair Meeting'. His cautious letter to Alexander Hay in Leiden is suggestive that he wanted more evidence in relation to their possible reaction if introduced to the Order. Given that high-ranking Jacobites were present at such gatherings and engaged in humorous activities that suggested they took the cause less than seriously, such caution was undoubtedly well founded.

While we can only speculate on the meaning of the Toboso motto, we are on firmer ground when it comes to the issue of the distribution of the membership. The Hay-Gordon letters, coupled with those of Ezekiel Hamilton, inform us of Toboso Knights based in a variety of locations. While we know that Admiral Gordon was made a member in 1732, there must already have been a membership in Russia in addition to Gordon and Henry Stirling, because when Hay sent greetings from George Keith to them with their rings he also added that:

> [George Keith] with Sir William Livingston the Grand Master whom I should have given the first place join in their hearty service to all our Brother Knights with you.[20]

We can certainly guess at who these 'Brother Knights' in Russia might be given the number of known Jacobite exiles in the country, but we can only name some for sure. However, there is also some confusion here as Livingston was not the Grand Master of the Order in 1732. The answer to this conundrum might lie in a simple error of punctuation, as the addition of a comma after 'Livingstone' would make the letter effectively read 'Sir William Livingstone *and* the Grand Master'. This speculation appears to be borne out by further correspondence from Hay in which the name of the actual Grand Master is revealed. In a letter confirming the acceptance of Captain Robert Little of the Russian navy into the Order, Sir Thomas Gordon and Sir Henry Stirling are again mentioned as members, along with the English Jacobite refugee, Admiral Sir Thomas Saunders. The letter was signed by Don Ezekiel del Toboso.[21] From a letter dated 22 April 1734, we learn that this was one of several pseudonyms for Reverend Ezekiel Hamilton, a secretary to the Duke of Ormonde, and self-proclaimed Grand Master of the Order from 1726.[22] As late as 1737 we still find George Keith referring to Hamilton as 'Great Master', clearly placing him in a position of superior authority within the Order.[23] Indeed, in no correspondence other than the 'Livingstone letter' is his place as *the* senior Tobosan challenged, adding credence to the conclusion that a missing comma may have sent us searching in the wrong direction for the Toboso hierarchy.[24]

That said, we know who the ruling cabal of the Order were. Among the other signatories to the April 1734 letter were Don G[eorge] Keith, 9th Earl Marischal of Scotland; Don Juan [John] Stewart; Don Gullielmo [William] Maxwell, 5th Earl of Nithsdale; Don Gulielmo [William] Hay, and Don Marcos Carse, thus giving us a strong indication of core membership of the organisation in Rome in the mid-1730s.[25] This also included, as Protectors of the Order, the two young Stuart princes, Charles and Henry Stuart. What role the Protectors of the Order actually played is unclear, but it seems that they are not mentioned again in this capacity after 1732. Thereafter, one person mentioned as a Protectress of Toboso was Lady Elizabeth Caryll (née Harrington), with whom Don Ezekiel conducted a correspondence over the 1734–1736 period.[26] We know the Order had concurrent Protectors, not least because of the two princes, but also due to a letter from one 'D.G.' to Ezekiel Hamilton in which the enigmatic author sent his regards to *El Maestro*, observing the fact that:

> Sir Patrick and I have very lately had the honour of paying our respects to the sister Protectresses of the Ancient and honourable order, and were received very graciously [...] I have many services to send you from the Companions of the most Ancient and honourable order.[27]

This letter clearly places two female Protectresses and other members in England, the author specifically being in London. Subsequently *'El Maestro'* wrote to Patrick Briscow noting a nest of Tobosans in Surry Street who were to receive Toboso necklaces, while others in England should receive rings of the Order.[28] Hamilton also contacted Captain John Urquhart in Rotterdam just before the latter embarked for London in 1736. Urquhart was instructed by Hamilton to call in at the Rainbow Coffee House in the city to meet with 'Mr Walter Price, Mr Child, Mr Drapier, Mr Waikburn and some more of our brethren who frequent that house'.[29] 'Our brethren' is suggestive of a Toboso connection, but it might also just mean fellow Jacobites – we simply cannot be sure. However, a known Toboso member, Dr. Hawely, took up residence in the Rainbow Coffee House when he moved to London in 1738, giving weight to the notion that it was a Toboso meeting place and that London had an active membership.[30]

Another hub of Toboso activity was the town of Spa in Wallonia (Austrian Netherlands). Ezekiel Hamilton noted that there had been a chapter meeting of Toboso in Spa in 1737.[31] He had also mentioned previous visits to the town and having met one Mr. Berkeley there in 1736, albeit he did not inform his recipient, the Duke of Ormonde, of any specific connection with the Order.[32] Indeed, the correspondence between Hamilton and Ormonde is devoid of any mention of the Order, specific or implied.[33] Nonetheless, from Hamilton's letters we know that other Jacobites in Spa included Mr. Alexander Hay (with whom Hamilton lodged), Sir Redmond Everard, Mr. Dicconson, two women, possibly sisters who were both known as Miss Digby and another young lady known as Miss Fanny, whose virtues Ezekiel extolled. Both Alexander Hay and Redmond Everard were certainly in Toboso, while it was probable the others were too.[34]

Definitive identification of Jacobites as members of the Order is quite problematic. Sometimes the fact that an individual is in Toboso comes from a simple one-off reference in a letter between members. For example, in one between the Keith brothers from 1731, George Keith suddenly addresses his brother as *Senor Don Diego*, which left the editor of the HMC *9th Report* confused and able only to insert that this must be 'a playful name given by the older brother to the younger'.[35] However, once established that this is a letter between Tobosans, we find their correspondence reveals others in the society. On 6 May and 12 June 1632 George Keith, again writing to his brother, mentioned both *Don Diego Tallboy* and *Don Marcos* (whom he also called *Senor Marks*). These, through a little detective work, we can identify as James Tallboy and Mark Carse of Cockpen.[36] Indeed, once made aware of their existence through the use of the *Don* or *Senor* titles, Tobosan Knights start to appear in other correspondence, such as the frustratingly titled *Don Andreas* at Avignon to whom Ezekiel Hamilton sent regards via Mr. George Kelly in 1738.[37] It is not clear if mention of a member of Toboso in this letter means that Kelly was also in Toboso, or if *Don Andreas* was simply universally known by that title to members and non-members alike. Certainly the letter contains no other hint that Kelly might be an initiate, but we cannot be certain. While such references are enticing we also have physical evidence of the Order that give us clues as to membership of the society. A Toboso ring exists in the National Museum of Scotland and is said to have belonged to Sir John Hynde Cotton, although the owner is more likely to have been John Cotton, Master of the Jacobite Lodge in Rome.[38] One person who it would really be interesting to tie into Toboso is the Irish Jacobite, Brigadier General Sir Charles Wogan. As governor of La Mancha, he must surely have been aware of the Quixote story. This is mere speculation, but it would certainly give an interesting twist to the story if the Order del Toboso actually included a known Jacobite as the governor of the region in Spain where Cervantes set his famous novel.

Setting aside the 'probable' membership to focus on the proven affiliates, some interesting facts can be established about the Order. The majority of members were Scots, about a dozen of them in total (Table 12.1), but this was not an exclusively Caledonian association. Of the twenty-six members identified to date, around 25% were English, including: Admiral Thomas Saunders, Mr Patrick Briscow, John Cotton, Dr. Hawley, William Howard Viscount Andover and Sir Redmond Everard. Of the Irish, Ezekiel Hamilton is the most important, being Grand Master of the Order, while at least two members – the Sempill brothers – were French-born, albeit with Scottish heritage.[39] Ethnic origins aside, we can also detail the confessions of faith of the Toboso Knights. It is quite evident that the overwhelming majority of them were Nonjurors, either Scottish Episcopalians or English and Irish Anglicans, although the admission of the Stuart princes shows that there was no bar to Catholic membership.

It can be categorically stated that membership of Toboso was not automatic to anyone. We should remember Ezekiel Hamilton's hesitation at admitting the Oxford Tories to 'a Fair Meeting', but there were others who were actually barred from the group, including influential Scottish Jacobites. In a veritable diatribe, Hamilton virulently attacked James Murray, Jacobite Earl of Dunbar, after he had made his application to join Toboso.[40] Henrietta Tayler believed that the decision not to admit Murray came from the young Stuart princes themselves, but there is compelling evidence to show that the blackballing came from Ezekiel Hamilton.[41] To begin with, Hamilton presented the Chevalier St. George with a petition against Lord Dunbar in 1733.[42] This was followed by a general missive to all Toboso Knights detailing the reasons why Hamilton felt Murray was 'incapable of being ever admitted into [Toboso]'.[43] Not least among the reasons cited for his rejection were two that are worthy of mention here. Firstly, Murray had, in the presence of Don Ezekiel Hamilton, failed 'in his respect to a right honourable lady who is the honour'd protectress of the most illustrious order of Toboso'.[44] Murray's disrespect to Lady Caryll was one thing, but more telling is perhaps the prospective candidate's ridicule of the Order itself. In the second reason given for Murray being disqualified from the Order, he took great exception to the fact that Murray, in the presence of several members, did:

> crack a dull joke on the design of reviving the said order, as if it were only to attack windmills, in which he shew'd the lightness and giddiness of his own head and that he himself was dispos'd to *turn* with every wind.[45]

In this document, Hamilton screams defiantly at those who decry the Order as something frivolous, because if it were, then how could he possibly take offence at Murray's suggestion? At the same time, we can see that there was some direct allusion to *Don Quixote* through his reference to 'tilting at windmills', although Murray clearly did not understand what that allusion represented. It must be said that the rest of the document is something of a personal rant against Murray, but the specific information giving insight into the Order is of considerable value. It shows that Hamilton controlled the Order in something of an autocratic fashion, albeit 'with the advice and consent of our brethren'. His application rejected, Murray was:

> Condemned to admire himself, to laugh at his own insipid jests and to read his own dull and malicious poems: and the said James Murray &c is by these presents declared to be forever incapable of any of the honours, rights, dignitys, privileges, preheminencys and authoritys belonging to the said order.[46]

While Toboso might well have been open to the concept of self-parody, it was anything but a 'mock order'. Some members clearly took themselves very seriously indeed, particularly Ezekiel Hamilton, who ultimately controlled admissions. On being approached to send Toboso rings to another member in France for distribution, Hamilton responded by clearly letting it be known that he would not even allow the Protectress to dictate who could join the Order, informing Sir Redmond Everard that:

> I am extremely concerned that ye rings you mention are not at my dis-posal, they have been long expected by the persons to whom they belong and you may easily believe that I can not Ask their consent to dispose of them to others: I beg you'll make my excuse to the fair Protectrice in ye best manner.[47]

Hamilton clearly believed that the membership should be expanded, but not without due process and careful consideration of the candidates, even if Lady Caryll was promoting them, or if they had strong Tory credentials like the Oxford graduates mentioned previously.

The above notwithstanding, hard facts regarding the Order remain quite scarce. Therefore, it is important that we establish what we can, and cannot, state for sure before drawing our conclusions. Taking one line of argument, it is alluring to think that the order might be one of the 1,000 side-degrees of Freemasonry mentioned by John Hamill, to see if this allows us any deeper insight into the group.[48] The quick answer is that it does not. Comparing the membership of Toboso with the Jacobite Masonic Lodge in Rome, and other Lodges elsewhere, there is a degree of overlap, with simul-taneous membership of both the Freemasons and the Order del Toboso being proven for the following individuals:

Mark Carse of Cockpen (Rome)
Mr. John Cotton (Grand Master, Rome)
George Keith (Prussia)
James Keith (Grand Master, Russia)
John Stewart of Grantully (Warden, Rome)

There is possibly a sixth dual member in the person of William Hay *if* the naval captain (who came from Russia and was a member of Toboso) and the individual of the same name in the Masonic Lodge in Rome are the same person. Hay's details as published by W. J. Hughan do not allow for this assumption.[49] Nonetheless, from Table 12.2, we can see that there were some thirty individuals with a Roman connection in the 1730s for whom we can ascribe a Masonic pedigree. Of these we can only prove that five were in Toboso, and of them, only three (possibly four with Hay) were in the Roman Lodge. Tobosan heavyweights, such as Ezekiel Hamilton, are not to be found on the list, although this might be due to the fact he left

Rome just at the time that the surviving minutes of the Roman lodge begin.

Of the non-Tobosan Masons it should be noted that some were treated with suspicion by members of the Order. James Murray (the surgeon) is described by Ezekiel Hamilton as 'a Canary Bird, false sly and insinuating'.[50] The absence of William Maxwell, 5th Earl Nithsdale, can possibly be explained by his ongoing conflict with George Seton, 5th Lord Wintoun, who became Master of the Lodge in 1736. Nevertheless, statistically, the Masonic-Toboso link looks pretty thin when the dual membership is compared, with only five out of thirty of the Freemasons with a Roman connection having a proven link with Toboso.

Further, with specific mention of at least two sister Protectresses (making a possible three females in total in this role, if the 'sisters' do not include Lady Caryll), we must continue to doubt the Masonic connection, which would not usually allow for female membership. There is some consideration to be given to the fact that the Protectors of the Order need not have been practising members, and perhaps were merely figureheads, which would allow for their status. Nonetheless, it is hard to ignore the statement by Hamilton explaining that:

> The Order [of the Knights of Tobosc (sic)] was much enlarged by making Necklaces with the Motto on them, I sent a few of them to England, as many as could be made during the time I stayed at Spa. I hope to get some more done the next season and I will not forget the Lady in Surry Street. I sent one to Sir William for his Lady which I hope he has received.[51]

The implication here is that the Order was enlarged by the provision of Toboso jewellery, some of which was clearly passed on to women, after which the Order was expanded. This in itself appears to reject the concept of a male-only membership, whether or not the female Protectresses were active participants in Toboso ritual or not. It can therefore be contended that being a Mason in the Jacobite Lodge in Rome (or elsewhere) was not any sort of prerequisite for membership of Toboso. Indeed, the Rome connection, while key at a certain juncture between 1732–35, seemed to lose any kind of defining role for the Order after chapters began to spring up elsewhere and Ezekiel Hamilton left the city.

Having established the identity of a cohort of Toboso Knights, and some of the locations they were to be found in, we can sketch a picture of the organisation, and surmise what it stood for. We can state for sure that the core of this group of British and Irish Jacobites found themselves scattered across Europe. Most had participated in the failed 1715 Jacobite uprising in Scotland, while some of the English had been at Preston. Through their participation they had lost their homes, their fortunes and many of their friends. By the 1730s, it was clear that another attempt to oust the Hanoverians from the British throne was being planned. While many Jacobites seriously plotted another uprising, some of the far-sighted exiles prophesised that such an endeavour would end in disaster for those considering an active part. Wishing neither to renounce their own political beliefs nor to encourage others to make the same mistakes that they had made, this group apparently came up with an ingenious solution by resorting to literary allegory. Taking *Don Quixote* as their inspiration, some Jacobite exiles formed a new Order that would allow for personal adherence to a cause whilst recognising the futility of supporting any insurrection aimed at forcing their beliefs on a society largely opposed or ambivalent to them.

Don Quixote's fantasy that the peasant girl, Aldonsa Lorenzo, was actually the 'Lady Dulcinea del Toboso' coupled with his agonising pursuit of her, came to symbolise the ill-advised quest that many Jacobites found themselves on during their exile. Aldonsa, though beautiful, was simply not what the gullible Quixote imagined her to be. Thus, to members of the society, Quixote's quest for the unattainable imaginary beauty represented their own pursuit of a Jacobite restoration. Once their fallacious plight was understood by Toboso initiates, they reflected on what they had lost and what they were unlikely to regain, and thereafter maintained their spirits by indulging in a degree of self-parody. That does not mean that they gave up their personal belief in Jacobitism, merely that they learned to live with the consequences of their actions in support of it.

Indeed, for those who actually participated in the 1715 uprising, it is clear that most, if not all, remained loyal in their adherence to the House of Stuart by not recognising the Hanoverian regime and rejecting offers of pardons from it. In November 1716, Lord Southesk wrote to the Earl of Mar telling him that Keith and his brother had had overtures of pardons made to them by British government agents in Paris.[52] A second overture came many years later during James Keith's convalescence in London in 1740. He remained in Britain for three months where 'in spite of his still notorious Jacobitism he was several times received by George II, though always in the guise and uniform of a Russian general'.[53] George Keith was eventually pardoned in the late 1750s, long after the Jacobite threat had fizzled out. However, during the 1730s, and despite the meetings of his brother with George II, George Keith is reported to have accepted the commission to serve as Commander-in-Chief of Jacobite forces in Scotland. How sincere he was in this quest is difficult to ascertain, given the intrigues that surrounded the operation. He maintained the position until 1744, although he did little by way of building an army, due to a growing distrust of the French and a dislike of his political superiors. Indeed, he is even said to have learned 'to hate' Prince Charles during this period and thereafter 'retired from Jacobitism'.[54] What his role in Toboso may confirm is that his disaffection with the movement may actually have had a much longer gestation period than hitherto understood.

We have sure evidence that while Marischal held a senior position in the fledgling Jacobite army in 1744, the Keith brothers were apparently actively *discouraging* Jacobites from becoming involved in the attempt.[55] Neither brother came home to participate once the rising started. James Keith later wrote that 'in 1744 the Court of France, then being at war with that of England [Great Britain], affected to make another attempt in favour of the Pretender, but did it so ineffectually, that the Lord Marischal saw through it, and endeavoured to prevail upon the Prince not to be a dupe'.[56] Given this statement, in combination with other information pertinent to Toboso, we cannot help but wonder just what George Keith *really* meant when he wrote to Ezekiel Hamilton in February 1737 that:

> I have three thousand livres lyfrent with which I propose to retire to some Village in a Protestant Canton in Switzerland: & chosing a Plan of cheapness according to my rent, I can find among that people a place where that small sum will be a Considerable estate, I am Naturally sober enough as to my eating, more as to my drinking, I do not game & am a *Knight Errant sin' Amor*; so that I need not Great Summs for my maintenance.[57]

Whilst undoubtedly being a general statement that he did not at that juncture have a spouse (the Earl Marischal never married), the description of himself as a *Knight Errant sin' Amor* in a letter to the Grand Master of the Order del Toboso should not go unnoticed. This is particularly pertinent because the statement was followed by a damning commentary in which Keith stated that:

> In a Word I have suckt in such Notions of liberty & independence & of ye meaness of Servile submission & flattery, for the sake of outward appearances, that I can not accustom My Self to follow such ways, I know few will approve this party: because most People are of different Principles from me & of those who are Not a great Number are carried on With the General current even against their own sentiments and Many others have not the Courage to take and follow the Party, they think best.

Thus our *Knight Errant* can be seen to be thoroughly disillusioned with the path of automatic loyalty to a social order he had previously accepted. Further, he was clearly perplexed that others, whom he believed should have known better, continued in their delusion, while admitting that many of his compatriots had yet to see the folly of their ways. By explaining his position in the way he did, Keith made it abundantly clear that a return to the Jacobite Court in Rome was not on his agenda, and strongly hinted at a growing rift between himself and the Jacobite movement. Therefore, when he described himself to Ezekiel Hamilton as a '*Knight Errant* without love', it can easily be read as his self-proclamation of having become a 'rebel without a cause'.

Certainly as forfeited veterans, the Keith brothers had done their bit for the House of Stuart, having been 'out' in the 1715 and 1719 uprisings. By the 1730s, both were established members of the Order del Toboso, having joined the Order in Spain, probably in the late 1720s. Upon arriving in Rome in 1732, George Keith with Grand Master Ezekiel Hamilton, William Hay and others sought to build the membership of the Order and open chapters across Europe, including Britain. That they invited the two Stuart princes to serve as Protectors to the Order might seem paradoxical with hindsight, given the spectacular success of the Jacobite army during the 1745 uprising under the command of Lord George Murray. However in 1732, success on the battlefield must have seemed a very distant prospect, while the ambition and undoubted charisma of Prince Charles Edward Stuart had yet to reveal itself. Rather, with the two failed risings of 1715 and 1719 as their benchmark for Stuart campaigning, many Jacobites became despondent with the cause, allowing members of Toboso to flirt with the princes as their patrons. Unfortunately we do not know if the princes ever took the Order del Toboso seriously, became initiated or formally left the group – only that there was a moment in 1732 where there was a connection.[58]

We are on safer ground when dealing with the long-term membership of the society. George Keith in particular felt future Jacobite attempts were futile and that the French were simply using the Stuarts as a means to secure their own agenda, perhaps even preparing to sacrifice them to gain some political advantage. He confirmed this view of French support during a further round of plotting in the 1750s in which both Keith and Lord George Murray were being mooted as leaders of another attempt on Scotland. Murray himself later wrote on the subject that:

> I take it as a very great favoure your writeing so particularly upon a certain subject, and I must own that it flatters me not a little to find that your sentiments were the same with those I had upon that head. I remember once in your presence to have told your brother, that if he had let me understand the *Carte de Pais* eleven years ago, which I was quite ignorant off, it would have prevented my ruin, and perhaps that of several others. As I never had the least thought of a back game, *Je pris mon parte en gallant homme* ... I thought it much more eligible to live in a country where I had no acquaintances, the language of which I know not a sillab, as in a country that had made the cats foot of

us [France] ... I could not brook living in a kingdom whose usage of us I thought barbarous. By what I have said your Excellency will easily perceive I have no intention to be made a tool of.[59]

Murray's opinion that George Keith knew of some French double-dealing during the planning of the 1745 uprising gives the impression that the Keith brothers kept Murray in the dark at the time, or subsequently had to remind him of how they viewed the French role in the attempt. Whatever Lord George is getting at in this letter, it is clear that the Keith brothers did not participate in the '45 and encouraged others not to go 'out' with Charles Edward Stuart.

Indeed, as an organisation, Toboso members are conspicuous by their absence in that campaign. For sure, Prince Charles himself was there, and George Kelly (if he was a member) also took part. But for the vast majority of the membership, their support for the cause appears to have taken the form of loyal toasts, perhaps in the Rainbow Coffee House in London or from the hot-baths at Spa. Certainly the membership remained intellectually attached to the Stuart cause, even maintaining correspondence with the court before, during and after the failure of the final campaign. Yet conclusively, they did not go 'out', and not through lack of military opportunity. Again the Keith brothers are instructive in this regard, with both serving in the field for European potentates for many years after the '45. They were respected generals, but apparently could not commit themselves, their families or friends to a cause they viewed as 'lost'. Thus the spread of the Order into Britain makes a great deal of sense, particularly as that is where Toboso might have made the greatest impact among those who had most to lose should there be another failed Jacobite uprising.

If this analysis is correct, Toboso served as a social network which bound certain of the expatriate community together while protecting others of Jacobite inclination in Britain from sharing in their own misfortune and exile. They encouraged each other to hold on to their personal political loyalty while at the same time being able to indulge in some light-hearted self-reflection and realistic analysis of what their loyalty had cost them. While neither the Tobosans nor most contemporaries could have predicted the initial spectacular success of the Stuart army in 1745, those at the core of the Order correctly anticipated that fighting for a 'Jacobite Restoration' in the mid-eighteenth century was simply tantamount to 'Tilting at Windmills'.

Table 12.1   Established Members of the 'Order del Toboso'

Initiated	Location	Freemason	Jacobite	Active 1745?
Anon. – *'Don Andreas'*	Avignon 1738		YES	
Sir Patrick *de la Ardicate Espada*	Rome 1734		YES	
Mr. Patrick Briscow	Paris 1738		YES	
Lady Elizabeth Caryll (nee Harrington) – *'Protectress'*	1734 England 1736		YES	NO
Mark Carse of Cockpen – *'Don Marcos'*	Rome 1733	YES Rome 1735	YES	NO (d.1736?)
Mr. John Cotton		YES Rome 1735	YES	NO
Sir Redmond Everard	Spa 1736		YES	
Admiral Thomas Gordon – *'Don Thomas'*	St. Petersburg (Russia) 1732		YES	NO (d.1741)
Rev. Ezekiel Hamilton, aka George Bennett (Grand Master) – *'Don Ezekiel del Toboso'*	Rome 1733 Spa 1736 Leiden 1736		YES	NO
Dr Hawley – *'Physician to the Order'*	Spa 1738 London 1738		YES	
Alexander Hay	Spa 1736		YES	NO
Captain William Hay *'Don Gullielmo'*	Rome 1732	PERHAPS	YES	NO
William Howard, Viscount Andover				
Field-Marshall George Keith – *'Don George'*	Valencia 1731 Rome 1733 Madrid 1736	YES	YES	NO
General James Keith – *'Don Diego'*	Russia 1731	YES	YES	NO
Captain Robert Little	Russia 1733		YES	NO
Sir William Livingston, 3rd Viscount Kilsyth (possibly mentioned as Grand Master, February 1732)	Rome 1732		YES	NO (d.1733)
William Maxwell, 5th Earl of Nithsdale – *'Don Gullielmo'*	Rome 1733		YES	NO (d.1744)

Table 12.1   Established Members of the 'Order del Toboso' – *continued*

Initiated	Location	Freemason	Jacobite	Active 1745?
Francis, Jacobite 2nd Lord Sempill	Paris 1736		YES	NO
Mr. Sempill	Paris 1736		YES	NO
Prince Charles Edward Stuart – *'Protector'*	Rome 1732		N/A	YES
Prince Henry Stuart – *'Protector'*	Rome 1732		N/A	NO
Sir John Stewart (Stuart) of Grantully – *'Don Juan'*	Rome 1733	Rome 1735	YES	NO (d.1739)
Rear Admiral Thomas Saunders	Russia 1733		YES	NO
Sir Henry [Harry] Stirling	Russia 1733		YES	NO
James Tallboy – *'Don Diego'*	Rome? 1732		YES	

Table 12.2   Masons at Rome (or Connected)

Initiated	Lodge	Toboso	Jacobite	Active 1745?
Howard Anderson	Rome			
Captain Thomas Archdeacon	Rome			
Mark Carse of Cockpen *'Don Marcos'*	Rome	YES		NO (d.1736?)
Mr. John Cotton, 'Master', 1735–1736	Rome	YES		
Alex Clerk	Rome			
Sir Marmaduke Constable of Eveningham	Rome			
'Compte' Carl Johan Cronstedt – Swedish Architect on Grand Tour	Rome		NO	NO
Mr. Captain de Croysman (French Officer)	Rome		NO	NO

Table 12.2   Masons at Rome (or Connected) – *continued*

Initiated	Lodge	Toboso	Jacobite	Active 1745?
Dr. Alexander Cunningham, aka ISir Alexander Dick of Priestfield	Rome			YES
James Dashwood	Rome			
Henry Fitzmaurice	Rome			
John Forbes (visitor)				
Mr. Haliburton	Rome			YES
Mr. Hay of Dumelziers (junior)	Rome			
Colonel William Hay* Possible confusion in source with Captain William Hay, of Toboso	Rome	PERHAPS		NO (d.1740)
William Howard 'Master', 1735	Rome			
Dr. James Irvin (physician)	Rome			
James Irvin (junior) 'Warden'	Rome			
George Keith, Earl Marischal of Scotland	Prussia (1747)	YES		NO
James Keith, Field Marshall	Russia (1732)			
	Sweden (1743)	YES		NO
Danie Kilmaster	Rome			
Will Mosman 'Deputy Warden'	Rome			
James Murray (surgeon)	Rome			
John Murray 'Junior Warden'	Rome			YES
Luis Nairn	Rome			
Allan Ramsay	Rome			
Comte Saudarini	Rome		NO	NO
George Seton 5th Lord Wintoun 'Master', 1736	Rome			

Table 12.2   Masons at Rome (or Connected) – *continued*

Initiated	Lodge	Toboso	Jacobite	Active 1745?
William Sheldon	Rome			
Charles Slezer	Rome			
Sir John Stewart (Stuart) of Grantully	Rome	YES		
Thomas Twisden	Rome			
Marquis C. A. Vasse (French Cavalry Officer)	Rome		NO	
De Bandy de Vis	Rome		NO	
Richard Younger	Rome			

Notes

1   The Order del Toboso was briefly discussed in S. Murdoch, *Network North: Scottish Kin, Commercial and Covert Associations in Northern Europe, 1603–1746* (Leiden, 2006), pp. 337–41. The present chapter has two main functions: to correct some errors of fact and to present a far more detailed and comprehensively researched interpretation of the Order than time or space permitted in the monograph. I would like to extend my thanks to Professor Edward Corp, Professor Allan Macinnes, Dr. Evelyn Lord, Dr. Alexia Grosjean and Alison Duncan for their helpful and constructive comments on this chapter.

2   W. M. Thackeray, *The History of Henry Esmond, Esq.* (London, 1852), Book II, Chapter II, final paragraph.

3   Miguel de Cervantes, *Don Quixote* (Madrid, 2 parts, 1605–1615). Certainly, the association with the Stuarts and Quixote had some pedigree. For example, Elizabeth of Bohemia (daughter of James VI and grandmother of George I of Great Britain), found herself in exile most of her life. She also likened her son, Prince Rupert, to Don Quixote on several occasions. See for example TNA, SP16/317 i.12, ff. 20–1 & SP16/352 & i.41, ff. 87–90. Elizabeth of Bohemia to Sir Thomas Roe, 4 April & 16 April 1637. For opponents making the link to Quixote in mockery of the Stuarts, see British Library, C115 I 3 (36). Jack Catch esq., *AN HUE and CRY AFTER THE PRETENDER* (Edinburgh, 1716), 'the said *James* [....] to the Continuance of his Raving and Madness; whereby he fancies himself a King, and makes Mock-Ministers; creating Sham Generals, Secretaries, Lords and Knights, in Scotland; and Dukes of Newcastle, and Greenwich, in his Hunting-Matches and Freaks at Bar-le-Duc, where he and the D_____ of L_____ are raving like Don Quixot and Sancho, about Kingdoms, and the Government of imaginary Islands, to the known Disturbance of their own Brains, and the certain Laughter of their Neighbours'. I thank Dr Nadine Akkerman and Kieran German respectively for bringing these sources to my attention.

4   R. L. Karter, 'Frederick the Great', in *The Yearbook of the Grand Lodge of Ancient Free and Accepted Masons of Scotland* (Edinburgh, 1985), p. 98: A. K. L. Nihtinen,

'Field Marshal James Keith: Governor of the Ukraine and Finland, 1740–1743', in A. Mackillop and S. Murdoch, eds, *Military Governors and Imperial Frontiers: A Study of Scotland and Empires, 1600–1800* (Leiden, 2003), p. 114.

5 A. Forey, 'The Military Order of Saint Thomas of Acre', *English Historical Review*, 92 (1977), pp. 481–503; For the 'Scots Club' see D. Szechi, ed., *Letters of George Lockhart of Carnwath, 1698–1732* (Edinburgh, 1989), pp. 246–7. George Lockhart to Allan Cameron, 5 October 1725; Same to John Hay, 13 October 1725.

6 R. F. Gould, *History of Freemasonry*, revised and edited by Dudley Wright (5 vols., London, 1930), IV, pp. 2–19; P. F. Anson, *Underground Catholicism in Scotland, 1622–1878* (Montrose, 1970), pp. 143–4; M. Baigent, 'The painting of the "Judgement of Solomon" at Culross "Palace", Fife', *Ars Quartuor Coronatorum: Transactions of the Quartuor Lodge No. 2076*, vol. 106 (1994), pp. 160–1; J. Hamill, 'The Jacobite Conspiracy', *Ars Quartuor Coronatorum*, vol. 113 (2000), pp. 99–100. Hamill disputes that Ramsay remained a Mason after the Papal Bull of 1738.

7 Hamill, 'The Jacobite Conspiracy', p. 100.

8 H. Tayler, *The Jacobite Court at Rome in 1719 from the original documents at Fettercairn House and at Windsor Castle* (Edinburgh, 1938), p. 138. See also D. F. Allen, 'Attempts to Revive the Order of Malta in Stuart England', in *The Historical Journal*, 33:4 (1990), p. 950.

9 R. Wills, *The Jacobites and Russia 1715–1750* (East Linton, 2002), pp. 146–7, 183.

10 Murdoch, *Network North*, p. 339.

11 Allen, 'Attempts to Revive the Order of Malta', p. 950.

12 HMC, *10th Report*, ed., Sir John Stirling Maxwell *et al.* (London, 1885), p. 178. William Hay to Admiral Thomas Gordon, 2 February 1732; HMC, *9th Report* (London, 1884), p. 222. George Keith to James Keith, n.d., but 1731.

13 HMC, *10th Report*, p. 178, William Hay to Admiral Thomas Gordon, 2 February 1732.

14 HMC, *10th Report*, p. 178. William Hay to Admiral Thomas Gordon, 2 February 1732.

15 Captain Hay's arrival in Rome is recorded in J. Ingamells, *A Dictionary of British and Irish Travellers in Italy, 1701–1800* (New Haven, 1997), p. 477.

16 British Library, Mackintosh Collections, vol. XXXVI, f. 83: *Journal de la Négociation de M [Thomas] Carte avec M. Robert Walpole*. Interview 23 September 1739, written up 23 October 1739.

17 Carte quoted in F. P. Lole, *A Digest of the Jacobite Clubs* (Royal Stuart Society, London, 1999), p. 70. I thank Professor Edward Corp for bringing this quote to my attention. This source puts the date of the journal at 1740, but the MSS is dated 1739 (see preceding reference).

18 HMC, *10th Report*, p. 502. Ezekiel Hamilton to Mr. Alexander Hay, Leiden, 25 June 1737.

19 Cervantes, *Don Quixote*, Part II: Chapter XXX. Depending on the edition and translation, it is also rendered 'Verdant Meadow'.

20 HMC, *10th Report*, p. 178. William Hay to Admiral Thomas Gordon, 2 February 1732.

21 HMC, *10th Report*, pp. 183–4. Ezekiel Hamilton to Admiral Thomas Gordon, 28 January 1733.

22 HMC, *10th Report*, p. 184. Ezekiel Hamilton to Admiral Thomas Gordon, 22 April 1734. That he was a secretary to Ormonde is derived from British

Library, Add Mss 33950, ff. 19–20. Letters to and from the Duke of Ormonde, 1719.

23 HMC, *10th Report*, p. 474. George Keith to Ezekiel Hamilton, Valencia, 30 January 1737.

24 It could be that each chapter had its own Grand Master, but from the evidence available it would appear that there was only one, and that was Ezekiel Hamilton.

25 Ingamells, *A Dictionary of British and Irish Travellers in Italy*, pp. 447, 477, 641, 690 and 911. He notes that George Keith remained in Rome between 1730–1732, William Hay between 1725–41, John Stuart arrived in 1733 and died there in 1739, while Ezekiel Hamilton also lived there in 1733, but left c. 1635.

26 For example see HMC, *10th Report*, p. 462. Ezekiel Hamilton to Lady Caryll, Leiden, 15 November 1736. It is yet uncertain as to what role a Protectress had within Toboso. If it was anything like a 'Lady Patroness' then we can be guided by the following definition: 'When local clubs and groups chose women to act as "Lady Patronesses" and preside over events, such as their annual feasts or banquets, the "distinction" was often little more than a lightly veiled statement of political intent. The woman who was chosen was honoured as a representative of a political family and her ceremonial services forged a connection between her family and the group.' See Elaine Chalus, '"That Epidemical Madness": women and electoral politics in the late eighteenth century', in H. Barker and E. Chalus (eds), *Gender in Eighteenth-Century England: Roles, Representations and Responsibilities* (Harlow, 1997), p. 159; Elaine Chalus, *Elite Women in English Political Life c. 1754–1790* (Oxford, 2005), chapter 4, 'Women and Patronage', pp. 139–40. I thank Alison Duncan for these most useful references.

27 HMC, *10th Report*, p. 472. D. G. to Ezekiel Hamilton, London, 15 February 1737. It is not made clear who Sir Patrick is in this instance. There is no indication as to who D. G. might be. This might be the initials of the author's real name, or stand for *Don Gullielmo* thus giving us several members of Toboso to consider as the author.

28 HMC, *10th Report*, pp. 516–17. Ezekiel Hamilton to Mr Patrick Briscow, Leiden, 26 March 1738.

29 HMC, *10th Report*, p. 459. Ezekiel Hamilton to Captain John Urquhart, Leiden, 31 October 1736. From a later letter of Urquhart to Hamilton we learn that Urquhart had carried letters from Hamilton to Drapier. See p. 463, 16 November 1736.

30 HMC, *10th Report*, p. 517. Ezekiel Hamilton to Patrick Briscow, Leiden, 26 March 1738.

31 HMC, *10th Report*, pp. 516–17. Ezekiel Hamilton to Patrick Briscow, Leiden, 26 March 1738. Hamilton had previously met with one Mr Berkeley at Spa in 1736, which might hint at a possible member, albeit the chapter meeting did not take place there until 1737.

32 See HMC, *10th Report*, p. 456. Ezekiel Hamilton to Duke of Ormonde, Leiden, 13 October 1736.

33 This was not because they did not discuss oath-bound societies – they certainly did. On one occasion, Hamilton related that a 'Quarrel' had broken out between the Duke of Richmond and a physician, both members of the 'Club of the Knights of St. George' at The Hague. When describing that 'Club', Hamilton said it was 'a sort of Society like the free Masons', which implies Ormonde would know what that meant. What Hamilton did not do was liken the 'Club of the Knights of St George' to Toboso, which suggests either that there was no

similarity between them or that Ormonde was not a Toboso initiate. For this letter see HMC, *10th Report*, p. 466. Ezekiel Hamilton to Duke of Ormonde, Leiden, 3 December 1736.

34 HMC, *10th Report*, pp. 458–9. Ezekiel Hamilton to Duke of Ormonde, Leiden, 21 November 1736. Of Miss Fanny he says 'the younger Miss Fanny had a Strong Constitution, she was reckoned to be the best Walker and the best dancer of all the Ladies in Spa, and was very much respected by Every Body for her good quality.' For Hamilton's correspondence with Alexander Hay see p. 460, Leiden, 6 November 1736, where he notes Mr. Dicconson still being at Spa. However, we cannot assume that all Scots in Spa were Jacobites, even if noted in friendly terms by Hamilton. For example, he also notes the presence of Lord Cathcart at Spa at this time, which is rather surprising given that Lord Charles Cathcart was first a groom, then a Gentleman of the Bedchamber to George II. Hamilton states 'this Evening Lord Cathcart, who is come hither to see his two Sons, told me that Publick Gazettes mention Mr [James] Keith's being in good health, and that he had his Winter Quarters in the Ukraine. Ld Cathcart is a well temper'd and well bred Man, I was known to him at Spa, he often speaks of your Lordship with all possible respect.' See *ibid.*, p. 506, Hamilton to George Keith, Leiden, 21 November 1737. For his status as a confirmed Hanoverian, see *The Greening Peerage of Scotland* (London, 1767), p. 201; Sir James Balfour Paul, *The Scots Peerage*, II, pp. 518–19. For the fact that there was no Jacobite Lord Cathcart with which he may have been confused see The Marquis of Ruvigny & Raineval, *The Jacobite Peerage: Baronetage, Knightage & Grants of Honour* (Edinburgh, 1904).

35 HMC, *9th Report*, p. 222. George Keith to James Keith, Nova Paulova, 3 August [1731?].

36 HMC, *9th Report*, p. 222. George Keith to James Keith, both Rome, 6 May and 12 June 1732.

37 HMC, *10th Report*, p. 517. Ezekiel Hamilton to Mr. George Kelly, Leiden, 18 April 1738.

38 Lole, *A Digest of the Jacobite Clubs*, p. 70. I thank Professor Edward Corp for his discussion with me regarding the likely owner of the ring.

39 Francis Sempill, Jacobite 2nd Lord Sempill, and his brother were born in France, the sons of Robert Sempill and Elizabeth Abercromby. 'There is no record of his ever having visited Scotland'. See *Oxford DNB*. Online edition, accessed May 2006.

40 For more on Murray see Szechi, *Letters of George Lockhart of Carnwath*, passim.

41 Tayler, *The Jacobite Court at Rome*, p. 138.

42 Ingamells, *A Dictionary of British and Irish Travellers in Italy*, p. 447.

43 HMC, *10th Report*, p. 184. Ezekiel Hamilton to 'all true Knights, Squires, &c.', Sierra di Radicofani, 22 April 1734 and passim.

44 HMC, *10th Report*, p. 184. Ezekiel Hamilton to 'all true Knights, Squires, &c.', Sierra di Radicofani, 22 April 1734.

45 HMC, *10th Report*, p. 184. Ezekiel Hamilton to 'all true Knights, Squires, &c.', Sierra di Radicofani, 22 April 1734.

46 HMC, *10th Report*, p. 184. Ezekiel Hamilton to 'all true Knights, Squires, &c.', Sierra di Radicofani, 22 April 1734.

47 HMC, *10th Report*, p. 470. Ezekiel Hamilton to Sir Redmund Everard, Leiden, 31 January 1737.

48 Professor Edward Corp first raised the possibility of a significant Toboso-Roman Lodge connection, and the analysis in the text results directly from his suggestion.

49 For Captain William Hay arriving in Russia with other Scottish naval officers (including the future Tobosan, Robert Little), see S. Murdoch, 'Soldiers, Sailors, Jacobite Spy: Russo-Jacobite Relations, 1688–1750', *Slavonica*, 1996/97. 3:1, p. 9; For Captain William Hay writing to Russia see HMC, *10th Report*, p. 178. William Hay to Admiral Thomas Gordon, 2 February 1732. For Colonel William Hay being in the Roman Lodge see W. J. Hughan, *The Jacobite Lodge at Rome, 1735–1737* (Torquay, 1910), pp. 16, 19. All details of the membership of the Lodge at Rome are derived from this volume, though it should be noted that Hughan mis-identifies several members of the Roman Lodge.

50 HMC, *10th Report*, p. 516. Ezekiel Hamilton to Patrick Briscow, Leiden, 26 March 1738.

51 HMC, *10th Report*, pp. 516–17. Ezekiel Hamilton to Patrick Briscow, Leiden, 26 March 1738. Which of the several 'Sir Williams' in Toboso is not made clear, and may indeed refer to a member not yet on our list. However, if English, Viscount Andover is most likely.

52 HMC, *Stuart Papers*, III, p. 166. Lord Southesk to Earl of Mar, 15 January 1717.

53 Gould, *History of Freemasonry*, IV, p. 174. Gould is quoting a source he describes as 'Buchan, *Account of the Keith Family*' which I have not seen.

54 For his 'retrial' from Jacobitism see F. J. McLynn, *France and the Jacobite Rising of 1745* (Edinburgh, 1981), p. 236. For the fact that Marischal and Prince Charles did not get on, see the same volume, p. 26. That Marischal 'hated' Prince Charles, see the biography by Edward M. Furgol, 'Keith, George, styled tenth Earl Marischal', *Oxford DNB*. Online edition, accessed 6 August 2008.

55 Lenman and Gibson, *The Jacobite Threat*, p. 185. As a ploy to prevent the creation of a 'rebel' army, the acceptance of a high ranking position is not without a Scottish precedent. In the 1620s Colonel Robert Stewart sought to build an army of Scots to invade Sweden on behalf of Sigismund Vasa of Poland-Lithuania. He appointed John Fairbairne as chief recruiter and Quarter-master General of the new Scots-Polish army. However, Fairbairne covertly worked for the Swedes, and diverted numerous recruits into Swedish service on behalf of his handler, Sir James Spens of Wormiston, British ambassador to Stockholm and a general in the Swedish army. Whilst not exactly analogous with the appointment of Keith as Commander-in Chief, it certainly demonstrates that the acceptance of a position does not necessarily demonstrate a commitment to the cause. For more on the operations of Fairbairne and Spens see Murdoch, *Network North*, pp. 260–7 in the chapter 'Espionage and the Subversive Network.'

56 J. Keith, *A Fragment of Memoir of Field-marshal James Keith, written by himself 1714–1734* (Berlin, 1789), p. xi. Several scholars have asserted this. See for example McLynn, *France and the Jacobite Rising*, p. 188 who states that 'The Earl Marischal returned to Paris in rare bad humour, disgusted with the French. By this time he was convinced that France had always been insincere over the invasion project, doubtless because it was considered at Versailles that Louis XV did not stand to gain enough from a Stuart restoration'. See also p. 25 in the same volume.

57 HMC, *10th Report*, p. 473. George Keith to Ezekiel Hamilton, 13 February 1737. The italics are mine.

58 It is an interesting point of 'membership' of any group that some people will join an organisation, only to lose interest quickly and either formally leave or simply not return to it. Others will remain lifelong members. In the case of the two Stuart princes, it is quite clear that Prince Charles had a very different view of his destiny to that of Toboso, and so the lack of any mention of him in

records of the Order in the post-1732 period are not surprising. It may also be that as a boy patron, he never really understood what the Order was actually about, although further research may reveal a different understanding.

59   HMC, *Report on the Muniments and Other Family Papers belonging to the Right Honourable William Buller Fullerton Elphinstone, Lord Elphinstone*, pp. 220–2. Lord George Murray to James Keith, 10 March 1756.

Index